Course	Annual Editions
	World History, Vol. 1
	World Prehistory to 1500, 12/e
Course Number	**by Mitchell/Mitchell**

http://create.mheducation.com

ISBN-10: 1121841880   ISBN-13: 9781121841888

Contents

Credits

Preface

History is a dialogue between the past and the present. As we respond to events in our own time and place, we bring the concerns of the present to our study of the past. It has been said that where you stand determines what you see. Those of us who stand within the Western world have sometimes been surprised to discover peoples and cultures long gone that seem quite "modern" and even a bit "Western." Other peoples and cultures in the complex narrative of World History can seem utterly "foreign."

At times, the West has felt that its power and dominance made only its own story worth telling. History, we are reminded, is written by the winners. For the Chinese, the Greeks, the Ottoman Turks, and many other victors from the past, the stories of other civilizations seemed irrelevant, and certainly less valuable than their own triumphal saga. From our perspective in the present, however, all these stories form a tapestry. No one thread or pattern tells the whole tale, and all seem to be equally necessary for assembling a complete picture of the past. As we are linked by capital, communications, and conflict with cultures whose histories, value systems, and goals challenge our own, *World History* can offer keys to understanding. As businesspeople and diplomats have always known, negotiations require a deep knowledge of the other's worldview. In an increasingly interconnected world, we ignore other civilizations at our own peril. As the dominant world power, we touch the lives of millions by decisions we make in the voting booth. Once-powerful cultures that have fallen can offer cautionary advice. Those that survived longer than their neighbors offer hints.

When we read the newspaper or surf the Internet, we find confusing political, economic, religious, and military clashes that make sense only within the context of lived history and historical memory. The role of the United States in Afghanistan and Iraq, the perennial conflicts in the Middle East, China's and India's emerging roles as economic superpowers, the threat posed by religious fundamentalism, Africa's political future, the possibility of viral pandemics—these concerns of the global village have roots in the past.

Understanding the origins of conflicts offers us the possibility of envisioning their solutions. Periodization, or the marking of turning points in history, cannot be done universally. Cultures mature on different timetables and rise and fall independently. We have followed a somewhat traditional structure, beginning with natural history, considering early civilizations to 500 BCE, later civilizations to 500 CE, and the world to 1500, pausing to examine the origins of the world's religions, and ending with exploration. Within this structure, one can read revisionist views of ancient civilizations. Warfare and methods of surviving it; the origins of writing, artwork; engineering marvels and planned cities—all of these commonplaces of modern life have ancient historical antecedents. The lives of female and male humans and deities are juxtaposed. We see Jews, Christians, and Muslims playing their parts on the world stage, as partners or adversaries.

The articles have been selected for balance, readability, and interest. They are offered to the instructor to broaden and deepen material in the assigned text as well as to provide a variety of focuses and writing styles. Our intention has been to offer the most current articles available.

The topic guide will help instructors navigate the volume and choose the readings that best complement a unit of study.

Editors

JOSEPH R. MITCHELL is a history instructor at Howard Community College in Columbia, Maryland, and a popular regional speaker. He co-authored a book on the history of the planned city of Columbia, Maryland, *New City on a Hill* (The History Press, 2006). He received an MA in history from Loyola College in Maryland and an MA in African American History from Morgan State University, also in Maryland. He is the principal co-editor of *The Holocaust: Readings and Interpretations* (McGraw-Hill, 2001) and *Taking Sides: Clashing Issues in Western Civilization* (McGraw-Hill, 2000). He currently serves on the Board of Trustees of the African Art Museum of Maryland.

HELEN BUSS MITCHELL is a professor of philosophy and director of the women's studies program at Howard Community College in Columbia, Maryland. She is the author of *Roots of Wisdom: A Tapestry of Philosophical Traditions,* 6th edition and *Readings from the Roots of Wisdom,* 3rd edition (Wadsworth/Cengage). *Roots of Wisdom* has twice been translated into Spanish and a Chinese translation is underway. She is also creator, writer, and host of a philosophy telecourse, *For the Love of Wisdom,* distributed nationally by Dallas TeleLearning. She has earned numerous degrees, including a PhD in intellectual and women's history from the University of Maryland.

Academic Advisory Board

Members of the Academic Advisory Board are instrumental in the final selection of articles for *Annual Editions* ExpressBooks. Their review of the articles for content, level, and appropriateness provides critical direction to the editor(s) and staff. We think that you will find their careful consideration reflected in this ExpressBook.

Mary Hovanec
Cuyahoga CC Western-Parma

Kimberly F. Jones
Long Island University

Carol A. Keller
San Antonio College

Charles A. Keller
Southern Arkansas University

Richard Kennedy
North Carolina Wesleyan College

Keith N. Knapp
The Citadel

Kenneth E. Koons
Virginia Military Institute

Ann Kuzdale
Chicago State University

Oscar Lansen
University of North Carolina–Charlotte

Jonathan Lee
San Antonio College

Senya Lubisich
Citrus College

Chris Mack
SUNY Oswego

Aran S. MacKinnon
University of West Georgia

Erik C. Maiershofer
Hope International University

Daniel S. Marrone
Farmingdale State College of the State University of NY

Frank D. McCann
University of New Hampshire

Phil McCaskey
Cape Fear Community College

Kate McGrath
Central Connecticut State University

David A. Meier
Dickinson State University

Maurice Melton
Albany State University

Ralph Menning
Kent State University-Stark

Richard M. Mickle
Blue Ridge Community College

Garold Mills
University of Oklahoma

William S. Morison
Grand Valley State University

Robert Morris
Western International University

Annette Morrow
Minnesota State University Moorhead

Tracy Musacchio
John Jay College/CUNY

Teresa Mushik
Empire State College

Tim Myers
Butler Community College

Raphael Chijioke Njoku
University of Louisville

Patricia O'Neill
Central Oregon Community College

Ray Ortensie
Palo Alto Community College

David S. Payne
Northern Kentucky University

David D. Peck
Brigham Young University

Armand Policicchio
Slippery Rock University

Mary Pratt
Southwest Tennessee Community College

Jason Ripper
Everett Community College

Pamela T. Roseman
Georgia Perimeter College

Chad Ross
East Carolina University

Steven J. Salm
Xavier University

Anthony R. Santoro
Christopher Newport University

Michele Scott-James
MiraCosta College

Haim Shaked
University of Miami

Narasingha P. Sil
Western Oregon University

Shelley A. Sinclair
University of Wisconsin–La Crosse

Shumet Sishagne
Christopher Newport University

David E. Skinner
Santa Clara University

John Stahler
Irvine Valley College

David Stefancic
Saint Mary's College

Richard Steigmann-Gall
Kent State University

Rachel L. Stocking
Southern Illinois University–Carbondale

Eric Strahorn
Florida Gulf Coast University

Michelle Tabit
Defiance College

Bart Talbert
Salisbury State University

James S. Taw
Valdosta State University

Timothy M. Teeter
Georgia Southern University

John E. Van Sant
University of Alabama-Birmingham

Della M. Vanhuss
Tri-County Technical College

Melanie H. Vansell
San Bernardino Valley College

Pamela Vaughan Knaus
Colorado State University

Heather Wadas
Shippensburg University of Pennsylvania

Jessica Wilkie
SUNY University at Buffalo

Hayrettin Yucesoy
Saint Louis University

Andrei Znamenski
The University of Memphis

Prepared by: Joseph R. Mitchell, *Howard Community College*
and Helen Buss Mitchell, *Howard Community College*

Correlation Guide

The *Annual Editions* series provides students with convenient, inexpensive access to current, carefully selected articles from the public press. **Annual Editions: World History, Volume 1—Prehistory to 1500, 12/e** is an easy-to-use reader that presents articles on important topics such as *ancient civilizations, religion, rulers, warfare,* and many more. For more information on other McGraw-Hill Create™ titles and collections, visit www. mcgrawhillcreate.com.

This convenient guide matches the units in **World History, Volume 1, 12/e** with the corresponding chapters in two of our best-selling McGraw-Hill World History textbooks by Bentley/Ziegler and Bentley et al.

Annual Editions: World History, Volume 1, 12/e	**Traditions & Encounters, Volume I: From The Beginning to 1500, 5/e by Bentley/Ziegler**	**Traditions & Encounters: A Brief Global History, Volume I, 3/e by Bentley et al.**
Unit: Natural History and the Spread of Humankind	**Chapter 1:** Before History	**Chapter 1:** The Foundations of Complex Societies
Unit: The Beginnings of Culture, Agriculture, and Cities	**Chapter 2:** Early Societies in Southwest Asia and the Indo-European Migrations **Chapter 3:** Early African Societies and the Bantu Migrations	**Chapter 1:** The Foundations of Complex Societies **Chapter 2:** Early African Societies and the Bantu Migrations
Unit: The Early Civilizations to 500 BCE	**Chapter 4:** Early Societies in South Asia **Chapter 5:** Early Society in East Asia **Chapter 6:** Early Societies in the Americas and Oceania	**Chapter 2:** Early African Societies and the Bantu Migrations **Chapter 3:** Early Societies in South and East Asia **Chapter 4:** Early Societies in the Americas and Oceania
Unit: The Later Civilizations to 500 CE	**Chapter 7:** The Empires of Persia **Chapter 8:** The Unification of China **Chapter 9:** State, Society, and the Quest for Salvation in India **Chapter 10:** Mediterranean Society: The Greek Phase **Chapter 11:** Mediterranean Society: The Roman Phase **Chapter 12:** Cross-Cultural Exchanges on the Silk Roads	**Chapter 5:** The Empires of Persia **Chapter 6:** The Unification of China **Chapter 7:** State, Society, and the Quest for Salvation in India **Chapter 8:** Mediterranean Society under the Greeks and Romans **Chapter 9:** Cross-Cultural Exchanges on the Silk Roads
Unit: The Great Religions	**Chapter 13:** The Expansive Realm of Islam **Chapter 16:** The Two Worlds of Christendom	**Chapter 10:** The Commonwealth of Byzantium **Chapter 11:** The Expansive Realm of Islam
Unit: The World of the Middle Ages, 500–1500	**Chapter 13:** The Expansive Realm of Islam **Chapter 14:** The Resurgence of Empire in East Asia **Chapter 15:** India and the Indian Ocean Basin **Chapter 16:** The Two Worlds of Christendom **Chapter 17:** Nomadic Empires and Eurasian Integration **Chapter 18:** States and Societies of Sub-Saharan Africa **Chapter 19:** The Increasing Influence of Europe **Chapter 20:** Worlds Apart: The Americas and Oceania	**Chapter 10:** The Commonwealth of Byzantium **Chapter 11:** The Expansive Realm of Islam **Chapter 12:** The Resurgence of Empire in East Asia **Chapter 13:** India and the Indian Ocean Basin **Chapter 14:** Nomadic Empires and Eurasian Integration **Chapter 16:** Western Europe during the Middle Ages
Unit: 1500: The Era of Global Expansion	**Chapter 21:** Reaching Out: Expanding Horizons of Cross-Cultural Interaction **Chapter 22:** Transoceanic Encounters and Global Connections	**Chapter 18:** Reaching Out: Cross-Cultural Interactions

Prepared by: Joseph R. Mitchell, *Howard Community College*
and Helen Buss Mitchell, *Howard Community College*

Topic Guide

Unit I

UNIT

Prepared by: Joseph R. Mitchell, *Howard Community College*
and Helen Buss Mitchell, *Howard Community College*

Natural History and the Spread of Humankind

The late astronomer Carl Sagan, in his famous book *The Dragons of Time* (1970), imagined all of time compressed into a single year. New Year's Day began fifteen billion years ago with the Big Bang, a moment when the universe emerged from an enormously powerful explosion of compressed matter and antimatter. The Earth formed in mid-September and life began near the end of that month. In Sagan's scenario, humans do not make an appearance until 10:30 PM on December 31st. The Akkadian Empire, the first we know about, formed in the last nine seconds of the year. When we think in cosmic time, as Sagan invites us to do, human existence seems both recent and fragile. It is this human story, nonetheless, that is the chief focus of world history. During our hour and a half of cosmic time, humans of various kinds have lived and flourished on our wet, green planet. Many of the branches of our family tree, however, have led to dead ends. What happened to Neanderthals, who shared Europe with more modern Cro-Magnons? Was it predators, environmental conditions, or warfare that ended their history? Only one species survived, but the story of its survivability is incomplete and some of it is lost in mystery. Bipedal locomotion—the ability to walk upright on two legs—was a huge advantage to some of our distant relatives. They saw expanded possibilities, and began a migration that now spans the globe.

Access to sophisticated tools of analysis has allowed anthropologists and genetic historians to peel back some of the layers of mystery. Studying dental records and styles of tool making has allowed us to trace the spread of peoples and cultures throughout the world. DNA analysis focusing on mitochondrial DNA (passed directly from mothers) and the Y-chromosome (inherited only from fathers) now permits people to trace their genetic ancestry into the distant past. These same techniques can shed light on where the first Americans began their long journey. Was it Mongolia, Southeast Asia, or somewhere else? Was there a single migration, or were there multiple ones with different starting points? And, is warfare inevitable?

The answers to questions such as these might affect how we feel about ourselves. Individually, we might be thrilled or appalled to discover who some of our distant ancestors were. And, larger language groups can have the same reactions. If we share blood with those who have become our traditional enemies, does this make warfare or negotiation easier or more difficult? Linguistic analysis can be increasingly precise on these points. So can DNA patterning. In the most general sense, we all share the same common ancestors. As our species has spread across the Earth, we have become quite diverse. Thousands of years of history have chronicled our cooperation and competition. In Carl Sagan's year, all of this has been accomplished in less than a minute.

Article

Prepared by: Joseph R. Mitchell, *Howard Community College*
and Helen Buss Mitchell, *Howard Community College*

Gone but Not Forgotten

RICHARD MONASTERSKY

Learning Outcomes

After reading this article, you will be able to:

- Determine what evidence is offered to support the claim that the Neanderthals made a substantial contribution to the modern gene pool of Europe.

Neanderthals, those long-lost cousins of modern humans, will not remain lost for long, at least from the prying eyes of geneticists.

Two teams of scientists announced in November that for the first time they had analyzed DNA from the nuclei of cells preserved in 37,000-year-old Neanderthal fossils. That, they say, lays the groundwork for determining the entire sequence of the Neanderthal genome within the next two years.

Because Neanderthals, who disappeared 28,000 years ago, are the closest relatives of modern humans, obtaining the genetic blueprint for those extinct people could reveal important clues about how our own species evolved, the researchers say.

The genetic evidence could also solve mysteries that have plagued anthropologists since the first Neanderthal skeleton was found 150 years ago: namely, what did the ancient people look like, could they speak, and why did they ultimately vanish? After successfully weathering ice ages in Europe for more than 150,000 years, Neanderthals went extinct soon after modern humans appeared there around 40,000 years ago. Some researchers have argued that modern humans wiped out the stockier Neanderthals. Others contend, however, that the two groups intermingled and that the more numerous modern humans simply engulfed the smaller Neanderthal populations.

The DNA sequences will profoundly alter studies of the enigmatic ancient people, said one of the team leaders, Edward M. Rubin, of the Lawrence Berkeley National Laboratory, a federal facility managed by the University of California. "Instead of it being a data-poor field largely based on bones and associated artifacts, it will be a data-rich field, associated with enormous amounts—billions of bits—of data available on the Internet," he says.

In an era when scientists are routinely publishing the genetic sequences of living animals and plants, Mr. Rubin and his colleagues said they would soon manage that feat for the extinct people. "We're going to be able to learn about their biology and learn about things we could never learn from the bones and the artifacts we have," says Mr. Rubin.

The results announced this week go far beyond previous work on Neanderthal DNA, which has focused exclusively on genetic material from mitochondria, the power plants inside cells. They carry their own snippets of DNA, which is passed down from mother to child, with no contribution from the father. In the new work, Mr. Rubin's team and a group led by Svante Paabo of the Max Planck Institute for Evolutionary Anthropology, in Leipzig, Germany, studied Neanderthal DNA that came from the nuclei of cells, where most of an organism's genetic information is housed.

Mr. Rubin's group published its analysis in *Science,* and Mr. Paabo's team published its paper in *Nature* in November. "These papers are perhaps the most significant contributions published in this field since the discovery of Neanderthals," according to a commentary in *Nature* written by David M. Lambert of Massey University and Craig D. Millar of the University of Auckland, both in New Zealand.

Finding the Right Bone

DNA degrades with time, and Mr. Paabo's team has searched for years to find bones that have preserved enough Neanderthal genetic material and are not contaminated by DNA from modern people. After testing 70 bone and tooth samples from fossils collected around Europe and Western Asia, the researchers eventually found a small bone from a cave in Croatia.

"One thing that is fortunate about this particular bone: It's rather small and uninteresting," Mr. Paabo says. "It was thrown in a big box of uninteresting bones and not handled very much." That kept it from being contaminated by the DNA of researchers.

Mr. Paabo and Mr. Rubin used different methods to sequence the Neanderthal DNA, but they came to generally similar conclusions about how recently the ancestors of modern humans and Neanderthals split apart, roughly 400,000 to 500,000 years ago.

DNA consists of long chains of nucleotide bases, the letters that make up the genetic code. Mr. Paabo's group sequenced one million bases of Neanderthal DNA, a tiny fraction of the total. People today have three billion bases. But he says he could complete a rough draft of the entire Neanderthal genome in two years, using less than one-tenth of an ounce of fossil material.

The researchers say their data do not support much mixing of Neanderthal genes into the modern human population during the time the two populations overlapped in Europe.

But supporters of that theory say the new data do not kill off the idea that Neanderthals and humans were interbreeding. In fact, they cite some evidence, reported by Mr. Paabo's team, that indicates human males might have been mating with Neanderthals and contributing DNA to that gene pool. "That's a very convincing demonstration of interbreeding between Neanderthals and humans," says Milford H. Wolpoff, a professor of anthropology at the University of Michigan at Ann Arbor.

Evidence for such interbreeding comes from two recent studies that looked at the genetic variation present in modern humans. In one paper, published in November in the Proceedings of the National Academy of Sciences, Bruce T. Lahn, a professor of human genetics at the University of Chicago, and his colleagues studied a gene called microcephalin that is involved in guiding brain formation. Mr. Lahn's group found that the gene comes in many variations, or alleles, with one class that differs markedly from the others. The degree of difference suggests that the unusual allele was introduced into the human population 37,000 years ago from a group of people that had been separated from humans for roughly a million years.

"We speculate that Neanderthals might have been the source for that new variant," says Mr. Lahn. "We know that 37,000 years ago, Neanderthals and humans coexisted." And the researchers have found more of this variant allele among people in Europe and Asia, where Neanderthals lived.

Mr. Lahn's group has looked at other genes and found one other possible set that might have come from interbreeding, which he takes as evidence that there was limited gene flow between the two groups. If interbreeding had happened commonly, the human genome would harbor more of these unusual genes, he says.

In another study, researchers from the University of California at Los Angeles looked at sequences of 135 genes in people today and estimated that 5 percent of the gene pool represents ancient admixture, meaning it came from extinct populations of people. "If the signal we observe is indeed the result of an admixture event, then these results would change our understanding of the origins of modern humans," the researchers write in the journal *Public Library of Science Genetics*. "it would argue that archaic populations such as Neanderthals must have made a substantial contribution to the modern gene pool in Europe."

Critical Thinking

1. As we sequence the Neanderthal genome, critically analyze how our written history of the period might change.

2. How might the discovery that the modern gene pool contains an admixture from extinct populations change the way we think about ourselves?

3. If genetic evidence reveals that we can all trace our family tree back to common ancestors, how might this potentially increase unity among all humans?

Create Central

www.mhhe.com/createcentral

Internet References

The Ancient World
www.omnibusol.com/ancient.html

Fossil Hominids
www.talkorigins.org/faqs/homs

Article

Prepared by: Joseph R. Mitchell, *Howard Community College*
and Helen Buss Mitchell, *Howard Community College*

Out of Africa

Somewhere between 80,000 and 50,000 years ago, Africa saved *Homo sapiens* from extinction. Charting the DNA shared by more than six billion people, a population geneticist—and director of the Genographic Project—suggests what humanity "owes" its first home.

SPENCER WELLS

Learning Outcomes

After reading this article, you will be able to:

- Determine what evidence is offered to prove that Africa was the birthplace of humankind and understand what implication this might have for the modern world.

Do you think you know who you are? Maybe Irish, Italian, Jewish, Chinese, or one of the dozens of other hyphenated Americans that make up the United States melting pot? Think deeper—beyond the past few hundred years. Back beyond genealogy, where everyone loses track of his or her ancestry—back in that dark, mysterious realm we call prehistory. What if I told you every single person in America—every single person on earth—is African? With a small scrape of cells from the inside of anyone's cheek, the science of genetics can even prove it.

Here's how it works. The human genome, the blueprint that describes how to make another version of you, is huge. It's composed of billions of sub-units called nucleotides, repeated in a long, linear code that contains all of your biological information. Skin color, hair type, the way you metabolize milk: it's all in there. You got your DNA from your parents, who got it from theirs, and so on, for millions of generations to the very beginning of life on earth. If you go far enough back, your genome connects you with bacteria, butterflies, and barracuda—the great chain of being linked together through DNA.

What about humanity, though? What about creatures you would recognize as being like you if they were peering over your shoulder right now? It turns out that every person alive today can trace his or her ancestry back to Africa. Everyone's DNA tells a story of a journey from an African homeland to wherever you live. You may be from Cambodia or County Cork, but you are carrying a map inside your genome that describes the wanderings of your ancestors as they moved from the savannas of Africa to wherever your family came from most recently. This is thanks to genetic markers—tiny changes that arise rarely and spontaneously as our DNA is copied and passed down through the generations—which serve to unite people on ever older branches of the human family tree. If you share a marker with someone, you share an ancestor with him or her at some point in the past: the person whose DNA first had the marker that defines your shared lineage. These markers can be traced to relatively specific times and places as humans moved across the globe. The farther back in time and the closer to Africa we get, the more markers we all share.

What set these migrations in motion? Climate change—today's big threat—seems to have had a long history of tormenting our species. Around 70,000 years ago it was getting very nippy in the northern part of the globe, with ice sheets bearing down on Seattle and New York; this was the last Ice Age. At that time, though, our species, *Homo sapiens,* was still limited to Africa; we were very much homebodies. But the encroaching Ice Age, perhaps coupled with the eruption of a super-volcano named Toba, in Sumatra, dried out the tropics and nearly decimated the early human population. While *Homo sapiens* can be traced to around 200,000 years ago in the fossil record, it is remarkably difficult to find an archaeological record of our species between 80,000 and 50,000 years ago, and genetic data suggest that the population eventually dwindled to as few as 2,000 individuals. Yes, 2,000—fewer than fit into many symphony halls. We were on the brink of extinction.

And then something happened. It began slowly, with only a few hints of the explosion to come: The first stirrings were art—tangible evidence of advanced, abstract thought—and a significant improvement in the types of tools humans made. Then, around 50,000 years ago, all hell broke loose. The human population began to expand, first in Africa, then leaving the homeland to spread into Eurasia. Within a couple of thousand years we had reached Australia, walking along the coast of South Asia. A slightly later wave of expansion into the Middle East, around 45,000 years ago, was aided by a brief damp period in the Sahara. Within 15,000 years of the exodus from Africa our species had entered Europe, defeating the Neanderthals in the process. (Neanderthals are distant cousins, not ancestors; our evolutionary lineages have been separate for more than 500,000 years.) We had also populated Asia, learning to live in frigid temperatures not unlike those on the Moon, and around 15,000 years ago we walked across a short-lived, icy land bridge to enter the Americas—the first hominids ever to set foot on the continents of the Western Hemisphere. Along the way we kept adapting to new climates, in some cases lost our dark tropical skin pigmentation, developed different languages, and generated the complex tapestry of human diversity we see around the world today, from Africa to Iceland to Tierra del Fuego. But the thing that set it all in motion, the thing that saved us from extinction, happened first in Africa. Some anthropologists call it the Great Leap Forward, and it marked the true origin of our species—the time when we started to behave like humans.

Africa gave us the tool we needed, in the form of a powerful, abstract mind, to take on the world.

Africa gave us the tool we needed, in the form of a powerful, abstract mind, to take on the world (and eventually to decode the markers in our DNA that make it possible to track our amazing journeys). Perhaps just a few small genetic mutations that appeared around 50,000 years ago gave humans the amazing minds we use to make sense of the confusing and challenging world around us. Using our incredible capacity to put abstract musing into practice, we have managed to populate every continent on earth, in the process increasing the size of our population from a paltry few thousand to more than six billion. Now, 50 millennia after that first spark, times have changed. A huge number of things have contributed to Africa's relative decline on the world stage, perhaps most important geography. As Jared Diamond describes in his masterly book *Guns, Germs, and Steel,* Eurasia, with its East-West axis, allowed the rapid latitudinal diffusion of ideas and tools that would give its populations a huge advantage after the initial leap out of Africa. Couple that with the results of colonial exploitation over the past five centuries, and Africa, despite many strengths and resources, is once again in need, as it was 70,000 years ago. This time, though, things are different.

The world population that was spawned in Africa now has the power to save it. We are all alive today because of what happened to a small group of hungry Africans around 50,000 years ago. As their good sons and daughters, those of us who left, whether long ago or more recently, surely have a moral imperative to use our gifts to support our cousins who stayed. It's the least we can do for the continent that saved us all thousands of years ago.

Critical Thinking

1. If humans were on the verge of extinction between 80,000 and 50,000 years ago and the advanced abstract thinking that saved us originated in Africa, how does this change the way you think about the African continent?

2. What theories does this article offer to explain Africa's "relative decline"?

3. How do genetic markers help us trace our origins?

Create Central

www.mhhe.com/createcentral

Internet References

Fossil Hominids
www.talkorigins.org/faqs/homs
The Human Origins Program at the Smithsonian
http://anthropology.si.edu/humanorigins/

Article

Prepared by: Joseph R. Mitchell, *Howard Community College*
and Helen Buss Mitchell, *Howard Community College*

Who Were the First Americans?

MICHAEL D. LEMONICK AND ANDREA DORFMAN

Learning Outcomes

After reading this article, you will be able to:

- Discuss how the discovery of Kennewick Man has changed the way we view the First Americans.

It was clear from the moment Jim Chatters first saw the partial skeleton that no crime had been committed—none recent enough to be prosecutable, anyway. Chatters, a forensic anthropologist, had been called in by the coroner of Benton County, Wash., to consult on some bones found by two college students on the banks of the Columbia River, near the town of Kennewick. The bones were obviously old, and when the coroner asked for an opinion, Chatters' off-the-cuff guess, based on the skull's superficially Caucasoid features, was that they probably belonged to a settler from the late 1800s. Then a CT scan revealed a stone spear point embedded in the skeleton's pelvis, so Chatters sent a bit of finger bone off to the University of California at Riverside for radiocarbon dating. When the results came back, it was clear that his estimate was dramatically off the mark. The bones weren't 100 or even 1,000 years old. They belonged to a man who had walked the banks of the Columbia more than 9,000 years ago.

In short, the remains that came to be known as Kennewick Man were almost twice as old as the celebrated Iceman discovered in 1991 in an Alpine glacier, and among the oldest and most complete skeletons ever found in the Americas. Plenty of archaeological sites date back that far, or nearly so, but scientists have found only about 50 skeletons of such antiquity, most of them fragmentary. Any new find can thus add crucial insight into the ongoing mystery of who first colonized the New World—the last corner of the globe to be populated by humans. Kennewick Man could cast some much needed light on the murky questions of when that epochal migration took place, where the first Americans originally came from and how they got here.

U.S. government researchers examined the bones, but it would take almost a decade for independent scientists to get a good look at the skeleton. Although it was found in the summer of 1996, the local Umatilla Indians and four other Columbia Basin tribes almost immediately claimed it as ancestral remains under the Native American Graves Protection and Repatriation Act (*see box*), demanding that the skeleton be reburied without the desecration of scientific study. A group of researchers sued, starting a legal tug-of-war and negotiations that ended only last summer, with the scientists getting their first extensive access to the bones. And now, for the first time, we know the results of that examination.

What the Bones Revealed

It was clearly worth the wait. The scientific team that examined the skeleton was led by forensic anthropologist Douglas Owsley of the Smithsonian Institution's National Museum of Natural History. He has worked with thousands of historic and prehistoric skeletons, including those of Jamestown colonists, Plains Indians and Civil War soldiers. He helped identify remains from the Branch Davidian compound in Texas, the 9/11 attack on the Pentagon and mass graves in Croatia.

In this case, Owsley and his team were able to nail down or make strong guesses about Kennewick Man's physical attributes. He stood about 5 ft. 9 in. tall and was fairly muscular. He was clearly right-handed: the bones of the right arm are markedly larger than those of the left. In fact, says Owsley, "the bones are so robust that they're bent," the result, he speculates, of muscles built up during a lifetime of hunting and spear fishing.

An examination of the joints showed that Kennewick Man had arthritis in the right elbow, both knees and several vertebrae but that it wasn't severe enough to be crippling. He had suffered plenty of trauma as well. "One rib was fractured and healed," says Owsley, "and there is a depression fracture on his forehead and a similar indentation on the left side of the head." None of those fractures were fatal, though, and neither was the spear jab. "The injury looks healed," says Owsley. "It wasn't a weeping abscess." Previous estimates had Kennewick Man's age as 45 to 55 when he died, but Owsley thinks he may have been as young as 38. Nothing in the bones reveals what caused his demise.

But that's just the beginning of an impressive catalog of information that the scientists have added to what was already known—all the more impressive given the limitations placed on the team by the U.S. Army Corps of Engineers, which is responsible for the skeleton because the Corps has jurisdiction over the federal land on which it was found. The researchers had to do nearly all their work at the University of Washington's Burke Museum, where Kennewick Man has been housed in a locked room since 1998, under the watchful eyes of representatives of both the Corps and the museum, and according to

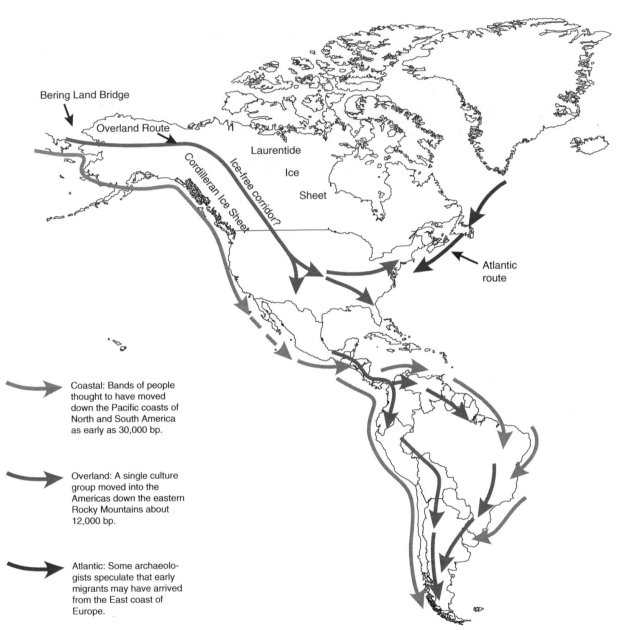

Bering Land Bridge

Overland Route

Laurentide

Ice

Sheet

Cordilleran Ice Sheet

Ice-free corridor?

Atlantic route

Coastal: Bands of people thought to have moved down the Pacific coasts of North and South America as early as 30,000 bp.

Overland: A single culture group moved into the Americas down the eastern Rocky Mountains about 12,000 bp.

Atlantic: Some archaeologists speculate that early migrants may have arrived from the East coast of Europe.

Hypothesized routes for the first settlement of the Americas.

a strict schedule that had to be submitted in advance. "We only had 10 days to do everything we wanted to do," says Owsley. "It was like a choreographed dance."

Perhaps the most remarkable discovery: Kennewick Man had been buried deliberately. By looking at concentrations of calcium carbonate left behind as underground water collected on the underside of the bones and then evaporated, scientists can tell that he was lying on his back with his feet rolled slightly outward and his arms at his side, the palms facing down—a position that could hardly have come about by accident. And there was no evidence that animal scavengers had been at the body.

The researchers could also tell that Kennewick Man had been buried parallel to the Columbia, with his left side toward the water: the bones were abraded on that side by water that eroded the bank and eventually dumped him out. It probably happened no more than six months before he was discovered, says team member Thomas Stafford, a research geochemist based in Lafayette, Colo. "It wouldn't have been as much as a year," he says. "The bones would have been more widely dispersed."

The deliberate burial makes it especially frustrating for scientists that the Corps in 1998 dumped hundreds of tons of boulders,

The Legal Battle: Who Should Own the Bones?

The Pawnee Indians tell a mordant story about the kinds of things scientists discover when they study sacred remains. After decades of watching researchers plunder its burial grounds for bodies and artifacts, the tribe finally forced Nebraska researchers and museums to return the items in 1989. Once the treasures were back in hand, the Pawnees asked the scientists what they had learned.

"You ate corn," they answered.

Kennewick Man, the most talked-about Native American remains uncovered in recent memory, may be revealing a lot more than that. But if it's a mother lode for scientists, it's also been a massive headache for the Federal Government, local tribes and the lawyers who represent them. At issue is the Native American Graves Protection and Repatriation Act (NAGPRA), a 1990 law intended to make up in some way for the generations of scientific strip-mining Indian lands have endured, by either selectively protecting artifacts still in Native American hands or returning those that have been carried off.

NAGPRA probably seemed straightforward enough to the legislators' eyes. It requires Indians who want to protect an artifact to show by a preponderance of archaeological, geological, historical or other evidence that they have some cultural affiliation to it. But what appears clear to lawyers can be devilishly hard to apply.

For one thing, the older an artifact is, the harder it becomes to show the neat nexus of affiliations that the law requires. "The evidence collapses as you go back in time," says Pat Barker, an archaeologist for the Bureau of Land Management (BLM) in Nevada, who is working on a similar case. "The first 500 years is pretty solid, by 1,000 it's getting dicey, and by 10,000 most of that stuff you just can't get at."

That would put Kennewick Man—more than 9,000 years old—firmly in the hands of the scientists. But lawyers and archaeologists aren't theologians, and for a lot of Native Americans, spirituality is what protecting artifacts is all about.

"Archaeologists always tell us where we came from," says Rochanne Downs, a coordinator for the dozens of Indian tribes that have banded together in the Great Basin Inter-Tribal NAGPRA Coalition. "Well, we know where we came from. Our people were made from mud, and then the tribes were sent out. Sometimes people think that's funny, but when I look at the immaculate Conception, that seems kind of odd to me." Not all Indians believe in the ancient-clay idea, but if those who do are going to be shown the same respect as the adherents of any other faith, then the age of the find becomes immaterial. "We don't have a prehistory," says Downs. "We have one continuous history."

Human remains that are returned to tribes are treated reverently. Several weeks ago, the Umatilla tribe in Washington reinterred 240 remains in a massive burial accompanied by traditional ceremonies and moving words from tribal elders. "It was hard to describe," says Audie Huber, a Native American—though not an Umatilla—who has monitored the Kennewick case for several tribes. "The sense of relief was palpable."

What makes these disputes more difficult is that modern archaeological methods often guarantee that an artifact will—in the eyes of the Indians at least—be defiled. Not only is the find seized from sacred land, but radiocarbon dating (which was used to estimate the age of Kennewick Man) requires that a portion of the find be destroyed. "We're always presented as antiscience Luddites," says Huber. "But we don't like seeing remains pulverized and irradiated."

Finally, ticklish as any NAGPRA case can be, the extreme age and importance of Kennewick Man practically guaranteed that it would be beset by legal maneuvering. Soon after the find was announced in 1996, the Umatilla tribes of Oregon and Washington claimed it. Eight anthropologists immediately sued for the right to study it, and archaeologists for the National Park Service were called in to study the skeleton and help settle the dispute. They found in favor of the Umatillas, but a federal district court disagreed, as did a circuit court, citing a lack of cultural and genetic evidence to link the bones to the claimants.

That stunned the tribes, since NAGPRA does not include a DNA requirement. Last year Senator John McCain proposed an amendment that might have smoothed things over by broadening NAGPRA to include Indians who were ever indigenous to a particular region. The measure appeared headed for approval until the Interior Department objected to it—a move that helped scuttle the change and only inflamed the situation further. Even if the McCain measure had passed, the Indians see it as merely a first step, citing another recent case in which the BLM ignored a NAGPRA committee recommendation without even a court ruling. "With NAGPRA," says Downs, "you get a judgment but no enforcement." With as many as 118,000 sets of Native American remains still awaiting repatriation, that problem is not going away.

The pity is that even in its current, imperfect state, NAGPRA can work (to date, about 30,000 remains and half a million funerary objects have been returned to tribes), provided that everyone turns down the heat and tries to reach consensus. However much knowledge scientists pry from the Kennewick bones, the goodwill lost and the contentious precedents set may make the next generation of NAGPRA cases a lot less friendly than the last.

—Jeffrey Kluger.
Reported by Dan Cray/Los Angeles.

dirt and sand on the discovery site—officially as part of a project to combat erosion along the Columbia River, although some scientists suspect it was also to avoid further conflict with the local tribes. Kennewick Man's actual burial pit had already been washed away by the time Stafford visited the site in December 1997, but a careful survey might have turned up artifacts that could have been buried with him. And if his was part of a larger burial plot, there's now no way for archaeologists to locate any contemporaries who might have been interred close by.

Still, the bones have more secrets to reveal. They were never fossilized, and a careful analysis of their carbon and nitrogen composition, yet to be performed, should reveal plenty about

Kennewick Man's diet. Says Stafford: "We can tell if he ate nothing but plants, predominantly meat or a mixture of the two." The researchers may be able to determine whether he preferred meat or fish. It's even possible that DNA could be extracted and analyzed someday.

While the Corps insisted that most of the bones remain in the museum, it allowed the researchers to send the skull fragments and the right hip, along with its embedded spear point, to a lab in Lincolnshire, Ill., for ultrahigh-resolution CT scanning. The process produced virtual slices just 0.39 mm (about 0.02 in.) thick—"much more detailed than the ones made of King Tut's mummy," says Owsley. The slices were then digitally recombined into 3-D computer images that were used to make exact copies out of plastic. The replica of the skull has already enabled scientists to clear up a popular misconception that dates back to the initial reports of the discovery.

Was Kennewick Man Caucasian?

Thanks to Chatters' mention of Caucasoid features back in 1996, the myth that Kennewick Man might have been European never quite died out. The reconstructed skull confirms that he was not—and Chatters never seriously thought otherwise. "I tried my damnedest to curtail that business about Caucasians in America early," he says. "I'm not talking about today's Caucasians. I'm saying they had 'Caucasoid-like' characteristics. There's a big difference." Says Owsley: "[Kennewick Man] is not North American looking, and he's not tied in to Siberian or Northeast Asian populations. He looks more Polynesian or more like the Ainu [an ethnic group that is now found only in northern Japan but in prehistoric times lived throughout coastal areas of eastern Asia] or southern Asians."

That assessment will be tested more rigorously when researchers compare Kennewick Man's skull with databases of several thousand other skulls, both modern and ancient. But provisionally, at least, the evidence fits in with a revolutionary new picture that over the past decade has utterly transformed anthropologists' long-held theories about the colonization of the Americas.

Who Really Discovered America?

The conventional answer to that question dates to the early 1930s, when stone projectile points that were nearly identical began to turn up at sites across the American Southwest. They suggested a single cultural tradition that was christened Clovis, after an 11,000-year-old-plus site near Clovis, N.M. And because no older sites were known to exist in the Americas, scientists assumed that the Clovis people were the first to arrive. They came, according to the theory, no more than 12,000 years B.P. (before the present), walking across the dry land that connected modern Russia and Alaska at the end of the last ice age, when sea level was hundreds of feet lower than it is today. From there, the earliest immigrants would have made their way south through an ice-free corridor that geologists know cut through what are now the Yukon and Mackenzie river valleys, then along the eastern flank of the Canadian Rockies to the continental U.S. and on to Latin America.

That's the story textbooks told for decades—and it's almost certainly wrong. The first cracks in the theory began appearing in the 1980s, when archaeologists discovered sites in both North and South America that seemed to predate the Clovis culture. Then came genetic and linguistic analyses suggesting that Asian and Native American populations diverged not 12,000 years ago but closer to 30,000 years ago. Studies of ancient skulls hinted that the earliest Americans in South America had different ancestors from those in the North. Finally, it began to be clear that artifacts from Northeast Asia dating from just before the Clovis period and South American artifacts of comparable age didn't have much in common with Clovis artifacts.

Those discoveries led to all sorts of competing theories, but few archaeologists or anthropologists took them seriously until 1997. In that year, a blue-ribbon panel of researchers took a hard look at evidence presented by Tom Dillehay, then at the University of Kentucky, from a site he had been excavating in Monte Verde, Chile. After years of skepticism, the panel finally affirmed his claim that the site proved humans had lived there 12,500 years ago. "Monte Verde was the turning point," says David Meltzer, a professor of prehistory at Southern Methodist University in Dallas who was on the panel. "It broke the Clovis barrier."

Why? Because if people were living in southern Chile 12,500 years ago, they must have crossed over from Asia considerably earlier, and that means they couldn't have used the ice-free inland corridor; it didn't yet exist. "You could walk to Fairbanks," says Meltzer. "It was getting south from Fairbanks that was a problem." Instead, many scientists now believe, the earliest Americans traveled down the Pacific coast—possibly even using boats. The idea has been around for a long time, but few took it seriously before Monte Verde.

One who did was Jon Erlandson, an archaeologist at the University of Oregon, whose work in Daisy Cave on San Miguel Island in California's Channel Island chain uncovered stone cutting tools that date to about 10,500 years B.P., proving that people were traveling across the water at least that early. More recently, researchers at the Santa Barbara Museum of Natural History redated the skeletal remains of an individual dubbed Arlington Springs Woman, found on another of the Channel Islands, pushing her age back to about 11,000 years B.P. Farther south, on Cedros Island off the coast of Baja California, U.C. at Riverside researchers found shell middens—heaps of kitchen waste, essentially—and other materials that date back to the same period as Daisy Cave. Down in the Andes, researchers have found coastal sites with shell middens dating to about 10,500 years B.P.

And in a discovery that offers a sharp contrast to the political hoopla over Kennewick Man, scientists and local Tlingit and Haida tribes cooperated so that researchers could study skeletal remains found in On Your Knees Cave on Prince of Wales Island in southern Alaska. "There's no controversy," says Erlandson, who has investigated cave sites in the same region. "It hardly ever hits the papers." Of about the same vintage as Kennewick Man and found at around the same time, the Alaskan bones, along with other artifacts in the area, lend strong support to the coastal-migration theory. "Isotopic analysis of the human remains," says James Dixon, the University of Colorado at Boulder anthropologist who found them, "demonstrates that the individual—a young male in his early 20s—was raised primarily on a diet of seafood."

Cruising Down the Kelp Highway

Erlandson has found one more line of evidence that supports the migration theory. While working with a group of marine ecologists, he was startled to learn that there were nearly continuous kelp forests growing just offshore all the way from Japan in the western Pacific to Alaska and down the West Coast to Baja California, then (with a gap in the tropics) off the coast of South America. In a paper presented three weeks ago, he outlined the potential importance to the earliest Americans of what he calls the "kelp highway."

"Most of the early sites on the west coast are found adjacent to kelp forests, even in Peru and Chile," he says. "The thing about kelp forests is they're extremely productive." They not only provide abundant food, from fish, shellfish, seals and otters that thrive there, but they also reduce wave energy, making it easier to navigate offshore waters. By contrast, the inland route along the ice-free corridor would have presented travelers with enormous ecological variability, forcing them to adapt to new conditions and food sources as they traveled.

Unfortunately, the strongest evidence for the coastal theory lies offshore, where ancient settlements would have been submerged by rising seas over the past 10,000 years or so. "Artifacts have been found on the continental shelves," says Dixon, "so I'm quite confident there's material out there." But you need submersible craft to search, and, he says, that type of research is a very hard sell to the people who own and operate that kind of equipment. "The maritime community is interested in shipwrecks and treasures. A little bit of charcoal and some rocks on the ocean floor is not very exciting to them."

Multiple Migrations

Even if the earliest Americans traveled down the coast, that doesn't mean they couldn't have come through the interior as well. Could there have been multiple waves of migration along a variety of different routes? One way scientists have tried to get a handle on that question is through genetics. Their studies have focused on two different types of evidence extracted from the cells of modern Native Americans: mitochondrial DNA, which resides outside the nuclei of cells and is passed down only through the mother; and the Y chromosome, which is passed down only from father to son. Since DNA changes subtly over the generations, it serves as a sort of molecular clock, and by measuring differences between populations, you can gauge when they were part of the same group.

Or at least you can try. Those molecular clocks are still rather crude. "The mitochondrial DNA signals a migration up to 30,000 years ago," says research geneticist Michael Hammer of the University of Arizona. "But the Y suggests that it occurred within the last 20,000 years." That's quite a discrepancy. Nevertheless, Hammer believes that the evidence is consistent with a single pulse of migration.

Theodore Schurr, director of the University of Pennsylvania's Laboratory of Molecular Anthropology, thinks there could have been many migrations. "It looks like there may have been one primary migration, but certain genetic markers are more prevalent in North America than in South America," Schurr explains, suggesting secondary waves. At this point, there's no definitive proof of either idea, but the evidence and logic lean toward multiple migrations. "If one migration made it over," Dillehay, now at Vanderbilt University, asks rhetorically, "why not more?"

Out of Siberia?

Genetics also points to an original homeland for the first Americans—or at least it does to some researchers. "Skeletal remains are very rare, but the genetic evidence suggests they came from the Lake Baikal region" of Russia, says anthropologist Ted Goebel of the University of Nevada at Reno, who has worked extensively in that part of southern Siberia. "There is a rich archaeological record there," he says, "beginning about 40,000 years ago." Based on what he and Russian colleagues have found, Goebel speculates that there were two northward migratory pulses, the first between 28,000 and 20,000 years ago and a second sometime after 17,000 years ago. "Either one could have led to the peopling of the Americas," he says.

Like just about everything else about the first Americans, however, this idea is open to vigorous debate. The Clovis-first theory is pretty much dead, and the case for coastal migration appears to be getting stronger all the time. But in a field so recently liberated from a dogma that has kept it in an intellectual straitjacket since Franklin Roosevelt was President, all sorts of ideas are suddenly on the table. Could prehistoric Asians, for example, have sailed directly across the Pacific to South America? That may seem far-fetched, but scientists know that people sailing from Southeast Asia reached Australia some 60,000 years ago. And in 1947 the explorer Thor Heyerdahl showed it was possible to travel across the Pacific by raft in the other direction.

At least a couple of archaeologists, including Dennis Stanford of the Smithsonian, even go so far as to suggest that the earliest Americans came from Europe, not Asia, pointing to similarities between Clovis spear points and blades from France and Spain dating to between 20,500 and 17,000 years B.P. (Meltzer, Goebel and another colleague recently published a paper calling this an "outrageous hypothesis," but Dillehay thinks it's possible.)

All this speculation is spurring a new burst of scholarship about locations all over the Americas. The Topper site in South Carolina, Cactus Hill in Virginia, Pennsylvania's Meadowcroft, the Taima-Taima waterhole in Venezuela and several rock shelters in Brazil all seem to be pre-Clovis. Dillehay has found several sites in Peru that date to between 10,000 and 11,000 years B.P. but have no apparent links to the Clovis culture. "They show a great deal of diversity," he says, "suggesting different early sources of cultural development in the highlands and along the coast."

It's only by studying those sites in detail and continuing to search for more evidence on land and offshore that these questions can be fully answered. And as always, the most valuable evidence will be the earthly remains of the ancient people themselves. In one 10-day session, Kennewick Man has added immeasurably to anthropologists' store of knowledge, and the next round of study is already under way. If scientists treat those bones with respect and Native American groups acknowledge the importance of unlocking their secrets, the mystery of how and when the New World was populated may finally be laid to rest.

Critical Thinking

1. In what specific ways does Spirit Cave Man challenge our understanding of the "first Americans?"

2. Karen Wright asserts that "none of the new stories are simple." Critically discuss the implications of this assertion.

3. How important is it to know the origin and culture of the "First Americans"? Why should we care?

Create Central

www.mhhe.com/createcentral

Internet References

The Origin and Evolution of Life
http://cmex-www.arc.nasa.gov/VikingCD/Puzzle/EvoLife.htm

Article

Prepared by: Joseph R. Mitchell, *Howard Community College*
and Helen Buss Mitchell, *Howard Community College*

Stone Age India

Does evidence buried by a super-volcano redraw the map of human migration?

Samir S. Patel

Learning Outcomes

After reading this article, you will be able to:

- Discuss how the discoveries at Andhra Pradesh will alter the way the history of India is written.

The great alchemy of prehistoric archaeology is the way it conjures our story—of modern humans, that is— from bits of stone and bone. But the tale of our evolution and migration to every corner of the planet is filled with gaps and guesswork. Scholars have been trying for decades to make sense of it. Much of their focus for the Middle and Upper Paleolithic eras, from roughly 250,000 to 30,000 years ago, has been on Africa, Europe, and the Levant (eastern Mediterranean). University of Oxford archaeologist Mike Petraglia sees an injustice there, which he and a diverse team of researchers from three continents are working to rectify. Specifically, they believe that India deserves a central place in our understanding of the Paleolithic. Their evidence suggests that modern humans arrived there rather early and thrived under some unusually grim conditions.

The missing chapter of our story that they have uncovered in the state of Andhra Pradesh has no clear beginning, but it has a rare bookmark, a hazy horizon of fine grit that marks what may be the most important event in human history. And there—around 74,000 years ago, well before Homo sapiens are thought to have arrived in India—is where we start.

The Jurreru Valley is wide on the bottom and steep on the sides. Now dammed, in the Middle Paleolithic its river lazily meandered and fed shallow lakes during the monsoon. The water attracted people—who they were is a critical matter of debate—and funneled them through the landscape. They hunted, gathered, and made tools from stone eroding out of the valley's south side. But one day 74,000 years ago their lives took a dramatic turn. A low, distant rumble rolled in from the south, followed hours later by horizon-spanning clouds stacked like thunderheads. Day turned darker than night,

a chill hit the air, and there began a blizzard of fine, abrasive particles—ash from 1,700 miles southeast on the Indonesian island of Sumatra. One of the most explosive events known, the Toba Volcano spewed 670 cubic miles of ash 25 miles into the atmosphere. In India there was nowhere to hide. Four inches of the stuff blanketed the subcontinent. The eruption also cast sulfur into the stratosphere, forming an aerosol that scattered sunlight. Some climatologists believe this touched off a thousand-year cold snap, and geneticists say humans underwent a drastic population drop, known as a bottleneck, some time in the Middle Paleolithic. A popular theory puts the two together; Toba almost wiped us out. Pity the poor people of Jurreru. Or should we?

When Petraglia, an American who recently left Cambridge for Oxford, started working in remote parts of India in 1987, he was frustrated by the difficulty of acquiring equipment, navigating bureaucracy, and getting just about anything done. Later, an Indian grad student advised, "Sir, adjustment." He took the advice and now faces the difficulties with a bemused chuckle. It's worth it, he says, somehow managing to be simultaneously pensive and effusive: "I've seen archaeological sites around the world, but I keep coming back to India because it's such an amazing place for its archaeology." For the Paleolithic, though, this is a minority view. The prevailing wisdom is that India's sites aren't well stratified, are near-impossible to date, and lack the greatest and sexiest of finds—human remains. It's not worth the "adjustment." So the subcontinent has had little place in the study of early humans. Petraglia's reply (minus the skeletal remains, so far) is the Jurreru Valley.

The small village of Jwalapuram sits where the valley spills onto the plain. With freshly swept lanes flanked by open sewers, it is both tidy and sloppy in the way of rural Indian villages. Archaeologists pour out of the truck and load equipment from a shed, while villagers who have been hired to work on the dig grab the roof rack and stand on the running boards. When the researchers first arrived in 2003, the locals thought they came for what all Westerners come for—land, gold, or women. Education efforts have helped change their attitude. "It turned from suspicion to now they're proactive about the history and prehistory," says Petraglia. The van makes a half-dozen stops around the valley to drop off an archaeologist or two and a couple of workers. The team has identified more than 180 sites, which Petraglia thinks provide a more or less unbroken record of the last 100,000 years of human occupation. "Basically, the entire valley is full of archaeology," he says.

Petraglia and his co-principal investigator, Ravi Korisettar of Karnataka University, began this project at the nearby Billa Surgam Caves, where they were following up on excavations dating to the 19th century. A graduate student, Sacha Jones, was interested in studying Toba ash, so Korisettar asked around to find out if any locals had seen fine white material in the ground. Someone pointed them to Jwalapuram. "Even from a distance it was clear that dust was rising in the air, and it could be nothing else but volcanic ash," says Korisettar.

The ash was in the air, actually, because of laundry. Washed into channels of the river soon after it fell, it accumulated in clean, white, eight-foot-thick beds that have hardened over the years. Today, heavy machinery scoops and crushes it, and villagers (including children), covered in ash from head to toe, sift and bag it by hand. The sacks of angular, abrasive particles are sold for use in laundry detergent. The haze that surrounds the miners is like a window into the valley of 74,000 years ago. Perhaps like the valley's earlier inhabitants, the villagers experience breathing and digestive problems, as well as linear brown stains on their teeth caused by excess fluoride that leeches from the ash into the groundwater.

The archaeologists have a different interest in the ash. Within sight of the ash-clouds, Petraglia and I climb into a deep square cut into the scrubby hard pan. As archaeologist Janardhana Bora from Karnataka University supervises the dig and I step lightly around stone tools awaiting documentation, Petraglia crouches to point out a narrow white line that runs around the pit's perimeter. Ashfall. To a prehistoric archaeologist, it is a thing of pure beauty, an answer to a vexing question—how old is this rock in the ground? The team can trace this moment across 160 acres of the valley, confident that anything under it is older than 74,000 years ago and anything above, younger. And this in a place notorious for difficult-to-date sites. "When I first started working in India, a big critique from Western paleoanthropologists was that there's nothing in India that is stratified or datable," says Petraglia. "And we're proving that it's everywhere."

As we walk between excavation sites, Petraglia picks up a rock that is fluted all the way around like the cylinder of a revolver. It is a core, a stone shaped so that small blades could be knocked off it easily and consistently. The initial survey of the valley turned up loads of things like this, probably exposed by ash mining. So they shifted most of their effort to the valley, and in five years have excavated hundreds of stone tools, such as flakes and scrapers, and prepared cores, which are indicative of Middle Paleolithic technology. Notably, the artifacts appear on both sides of the ash horizon. "No one had ever found artifacts associated with Toba in such a beautiful way," Petraglia says. With a dating technique called optically stimulated luminescence (OSL)—useful, but with a rather wide margin of error—they found that the artifacts below the ash date to around

77,000 years ago, and above it to 74,000 years ago. And the artifacts on both sides are remarkably similar, demonstrating an unexpected continuity and resilience. Contrary to the team's expectations, whoever was here survived Toba, culture intact.

Later, I join the archaeologists for their regular communal dinner in a hotel room. Over rice wrapped in banana leaves and watery, spicy South Indian curries served in plastic bags, they crack open beers and laptops. There's a lot to discuss: a half-dozen valley sites, two in the caves, and another in the hills. There's a volcanologist, lithic experts, a flintknapper experimenting with what happens when cows trample stone tools, a community outreach team, and several other specialists soon to arrive. Petraglia and I begin to discuss a critical question: Who made the tools? It is known that India was occupied by archaic humans going back 700,000 years or more, and that later they might have started using Middle Paleolithic tools. The earliest modern humans were thought to have arrived not long before 50,000 years ago, basically passing through on the way to Australia. This would suggest that the residents of the ancient Jurreru Valley who saw the sky go dark were not moderns. But Petraglia, Korisettar, and Chris Clarkson, the team's lithic specialist from the University of Queensland, think they were. If they're right, they'll add a major new arrow on the map of human migration.

Clarkson is working on an extensive analysis of the artifacts from the Jurreru Valley. He compared the cores with European, African, and Levantine examples, with a variety of factors related to their shape, dimensions, and usage. Statistically, he says, they appear most closely related to cores from southern Africa that were made by Homo sapiens (versus European Middle Paleolithic tools, which are most commonly associated with Neanderthals). Typically, outside of Africa, modern humans are associated with so-called Upper Paleolithic technology, which includes thin blades and bone tools. But in India, there's no clear Upper Paleolithic—in fact, there's no change in stone tools there at all until around 35,000 years ago. There's a continuity, and no reason to think that moderns didn't arrive there far earlier.

Modern humans first left Africa 125,000 to 100,000 years ago, spreading into the Levant. This is considered a failed dispersal—moderns there gave way to Neanderthals around 70,000 years ago and didn't reappear until the Upper Paleolithic, by which time humans had just started on their way to Australia and had begun to enter Europe. Based on their analysis, Petraglia theorizes that the first dispersal was no failure, but that we had also moved at that time to the Arabian Peninsula— where promising sites are being investigated—and then to India, bearing African-style tools. "If moderns were in the Levant circa 100,000 years ago, they should also have been in southern Arabia and could thus have started eastward to India," says Robin Dennell of the University of Sheffield and author of the 2009 book, The Palaeolithic Settlement of Asia. "My personal hunch is that moderns were in India by 70,000 years ago and possibly 100,000 years ago."

Ofer Bar-Yosef of Harvard University thinks Petraglia has indeed found evidence of moderns. "His current discovery of this data in this place is extremely important," he says, "and it fills an important gap in our geographic knowledge of the dispersal of the modern human."

Not everyone is convinced, however, especially in the absence of human fossils. Petraglia's arguments for cultural continuity also defy one of the more dramatic theories regarding the Middle Paleolithic—that Toba almost wiped humans out.

The Toba bottleneck theory is the brainchild of prehistoric anthropologist Stanley Ambrose of the University of Illinois, climatologist Michael Rampino of New York University, and others. In 1992, Rampino speculated that the sulfuric veil from Toba led to a "volcanic winter," with mean global cooling of five to nine degrees Fahrenheit. He thinks this change caught a climate on the brink, creating a feedback loop of snow cover that started a mini Ice Age. Ice cores from Greenland confirm what appears to be a spike of sulfur around the time of the eruption, followed by 1,000 years of cold (and then 2,000 warmer years before the last Ice Age). The most recent models, by Alan Robock of Rutgers University, find global cooling of 20 degrees Fahrenheit or more, but not enough to start a mini Ice Age. "But it would be decades before things returned to close to normal," says Robock. "You'd have to be very smart, adaptive, and lucky to survive that."

Genetic data may also support Ambrose's theory. Studies of mitochondrial DNA appear to show a population drop of 75 to 90 percent—down to as few as 10,000 individuals, the capacity of a minor-league baseball park—followed by a population rebound sometime in the last couple hundred thousand years. Ambrose even thinks this decline and expansion might have helped differentiate the human races. Warm, wet environments, specifically those in Africa, would have offered the best chance for survival. While India might have made a good refuge from the Toba winter, the entire subcontinent was blanketed in ash. Could anyone have survived there?

Adam Durant, a volcanologist on Petraglia and Korisettar's team, leads me through the ash miners' deep gashes in the Jurreru Valley, so bright white that they make me squint through my sunglasses. This ash accumulated as it washed down from the hillsides for six or seven years following the eruption, covering and fossilizing riverside trees that now form a ghost forest of branches and roots. Atop the ash are windblown deposits that suggest the monsoon shifted after the eruption. It certainly was a catastrophe, but perhaps a relatively brief one. Korisettar says the valley would have been a good place to weather the storm; springs in the mountains offer untainted water and the steep valley walls might have sloughed off ash before it could kill plant life. "It did not cover the entire landscape like a mantle," he says.

Regarding the climatic impact, Cambridge volcanologist Clive Oppenheimer, who is on the research team, says we know few specifics. He theorizes that the Toba eruption, though still massive, produced far less sulfur than has been assumed—100 times less than Robock used in his model—meaning it may have merely nudged the climate by a degree or so. And the Greenland ice core, he says, has no ash and no clear link between Toba and the sulfur spike, which might have come from a much smaller eruption nearby, in Iceland perhaps. "We're lacking evidence to say whether it was a large or small impact," he says. Furthermore, estimates of the timing of the genetic bottleneck and release vary widely from 60,000 to 2 million years ago.

Petraglia and Korisettar's discovery of the first archaeological evidence associated with Toba ash suggests that the eruption was survivable, even for those relatively close by. "The whole, appealing, sexy theory—we're questioning it," says Petraglia. "I'm just saying that the story is more complicated than the simplistic scenario that has been put out."

In response, Ambrose is critical of both Petraglia's approach and findings. "Right at the beginning he was really selling this stuff so hard and making such firm conclusions that I was like, 'I need to see evidence for this,'" he says. In his estimation, the evidence presented so far is not enough. The archaeological deposits in the Jurreru Valley, he finds, don't appear to be in their original context (they might have eroded into deposits from elsewhere). "The basis for the continuity of stone tool industries before and after the eruption is really, really weak," he says. Also, the lithic analysis is too limited to prove anything—the tools simply aren't distinctive enough to be indicative of an African origin—and there is no evidence of such an old lineage in the modern Indian genome. Ambrose wants to see more samples and some human remains. "You cannot prove one way or the other until you have actual skeletons," he says. "It's the only way."

Petraglia agrees on that point. "I would love to provide everyone with the smoking gun, but other than a fossil, it's going to be hard," he says. "How convincing are we? Well, that's a matter of doing more work." In Jurreru, however, the ash makes the soil acidic, destroying animal bones—human or otherwise. That said, Petraglia defends the integrity of the stratigraphy there and says that additional finds made since he first reported his results continue to support the theories of cultural continuity and the presence of modern humans. And with regard to the genetic information, Petraglia argues that these old bloodlines may have been swamped by population booms, especially in the last 5,000 years. According to Cambridge geneticist Toomas Kivisild, it is possible that up to 5 percent of the modern genome was contributed by lineages that are no longer detectable. "I understand that this is nonconventional. I'm okay with that because big chunks of the world, like India, have never been thought about in terms of human evolutionary processes," Petraglia says. "Just the fact that we are doing it is a serious advance in Indian prehistory."

This is one of the first modern, large-scale, interdisciplinary prehistoric projects in India. There could be countless other sites across the country to help refine the story. The research team has already spent a field season in the Son Valley of Madhya Pradesh to the north, where they also found ash and artifacts. Indian archaeologists traditionally have focused on surveys and have identified scores of other Paleolithic sites, but they often lack the resources for big interdisciplinary projects or in-depth artifact analysis. Petraglia and Korisettar hope some of the young Indian archaeologists on this excavation will change that. But the passing over of India and other regions as important sites for prehistoric archaeology goes deeper than that.

Western thinking has long dominated Paleolithic archaeology, and defined the Middle and Upper Paleolithic sequences in Europe and the Middle and Late Stone Ages of Africa as the keys to understanding how modern human technology and thought evolved. "That was the framework we had for a long time," says Korisettar. So when Paleolithic archaeology began in India more than a century ago, Indians and Englishmen alike were looking for analogues to Europe. In fact, claims about Upper Paleolithic evidence first drove this project. The Billa Surgam Caves were discovered and excavated by the English in the 19th century. They determined, as did Indian archaeologists who dug there in the 1970s, that it was an Upper Paleolithic site with scores of bone tools.

Their conclusions were called into question as early as the 19th century and as recently as the 1960s. "I thought, ooh boy, if we could look at this area in a new way with all the approaches and techniques we have now," says Petraglia. In the caves, in a dig supervised by archaeologist Jinu Koshy of Karnataka University, the team has found very few items that are clearly human artifacts. The worked bone previously reported might have been gnawed by porcupines, and the stone artifacts might be the natural result of rockfall from cave walls. They have continued to dig, even after shifting to the valley, for the paleoenvironmental data the caves have protected, particularly bones of mammals. "Find me a hominid," Petraglia says to Koshy, "even if it proves all my theories wrong."

But decades of looking for that European sequence—rather than a distinct, indigenous model—had already affected Indian Paleolithic archaeology. "The way in which the occupation history of modern humans played out is different in different places," says Petraglia. "The Western European model is very biased. People have tried to throw it onto huge areas of the world and it just doesn't work."

This new chapter in the story of early *Homo sapiens* will pick up plot points and details as a new generation of Indian archaeologists and interested outsiders remake the country in the image of Europe and Africa—not in the conclusions they draw or the lithic sequence they define, but as a place with thousands of sites, clear chronology, and a long history of excavation. Petraglia and Korisettar are working on a continuing reevaluation of India's prehistory, one that is distinct from—and every bit as important as—Europe's. "I think we have a new, alternative model here," he says.

India never experienced an Upper Paleolithic like Europe's, they reason, with its technological and cultural shifts, but stayed with Middle Paleolithic tools until 35,000 years ago. Then technology changed, at a time unique to India, to a microlithic style marked by the use of tiny, easy-to-replace blades mounted on wooden tools. On the north side of the Jurreru Valley, the team found a rock shelter containing well-stratified microlithic deposits—seven layers and 53,000 artifacts. Such sites have long been considered to be less than 10,000 years old, but Petraglia's team has radiocarbon dated this one to 35,000 years ago, later than microlithic tools appear in Africa, but earlier than in Europe. There is no known migration event at that time, so Petraglia argues this technology developed independently in India. The shift also coincides with genetic evidence for a major demographic change with rapidly rising populations (it is India, after all), symbolism, and group dynamics.

India's evolution is distinct, and occurs in a crucial place in the world, between early and late adopters (West and East) of modern human technology and culture. Understanding it will illuminate all the prehistory around it, both chronologically and geographically. "I think India's central problem here is that it is not seen as a bridge, but as a place in the middle of nowhere," says Dennell. "Unless we understand this bridge, it's hard to know what's happening on either side."

Critical Thinking

1. What might a study of ancient India tell us about human migration patterns?

2. What role might the Toba volcanic eruption of 74,000 years ago have played in India's prehistory?

3. Is India a "bridge" that we must understand in order "to know what's happening on either side"? Critically discuss.

Create Central

www.mhhe.com/createcentral

Internet References

Talk-Origins
www.talkorigins.org

SAMIR S. PATEL is a senior editor at *Archaeology*.

From *Archaeology*, January/February 2010, pp. 28, 30–34. Copyright © 2010 by Archaeological Institute of America. Reprinted by permission of *Archaeology Magazine*. www.archaeology.org

Prepared by: Joseph R. Mitchell, *Howard Community College*
and Helen Buss Mitchell, *Howard Community College*

Article

Is War Inevitable?

E. O. WILSON

Learning Outcomes

After reading this article, you will be able to:

- Understand the arguments for and against the inevitability of warfare among humans.

"istory is a bath of blood," wrote William James, whose 1906 antiwar essay is arguably the best ever written on the subject. "Modern man inherits all the innate pugnacity and all the love of glory of his ancestors. Showing war's irrationality and horror is of no effect on him. The horrors make the fascination. War is the strong life; it is life in extremis; war taxes are the only ones men never hesitate to pay, as the budgets of all nations show us."

Our bloody nature, it can now be argued in the context of modern biology, is ingrained because group-versus-group competition was a principal driving force that made us what we are. In prehistory, group selection (that is, the competition between tribes instead of between individuals) lifted the hominids that became territorial carnivores to heights of solidarity, to genius, to enterprise—and to fear. Each tribe knew with justification that if it was not armed and ready, its very existence was imperiled. Throughout history, the escalation of a large part of technology has had combat as its central purpose. Today the calendars of nations are punctuated by holidays to celebrate wars won and to perform memorial services for those who died waging them. Public support is best fired up by appeal to the emotions of deadly combat, over which the amygdala—a center for primary emotion in the brain—is grandmaster. We find ourselves in the "battle" to stem an oil spill, the "fight" to tame inflation, the "war" against cancer. Wherever there is an enemy, animate or inanimate, there must be a victory. You must prevail at the front, no matter how high the cost at home.

Any excuse for a real war will do, so long as it is seen as necessary to protect the tribe. The remembrance of past horrors has no effect. From April to June in 1994, killers from the Hutu majority in Rwanda set out to exterminate the Tutsi minority, which at that time ruled the country. In a hundred days of unrestrained slaughter by knife and gun, 800,000 people died, mostly Tutsi. The total Rwandan population was reduced by 10 percent. When a halt was finally called, 2 million Hutu fled the country, fearing retribution. The immediate causes for the bloodbath were political and social grievances, but they all stemmed from one root cause: Rwanda was the most overcrowded country in Africa. For a relentlessly growing population, the per capita arable land was shrinking toward its limit. The deadly argument was over which tribe would own and control the whole of it.

Universal Conflict

Once a group has been split off from other groups and sufficiently dehumanized, any brutality can be justified, at any level, and at any size of the victimized group up to and including race and nation. And so it has ever been. A familiar fable is told to symbolize this pitiless dark angel of human nature. A scorpion asks a frog to ferry it across a stream. The frog at first refuses, saying that it fears the scorpion will sting it. The scorpion assures the frog it will do no such thing. After all, it says, we will both perish if I sting you. The frog consents, and halfway across the stream the scorpion stings it. Why did you do that, the frog asks as they both sink beneath the surface. It is my nature, the scorpion explains.

War, often accompanied by genocide, is not a cultural artifact of just a few societies. Nor has it been an aberration of history, a result of the growing pains of our species' maturation. Wars and genocide have been universal and eternal, respecting no particular time or culture. Archaeological sites are strewn with the evidence of mass conflicts and burials of massacred people. Tools from the earliest Neolithic period, about 10,000 years ago, include instruments clearly designed for fighting. One might think that the influence of pacific Eastern religions, especially Buddhism, has been consistent in opposing violence. Such is not the case. Whenever Buddhism dominated and became the official ideology, war was tolerated and even pressed as part of faith-based state policy. The rationale is simple, and has its mirror image in Christianity: Peace, nonviolence, and brotherly love are core values, but a threat to Buddhist law and civilization is an evil that must be defeated.

Since the end of World War II, violent conflict between states has declined drastically, owing in part to the nuclear standoff of the major powers (two scorpions in a bottle writ large). But civil wars, insurgencies, and state-sponsored terrorism continue unabated. Overall, big wars have been replaced around the world by small wars of the kind and magnitude more typical of hunter-gatherer and primitively agricultural societies. Civilized societies have tried to eliminate torture, execution, and the murder of civilians, but those fighting little wars do not comply.

Archaeologists have determined that after populations of *Homo sapiens* began to spread out of Africa approximately 60,000 years ago, the first wave reached as far as New Guinea and Australia. The descendants of the pioneers remained as hunter-gatherers or at most primitive agriculturalists, until reached by Europeans. Living populations of similar early provenance and archaic cultures are the aboriginals of Little Andaman Island off the east coast of India, the Mbuti Pygmies of Central Africa, and the !Kung Bushmen of southern Africa. All today, or at least within historical memory, have exhibited aggressive territorial behavior.

Lethal Legacy

Tribal aggressiveness goes back well beyond Neolithic times, but no one as yet can say exactly how far. It could have begun at the time of *Homo habilis,* the earliest known species of the genus *Homo,* which arose between 3 million and 2 million years ago in Africa. Along with a larger brain, those first members of our genus developed a heavy dependence on scavenging or hunting for meat. And there is a good chance that it could be a much older heritage, dating beyond the split 6 million years ago between the lines leading to modern chimpanzees and to humans.

A series of researchers, starting with Jane Goodall, have documented the murders within chimpanzee groups and lethal raids conducted between groups. It turns out that chimpanzees and human hunter-gatherers and primitive farmers have about the same rates of death due to violent attacks within and between groups. But nonlethal violence is far higher in the chimps, occurring between a hundred and possibly a thousand times more often than in humans.

The patterns of collective violence in which young chimp males engage are remarkably similar to those of young human males. Aside from constantly vying for status, both for themselves and for their gangs, they tend to avoid open mass confrontations with rival troops, instead relying on surprise attacks. The purpose of raids made by the male gangs on neighboring communities is evidently to kill or drive out their members and acquire new territory. There is no certain way to decide on the basis of existing knowledge whether chimpanzees and humans inherited their pattern of territorial aggression from a common ancestor or whether they evolved it independently in response to parallel pressures of natural selection and opportunities encountered in the African homeland. From the remarkable similarity in behavioral detail between the two species, however, and if we use the fewest assumptions required to explain it, a common ancestry seems the more likely choice.

The principles of population ecology allow us to explore more deeply the roots of mankind's tribal instinct. Population growth is exponential. When each individual in a population is replaced in every succeeding generation by more than one—even by a very slight fraction more, say 1.01—the population grows faster and faster, in the manner of a savings account or debt. A population of chimpanzees or humans is always prone to grow exponentially when resources are abundant, but after a few generations even in the best of times it is forced to slow down. Something begins to intervene, and in time the population reaches its peak, then remains steady, or else oscillates up and down. Occasionally it crashes, and the species becomes locally extinct.

What is the "something"? It can be anything in nature that moves up or down in effectiveness with the size of the population. Wolves, for example, are the limiting factor for the population of elk and moose they kill and eat. As the wolves multiply, the populations of elk and moose stop growing or decline. In parallel manner, the quantity of elk and moose are the limiting factor for the wolves: When the predator population runs low on food, in this case elk and moose, its population falls. In other instances, the same relation holds for disease organisms and the hosts they infect. As the host population increases, and the populations grow larger and denser, the parasite population increases with it. In history diseases have often swept through the land until the host populations decline enough or a sufficient percentage of its members acquire immunity.

There is another principle at work: Limiting factors work in hierarchies. Suppose that the primary limiting factor is removed for elk by humans' killing the wolves. As a result the elk and moose grow more numerous, until the next factor kicks in. The factor may be that herbivores overgraze their range and run short of food. Another limiting factor is emigration, where individuals have a better chance to survive if they leave and go someplace else. Emigration due to population pressure is a highly developed instinct in lemmings, plague locusts, monarch butterflies, and wolves. If such populations are prevented from emigrating, the populations might again increase in size, but then some other limiting factor manifests itself. For many kinds of animals, the factor is the defense of territory, which protects the food supply for the territory owner. Lions roar, wolves howl, and birds sing in order to announce that they are in their territories and desire competing members of the same species to stay away.

Wars Past, Present, Future

Humans and chimpanzees are intensely territorial. That is the apparent population control hardwired into their social systems. What the events were that occurred in the origin of the chimpanzee and human lines—before the chimpanzee-human split of 6 million years ago—can only be speculated. I believe that the evidence best fits the following sequence. The original limiting factor, which intensified with the introduction of group hunting for animal protein, was food. Territorial behavior evolved as a device to sequester the food supply. Expansive wars and annexation resulted in enlarged territories and favored genes that prescribe group cohesion, networking, and the formation of alliances.

For hundreds of millennia, the territorial imperative gave stability to the small, scattered communities of *Homo sapiens,* just as they do today in the small, scattered populations of surviving hunter-gatherers. During this long period, randomly spaced extremes in the environment alternately increased and decreased the population size so that it could be contained within territories. These demographic shocks led to forced emigration or aggressive expansion of territory size by conquest, or both together. They also raised the value of forming alliances outside of kin-based networks in order to subdue other neighboring groups.

Ten thousand years ago, at the dawn of the Neolithic era, the agricultural revolution began to yield vastly larger amounts of food from cultivated crops and livestock, allowing rapid growth in human populations. But that advance did not change human nature. People simply increased their numbers as fast as the rich new resources allowed. As food again inevitably became the limiting factor, they obeyed the territorial imperative. Their descendants have never changed. At the present time, we are still fundamentally the same as our hunter-gatherer ancestors, but with more food and larger territories. Region by region, recent studies show, the populations have approached a limit set by the supply of food and water. And so it has always been for every tribe, except for the brief periods after new lands were discovered and their indigenous inhabitants displaced or killed.

The struggle to control vital resources continues globally, and it is growing worse. The problem arose because humanity failed to seize the great opportunity given it at the dawn of the Neolithic era. It might then have halted population growth below the constraining minimum limit. As a species we did the opposite, however. There was no way for us to foresee the consequences of our initial success. We simply took what was given us and continued to multiply and consume in blind obedience to instincts inherited from our humbler, more brutally constrained Paleolithic ancestors.

Critical Thinking

1. What are the strongest arguments put forth by E.O. Wilson for the biological and cultural roots of warfare?

2. How does Wilson use the fable of the Scorpion and the Frog to support his argument that war is inevitable?

Create Central

www.mhhe.com/createcentral

Internet References

WWW-VL Prehistoric Web Index
   http://easyweb.easynet.co.uk/~aburnham/database/index.htm

Wilson, E.O.; Horgan, John. From *Discover*, June 2012, pp. 53–57. Copyright © 2012 by Discover Syndication. Reprinted by permission via PARS International.

Unit II

UNIT

Prepared by: Joseph R. Mitchell, *Howard Community College*
and Helen Buss Mitchell, *Howard Community College*

The Beginnings of Culture, Agriculture, and Cities

Most of what we take for granted as essential to human flourishing had its beginnings during this time period. As our distant ancestors moved from a hunter-gatherer, nomadic lifestyle to horticulture, the intentional planting and harvesting of plants, and the domestication of animals, rather than the hunt, culture became possible. With this shift came permanent settlements, usually near water, as we see in the Fertile Crescent of Mesopotamia— literally, the place between two rivers, the Tigris and Euphrates. As farmers remained close by to tend crops and raise animals, cities were born, beginning some 10,000 years ago.

Culture arises when people observe the natural environment around them and imagine ways to shape it. The annual flooding of the Nile River in Egypt made a rich civilization possible, and it sharpened the skills of those who "read" the heavens to find the star Sirius that signaled the river's rise and the beginning of the harvest season. When humans discovered ways to manipulate their environment, a great transformation was under way. Trial and error probably led to the establishment of the great grain crops—corn in the Western Hemisphere, wheat in the Middle East, and rice in Asia. Each seems to have developed independently.

Peaceful coexistence is much more likely when resources are plentiful. Scarcity creates competition and can lead to warfare. Myths and stories, honed and embellished over time, establish what is vital and worth protecting. What circumstances would have been extreme enough to cause a culture to make war on a neighbor? And, who would have had the power to make such a decision? Nomads can always move on. In a city, major decisions touch everyone. So, collective decisionmaking would have been required for anything affecting the common good. Windows into these ancient cultures open once writing is established. Sumerians were among the first to experiment with, first, business transactions and, later, poetry and prayer, using their characteristic cuneiform style. Prominent in myth and story, the Goddess Innana ruled the heavens, making powerful roles for human women seem "natural." And, Egyptian mariners sailed great distances in search of spices.

As cities mature and cultures exchange goods, barter or trade of one item for another works for a while. Eventually, however, a marketplace of many items of differing values requires what economists call a medium of exchange—something with a fixed value, against which a wide range of goods can be priced. Precious metals such as gold and silver served as the first money, making possible sophisticated transfers of goods and services as early as 2500 BCE. Agriculture and cash had created new possibilities for early humans.

Article

Prepared by: Joseph R. Mitchell, *Howard Community College*
and Helen Buss Mitchell, *Howard Community College*

Who Were the Hurrians?

New discoveries in Syria suggest a little-known people fueled the rise of civilization.

ANDREW LAWLER

Learning Outcomes

After reading this article, you will be able to:

- Discuss how the history of the Hurrians changes the history of Mesopotamia.

With its vast plaza and impressive stone stairway leading up to a temple complex, Urkesh was designed to last. And for well over a millennium, this city on the dusty plains of what is now northeastern Syria was a spiritual center for a puzzling people called the Hurrians. All but forgotten by history, their origin remains obscure, but new research shows they maintained a remarkable continuity during turbulent times—and that their beliefs and traditions echoed across the Near East long after they themselves had vanished.

Excavations led by husband-and-wife UCLA archaeologists Georgio Buccellati and Marilyn Kelly-Buccellati over the past quarter century reveal that the Hurrians were far more than just another wandering tribe in the fractious Middle East. And during last year's season, they found compelling evidence that the Hurrians not only strongly influenced the language, culture, and religion of later peoples, but also may have been present 1,000 years earlier—just as nearby Mesopotamians began to create the first cities.

That idea is at odds with a long-held belief among scholars that the Hurrians arrived much later from the Caucasus or some other distant region to the northeast, a theory based on linguistic associations with Caucasus' languages and the fact that Hurrian names are absent from the historical record until Akkadian times. But Piotr Michaelowski, an Assyriologist at the University of Michigan, notes that Hurrian, like Sumerian, is a language unrelated to Semitic or Indo-European tongues that dominated the region during and after the third millennium B.C. Perhaps, he suggests, the Hurrians were earlier inhabitants of the region, who, like the Sumerians, had to make room for the Semitic-speaking people who created the world's first empire based at Akkad in central Mesopotamia around 2350 B.C.

The Hurrians were long dismissed as a marginal tribe from the north, drawn to the fringes of civilization after the rise of the great southern Sumerian centers of Ur, Uruk, and Nippur. Scholars long assumed that the Hurrians arrived in the middle of the third millennium B.C., and eventually settled down and adopted cuneiform as a script and built their own cities. By 1200 B.C., their lands had been swallowed by the Hittites, an expanding empire from Anatolia. The Hurrians then vanished from the Near Eastern stage.

Amid the grand backdrop of empires, wars, and migrations at the heart of Near Eastern history, the Hurrians were not even a footnote until the 1920s, when epigraphers translated Hittite texts dating to the second millennium B.C. Those texts and tablets revealed powerful empires like the Mitanni that struck fear into the Hittites, corresponded with Egyptian kings, and wrote musical compositions. Those compositions, the oldest yet known, were performed as far away as Ugarit on the Mediterranean coast. The Hurrians had a distinct pantheon of deities, led by Kumbari, the god of the underworld. His storm-god son Teshub is associated with a sacred bull, carries a thunderbolt, and may have influenced Greek conceptions of Zeus, Semitic ideas about Baal (the great god of the Canaanites and Phonenicians), and Indian views of Indra, king of the Hindu gods and lord of wind and weather. Each is associated with the same symbols. Yet despite these tantalizing hints of widespread influence, archaeological evidence of the Hurrians remained elusive. Even the location of the ancient Hurrian capital of Urkesh, mentioned frequently in texts, was unknown.

British archaeologist Max Mallowan came tantalizingly close to discovering Urkesh in the 1930s, when he briefly wandered onto a remote mound called Tell Mozan in northeastern Syria close to the Turkish and Iraq borders—an area that marks the boundary between the highlands of Anatolia and the plains of Mesopotamia. But he concluded there were Roman layers that would take too much time and money to remove.

So Tell Mozan lay undisturbed for another half-century, until the Buccellatis picnicked at the site. Intrigued by a mound that towers nearly 90 feet above the plain and had never been investigated, they took a closer look. What Mallowan thought were Roman sherds, they determined, were actually remains of pots from the third millennium B.C. There was a hint that the site might be ancient Urkesh; two bronze lions were sold in the marketplace at Amuda, the closest town, in the 1940s and ended up at the Louvre in Paris and the Metropolitan Museum of Art in New York. The inscription on each read: "The king of Urkesh built the temple of the lion." But the exact provenance of the finds was uncertain, given that there are numerous tells, or mounds, in the area.

The Buccellatis started digging in the early 1980s, but proof that the site was indeed Urkesh evaded them for a decade. They uncovered a mid-third-millennium B.C. structure at the tells high point with a stone ramp and a large stone block in the center that appears to be an altar. The most intriguing find, however, was a stone statue of a lion similar to the bronze ones sold in Amuda. They suspected this complex

was the temple of the lion mentioned in the inscriptions, but lacked concrete evidence. Then one day the team discovered a storehouse near the city gate that contained hundreds of delicate and fragmentary clay seal impressions with pictographic images. After painstaking work, Marilyn found one that read "Tupkish, king of Urkesh" in cuneiform script from approximately 2300 B.C. This find, along with the other seal impressions, led the Buccellatis to conclude they had indeed found the long-lost Hurrian capital.

Tupkish is a classic Hurrian name. Since the Hurrians adapted Akkadian cuneiform to their language, scholars are able to read the cuneiform script they carved into their seals— and the Buccellatis have found more than 100 seals with the name of Tupkish's foreign queen, Uqnitum, Akkadian for "girl of lapis lazuli," the precious stone mined in Afghanistan that was a symbol of royalty and wealth in ancient Mesopotamia. The storeroom appeared to be the place where her property was kept, a sign of her prominent role in the court. The queen may

Gate to the Underworld

Though the Urkesh palace resembles other Akkadian-style royal residences in the region, there is one feature adjacent to the structure that appears unique to this site. Tucked into the ground near the royal residence is an unusual stone-lined pit built sometime before the palace was constructed. The pit's large underground room has a square antechamber facing west and a deeper circular pit. Discovered in 1999 as the team was tracing the southern wall of the palace, the pit bears no similarity to anything known from this era.

Examining the pit more carefully, UCLA archaeologists Giorgio Buccellati and Marilyn Kelly-Buccellati determined that it was originally covered with a roof and had a single, easily closed entrance facing west. At first, they thought they had stumbled on a royal tomb, but no human remains could be identified. Then they speculated it was a ritual well or a holy place in which the king and queen might make funerary offerings—*kipsum* in Hurrian. Within the pit they found silver rings, an obsidian blade, clay animal figurines, and copper and bronze pins, along with a scattering of other small artifacts, including an unusual jar depicting a nude woman with long braided hair. Only one readable seal fragment was found, from the 22nd century B.C., depicting a seated deity identified as the sun god Shamash.

But it was the mass of animal bones that made them consider a more radical idea. The largest number of animal remains were piglets followed by puppies; dogs were considered unclean by the Hurrians and by the later Hittites as well. Sheep, goat, and donkey bones also were found, but in smaller numbers. In many cases, the remains of entire animals were intact.

This led Marilyn to propose that the structure was in fact an *api*—a ritual place for transmitting troublesome demons and spirits into the underworld, a ritual detailed in many

later Hittite texts. "The gods of the underworld are dead, so they can't be threatened by death or evil," explains Gernot Wilhelm, an archaeologist and philologist at the University of Würzburg in Germany. Therefore, pig and dog sacrifices would have been perfectly fine for those deities *not* bound by the rules of the living.

In the Hurrian world—and in the later Hittite culture— the purpose of calling on the underworld forces was to seal away bad spirits. For example, a priest might perform a ritual at sunset in a house that was the site of a murder, Wilhelm says. Typically this would involve digging or tracing a circular hole in the floor so that the gods of the netherworld could suck down the evil.

But the Hittite and Hurrian texts about the api ritual were written 1,000 years after construction of the pit in Urkesh. And aside from a couple of small holes near the Hittite capital of Hatusa, there is little archaeological evidence for their existence as permanent structures. Some Near Eastern specialists are far from convinced. The Urkesh pit "could be anything," insists Piotr Michaelowski, an Assyriologist at the University of Michigan—for example, a well in which animals drowned. Basing the function of the pit on texts dating to a millennium later is highly questionable, he adds.

The Buccellatis argue that the long history of animal bones in the Urkesh pit, the door facing the setting sun, and the circular and underground nature of the structure— combined with the later texts—provide compelling evidence that the elite of Urkesh used the pit to rid themselves of evil. Billie Jean Collins, a Hittite specialist at Emory University in Atlanta, notes that Hittites saw Kumbari, whose hometown was Urkesh—as the god of the underworld. Collins, who studied the Urkesh pit, thinks that its use as an api is the best explanation of the structure.

—AL

have been an Akkadian princess at a time when Akkad was at its height, extending from just south of Urkesh to the Persian Gulf, some 600 miles away. Her time in Urkesh appears to have been pleasant: one seal shows her enjoying a performance by a lyre player and a singer while surrounded by her daughters and servants.

Nor was Uqnitum the only Akkadian in Urkesh. Tar'am-Agade, the daughter of the great Akkadian king Naram-Sin, left behind her own seal, along with that of an Akkadian official named Isharbeli. If Naram-Sin's daughter lived at the Urkesh court, the Buccellatis believe it would be convincing evidence that Akkad chose an alliance rather than a costly conquest of the Hurrian capital. That may illustrate the strength and independence of Urkesh, since other cities, from Ur in the south to Brak in the north, were clearly overwhelmed by the Akkadian military.

Three generations of royal family, starting with Tupkish and Uqnitum, lived in the mud-brick palace built around 2250 B.C. just west of a slightly older temple. The Buccellatis found intriguing evidence of daily life in the court when they uncovered a service wing of the palace that included a kitchen. Tuli, "the female cook of the queen," mentioned on a seal impression, appeared to manage a team of servants tasked to come up with a variety of dishes. Nearby are the storerooms where the seal impressions were found as well as work areas. Only a portion of the formal part of the palace, where the royals lived and entertained, has been excavated, but the team has uncovered remains of a toilet, a substantial drain system, and a stone-paved courtyard. The archaeologists also found a tablet that appears to show the floor plan of three rooms in this part of the palace, possibly an architects guide used by the builders.

The Urkesh finds are also helping remake our view of the ancient Near East. The continuity of the city is amazing, given the dangers that smaller urban areas faced in a region famous for the movements of nomads and armies. "It's a tribute to the people of Urkesh that they defended themselves so well and so long," says Michaelowski. "Places like this tend to get zapped." Even today, the region is tense. Just a few minutes from Urkesh is the heavily guarded Turkish border, with its sinister barbed wire fence and watchtowers. And a short distance in the other direction is war-torn Iraq. But despite the politics, the location still has its advantages. The road to Iraq is lined for miles with tractor-trailer trucks hauling supplies from Turkey and Syria. Though often at odds, Anatolians and Mesopotamians have always been eager to do business with one another—and the Hurrians sat at that very juncture.

In its heyday at the end of the third millennium B.C., Urkesh was a thriving capital of up to 20,000 residents. And though its power waned over the centuries, it remained a sacred center during the rise of the Hurrian-speaking Mitanni Empire that dominated the region during the 14th century B.C. By 1200, however, the Hittites had crushed the Mitannis, ending Hurrian independence. Even then, Urkesh and Hurrian traditions continued to influence the Hittites in Anatolia, just as Greek culture continued to influence Rome after it was conquered. "The Hittites conquered Mitanni, but ultimately the

Hurrians won the day," says Billie Jean Collins, a Hittite specialist at Emory University. Though a small town by then, Urkesh continued to be known as a sacred center respected by the Hittites—perhaps in the same way that imperial Romans respected the Oracle of Delphi or Persians honored the ancient foreign deities worshiped in the crumbling city of Uruk in southern Mesopotamia.

The holy area was at the heart of Urkesh. While the palace nearby was covered over with new houses within a century or two, the sacred precinct remained surprisingly unaltered over at least 1,000 years. The complex is made up of the temple atop a walled acropolis reached by the massive stairway. Until the past field season, the Buccellatis believed the high mound was originally oval-shaped, but recent data shows it more likely to have been an asymmetrical polygon. Giorgio says this shape resembles sites to the north in Anatolia more than those just to the south and east in northern Mesopotamia—a sign that the Hurrians were able to incorporate ideas drawn from both regions in their architecture. The complex dates to at least 2400 B.C.

That early date was surprising enough to archaeologists and epigraphers who assumed the Hurrians had only just arrived in the region then. But this past season, the excavators have found remains of even earlier structures. Immediately below a third-millennium B.C. terrace, the team found seals and pottery that date to the mid-fourth millennium B.C. Giorgio downplays the finds, which he insists are preliminary.

The implications, however, excite other scholars. Recent excavations at Tell Brak and Tell Hamoukar just a short drive across the plain, show an urban revolution brewing during the early and mid-fourth millennium in the region, a development that appears separate and independent from the development of southern Mesopotamian centers. Did the Hurrians play a part in this nascent civilization? If they did, the conclusion flies in the face of conventional scholarly wisdom about a Caucasus origin. "The school of thought that says the Hurrians emigrated to the plains is just a theory, and not well founded" says Gernot Wilhelm, an archaeologist and philologist at the University of Würzburg in Germany. But archaeological data is sparse: though a few other sites with Hurrian occupation have been excavated, all of them date to a later period than Urkesh.

The discovery of a sophisticated city with monumental architecture, plumbing, stonework, and a large population contradicts the idea that Hurrians were a roving mountain people in a strange land. And if Urkesh existed as many as 1,000 years earlier than previously thought—and was populated with Hurrian speakers—then the Hurrians may have been far from latecomers on the stage of the ancient Near East. Since historical records pertaining to northern Mesopotamia are sparse until Akkadian times, the absence of references to Hurrians does not mean they were not there, Wilhelm adds.

He proposes a more radical notion based on admittedly circumstantial linguistic evidence that complements the finds at Urkesh. He notes that the style of Hurrian personal names resembles that of the Akkadians. "Hurrian- and Semitic-speaking peoples may have lived together for a long time," Wilhelm suggests, because naming typically changes slowly. Those Semitic speakers seem to have appeared in large numbers in Mesopotamia in the third millennium B.C., though exactly from where is a matter of controversy. Given the evidence that Urkesh was settled as early as 3500 B.C., he suggests that Hurrians may have spread across the Fertile Crescent in prehistory.

All these scholars acknowledge there is not yet enough information to say with any certainty where the Hurrians came from and when they arrived at Urkesh, and all say they hope the Buccellatis will uncover a trove of tablets that might reveal the secrets of Hurrian history. "Before the mid-1990s, the Hurrians only existed as a few personal names," notes Gonzalo Rubio, a philologist at the Pennsylvania State University. "We are still missing huge pieces of the picture, but the finds at Urkesh are incredible."

Far from being yet another rough nomadic tribe, such as the Amorites or Kassites who were latecomers to the Mesopotamian party, the Hurrians and their unique language, music, deities, and rituals may have played a key role in shaping the first cities, empires, and states. The language has died, the music faded, and the rituals are forgotten. But thanks to the sculptors, stone masons, and seal carvers at Urkesh, Hurrian creativity can shine once again.

Critical Thinking

1. How do recent archaeological findings contradict long held assumptions about the Hurrians?
2. What features suggest sophisticated city life in Urkesh?
3. It has been suggested that history is the story told by the winners. What might we learn by studying "losers," such as the Hurrians?

Create Central

www.mhhe.com/createcentral

Internet References

Urkesh and the Hurrians
http://128.97.6.202/urkeshpublic/hurrians.htm

ANDREW LAWLER is a staff writer for Science.

Article   Prepared by: Joseph R. Mitchell, *Howard Community College*
                                         and Helen Buss Mitchell, *Howard Community College*

Dawn of the City

Excavations Prompt a Revolution in Thinking about the Earliest Cities

BRUCE BOWER

Learning Outcomes

After reading this article, you will be able to:

• Discuss how the discovery of the ancient city of Tell Brak has forced scientists to rethink how urbanism originated in the Near East.

A massive earthen mound rises majestically and rather mysteriously above agricultural fields in northeastern Syria. From a distance, the more than 130-foot-tall protrusion looks like a jagged set of desolate hills. But up close, broken pottery from a time long past litters the mound's surface. The widespread debris vividly testifies to the large number of people, perhaps as many as 10,000, who once congregated on and around this raised ground.

Known as Tell Brak, the mound and its surrounding fields contain the remnants of the world's oldest known city. The word *tell* refers to an ancient Near Eastern settlement consisting of numerous layers of mud-brick construction. Generation after generation of residents cut down, leveled, and replaced each layer with new buildings, eventually creating an enormous mound.

At the city of Brak, the first *tell* layers were built more than 6,000 years ago. At that time, the settlement emerged as an urban center with massive public structures, mass-produced crafts and daily goods, and specially made prestige items for socially elite citizens.

Surprisingly, the evidence for Brak's rise as a major city predates, by as many as 1,000 years, evidence for comparable urban centers hundreds of miles to the south, in what's now southern Iraq. Like those southern cities, Brak lay between the Tigris and Euphrates rivers in the ancient land of Mesopotamia. But scholars have long assumed that southern Mesopotamia's fertile crescent, blessed with rich soil and copious water, represented the "cradle of civilization." In the traditional scenario, fast-growing southern cities established colonies that led to a civilization of the north. Southern immigrants sought timber, metal, and other resources that were absent in their homeland.

Excavations at Tell Brak and at the nearby remains of a comparably ancient city, Hamoukar, may turn that model on its head. New discoveries indicate that the world's first cities either arose in northern Mesopotamia or developed independently and at roughly the same time in the region's northern and southern sectors. The idea that urbanites radiated out of the south and triggered the construction of major northern settlements now rests on shaky ground.

"As yet, no other large site, indeed no other Near Eastern site, has yielded evidence of early urban growth comparable to that at Tell Brak," says archaeologist Augusta McMahon of the University of Cambridge in England. McMahon directs excavations at the Syrian site.

Researchers have also discovered dramatic signs of ancient warfare at Brak and Hamoukar. Further analysis of these discoveries may illuminate the nature of contacts and conflict between northern and southern Mesopotamians.

"Excavations at Brak and Hamoukar are the biggest thing to happen in Mesopotamian research in a long time," comments archaeologist Guillermo Algaze of the University of California, San Diego.

U rban sprawl Excavations at Tell Brak started modestly enough about 70 years ago. Archaeologist Max Mallowan, husband of author Agatha Christie, led a team that uncovered the ruins of a religious temple. Thousands of small stone idols depicting eyes littered its floor. The investigators dubbed the poorly dated structure the Eye Temple.

A husband-and-wife team from Cambridge, David Oates and Joan Oates, initiated a new series of Tell Brak excavations in 1976. At the time, they suspected that the site held remnants of urban development from perhaps as early as 5,000 years ago, when, evidence suggested, the Eye Temple had been built.

But as years of field work accumulated, unexpectedly deep tell levels came to light. By 2006, the investigators realized that they were digging into something special. Sediment from 6,000 years ago or more, when the earliest known southern Mesopotamian cities had not yet been built, started to surrender the remains of huge public buildings.

In the September 2007 *Antiquity,* McMahon, Joan Oates, and their colleagues describe these discoveries. (David Oates is now deceased.)

The oldest structure found so far, dating to about 6,400 years ago, featured a massive entrance framed by two towers and an enormous doorsill made of a single piece of basalt. Excavations revealed parts of two large rooms inside, a group of small rooms near the front, and a pair of guard rooms just outside the entrance. Despite its size, it was likely not a temple, but rather an administrative center, McMahon says. With a central room and several satellite areas, its layout is not that of a standard Mesopotamian temple.

"Whatever its formal functions, this is the earliest Mesopotamian example of a genuinely secular monumental building," McMahon says.

A second ancient structure, with red mud-brick walls surrounding three floors, housed potters and other artisans. These workers had access to several large, clay ovens inside the building.

Pottery finds include large, open bowls, small bowls with incised craftsman's marks, and a basic type of mass-produced bowl.

The scientists also uncovered huge piles of raw flint, obsidian, and a variety of colored stones used to make beads and other stone objects. Some areas contained caches of clay spindle whorls situated near the bones of sheep or possibly goats. These finds resulted from wool weaving, according to the investigators.

To their surprise, this building also yielded an unusual obsidian and white marble chalice. A piece of obsidian had been hollowed out to form a drinking vessel and attached with sticky bitumen to a white marble base. This fancy cup contrasts with mass-produced bowls found throughout the building and points to the presence of at least a small number of social elites in ancient Brak, McMahon holds.

Workshop rooms also contained numerous clay stamp seals, including one bearing the impression of a lion and another showing a lion caught in a net. Such seals signified a ruler's total ownership or control in southern Mesopotamian cities, and probably meant much the same at Brak.

The researchers refer to a third huge structure from roughly 6,000 years ago as "the feasting hall." It contained several large ovens for grilling or baking huge amounts of meat. The bones of goats and other medium-sized game, as well as pieces of mass-produced plates, littered the floors of adjacent rooms.

Either this building was designed for feasting or it served as a kind of ancient cafeteria for nearby workers and bureaucrats, the scientists speculate.

One of the most intriguing insights at Tell Brak came not from excavations but from an analysis of how pottery fragments accumulated across the entire site, from the city center to adjacent suburbs. Brak's urban expansion began more than 6,000 years ago in a set of small settlements that now surround the central mound, according to the pottery study (*SN: 9/15/07, p. 174*). As these villages ballooned in size, they expanded inward. Construction of the city center's massive buildings followed.

In other words, Brak's urban ascent was not planned and directed by a ruling class that first built an imposing group of core structures, as happened at southern Mesopotamian sites. McMahon's team argues that decentralized growth characterized the northern city, as inhabitants of nearby settlements interacted to cultivate a metropolis without necessarily planning to do so.

Brak attack Sometimes archaeologists make major finds serendipitously. In 2006, local residents bulldozed a grain-storage trench along the mound's border. The shocked farmers dug into a pit crammed with human skeletons, pottery, and animal bones. They had uncovered a mass grave.

Last year, McMahon's team excavated the area and found two mass graves containing parts of at least 70 bodies.

Radiocarbon measurements and assessments of pottery scattered among the bones place their age at about 5,800 years, a time of intense growth at Brak.

These graves probably held the victims of warfare, McMahon says. The bodies primarily come from young and middle-aged adults who apparently died at the same time. Many individuals lack hands and feet, possibly due to scavenging of the dead by rats and dogs on the battlefield.

Skirmish survivors apparently dumped dead bodies of their comrades, or perhaps of their enemies, into the pits. It wasn't an entirely haphazard operation, however. In one cavity, a pile of human skulls rises from the skeletal carnage.

Animal bones that held choice pieces of meat were thrown into one burial pit after ancient residents held some sort of ceremonial feast on top of it, McMahon adds.

"It's a little bit gruesome, but very exciting," she says. "It's also frustrating that we don't yet know anything about normal ways of death at Brak."

The unearthing of mass burials at Brak follows the 2005 discovery of an ancient war zone at Hamoukar. A major battle destroyed the city around 5,500 years ago, says archaeologist and excavation codirector Clemens Reichel of the University of Chicago.

Reichel's team noted extensive destruction of a 10-foot-high mud-brick wall that protected Hamoukar. Bombardment by thousands of inch-long clay bullets shot out of slings weakened the wall, which then collapsed in a fire.

Southerners likely contributed to the attack on Hamoukar, Reichel says. Destruction debris strewn across the site contains numerous large pits stocked with southern Mesopotamian pottery. Southerners either led the charge against the northern city or assumed control of it afterward, in Reichel's view.

Investigators have also discovered a site for making obsidian tools on Hamoukar's outskirts, dating to more than 6,000 years ago. The nearly 800-acre site roughly equals the size of Uruk, the largest known southern Mesopotamian city.

Hamoukar residents built this enormous workshop primarily to export tools, Reichel proposes. It sits on an ancient trade route that led to southern Mesopotamia.

"Urbanism in northern Mesopotamia started much earlier than we previously realized and wasn't imposed by the south," Reichel says.

Southern secrets Ironically, new insights into northern Mesopotamian cities gleaned from work at Brak and Hamoukar highlight huge gaps in what researchers know about urban origins in the south.

No archaeological projects have occurred in southern Iraq for nearly 20 years because of political instability and war. Moreover, periodic flooding in that region has covered ancient sites in layers of river sediment.

"I don't believe we're seeing earlier urban development in the north than in the south," Reichel remarks. "We don't know what happened in the south at the time of Brak and Hamoukar."

UCSD's Algaze agrees. He formerly advanced the view that urbanism spread from southern Mesopotamia to the rest of the Near East, but he has changed his mind in light of the new northern discoveries.

Ancient urban centers in the north and south likely developed at roughly the same time, Algaze theorizes. For now, much more data exist for early northern cities, making regional comparisons difficult.

"Tell Brak is an archaeological gold mine," Algaze says. "The picture of Mesopotamian urbanism is now more complex and interesting than ever."

Consider the puzzle of the decline of northern cities such as Brak beginning around 5,000 years ago, accompanied by continued growth of southern settlements. No one knows why urbanism initially reached massive heights in both regions only to wither in the north and flower in the south.

For that matter, it remains a mystery why northern Mesopotamian cities emerged in the first place, Reichel adds.

New hypotheses for when and how Brak transformed into a major city need to be tested in further work, including excavations of additional northern and southern Mesopotamian cities, according to Algaze.

"We need to go back to the drawing board," Algaze remarks, "and rethink how urbanism originated in the Near East."

Critical Thinking

1. In this northern city, growth appears to be decentralized, beginning with scattered settlements that interacted to form a metropolis. What might this tell us about the people of ancient northeastern Syria?
2. Why might the "World's oldest known city" have developed so far north of the Fertile Crescent? Be a detective and speculate.
3. Why have archaeological projects in southern Iraq been "on hold" for the past two decades?

Create Central

www.mhhe.com/createcentral

Internet References

Tell Brak Home Page
www.learningsites.com/Brak/Tell-Brak_home.html

Prepared by: Joseph R. Mitchell, *Howard Community College*
and Helen Buss Mitchell, *Howard Community College*

Article

The Dawn of Art

A controversial scholar claims modern culture was born in the foothills of the Alps.

ANDREW CURRY

Learning Outcomes

After reading this article, you will be able to:

- Determine whether it is possible that figurative art and music developed 40,000 years ago in Swabia, which is today a thriving, prosperous area in Germany.

The search for the origins of civilization has taken archaeologists to less pleasant places than Swabia. Nestled between France, Switzerland, and Bavaria, the German region is the heart of Baden-Württemburg, a state that markets itself as a center for creativity and innovation. It's no idle boast. Hundreds of small high-tech firms dot the region. Giants such as Mercedes-Benz, Porsche, and Zeiss are all based in the gleaming, modern state capital, Stuttgart.

American archaeologist Nicholas Conard is convinced Swabia's tradition of innovation goes back a long way: 40,000 years, give or take a few thousand. Excavating in caves east of Tübingen, a medieval town 20 miles south of Stuttgart, Conard has unearthed expertly carved figurines and the oldest musical instruments in the world. The finds are among the earliest art ever discovered, and they're extremely sophisticated in terms of craftsmanship, suggesting a surprising degree of cultural complexity.

most helpful — Conard claims his finds are evidence of an intense flowering of art and culture that began in southwestern Germany more than 35,000 years ago. Although older art and decorations have been found—including geometric patterns on stones and personal ornaments in South Africa, as well as drilled shell beads on the shores of the Mediterranean—the figurines and instruments in Conard's caves are symbolic representations that reflect a state of mind with which modern humans can easily identify. "Figurative art began in Swabia, music began in Swabia," he says. "It couldn't have developed elsewhere, because the dates are just later elsewhere."

If he's right, it could change the way we look at the development of humanity. But Conard's conclusions have been controversial from the start, and he's still fighting an uphill battle to convince colleagues that the evidence backs him up.

most interesting

The Swabian Jura, a limestone plateau about the size of Rhode Island, forms part of the foothills of the Alps. The Danube's headwaters are in the nearby Black Forest, and over the last 50 million years the river and its tributaries carved narrow, high-walled canyons that are dotted with thousands of caves.

Archaeologists believe the Danube, sweeping west across Europe, was the path of least resistance for early humans migrating north. Searching for open space and new hunting grounds, they followed the receding glaciers. Eventually, they would have reached the Swabian Jura and stopped. "If modern humans are coming up the Danube, at some point the Danube ends," Conard says. "That happens to be here."

Forty thousand years ago, glaciers a mile or more thick still covered northern Europe. Present-day Swabia was at the edge of the habitable world. In the region's caves, archaeologists have found animal remains—bones from woolly mammoths, woolly rhinoceroses, reindeer, snow hares, and arctic lemmings—that indicate a tundra-like environment.

Researchers have been systematically working in Swabia's Lone and Ach valleys since the early 1880s. In the 1930s, excavators found hundreds of stone and bone tools, as well as small figurines carved from mammoth ivory. When World War II began, hundreds of artifacts were put in storage at regional museums and essentially forgotten about until the 1960s. If not for a career-making stroke of luck, the artifacts might still be there.

In 1969, Tübingen archaeologist Joachim Hahn began rummaging through uninventoried finds. From more than 200 fragments of mammoth ivory, he reconstructed a half-man, half-lion sculpture almost a foot tall: the "Löwenmensch," or "Lion Man." Hahn spent the next 25 years working on the Swabian caves, until his death in 1997.

After Hahn died, Conard, who has been chair of the archaeology department at the University of Tübingen since 1995, took over work in the Swabian Jura. He quickly attracted motivated young researchers from Germany, France, the United States, and elsewhere and led them in a hunt for more evidence of the area's prehistoric inhabitants.

The results have been impressive. In 2003, Conard announced three finds from a cave called Höhle Fels, sophisticated and artful, the ivory sculptures—a horse head, bird, and mysterious humanoid figurine—each fit in the palm of a hand. According to Conard, they were carved at least 30,000 and perhaps as many as 40,000 years ago, making them the oldest figurines in the world. "Nobody imagined the earliest representational art could be so perfect," Conard says.

At Geißenklösterle, a cave not far from Höhle Fels, his team uncovered a carved mammoth-ivory flute almost seven inches long. Reconstructed from 31 fragments, the three-hole flute was both the oldest musical instrument ever found and an unparalleled example of craftsmanship. Hahn had discovered flutes made from hollow swan bones at Geißenklösterle, but this one was carved from solid ivory. The instrument, Conard announced, was between 30,000 and 37,000 years old.

Höhle Fels is a 15-minute walk from the tiny town of Schelklingen, past the Heidelberger Cement plant and up a dirt path that winds around the local swimming pool. The cave entrance is gated with steel bars. Inside, a metal walkway is suspended over a floodlit pit in the cave's entrance passageway. The pit walls, made of sand and loose limestone pebbles, are reinforced by sandbags.

Despite warm weather outside, the cave is wet and chilly. Clad in jackets, boots, and long pants, a half-dozen researchers from the United States, Germany, and South Africa are at work in the pit. Conard arrives wearing a wrinkled plaid shirt, khakis, and battered green Converse sneakers, and swings into the pit to inspect the day's work.

The Höhle Fels dig is divided into three layers. At the bottom, a sheet of paper in a plastic sleeve reads "Middle Paleolithic," marking the cave's lowest, and therefore oldest, layer. It contains tools and bones left by Neanderthals, who occupied Europe for about 200,000 years before modern humans arrived. A barren, or sterile, layer sits atop the Middle Paleolithic.

About four feet higher, a sheet labeled "Aurignacian" modestly marks a critical shift in human history. Across Europe, the beginning of the Aurignacian marked a significant step forward: art, sophisticated bone and ivory tools, jewelry, cave paintings, musical instruments, and other "hallmarks of modernity" all appear for the first time in this layer. Although the definition of "modernity" is hotly debated, Conard sees it as a state of mind that people today would recognize. "If you were transported back in time, you'd have to learn a new language, you'd have to learn how to knap flint and maybe hunt mammoth, but you and those people are the same" he says. "That's certainly the case with the Aurignacian in Swabia." The final level is the Gravettian, an era best known for Venus figurines found at sites in France and elsewhere.

Although Conard had been working on European Paleolithic sites for more than 20 years, he wasn't an expert on the Swabian Jura until he took over Hahn's work in the late 1990s. The first thing he did was review data from local digs, including dozens of radiocarbon dates.

Conard says the timing of the Aurignacian and Gravettian artifacts found in the Swabian caves immediately leapt out at him. While most archaeologists think that the Aurignacian began about 36,000 years ago, Conard is convinced that the Swabian Aurignacian began thousands of years before it emerged elsewhere in Europe—perhaps even 10,000 years before. "The Aurignacian developed here, the Gravettian developed here," he says now.

A significantly older Aurignacian might overlap with the Neanderthal era, or Middle Paleolithic. But when Conard reopened digs at Höhle Fels and Geißenklösterle, he found a sterile layer between the Middle Paleolithic and the Aurignacian levels, a critical indicator of the lack of human occupation as clear as a roadside motel's blinking neon "vacancy" sign. "Judging by the low artifact density in the Middle Paleolithic and sterile layers, we conclude modern people came into a nearly empty region," says Michael Bolus, a German archaeologist who works closely with Conard. "In our region there's no continuity between Neanderthals and modern humans."

As Conard, Bolus, and others dug deeper into the caves and sifted through Hahn's decades of data, they came up with a daring theory to explain the Swabian Jura's sophisticated tools and incredible carved figurines. "Looking at it from a physics background, if you have a vacuum, something's going to get sucked in," Conard says.

As humans followed the Danube into the region, the theory goes, they found an area at once abundant with animal life and virtually empty of competitors— so they began to settle it. The cold climate forced early inhabitants to be creative in order to survive. In response, they developed new tools and hunting strategies. The modern human population then surged, prompting still more innovation, including what Conard and his colleagues believe is the world's earliest representational art.

Conard and Bolus say the region served first as an incubator and then as a sort of piston, pushing its cultural and technological innovations out into the rest of Europe. They have dubbed the theory "Kulturpumpe," or culture pump. "Swabians may have been inventors all these years ago," Bolus says. "People sitting here got ideas from outside, but developed new things and spread them to other regions. It's a point our French colleagues don't want to accept."

The Kulturpumpe theory means more than just bragging rights for Swabia. On one level it's a bold claim to a set of prehistoric "firsts." But it's also a controversial vision of the beginnings of cultural modernity: all at once, and all in one place, rather than in slow evolutionary steps across Africa and Europe over tens of thousands of years.

When you're talking about the issue of where human beings come from, who's going to answer that except for a paleoarchaeologist? You can talk to a priest, or you can talk to us.

least helpful

The theory is an ambitious stab at one of the most important questions only archaeology can answer: When, how, and where did anatomically modern humans make the mental leap to true modernity? As Conard puts it, "When did people become like ourselves? When you're talking about the issue of where human beings come from, who's going to answer that except for a paleoarchaeologist? You can talk to a priest, or you can talk to us."

You'll certainly get a more straightforward answer from a priest. While Conard was making waves in the popular press for a string of "firsts" for the Swabian Jura, a storm was building in the world of paleoanthropology. Conard's colleagues read the publications flooding out of Tübingen with admiration—and consternation. "I think Nick is doing a great job in Tübingen," says João Zilhão, a paleoanthropologist at Bristol University who is one of Conard's main sparring partners. "He's going back to the sites and extracting data we can all use—even to disagree with him."

Zilhão says the Kulturpumpe theory has been controversial from the start. Critics have attacked everything from the accuracy of the radiocarbon dates to Conard's interpretation of the stratigraphy layers at key sites such as Höhle Fels and Geißenklösterle. More than five years after he floated the idea, few outside Conard's Tübingen department are willing swallow his argument. "The whole Kulturpumpe thing is very heated. Everybody has their belief in how things were, and they tend to stick to the beliefs pretty strongly," says Laura Niven, a researcher at the Max Planck Institute for Human Evolution in Leipzig (and one of Conard's former students).

If you look at the layers of an ideal excavation, the radiocarbon dates of the finds should match their physical locations, with the youngest pieces on top and the oldest at the bottom. Geißenklösterle, the first cave to be systematically excavated by Conard's team, has the best chronological evidence for the Kulturpumpe—and yet the site's layering is far from ideal. Deer bones that Conard dated to 41,000 years ago, for example, were uncovered above pieces that are only 29,000 years old.

Meanwhile, artifacts from the Middle Paleolithic layers came back with dates thousands of years younger than pieces from the Aurignacian. Bones with cut marks and other clear signs of human use are sometimes mixed with "unmodified" bones that seem much older. And the pieces themselves can't be directly tested. Even if Conard was willing to pulverize parts of the world's oldest sculptures to date them, mammoth ivory has very little organic matter to extract.

Conard's explanation relies on the intricacies of radiocarbon (C-14) dating. Especially with older artifacts, C-14 dates don't always correspond to the calendar. Climate change, rising and lowering sea levels, the earth's magnetic field, and cosmic rays can all change C-14 levels, making artifacts seem older or younger than they actually are. So scientists must calibrate radiocarbon dates, comparing them to tree rings, glacial ice cores, and lake sediments.

In the critical period Conard is investigating—between 30,000 and 50,000 years ago—some radiocarbon experts have observed wildly fluctuating levels of C-14 in the earth's atmosphere. Conard and Bolus argue that the fluctuations explain the odd dates at Geißenklösterle. "In some cases," Conard wrote last year, "these production spikes can lead to younger dates stratigraphically underlying older dates from secure contexts."

Ordinarily, Conard would cross-reference results with other local sites. But many of the caves that could corroborate his theory were excavated in the 1930s, before modern archaeological techniques were developed. "So many of these dates depend on old sites, and there are so many problems with old sites," says Niven. In 1931, for example, all 170 square meters of Vogel-herd Cave were excavated in 10 weeks flat by 31-year-old German archaeologist Gustav Riek, who employed mostly local laborers with shovels and pickaxes. None of his field notes survived.

Without other sites to back him up, Conard is vulnerable to another charge. Some suggest that the odd dates aren't the result of cosmic rays, but something more mundane. "German sites are used by carnivores as much as by humans," Zilhão points out. A restless bear could have dug into the coarse limestone rubble of a cave floor, churning up pieces of bone from lower layers and creating dating havoc.

If that's the case, the artifacts supporting the Kulturpumpe idea could simply be in the wrong place. Conard concedes the difficulties—and dismisses them. "Overall, the mixing is not so great" he says.

Critics say Conard based his estimates of each layer's age on the oldest artifacts—rather than looking at the finds as a whole. "There are dozens of dates in Europe for the Aurignacian, nothing older than 36,500 [years]. This is the only case with a date of 40,000. It seems unlikely that people bearing the same culture were at Geißenklösterle 4,000 years ahead of the rest of Europe," says Francesco d'Errico, an archaeologist at the University of Bordeaux. "If you really work on the dates and the site stratigraphy, you come up with the conclusion that this Aurignacian is 35,000–33,000 years old, the same as the rest of Europe."

Conard refuses to give any ground on his interpretations. "They're willfully misunderstanding the data," he says, frustrated. "That's just ignorance on their part."

But Conard refuses to give any ground on his interpretations. "They're willfully misunderstanding the data," he says, frustrated. "That's just ignorance on their part." When it comes to radiocarbon dating, there's no shaking his confidence: Conard's entire career has been based on the technique. As an undergraduate at the University of Rochester in the early 1980s, one of his mentors was Harry Gove, a nuclear physicist who was in the process of inventing the accelerated mass spectrometry (AMS) method of carbon dating.

The technique, capable of accurately dating a few milligrams of organic matter, was a breakthrough for archaeologists. And Conard was the first person to apply AMS to an archaeological find. His undergraduate thesis on radiocarbon dating of prehistoric horticulture in Illinois was published in *Nature* in 1984 and his background in the natural sciences continues to inform his work today. "An excavation's like a laboratory,"

Conard says. "My role models are physicists—in physics, what you do and your experimental data carry the day."

Yet many colleagues feel Conard's faith in radiocarbon dating is too strong. "Data produced from the natural sciences is often seen as more solid. But errors can happen," says archaeologist Olaf Jöris of the Roman-Germanic Museum in Mainz, Germany. "I highly esteem the work he's doing, but you can't just take dates for granted."

Two years ago, Conard decided to take another look at Vogelherd, the cave Gustav Riek excavated in 1931. The cave sits atop a steep hill, and spilling down from its mouth are the remains of Riek's dig—more than 4,000 bags worth of soil from the cave hastily pushed down the hill by workmen. Sifting the dirt, Tübingen graduate students trained in a more patient era have uncovered thousands of fragmentary artifacts missed during the first excavation.

This summer, Conard announced the first finds: fragments of an ivory flute, four fragmentary sculptures, and a complete carving of a mammoth. "This doesn't change anything, it just reinforces my position," he says. "People here dealt with figurative representations in ordinary life and routinely created music. From my point of view, that's overwhelming evidence of modernity."

It remains to be seen whether Conard can convince his colleagues that Swabian modernity came first. In the meantime, he hasn't stopped looking. "We're very much in the new data line of work here," Conard says. "We're dealing with a giant landscape, and all we've got is a few square meters. We haven't seen the whole picture."

Critical Thinking

1. What does the presence of art, such as an ivory flute and carved figures suggest to you about life in Swabia 35,000 to 40,000 years ago?
2. What theory does the author offer to explain these artifacts of a vanished civilization?

Create Central

www.mhhe.com/createcentral

Internet References

Schwaben Resources
   www.danube.swabians.org/

ANDREW CURRY is a freelance writer in Berlin, Germany, and a frequent contributor to *Archaeology*.

Prepared by: Joseph R. Mitchell, *Howard Community College*
and Helen Buss Mitchell, *Howard Community College*

Article

Prehistory *of* Warfare

Humans have been at each others' throats since the dawn of the species.

STEVEN A. LEBLANC

Learning Outcomes

After reading this article, you will be able to:

- Determine to what extent warfare was prevalent during the prehistoric era and evaluate the evidence that is offered to support the article's thesis.

In the early 1970s, working in the El Morro Valley of west-central New Mexico, I encountered the remains of seven large prehistoric pueblos that had once housed upwards of a thousand people each. Surrounded by two-story-high walls, the villages were perched on steep-sided mesas, suggesting that their inhabitants built them with defense in mind. At the time, the possibility that warfare occurred among the Anasazi was of little interest to me and my colleagues. Rather, we were trying to figure out what the people in these 700-year-old communities farmed and hunted, the impact of climate change, and the nature of their social systems—not the possibility of violent conflict.

One of these pueblos, it turned out, had been burned to the ground; its people had clearly fled for their lives. Pottery and valuables had been left on the floors, and bushels of burned corn still lay in the storerooms. We eventually determined that this site had been abandoned, and that immediately afterward a fortress had been built nearby. Something catastrophic had occurred at this ancient Anasazi settlement, and the survivors had almost immediately, and at great speed, set about to prevent it from happening again.

Thirty years ago, archaeologists were certainly aware that violent, organized conflicts occurred in the prehistoric cultures they studied, but they considered these incidents almost irrelevant to our understanding of past events and people. Today, some of my colleagues are realizing that the evidence I helped uncover in the El Morro Valley is indicative warfare endemic throughout the entire Southwest, with its attendant massacres, population decline, and area abandonments that forever changed the Anasazi way of life.

When excavating eight-millennia-old farm villages in southeastern Turkey in 1970, I initially marveled how similar modern villages were to ancient ones, which were occupied at a time when an abundance of plants and animals made warfare quite unnecessary. Or so I thought. I knew we had discovered some plaster sling missiles (one of our workmen showed me how shepherds used slings to hurl stones at predators threatening their sheep). Such missiles were found at many of these sites, often in great quantities, and were clearly not intended for protecting flocks of sheep; they were exactly the same size and shape as later Greek and Roman sling stones used for warfare.

The so-called "donut stones" we had uncovered at these sites were assumed to be weights for digging sticks, presumably threaded on a pole to make it heavier for digging holes to plant crops. I failed to note how much they resembled the round stone heads attached to wooden clubs—maces—used in many places of the world exclusively for fighting and still used ceremonially to signify power. Thirty years ago, I was holding mace heads and sling missiles in my hands, unaware of their use as weapons of war.

We now know that defensive walls once ringed many villages of this era, as they did the Anasazi settlements. Rooms were massed together behind solid outside walls and were entered from the roof. Other sites had mud brick defensive walls, some with elaborately defended gates. Furthermore, many of these villages had been burned to the ground, their inhabitants massacred, as indicated by nearby mass graves.

Certainly for those civilizations that kept written records or had descriptive narrative art traditions, warfare is so clearly present that no one can deny it. Think of Homer's *Iliad* or the Vedas of South India, or scenes of prisoner sacrifice on Moche pottery. There is no reason to think that warfare played any less of a role in prehistoric societies for which we have no such records, whether they be hunter-gatherers or farmers. But most scholars studying these cultures still are not seeing it. They should assume warfare occurred among the people they study, just as they assume religion and art were a normal part of human culture. Then they could ask more interesting questions, such as: What form did warfare take? Can warfare explain some of the material found in the archaeological record? What were people fighting over and why did the conflicts end?

> **Scholars should assume warfare occurred among the people they study, just as they assume religion was a normal part of human culture. Then they would ask more interesting questions, such as: What form did warfare take? Why did people start and stop fighting?**

Today, some scholars know me as Dr. Warfare. To them, I have the annoying habit of asking un-politic questions about their research. I am the one who asks why the houses at a particular site were jammed so close together and many catastrophically burned. When I suggest that the houses were crowded behind defensive walls that were not found because no one was looking for them, I am not terribly appreciated. And I don't win any popularity contests when I suggest that twenty-mile-wide zones with no sites in them imply no-man's lands—clear evidence for warfare—to archaeologists who have explained a region's history without mention of conflict.

Virtually all the basic textbooks on archaeology ignore the prevalence or significance of past warfare, which is usually not discussed until the formation of state-level civilizations such as ancient Sumer. Most texts either assume or actually state that for most of human history there was an abundance of available resources. There was no resource stress, and people had the means to control population, though how they accomplished this is never explained. The one archaeologist who has most explicitly railed against this hidden but pervasive attitude is Lawrence Keeley of the University of Illinois, who studies the earliest farmers in Western Europe. He has found ample evidence of warfare as farmers spread west, yet most of his colleagues still believe the expansion was peaceful and his evidence a minor aberration, as seen in the various papers in Barry Cunliffe's *The Oxford Illustrated Prehistory of Europe* (1994) or Douglas Price's *Europe's First Farmers* (2000). Keeley contends that "prehistorians have increasingly pacified the past," presuming peace or thinking up every possible alternative explanation for the evidence they cannot ignore. In his *War Before Civilization* (1996) he accused archaeologists of being in denial on the subject.

Witness archaeologist Lisa Valkenier suggesting in 1997 that hilltop constructions along the Peruvian coast are significant because peaks are sacred in Andean cosmology. Their enclosing walls and narrow guarded entries may have more to do with restricting access to the *huacas,* or sacred shrines, on top of the hills than protecting defenders and barring entry to any potential attackers. How else but by empathy can one formulate such an interpretation in an area with a long defensive wall and hundreds of defensively located fortresses, some still containing piles of sling missiles ready to be used; where a common artistic motif is the parading and execution of defeated enemies; where hundreds were sacrificed; and where there is ample evidence of conquest, no-man's lands, specialized weapons, and so on?

A talk I gave at the Mesa Verde National Park last summer, in which I pointed out that the over 700-year-old cliff dwellings were built in response to warfare, raised the hackles of National Park Service personnel unwilling to accept anything but the peaceful Anasazi message peddled by their superiors. In fact, in the classic book *Indians of Mesa Verde,* published in 1961 by the park service, author Don Watson first describes the Mesa Verde people as "peaceful farming Indians," and admits that the cliff dwellings had a defensive aspect, but since he had already decided that the inhabitants were peaceful, the threat must have been from a new enemy—marauding nomadic Indians. This, in spite of the fact that there is ample evidence of Southwestern warfare for more than a thousand years before the cliff dwellings were built, and there is no evidence for the intrusion of nomadic peoples at this time.

Of the hundreds of research projects in the Southwest, only one—led by Jonathan Haas and Winifred Creamer of the Field Museum and Northern Illinois University, respectively—deliberately set out to research prehistoric warfare. They demonstrated quite convincingly that the Arizona cliff dwellings of the Tsegi Canyon area (known best for Betatakin and Kiet Siel ruins) were defensive, and their locations were not selected for ideology or because they were breezier and cooler in summer and warmer in the winter, as was previously argued by almost all Southwestern archaeologists.

For most prehistoric cultures, one has to piece together the evidence for warfare from artifactual bits and pieces. Most human history involved foragers, and so they are particularly relevant. They too were not peaceful. We know from ethnography that the Inuit (Eskimo) and Australian Aborigines engaged in warfare. We've also discovered remains of prehistoric bone armor in the Arctic, and skeletal evidence of deadly blows to the head are well documented among the prehistoric Aborigines. Surprising to some is the skeletal evidence for warfare in prehistoric California, once thought of as a land of peaceful acorn gatherers. The prehistoric people who lived in southern Californian had the highest incident of warfare deaths known anywhere in the world. Thirty percent of a large sample of males dating to the first centuries A.D. had wounds or died violent deaths. About half that number of women had similar histories. When we remember that not all warfare deaths leave skeletal evidence, this is a staggering number.

There was nothing unique about the farmers of the Southwest. From the Neolithic farmers of the Middle East and Europe to the New Guinea highlanders in the twentieth century, tribally organized farmers probably had the most intense warfare of any type of society. Early villages in China, the Yucatán, present-day Pakistan, and Micronesia were well fortified. Ancient farmers in coastal Peru had plenty of forts. All Polynesian societies had warfare, from the smallest islands like Tikopia, to Tahiti, New Zealand (more than four thousand prehistoric forts), and Hawaii. No-man's lands separated farming settlements in Okinawa, Oaxaca, and the southeastern United States. Such societies took trophy heads and cannibalized their enemies. Their skeletal remains show ample evidence of violent deaths. All well-studied prehistoric farming societies had warfare. They may have had intervals of peace, but over the span of hundreds of years there is plenty of evidence for real, deadly warfare.

When farmers initially took over the world, they did so as warriors, grabbing land as they spread out from the Levant through the Middle East into Europe, or from South China down through Southeast Asia. Later complex societies like the Maya, the Inca, the Sumerians, and the Hawaiians were no less belligerent. Here, conflict took on a new dimension. Fortresses, defensive walls hundreds of miles long, and weapons and armor expertly crafted by specialists all gave the warfare of these societies a heightened visibility.

There is a danger in making too much of the increased visibility of warfare we see in these complex societies. This is especially true for societies with writing. When there are no texts, it is easy to see no warfare. But the opposite is true. As soon as societies can write, they write about warfare. It is not a case of literate societies having warfare for the first time, but their being able to write about what had been going on for a long time. Also, many of these literate societies link to European civilization in one way or another, and so this raises the specter of Europeans being warlike and spreading war to inherently peaceful people elsewhere, a patently false but prevalent notion. Viewing warfare from their perspective of literate societies tells us nothing about the thousands of years of human societies that were not civilizations—that is, almost all of human history. So we must not rely too much on the small time slice represented by literate societies if we want to understand warfare in the past.

The Maya were once considered a peaceful society led by scholarly priests. That all changed when the texts written by their leaders could be read, revealing a long history of warfare and conquest. Most Mayanists now accept that there was warfare, but many still resist dealing with its scale or implications. Was there population growth that resulted in resource depletion, as throughout the rest of the world? We would expect the Maya to have been fighting each other over valuable farmlands as a consequence, but Mayanist Linda Schele concluded in 1984 that "I do not think it [warfare] was territorial for the most part," this even though texts discuss conquest, and fortifications are present at sites like El Mirador, Calakmul, Tikal, Yaxuná, Uxmal, and many others from all time periods. Why fortify them, if no one wanted to capture them?

Today, more Maya archaeologists are looking at warfare in a systematic way, by mapping defensive features, finding images of destruction, and dating these events. A new breed of younger scholars is finding evidence of warfare throughout the Maya past. Where are the no-man's lands that almost always open up between competing states because they are too dangerous to live in? Warfare must have been intimately involved in the development of Maya civilization, and resource stress must have been widespread.

Demonstrating the prevalence of warfare is not an end in itself. It is only the first step in understanding why there was so much, why it was "rational" for everyone to engage in it all the time. I believe the question of warfare links to the availability of resources.

> **Demonstrating the prevalence of warfare is not an end in itself. It is only the first step in understanding why there was so much of it, why it was "rational" for everyone to engage in it all the time. I believe the question of warfare links to the availability of resources.**

During the 1960s, I lived in Western Samoa as a Peace Corps volunteer on what seemed to be an idyllic South Pacific Island—exactly like those painted by Paul Gauguin. Breadfruit and coconut groves grew all around my village, and I resided in a thatched-roof house with no walls beneath a giant mango tree. If ever there was a Garden of Eden, this was it. I lived with a family headed by an extremely intelligent elderly chief named Sila. One day, Sila happened to mention that the island's trees did not bear fruit as they had when he was a child. He attributed the decline to the possibility that the presence of radio transmissions had affected production, since Western Samoa (now known as Samoa) had its own radio station by then. I suggested that what had changed was not that there was less fruit but that there were more mouths to feed. Upon reflection, Sila decided I was probably right. Being an astute manager, he was already taking the precaution of expanding his farm plots into some of the last remaining farmable land on the island, at considerable cost and effort, to ensure adequate food for his growing family. Sila was aware of his escalating provisioning problems but was not quite able to grasp the overall demographic situation. Why was this?

The simple answer is that the rate of population change in our small Samoan village was so gradual that during an adult life span growth was not dramatic enough to be fully comprehended. The same thing happens to us all the time. Communities grow and change composition, and often only after the process is well advanced do we recognize just how significant the changes have been—and we have the benefit of historic documents, old photographs, long life spans, and government census surveys. All human societies can grow substantially over time, and all did whenever resources permitted. The change may seem small in one person's lifetime, but over a couple of hundred years, populations can and do double, triple, or quadruple in size.

The consequences of these changes become evident only when there is a crisis. The same can be said for environmental changes. The forests of Central America were being denuded and encroached upon for many years, but it took Hurricane Mitch, which ravaged most of the region in late October 1998, to produce the dramatic flooding and devastation that fully demonstrated the magnitude of the problem: too many people cutting down the forest and farming steep hillsides to survive. The natural environment is resilient and at the same time delicate, as modern society keeps finding out. And it was just so in the past.

These observations about Mother Nature are incompatible with popular myths about peaceful people living in ecological balance with nature in the past. A peaceful past is possible only if you live in ecological balance. If you live in a Garden of Eden surrounded by plenty, why fight? By this logic, warfare is a sure thing when natural resources run dry. If someone as smart as Sila couldn't perceive population growth, and if humans all over Earth continue to degrade their environments, could people living in the past have been any different?

A study by Canadian social scientists Christina Mesquida and Neil Wiener has shown that the greater the proportion of a society is composed of unmarried young men, the greater the likelihood of war. Why such a correlation? It is not because the young men are not married; it is because they cannot get married. They are too poor to support wives and families. The idea that poverty breeds war is far from original. The reason poverty exists has remained the same since the beginning of time: humans have invariably overexploited their resources because they have always outgrown them.

From foragers to farmers to more complex societies, when people no longer have resource stress they stop fighting. When climate greatly improves, warfare declines. The great towns of Chaco Canyon were built during an extended warm—and peaceful—period.

There is another lesson from past warfare. It stops. From foragers to farmers, to more complex societies, when people no longer have resource stress they stop fighting. When the climate greatly improves, warfare declines. For example, in a variety of places the medieval warm interval of ca. 900–1100 improved farming conditions. The great towns of Chaco Canyon were built at this time, and it was the time of archaeologist Stephen Lekson's *Pax Chaco*—the longest period of peace in the Southwest. It is no accident that the era of Gothic cathedrals was a response to similar climate improvement. Another surprising fact is that the amount of warfare has declined over time. If we count the proportion of a society that died from warfare, and not the size of the armies, as the true measure of warfare, then we find that foragers and farmers have much higher death rates—often approaching 25 percent of the men—than more recent complex societies. No complex society, including modern states, ever approached this level of warfare.

If warfare has ultimately been a constant battle over scarce resources, then solving the resource problem will enable us to become better at ridding ourselves of conflict.

There have been several great "revolutions" in human history: control of fire, the acquisition of speech, the agricultural revolution, the development of complex societies. One of the most recent, the Industrial Revolution, has lowered the birth rate and increased available resources. History shows that peoples with strong animosities stop fighting after adequate resources are established and the benefits of cooperation recognized. The Hopi today are some of the most peaceful people on earth, yet their history is filled with warfare. The Gebusi of

lowland New Guinea, the African !Kung Bushmen, the Mbuti Pygmies of central Africa, the Sanpoi and their neighbors of the southern Columbia River, and the Sirionno of Amazonia are all peoples who are noted for being peaceful, yet archaeology and historical accounts provide ample evidence of past warfare. Sometimes things changed in a generation; at other times it took longer. Adequate food and opportunity does not instantly translate into peace, but it will, given time.

The fact that it can take several generations or longer to establish peace between warring factions is little comfort for those engaged in the world's present conflicts. Add to this a recent change in the decision-making process that leads to war. In most traditional societies, be they forager bands, tribal farmers, or even complex chiefdoms, no individual held enough power to start a war on his own. A consensus was needed; pros and cons were carefully weighed and hotheads were not tolerated. The risks to all were too great. Moreover, failure of leadership was quickly recognized, and poor leaders were replaced. No Hitler or Saddam Hussein would have been tolerated. Past wars were necessary for survival, and therefore were rational; too often today this is not the case. We cannot go back to forager-band-type consensus, but the world must work harder at keeping single individuals from gaining the power to start wars. We know from archaeology that the amount of warfare has declined markedly over the course of human history and that peace can prevail under the right circumstances. In spite of the conflict we see around us, we are doing better, and there is less warfare in the world today than there ever has been. Ending it may be a slow process, but we are making headway.

Critical Thinking

1. What does Steven A. Leblanc mean when he writes, "... we must not rely so much on the small time slice represented by literate societies if we want to understand warfare in the past"?

2. What are the implications for warfare of this statement: "the change may seem small in one person's lifetime, but over a couple of hundred years, populations can and do double, triple, or quadruple in size"?

3. How does the author explain this claim: "... the greater the proportion of a society that is composed of unmarried young men, the greater likelihood of war"? Do you agree or disagree? Why?

Create Central

www.mhhe.com/createcentral

Internet References

Tell Brak Home Page
   www.learningsites.com/Brak/Tell-Brak_home.html

© 2003 by **Steven A. LeBlanc.** Portions of this article were taken from his book *Constant Battles,* published in April 2003 by *St. Martin's Press.* LeBlanc is director of collections at Harvard University's Peabody Museum of Archaeology and Ethnology.

From *Archaeology,* May/June 2003, pp. 18–25. Copyright © 2003 by Steven A. LeBlanc. Reprinted by permission of the author.

Article

Prepared by: Joseph R. Mitchell, *Howard Community College*
and Helen Buss Mitchell, *Howard Community College*

Writing Gets a Rewrite

Recent discoveries in the Near East and Pakistan are forcing scholars to reconsider traditional ideas about writing's evolution. But a lack of fresh data is making their task difficult.

ANDREW LAWLER

Learning Outcomes

After reading this article, you will be able to:

- Define the significance of writing for societies and for the study of history.

T he inventor of writing, according to Mesopotamian legend, was a high priest from the great city of Uruk who one day began making marks on wet clay. Five thousand years later, German archaeologists triumphantly discovered the oldest examples of writing—called cuneiform—200 kilometers south of here in a long-buried Uruk temple, providing what seemed to be scientific confirmation of the ancient myth.

But that heroic story is quietly being shelved by scholars as new finds in Egypt and Pakistan over the past decade, and a radical reinterpretation of clay objects found in Mesopotamia's heartland and its periphery—today's Iraq, Syria, and Iran—have necessitated a different account. Most researchers now agree that writing is less the invention of a single talented individual than the result of a complex evolutionary process stretching back thousands of years before the first hard evidence of writing surfaced in Mesopotamia, Egypt, and the Indus River valley about 3300 B.C. "The prehistoric communication revolution began some 9000 years ago," says Joan Oates, an archaeologist at the University of Cambridge, U.K. "In a sense, writing appears as the last step in the long line of evolution of communication systems."

The revised text on writing's history, however, is far from complete. Scholars say they are hampered by a lack of fresh data from Near Eastern sites, the reluctance of museum curators to allow potentially destructive testing of critical artifacts, and the limitations of radiocarbon dating. Moreover, the 1989 discovery in Egypt of an ancient and sophisticated writing system has fueled a new debate: Did Mesopotamia's literacy trigger that of Egypt, as is traditionally supposed, or was it the other way around—or neither? More recent finds showing that the Indus script likely was evolving around 3300 B.C.—at about the same time as its Near East counterparts began to coalesce—have deepened the mystery. Some researchers, pondering the near-simultaneous appearance of seemingly separate protowriting systems in three distinct civilizations, suggest that they may have developed independently in response to similar circumstances.

But tracing the predecessors of cuneiform, hieroglyphics, and Indus River valley script becomes increasingly tricky the farther back in prehistory researchers probe. "We really have very little information prior to 3500 B.C.," says Piotr Michalowski, a cuneiform scholar at the University of Michigan, Ann Arbor. "It comes down to a matter of faith."

Token Theory

For decades, archaeologists in Iraq, Syria, and Iran dug up curious ceramic pieces—numerous small tokens in diverse geometric shapes. They also found hollow clay spheres with markings on the outside from later periods and with these same small ceramic pieces inside. Those ranged in age from about 9000 to 4000 years old but were dismissed by most researchers as ancient games and relegated to museum storage bins.

But Pierre Amiet, an archaeologist at the Louvre in Paris, suspected as early as the 1960s that the mysterious objects were actually used to count goods. Since then, his student Denise Schmandt-Besserat, now at the University of Texas, Austin, has elaborated on that theory. After studying thousands of tokens, she proposed in the 1980s that different shapes signified different commercial objects—a cone shape, for example, represented a measure of grain; a cylinder connoted an animal. The number of tokens indicated quantity. "It was the first visual code, the first system of artifacts created for the sole purpose of communicating information," she says.

Despite her colleagues' skepticism, Schmandt-Besserat went on to theorize that the system grew and evolved over thousands of years. By the end of the fourth millennium B.C., tokens represented different animals; processed foods such as oil, trussed ducks, or bread; and manufactured and imported goods such as textiles and metal, she says. By about 3500 B.C., concurrent with the growth of major cities like Uruk, the tokens were often found in hollow clay spheres, like envelopes; markings on the outside indicated the sorts and quantities of tokens within.

Ultimately, the tokens were dispensed with altogether, and the clay spheres became clay tablets with impressed marks representing objects—marks that evolved into early cuneiform, according to Schmandt-Besserat. By 3100 B.C., someone—perhaps indeed an Uruk priest—began to use a reed stylus on wet clay to make the more precise markings that comprise cuneiform. This form of writing continued at Uruk and other Mesopotamian sites until the latter days of the Roman Empire, much as Latin survived as an elite and holy language in Europe for more than 1000 years after Rome's fall.

The token theory, according to some scholars, helps solve a nagging puzzle. "The great mystery until now was how a full-fledged system emerged so suddenly," says William Hallo, an Assyriologist at Yale University. "Now we can see a progression of successive steps [over] a fairly extended time."

But many Assyriologists say Schmandt-Besserat goes too far in postulating a sophisticated representational system before 3500 B.C. Oates prefers to call the tokens "a means of remembering rather than a genuine recording device." Eleanor Robson, an Assyriologist at Oxford University, U.K., says the later arrangements of tokens in spheres clearly are "a coherent system"; even so, she says, it is hard to identify the inside objects definitively from before 3500 B.C. "Most are little blobby lumps," she says, "and it's hard to know which are tokens and which are beads or weights."

Skeptics also insist that there is little evidence that cuneiform grew directly out of this system, as Schmandt-Besserat maintains. Token shapes and the impressions made on the spheres, she says, inspired cuneiform's representations for objects such as sheep and oil. But others are not so sure. "I accept the tokens as the earliest form of writing, but I see no good evidence that incised tokens are precursors" to cuneiform, says Robert Englund, a Sumerian scholar at the University of California, Los Angeles. Paul Zimansky, a Boston University archaeologist, agrees. "There's no indication of linkage," he says.

A few scholars take a harder line. Michalowski holds to the idea that cuneiform is a separate development that may have been influenced by tokens and cylinder seals—also widely used in ancient Mesopotamia—but that is unique and distinct. "I joke that cuneiform had to be invented by one person because it was too good to be invented by a committee," he says, arguing that the system is the result of a "quantum leap" that drew on many traditions.

More data would clearly be welcome. Englund and Robson assert that more research should be done on the sealed hollow spheres, more than 100 of which are in museums around the world. Englund and his colleagues have already done x-rays and computerized tomography scans on these objects at the University of Heidelberg in Germany, but, they say, the time, expense, and low resolution of these procedures make them a poor substitute for splitting open the spheres and studying them directly. Curators, however, are reluctant to see their artifacts tampered with and possibly destroyed. "It's an unpleasant situation," Englund says.

Dating Troubles

Egypt is only 1000 kilometers west of Mesopotamia, and there is a long history of trade between the two great civilizations. So scholars have long accepted the idea that hieroglyphics—which were thought to have appeared a century or so after cuneiform—were inspired by the Uruk concept of storing information.

But a 1989 discovery by Gunther Dreyer of Cairo's German Archeological Institute and his subsequent findings at Abydos in upper Egypt have threatened Mesopotamia's ancient claim as the source of the first writing system. Opening a royal tomb dubbed U-j in 1989, Dreyer's team found a large trove of objects bearing inscriptions that are more than a century older than the oldest written materials previously discovered in Egypt. The finds, which include nearly 200 small bone and ivory objects, are from roughly the same era as Uruk's earliest tablets—around 3200 B.C. A rougher set of similar inscriptions was found on nearby vessels. About 50 signs seem to represent humans, animals, and a palace façade. Later findings nearby included pot marks dating to about 3500 B.C.

Dreyer argues that the symbols represent a single well-developed system that led to hieroglyphics. But other researchers are skeptical of this claim. "The pot marks can't be interpreted," and so the data "are insufficient" to draw wide-ranging conclusions, says John Baines, an Egyptologist at Oxford University, although he agrees that the inscriptions on bone and ivory clearly are writing.

Meanwhile, attempts to accurately date materials from both Egypt and Mesopotamia have proven inconclusive. Recent radiocarbon dating in Heidelberg of charcoal from both an Uruk temple, where early cuneiform tablets were found, and the Abydos tomb showed a date of approximately 3450 B.C. for Uruk and 3320 B.C. for Abydos—pushing back the previous dates, based on well-known Egyptian chronologies, about 150 years.

Margarete van Ess of Berlin's German Archeological Institute, for one, accepts those dates, which push the origin of cuneiform back by a century or so, giving Mesopotamia the edge. But other scholars say such precision is not possible in radiocarbon dating. Researchers are looking for additional clues, both in situ and on the tablets and vessels that record the early writing; Van Ess, for example, recently began digging at Uruk after the decade-long hiatus resulting from international sanctions against Iraq.

Those clues are hard to come by, however. Because builders at Uruk often used old tablets as fill, pinpointing their date and context is difficult. "Uruk is such a mess," says Englund. "The stratigraphic record is really quite horrible." And Dreyer—who continues his excavations—has yet to find significant material at Abydos that may shed more light on hieroglyphic evolution.

Three at Once?

Archaeologists in Pakistan have had more luck in recent years. A team of U.S. researchers discovered compelling evidence in the late 1990s that the script from the Indus River valley also has a long and complex history. The Harappan civilization flourished there from 2800 B.C. to 1700 B.C. before collapsing; its script ceased to be used afterward, and the meanings of the signs remain a mystery. But although it never attained the complexity of the Mesopotamian or Egyptian writing systems, the Indus script nevertheless developed into a formidable grouping of signs.

The recent finds suggest that the script arose more than half a millennium earlier than previously believed. Pottery discovered at the site of Harappa includes markings that date from 3500 B.C. to 3300 B.C. and that appear to be precursors to that script. "I wouldn't call these signs writing," says Richard Meadow, a Harvard archaeologist who works at the site. "But these could be seen as part of an evolution of signs that continue to the Harappan period."

The Harappan and Abydos finds pose a major challenge to the traditional theory that writing diffused gradually from Mesopotamia to Egypt and perhaps to the Indus. All three areas were linked by trade in pre-history—Egypt to Mesopotamia through the Levant, and Mesopotamia to the Indus through modern-day Iran and the Persian Gulf coast. But the dominance of Mesopotamia is now in question.

"That the idea [of writing] passed from Egypt to Mesopotamia is quite a possibility now," maintains Dreyer. Others are not so quick to make that leap. "I'm undecided," says Baines, "but I don't think that's likely." Still other Mesopotamian scholars largely adhere to the old school of east-to-west influence, given what they say is the long evolution apparent from cylinder seals and the clay spheres.

Baines, however, posits a third possibility: that the two systems developed independently at about the same time. And if Harappa is included, then the evidence suggests that three separate systems with their own evolutionary paths began to mature nearly simultaneously. That would appear a stunning coincidence, but some researchers say contact with other groups, combined with an indigenous need to convey more complex information, might have been the not-so-coincidental common ingredients that made the Near East and the Indus advance so quickly.

"Writing develops in areas where people are interacting," says Jonathan Kenoyer, an archaeologist at the University of Wisconsin, Madison, who has dug along the Indus. "Yet these regions also developed their own unique forms of expression." This is true not only for the scripts, which are unrelated, but also for their function. In Egypt, for example, writing typically was focused on ceremonial uses, while accounting dominated Mesopotamian tablets.

However writing matured, scholars are left with the more daunting mystery of who laid the foundation for the artisans at Abydos, priests at Uruk, and the unknown makers of Indus script. "No one expected writing had such deep roots in prehistory," says Schmandt-Besserat. Deciphering that long and complex story is proving a formidable and controversial task, with no Rosetta Stone in sight.

Critical Thinking

1. What is the evidence for each of these civilizations being the discoverer of writing: Mesopotamian, Egyptian, Indus?
2. Arguing that the revolution in communication began up to 9,000 years ago, archaeologist Joan Cook writes: "In a sense, writing appears as the last step in a long line of evolution of communication systems." Support or challenge this thesis.
3. Why would being the first civilization to develop writing be significant?

Create Central

www.mhhe.com/createcentral

Internet References

National Geographic's Egyptian Pyramids
www.nationalgeographic.com/search/?proxyreload=1&search=egyptian+pyramids

Prepared by: Joseph R. Mitchell, *Howard Community College*
and Helen Buss Mitchell, *Howard Community College*

Article

Egypt's Lost Fleet

ANDREW CURRY

Learning Outcomes

After reading this article, you will be able to:

- Understand the implications of recent discoveries that prove ancient Egyptians could undertake 2,000 mile (roundtrip) voyages over land and sea.

The scenes carved into a wall of the ancient Egyptian temple at Deir el-Bahri tell of a remarkable sea voyage. A fleet of cargo ships bearing exotic plants, animals, and precious incense navigates through high-crested waves on a journey from a mysterious land known as Punt or "the Land of God." The carvings were commissioned by Hatshepsut, ancient Egypt's greatest female pharaoh, who controlled Egypt for more than two decades in the 15th century B.C. She ruled some 2 million people and oversaw one of the most powerful empires of the ancient world.

The exact meaning of the detailed carvings has divided Egyptologists ever since they were discovered in the mid-19th century. "Some people have argued that Punt was inland and not on the sea, or a fictitious place altogether," Oxford Egyptologist John Baines says. Recently, however, a series of remarkable discoveries on a desolate stretch of the Red Sea coast has settled the debate, proving once and for all that the masterful building skills of the ancient Egyptians applied to oceangoing ships as well as to pyramids.

Archaeologists from Italy, the United States, and Egypt excavating a dried-up lagoon known as Mersa Gawasis have unearthed traces of an ancient harbor that once launched early voyages like Hatshepsut's onto the open ocean. Some of the site's most evocative evidence for the ancient Egyptians' seafaring prowess is concealed behind a modern steel door set into a cliff just 700 feet or so from the Red Sea shore. Inside is a man-made cave about 70 feet deep. Lightbulbs powered by a gas generator thrumming just outside illuminate pockets of work: Here, an excavator carefully brushes sand and debris away from a 3,800-year-old reed mat; there, conservation experts photograph wood planks, chemically preserve them, and wrap them for storage.

Toward the back, a padlocked plywood door seals off an adjacent cave. As soon as the door is unlocked, a sweet, heavy, grassy smell like that of old hay wafts out, filling the area with the scent of thousands of years of decay. In the thin beam of a headlamp, one can make out stacked coils of rope the color of dark chocolate receding into the darkness of the long, narrow cave. Some of the bundles are as thick as a man's chest, and the largest may hold up to 100 feet of rope.

The rope is woven from papyrus, a clue that it may have come from the Nile Valley, where the paperlike material was common. Archaeologists found it neatly, professionally coiled and stacked, presumably by ancient mariners just before they left the shelter of the cave for the last time.

Boston University archaeologist Kathryn Bard and an international team have uncovered six other caves at Mersa Gawasis. The evidence they have found, including the remains of the oldest seagoing ships ever discovered, offers hard proof of the Egyptians' nautical roots and important clues to the location of Punt. "These new finds remove all doubt that you reach Punt by sea," Baines says. "The Egyptians must have had considerable seagoing experience."

Digging in Egypt was supposed to be a side project for Bard and her longtime research partner Rodolfo Fattovich, an archaeologist at the Orientale University of Naples. The two scholars have spent much of their careers excavating far to the south of Mersa Gawasis, uncovering the remains of ancient Axum, the seat of a kingdom that arose around 400 B.C. in what is now northern Ethiopia and Eritrea. When a 17-year civil war in Ethiopia ended in the early 1990s, Fattovich and Bard were among the first archaeologists to return to digging there.

Neither is a stranger to sketchy situations. Fattovich was working in the Ethiopian capital, Addis Ababa, in 1974 when a coup toppled the country's monarchy. Bard, who has degrees in art and archaeology, spent a year making the sometimes dangerous overland trip from Cairo to Capetown in the mid-1970s. She often wears a red T-shirt reading "Don't Shoot—I'm an Archaeologist" in more than a dozen languages.

Their time at Axum was cut short by another war. In 1998 fighting between Ethiopia and Eritrea flared up while Fattovich and Bard were excavating a collection of tombs just 30 miles from the border. The archaeologists were forced to flee, driving more than 200 miles south through the Simian mountains of Ethiopia on a one-lane dirt road.

With the instability in Ethiopia, Fattovich and Bard were unsure if they would be able to resume digging there. They decided to head to Egypt, where archaeologists had long been searching for evidence of maritime trade links between that nation and the possibly mythical kingdom of Punt. Fattovich, a voluble Italian with a bum knee, remembered reading about some scattered rock mounds found in the 1970s along the Red Sea. "We decided, why not go investigate?" Fattovich says. "But when we got there, the site looked very disappointing. There were just a few shrines, nothing impressive."

Beginning in 2002, they spent several weeks each year searching the coastal cliffs and the dried-up lagoon for signs of a harbor that might have sheltered merchant ships like those depicted in Hatshepsut's wall carvings. Then, on Christmas morning in 2004, Bard was clearing what she thought might be the back wall of a rock shelter when she stuck her hand through the sand into an open space. Clearing away the drifts of sand and rock revealed a hemispherical cave about 16 feet across and 6 feet high. Its entrance was a carved rectangular opening, clearly not a natural formation.

Inside, the archaeologists found shattered storage jars, broken boxes fashioned out of cedar planks, and five grinding stones. A piece of pottery inscribed with the name of Amenemhat III, a pharaoh who ruled Egypt around 1800 B.C., helped the team pinpoint the cave's age.

Not long afterward, another cave entrance emerged from the loose sand underneath a coral overhang. Inside was a chamber that made the first discovery look cramped: a gallery about 15 feet across, some 70 feet long, and tall enough for a short man to move around freely. The cave's entrance was reinforced with old ship timbers and reused stone anchors, the first conclusive evidence of large-scale Egyptian seafaring ever discovered.

More planks had been reused as ramps, and the cave floor was covered in wood chips left by ancient shipwrights. Other debris included shattered cups, plates, and ceramic bread molds, as well as fish bones. The cave's dimensions resembled those of standard Egyptian workers' barracks such as those found near the pyramids at Giza.

Over the past seven years, Fattovich and Bard have uncovered the hidden remnants of the ancient harborside community, which overlooked a lagoon more than a mile across. In addition to eight caves, they have found remains of five mud-brick ramps that might have been used to ease ships into the water and a shallow rock shelter used for storage and cooking. They work in the winter, when temperatures in the desert hover in the high 70s and the poisonous vipers that infest the caves are hibernating. Neither scientist was eager to spend much time in the caves: Fattovich describes himself as claustrophobic, and Bard has a deep-seated fear of snakes.

Evidence connecting Mersa Gawasis to Punt piled up both inside and outside the caves. A few hundred yards from the cliffs, piles of crumbled stone and conch shells a few feet high are evidence of altars the seafarers built north of the harbor entrance. They included stones carved with inscriptions that specifically mention missions to Punt. Timbers and steering oars similar to those on ships depicted in Hatshepsut's wall carvings were recovered in sand both inside and outside the caves. Many of the artifacts were riddled with telltale holes made by saltwater shipworms. The team even found fragments

of ebony and pottery that would have come from the southern Red Sea, 1,000 miles away.

As if that weren't enough, among the remnants of 40 smashed and empty crates found outside one cave were two sycamore planks marked with directions for assembling a ship. One of them bore an inscription still partly legible after 3,800 years: "Year 8 under his majesty/the king of Upper and Lower Egypt . . . given life forever/. . . .of wonderful things of Punt."

"It's really rare that you have all the evidence that fits together so nicely," Bard says.

While the windfall of Mersa Gawasis artifacts has answered some questions, it has raised others. For instance, how did the expeditions to Punt actually work, and how did the Egyptians construct vessels that could make a round-trip voyage of up to 2,000 miles?

Squatting in the humid heat of one of the Mersa Gawasis caves, Cheryl Ward unwraps a huge chunk of cedar as thick as a cinder block. Salt crystals on the wood glitter in the light of her headlamp. Ward turns the block in her hands and explains that it was once part of a plank from a ship's hull. From its width and curvature, she estimates the original ship would have been almost 100 feet long. "The size and magnitude of this piece are larger than anything we have for any [other] Egyptian ship, anywhere," she says.

Ward, a maritime archaeologist at Coastal Carolina University in Conway, South Carolina, spent three years building a full-scale reconstruction of a ship that would have docked in the lagoon of Mersa Gawasis. Ward has determined that unlike modern vessels, which are built around a strong internal frame, the Egyptian ship was essentially one giant hull. The curious construction meant that the craft required much larger timbers for strength. The wood was also cut thicker, with enough extra width to compensate for damage by shipworms. Some of the ship parts preserved in the Mersa Gawasis caves are more than a foot thick. "One of the features of Egyptian architecture is overbuilding," Ward says. "You can see similar safety features in the construction of these ships." Ward's archaeological experiment needed 60 tons of Douglas fir as a stand-in for the Lebanese cedar used by the ancient Egyptians.

The Egyptian ships were also unique in that they were held together with mortise-and-tenon joints, tab-and-slot fittings that needed no metal fasteners and could be taken apart and put back together again. For added strength, the individual timbers were carved with curves that nested into adjacent parts, a little like puzzle pieces. "From the very beginning, the Egyptians were building boats that could be disassembled, and that makes them different from anyone else," Ward says. "They were using the shapes of the planks to lock each of the pieces into place."

Shadowed by a support boat for safety, Ward and a crew of 24—including her two sons—sailed their 66-foot reconstruction, called *Min of the Desert*, on the Red Sea for two weeks, setting out from Safaga, a modern port not far from Mersa Gawasis. The team had low expectations; the professional long-distance sailor who captained the two-week-long voyage likened the wide, flat-bottomed craft to "a giant wooden salad bowl" the first time he saw it.

Yet once under way, the ship proved agile and fast. During an unexpected storm, it weathered 10-foot waves and winds over 20 knots, and the two massive steering oars trailing the ship's hull helped keep it on course. "In stormy weather it just surfed," Ward recalls, hefting the plank in her hands. At one point, the ship hit 9 knots, or about 10 miles an hour, with most of its sails furled. That's about three times as fast as an average modern sailboat, not too shabby for a craft carved with stone and copper tools.

For all the skill and craftsmanship evident in the Mersa Gawasis caves, ancient Egypt's ocean voyages were most likely an exception to the usual modes of trade, born out of necessity in order to obtain exotic raw materials. For most of Egypt's history, goods from Punt moved along established caravan routes via the upper Nile and across the eastern desert before cutting through modern-day Sudan. But around the time Mersa Gawasis came into use, it seems a hostile new kingdom to the south cut Egypt off from its supply of aromatic incense and resins. "If they could have gone overland, it was much easier than bringing timbers from Lebanon, building ships on the upper Nile, taking them apart and carrying them across the desert," Bard says. "They weren't stupid—no one wants to do things the hard way. But geopolitically, they had no other choice."

On the basis of the speeds *Min of the Desert* reached on its experimental voyage, Ward estimates that the endeavor would have taken at least four months, and probably more: a month to assemble the ships, a month to sail to Punt, a month and a half or more to sail back against the prevailing winds, and a month to disassemble the ships and prepare for the trek back across the desert. Fattovich suggests that there were probably just 15 to 20 expeditions over some 400 years, about one every two decades.

Even for a civilization that built the pyramids, these expeditions would have been a tremendous logistical challenge. The closest shipyards were in Qena, a city on the Nile not far from the great temples of Luxor, Karnak, and Thebes. Four hundred miles south of modern Cairo, Qena was the closest point on the Nile to the Red Sea and probably the starting point for voyages to Punt.

From Qena, expeditions would have had to trek east across 100 miles of desert, following channels cut by rare rainstorms— or *wadis*—until they arrived at the coast. Mersa Gawasis was an intermediate staging point where the expeditions could reassemble their ships and prepare for the long voyage south.

Today Egypt's Red Sea coast is almost completely lifeless, as though the sandy beach is simply an extension of the desert that stretches 100 miles inland to the Nile. "Here we are, in the middle of nowhere," Fattovich says. "For Egyptians this was the equivalent of what a moon base will be in 100 years—very strange, very difficult."

The carefully chosen harbor met a number of requirements for ancient sailors. It was sheltered from the waves and wind, its mouth was deep enough to clear the reefs that line the Red Sea coast, and the fossilized coral cliffs could be dug out easily. To top it off, Mersa Gawasis was a sort of marine oasis. Organic remains excavated in and around the caves helped the archaeologists reconstruct an environment very different from the expanse of sand and stone that surrounds the dig today. The inlet was once lined with mangrove trees and reeds. Shallow, calm water would have been perfect for launching ships. "Four thousand years ago, this was an ideal harbor. It's a perfect place for ships to be built," Bard says. "And it's the shortest distance between Qena and the Red Sea."

Like a modern space mission, the expeditions had to be entirely self-sufficient. Though the team did find freshwater sources not too far from the caves, everything else would have been carried across the desert. The ships themselves were disassembled plank by plank and probably loaded onto donkeys for the long trek. And each expedition brought with it not just the ships themselves but months' worth of food, rope, tools, and provisions for the voyage south.

All this took tremendous manpower. An inscription on a stone found atop the cliff commemorating a voyage that set sail around 1950 B.C. lists a labor force of 3,756 men, 3,200 of them conscripted workers. "These were complicated and expensive operations in Egyptian times," Fattovich says.

After about 400 years, Mersa Gawasis fell out of use. It was probably abandoned because there was no longer enough water in the lagoon to float ships, and perhaps overland links improved or other harbors were used. The last sailors to use the lagoon sealed up their ropes and shelters behind mud brick and sand to await expeditions that never came. For four millennia, the caves remained perfectly intact.

This year's dig at Mersa Gawasis may well be the last. The wood found in the caves has been carefully photographed, cleaned, and sealed in special vacuum bags for storage on shelves at the back of the caves. Of the eight caves the team has located, six have been thoroughly studied. The last two are blocked by fallen rock and sand. Clearing them out could cause a total collapse. Not long before the team finished for the season, they dispatched a three-foot-long robotic snake equipped with a camera built by a team from Carnegie Mellon University to look inside. But a small pile of rubble a few feet inside the cave opening proved the snakebot's undoing—it couldn't make it up the 45-degree slope. The robot's handlers hope to return and try again with a different design; if they find something remarkable, say, huge pieces of timber or even a whole vessel, there is a chance the caves would be opened.

In the meantime, the site is guarded 24 hours a day, and Bard says locals know there's no gold inside, just old pieces of wood. So even with political chaos engulfing Egypt, it should be safe from looters. She and Fattovich are now heading south for one last search, determined to find the trading fleet's actual destination. "I've spent my life searching for Punt," Fattovich says. "I would like to conclude my career with a final excavation to locate the harbor of Punt."

Sitting on the shore a short walk from the caves, waves gently lapping at the stony beach, Bard says she's been studying satellite images of the southern Red Sea to pinpoint harbors Egyptian sailors might have used to trade for the "wonderful things of Punt." "We're already thinking about where we might go next," she says, looking out to the sea.

Critical Thinking

1. Before recent archaeological findings confirmed the existence of Egyptian maritime voyages, what evidence strongly suggested it? Why was it doubted?
2. How did the Egyptians make roundtrip voyages of 2,000 miles that crossed land and sea? Do these accomplishments rival the building of pyramids?
3. Andrew Curry writes: "Ancient Egypt's ocean voyages were most likely . . . born of necessity in order to obtain exotic raw materials." What might have disrupted the usual patterns and motivated ancient Egypt to abandon overland caravan routes and "do things the hard way"?
4. In what ways was the launching of ships from the harbor at Mersa Gawasis "like a modern space mission"?

Create Central

www.mhhe.com/createcentral

Internet Reference

National Geographic's Egyptian Pyramids
http://www.nationalgeographic.com/search/?proxyreload=1&search=egyptian+pyramids

Unit III

UNIT

Prepared by: Joseph R. Mitchell, *Howard Community College*
and Helen Buss Mitchell, *Howard Community College*

The Early Civilizations to 500 BCE

What constitutes a civilization? Some characteristics might include urbanization; complex economic, political, and social systems; sophisticated technology; and literacy. If we use these criteria as a standard, evidence of cities, writing, and metallurgy would indicate the presence of civilization. But suppose one of these ingredients is missing. If we consider the sacred cosmology of ancient Ireland, might we have to broaden our criteria for defining and evaluating the sophistication of civilizations? Should we conclude, for example, that a group or society that does not write is uncivilized? Because most historians rely on written records, are illiterate people prehistoric?

Judgments about what is a civilization and what is not imply value rankings. And, because world history texts are organized around a history of civilizations, only those societies that are considered civilizations are included in the story. Mesopotamia, the ancient Greek name for the area "between the rivers"—the Tigris and Euphrates in modern Iraq—was home to the Bronze Age civilizations of Assyria, Akkad, and Sumer. In that "cradle of civilization," as well as on the Greek island of Crete, we find systems of writing, decorated pottery, paved streets, elaborate metal working, and sophisticated trading networks.

You know about the Incas because historians broadened the definition of civilization to include this complex society. But, you may know little about the Nubians, a powerful, literate society that once controlled all of ancient Egypt. The Greeks and Romans considered Nubia one of the foremost civilizations of the world, and valued its gold, frankincense, ebony, ivory, and animal skins. Herodotus admired the Nubians for their height, beauty, and longevity.

And, in the Indus River Valley, two of the earliest planned cities—Harappa and Mohenjo-Daro—featured water conduits, toilets, straight streets, and standard-sized building bricks four thousand years ago. Archaeologists have unearthed orderly walled cities and evidence of one of the world's first written languages in a civilization twice the size of Egypt and Mesopotamia that lasted for 700 years. Until the nineteenth century, however, we knew nothing of these peoples or their thriving, prosperous cultures.

Borrowing the methods and findings of archaeology has permitted historians to add to the list of civilizations. Most ancient cities and their civilizations have not survived, conquered either by competing civilizations or by nature. So, what is called material culture is often our only window into the lives of ancient peoples. Potsherds and even gold jewelry provide some insights about daily life and wealth, but tell us nothing about the thoughts and attitudes of the people who used these artifacts. Access to the inner life is possible only through the written word. And legacies from these ancient languages endure today, in our use of Assyrian words for many plants and minerals, as well as in our borrowing of the Sumerian system of astronomy and timekeeping, based on the number six. Our 60-second minutes and 60-minute hours have their roots in ancient Sumer.

Article

Prepared by: Joseph R. Mitchell, *Howard Community College*
and Helen Buss Mitchell, *Howard Community College*

Uncovering Ancient Thailand

Charles Higham's 40-year career has transformed our understanding of prehistoric Southeast Asia.

TOM GIDWITZ

Learning Outcomes

After reading this article, you will be able to:

- Discuss the contributions the work of Charles Higham has made to the archaeology of ancient Southeast Asia.

Eleven skeletons lie exposed at the bottom of a yawning ten-foot-deep hole in the village of Ban Non Wat, Thailand. Two dozen people swarm over them, troweling the earth in search of more graves, hoisting up the soil bucket by bucket. Workers kneel over the 3,000-year-old bones, coaxing them free with dental picks, still others sketch, bag, and carry them away. A white fabric roof hangs over the 40-foot-square pit; outside its shelter, more workers screen soil, sort artifacts, and reassemble countless sherds into graceful, ancient pots.

One man in shorts, sandals, and floppy gray hat seems to be everywhere. Charles Higham is in charge of this dig, leading his army of archaeologists, villagers, and Earthwatch volunteers by inspiration and example. One moment he's lying in the dirt, scraping at a wrist bone thick with shell bangles, and the next he's huddling over field notes with one of his students or joking with the locals in Thai. When traces of a new grave are discovered, he sometimes darts into the crowd of excavators and, with a few sweeps of his trowel, exposes a pot or a skull.

Higham, 66, an ebullient Englishman with a fringe of graying hair and a ready laugh, is a professor at the University of Otago in Dunedin, New Zealand. Since 1969 he has set his sights on filling in what he calls "the tabula rasa" of Southeast Asian prehistory by probing its most profound transformations: how its hunter-gatherers became farmers, its farmers became metalworkers, and its village elders became kings. His discoveries and books have illuminated a culture that stretches back 30,000 years.

"Until 30 years ago our knowledge of this area was very sparse indeed," Higham says, "but now Southeast Asia has become a major place in the world for understanding human history,

not just prehistory, but the history of our species. If anyone is remotely interested in that, then don't ignore Southeast Asia."

Higham has been one of the few English-speaking archaeologists working year after year in the region. "Everybody flocks like lemmings into Maya country and western Europe or the Near East," says Brian Fagan, emeritus professor of anthropology at the University of California, Santa Barbara, but Higham has hunkered down "in one of the seminal areas of early civilization."

"He's very much an archaeologist's archaeologist," says Graeme Barker, of Cambridge University. "What Charles writes we all want to read."

And here at Ban Non Wat, he has found plenty to write about. The village is on the Khorat Plateau, a rolling plain in northeast Thailand with a rich past; occupied since 2100 B.C., the site is only 30 miles from Phimai, once a temple city of the Angkor civilization. Over the past five years, Higham and Thai archaeologist Rachanie Thosarat have returned each dry season. So far, they have unearthed more than 460 Neolithic, Bronze, and Iron Age graves, offering an unparalleled view of the region's prehistoric past. "Every time we dig here," Higham says with relish, "it's a new surprise."

Higham fell in love with archaeology when he was 14 years old, after his aunt gave him W. Ceram's classic *Gods, Graves, and Scholars* for Christmas. The next summer he and his older brother Richard volunteered to dig at Snail Down, an Early Bronze Age cemetery near Stonehenge. By 1959, when Higham entered Cambridge, he had also dug in France and Greece and studied archaeology at the University of London.

The son of an architect, Higham had two burning goals at Cambridge: to win the highest academic honors and thus earn a full scholarship, and to play against Oxford in the annual rugby match. Although only 5'9" tall, he was a star player on the university's unbeaten rugby team and, in its victory over Oxford, put the first points on the board. In the classroom, he shone in a group of gifted young scholars studying under archaeologist Grahame Clark.

Clark pioneered the field of economic prehistory, the study of how early societies survived in their environments using evidence gleaned from the seeds, sticks, bones, and soil that most archaeologists at the time simply threw away. For his doctorate, Higham used domesticated cattle bones to reconstruct prehistoric life in Denmark and Switzerland. Says Norman Hammond, a fellow student at Cambridge and now professor of archaeology at Boston University, "His natural gift is for seeing promise in an unpromising situation. Nobody really thought of cattle bones in central Europe as being sexy. Charles was able to turn them into a major piece of work." While he researched he shrewdly submitted his findings to local and national journals. "By the time he got his Ph.D., he had a string of publications as long as your arm in six languages, and he was able to walk straight into a job at the University of Otago in New Zealand to teach European prehistory."

The Otago appointment was also due to Clark, who worked hard to spread his influence by placing his students in jobs around the world. "He got it into his head that because I was a rugby player and the [New Zealand] All Blacks were the best rugby team in the world, that I was the right person for New Zealand," Higham says.

Higham, his wife, Polly, and son Tom, the first of four children, arrived in 1967, and Higham swiftly made his mark. New Zealand has no prehistoric pottery, so its past can be difficult to decipher. Higham, with a landmark study, used the shells in an ancient midden to reveal the seasonal migrations of prehistoric Maori tribes. Two years after arriving, at only 28 years old, Higham became the first professor of prehistoric archaeology in Australasia.

Until then, prehistoric excavations in Southeast Asia had been few, and finds meager. Instead, scholars had focused on the stone ruins and inscriptions of ancient kingdoms that arose in the first centuries A.D.—Funan in the Mekong Delta, Champa in coastal Viet Nam, Dvarivati in central Thailand, and above all the magnificent Angkor civilization that thrived in Cambodia, Laos, and Thailand from the ninth to fifteenth centuries. These scholars thought Indian Brahmins and seafaring merchants had brought India's sophisticated Hindu culture to docile, primitive clans.

In the late 1960s, archaeologists began to focus anew on the region's prehistory. In 1969, Higham went to Thailand to meet American archaeologists Wilhelm Solheim, Donn Bayard, and Chester Gorman, who had discovered what were thought to be Asia's oldest bronze artifacts on the Khorat plateau. Soon, he was digging with Gorman in remote Thai caves, looking in vain for the region's first farmers.

In 1974, Higham was with Gorman and Thai archaeologist Prisit Charoenwongsa at Ban Chiang, a Khorat plateau village where looters had been plundering extraordinarily beautiful pots. Thermoluminescence dating suggested the pottery was 6,000 years old, and the University of Pennsylvania sponsored an excavation to rescue what was left. "We were in very heady, exciting times," Higham recalls.

Two years later, Gorman and Charoenwongsa announced Ban Chiang's bronze dated to 3600 B.C. and its iron to 1600 B.C., making them the earliest in the world. Extraordinarily, these advances had arisen in an egalitarian rural village. Elsewhere, metalworking had developed hand in hand with stratified societies, warfare, and specialized labor.

The discovery sparked a sensation. Ban Chiang artifacts appeared in newspapers around the globe, in *Time* and *Newsweek* cover stories, and in a traveling Smithsonian Institution show. But it also featured in heated debate.

"It led to two groups," Higham recalls, "one of which believed it, and one of which said, 'It's a whole lot of hooey, and this can't be the case'."

In 1980 Higham teamed up with Thai archaeologist Amphan Kijngam. At Ban Na Di, 14 miles southwest of Ban Chiang, they uncovered chunks of melted bronze and casting molds from a cultural phase almost certainly contemporary with Ban Chiang's famous bronze. Higham sent the Charcoal dating samples to a New Zealand lab.

"When they came back I got quite a shock. They were a thousand, two thousand years later than I imagined." The site's earliest bronze was dated to about only 1300 B.C., which pushed the site's iron to an even more recent date. "Beyond any doubt the radiocarbon results from Ban Chiang were far too early." The charcoal samples from this site, some of which Higham had gathered, had come from grave fill, which can include charcoal unearthed at the time of burial and far older than the graves themselves.

Later tests showed Ban Chiang's earliest pottery to be only about 4,000 years old, and most archaeologists now agree with Higham's dates. He is convinced bronze is a Middle Eastern innovation, carried into China along the Silk Road; the Thais learned it in the later second millennium B.C. from Shang Dynasty merchants who ventured south to swap bronze vessels for local goods.

Early in his career, before he had the resources to lead his own expeditions, Higham published a paper describing how best to explore what he called the "terra incognita" of prehistoric Southeast Asia. "He then moved like a general," says Hammond, "marshalling his forces across the area of central and northern Thailand, identifying a series of problems, and the sites at which they might be resolved, digging them, publishing them in depth, and promptly."

In the 1980s he aimed his sights on the hundreds of mounds that dot rice paddies in Thailand and northeast Cambodia. Often surrounded with ancient moats and banks, with villages perched on top, the mounds can cover 100 acres and reach 30 feet high. They formed during generations of human occupation, in a steady accumulation of cultural debris.

An hour east of Bangkok is a steep mound known as Khok Phanom Di. It was thought to be a natural hill until 1978, when a bulldozer, cutting a new path to the Buddhist temple atop it, unearthed beads, bracelets, and bones. A Thai archaeologist sank a test pit into the mound, and in 1980 showed Higham shellfish, rice, and radiocarbon dates suggesting it had been occupied for thousands of years.

Sea levels have risen and fallen several times over the past ten millennia, and although Khok Phanom Di now lies 14 miles from the Gulf of Siam, the test pit's shellfish were saltwater varieties. The mound seemed an ideal place to study the relationship between the resource-rich coast and early rice cultivation.

In 1984, Higham and Thosarat returned and dug for seven months, down 26 feet to the natural soil, removing 155 skeletons and enough pots, jewelry, stone tools, seeds, and dirt to fill more than five railroad boxcars.

The team subjected the material to an investigation that was unprecedented in Southeast Asia. They performed detailed forensic analyses of all the skeletons, even testing for strontium isotopes in their teeth—which vary depending on one's childhood environment—to spot newcomers to the settlement. They looked at food remains in the ingestive tracts of two especially well-preserved bodies to discover what they had eaten. They drilled the soil around the mound for ancient seeds, pollen, and sediments. The analyses filled seven volumes.

What they discovered was the first settlers arrived in 2000 B.C. at what was then a major river estuary near the open sea. They made a living as hunter-fisher-gatherers, using weighted nets and bone fishhooks to snare crabs, fish, porpoises, sharks, and rays. They were also skillful potters, and since the surrounding mud flats were too salty to farm, they traded ceramics for rice with farmers who lived on higher ground. They suffered from malarial mosquitoes and an inherited anemia that killed most of their children in infancy, but the surviving adults—some lived into their 40s—were generally in good health.

After about six generations sea levels fell, and the surrounding swamps silted up. Women from outside the community joined the site, and the people of Khok Phanom Di began to farm rice on the floodplain, digging with granite hoes, harvesting with shell knives. In time, the sea rose again, the salt marshes returned, and the villagers made their livelihood once more from ceramics.

The team found an astonishing grave dated to roughly 1500 B.C., when a woman was reverently interred under stacked pots and cylinders of raw potter's clay. The team dubbed her "the Princess." She was covered in red ochre and wore a shell headdress and two garments embroidered with more than 120,000 beads. Nearby lay a 15-month-old infant, undoubtedly her child, beneath the same clay forms, in the same red ochre, in a miniature version of her spectacular beaded garments. Beside the Princess's ankle a shell container held a ceramic anvil for shaping pots. Beside the infant, in exactly the same position, was a little anvil no bigger than a thimble.

The Princess died in her mid thirties, a wealthy master potter in the largest prehistoric grave Higham had yet seen. But she was only one of many thriving villagers. The team traced inherited skeletal traits in the clustered graves and discovered that two families endured for 17 generations. These families' fortunes fluctuated, with some generations rich in grave goods, others with little, proof that personal achievement, not inheritance, was the community's key to wealth.

"Only when a mortuary tradition in a single community can be followed over so many generations can we gain such an intimate glimpse into its operating principles," Higham wrote.

In 1994, Higham and Thosarat launched the Origins of Angkor, a multidisciplinary study in search of the region's Iron Age, a time around 500 B.C. when chiefdoms began to coalesce into the civilization of Angkor.

So far, they have excavated four sites in Thailand, and expanded to encompass two Cambodian digs. But the finds at Noen U-Loke, a village three miles from Ban Non Wat, stand out.

Noen U-Loke is a 30-acre mound ringed with five moats jutting 600 feet into the rice fields. The team dug for two seasons, revealing Southeast Asia's longest Iron Age mortuary sequence, more than 120 graves revealing an eight-century-long narrative of growing wealth, power, and eventual strife.

Iron was used at Noen U-Loke from the start, at first primarily for jewelry, then increasingly for farm tools and weapons. The early men and women wore Bronze Age-style shell and marble jewelry, but adopted beads of carnelian, jade, glass, and silver as well as gold earrings, tiger-tooth necklaces, and agate pendants imported from India. As time went on, the settlement grew rich, with some members buried in rice-filled coffins, wearing so many bronze toe rings, finger rings, bangles, and bracelets that they must have blazed in the sun.

Between 1 and 300 B.C., the community's leaders ordered construction of the moats and banks. But not long after, signs of warfare—iron spears and arrowheads—appear in abundance. In the mound's last years, one youth was laid to rest with an iron arrowhead piercing his spine, a victim.

Higham believes the increasingly elaborate burials demonstrate fine emergence of princely elites. And although the site was abandoned early in the first millennium, elsewhere lords like these soon began to construct brick temples, worship Hindu deities, adopt Sanskrit names, and, in time, swear fealty to the Khmer god-kings.

Excavations in southeast asia take place in the dry season from December to March, and to Higham, time is precious. "When we find nothing except soil and potsherds we have to work very hard and fast, like a battlefield, like a war," says Warrachai Wiriyaromp, an associate professor at Bangkok's Kasetsart University, a doctoral student of Higham's who has worked with him since 1979. "But when we reach the skeleton layer, we slow down, and work like hearing an orchestra, slowly, bit by bit."

Now it is March 1, and the diggers at Ban Non Wat have come to the undisturbed soil beneath the mound. This year Higham's team has found Iron Age butchering floors, a collapsed wattle and daub house, and a cemetery with 60 bodies crammed like sardines. The site's Bronze Age layers have yielded what he calls "super burials," high-status individuals interred together in single graves as long as 15 feet, laden with jewelry, beaded garments, bronze tools, and as many as 150 pots. These burials, near relatively poor, unadorned graves, have "revolutionized our thinking on the Bronze Age and its social structure," he says triumphantly, for they offer firm proof that, as elsewhere in the world, "there is a social hierarchy, a marked one, in the Bronze Age of Southeast Asia."

But as the season nears its end, he is encountering new puzzles. Until now the team has found bodies interred flat on their backs, the custom with farming cultures. But for the last two days three adults of unknown gender and a baby cradled in its mother's arms have emerged, buried on their sides with their knees drawn up in the crouching position favored by hunter-gatherers, with pots and shell jewelry unlike any found in the Neolithic graves. They're the first flexed bodies discovered on the Khorat plateau.

"They shouldn't be there. We've never found one before, and now we have five of them," says Higham. "We're nonplused, is the only way to put it."

These flexed burials support a bold theory. In 1987, Higham's former classmate, Cambridge professor Colin Renfrew, proposed that farmers in the Near East moved into new lands occupied by hunter-gatherers, spreading agriculture and Indo-European languages west to Ireland, east to China, and south into India. Linguists and archaeologists have proposed a similar diaspora for the spread of Austroasiatic and Austronesian languages in Asia, as farmers in China's Yangtze River valley began a migration in about 6000 B.C. that took human pioneers to eastern India, the Pacific Islands, and into Southeast Asia around 2500–200 B.C.

Higham notes that agriculture and metalworking arise later and later with further distance from the Yangtze, and that across the region pottery decoration, burial practices, and language are intriguingly similar.

He is already toying with scenarios for the flexed burials. Did Neolithic farmers move onto the mound where a hunter-gatherer cemetery already existed, or did arriving farmers and local, hunter-gatherers intermarry and bury their dead in the hunter-gatherer style?

But as Higham looks down at the gray bones of the clinging infant and its mother, he knows that future excavations could easily prove his theories wrong. "If we were to start opening up an area of this size at another site," he says, "God knows what we'd find."

Critical Thinking

1. In what significant ways has Charles Higham filled in the "tabula rasa" [blank tablet] of Southeast Indian prehistory?

2. Why would the discovery of "super burials" have "revolutionized our thinking of the Bronze Age and its social structure"?

3. What "bold theory" does the existence of "flexed burials" support?

Create Central

www.mhhe.com/createcentral

Internet References

Exploring Ancient World Cultures
http://eawc.evansville.edu

___

TOM GIDWITZ is a contributing editor for *Archaeology*.

Prepared by: Joseph R. Mitchell, *Howard Community College*
and Helen Buss Mitchell, *Howard Community College*

Article

Black Pharaohs

An ignored chapter of history tells of a time when kings from deep in Africa conquered ancient Egypt.

ROBERT DRAPER

Learning Outcomes

After reading this article, you will be able to:

- Determine what effect Nubian pharaohs have had on Egyptian history and on African history.

In the year 730 B.C., a man by the name of Piye decided the only way to save Egypt from itself was to invade it. Things would get bloody before the salvation came.

"Harness the best steeds of your stable," he ordered his commanders. The magnificent civilization that had built the great pyramids had lost its way, torn apart by petty warlords. For two decades Piye had ruled over his own kingdom in Nubia, a swath of Africa located mostly in present-day Sudan. But he considered himself the true ruler of Egypt as well, the rightful heir to the spiritual traditions practiced by pharaohs such as Ramses II and Thutmose III. Since Piye had probably never actually visited Lower Egypt, some did not take his boast seriously. Now Piye would witness the subjugation of decadent Egypt firsthand—"I shall let Lower Egypt taste the taste of my fingers," he would later write.

North on the Nile River his soldiers sailed. At Thebes, the capital of Upper Egypt, they disembarked. Believing there was a proper way to wage holy wars, Piye instructed his soldiers to purify themselves before combat by bathing in the Nile, dressing themselves in fine linen, and sprinkling their bodies with water from the temple at Karnak, a site holy to the ram-headed sun god Amun, whom Piye identified as his own personal deity. Piye himself feasted and offered sacrifices to Amun. Thus sanctified, the commander and his men commenced to do battle with every army in their path.

By the end of a yearlong campaign, every leader in Egypt had capitulated—including the powerful delta warlord Tefnakht, who sent a messenger to tell Piye, "Be gracious! I cannot see your face in the days of shame; I cannot stand before your flame, I dread your grandeur." In exchange for their lives, the vanquished urged Piye to worship at their temples, pocket their finest jewels, and claim their best horses.

He obliged them. And then, with his vassals trembling before him, the newly anointed Lord of the Two Lands did something extraordinary: He loaded up his army and his war booty, and sailed southward to his home in Nubia, never to return to Egypt again.

When Piye died at the end of his 35-year reign in 715 B.C., his subjects honored his wishes by burying him in an Egyptian-style pyramid, with four of his beloved horses nearby. He was the first pharaoh to receive such entombment in more than 500 years. A pity, then, that the great Nubian who accomplished these feats is literally faceless to us. Images of Piye on the elaborate granite slabs, or stelae, memorializing his conquest of Egypt have long since been chiseled away. On a relief in the temple at the Nubian capital of Napata, only Piye's legs remain. We are left with a single physical detail of the man—namely, that his skin was dark.

Piye was the first of the so-called black pharaohs—a series of Nubian kings who ruled over all of Egypt for three-quarters of a century as that country's 25th dynasty. Through inscriptions carved on stelae by both the Nubians and their enemies, it is possible to map out these rulers' vast footprint on the continent. The black pharaohs reunified a tattered Egypt and filled its landscape with glorious monuments, creating an empire that stretched from the southern border at present-day Khartoum all the way north to the Mediterranean Sea. They stood up to the bloodthirsty Assyrians, perhaps saving Jerusalem in the process.

Until recently, theirs was a chapter of history that largely went untold. Only in the past four decades have archaeologists resurrected their story—and come to recognize that the black pharaohs didn't appear out of nowhere. They sprang from a robust African civilization that had flourished on the southern banks of the Nile for 2,500 years, going back at least as far as the first Egyptian dynasty.

Today Sudan's pyramids—greater in number than all of Egypt's—are haunting spectacles in the Nubian Desert. It is possible to wander among them unharassed, even alone, a world away from Sudan's genocide and refugee crisis in Darfur or the aftermath of civil war in the south. While hundreds of miles north, at Cairo or Luxor, curiosity seekers arrive by the busload to jostle and crane for views of the Egyptian wonders, Sudan's seldom-visited pyramids at El Kurru, Nuri, and Meroë stand serenely amid an arid landscape that scarcely hints of the thriving culture of ancient Nubia.

Now our understanding of this civilization is once again threatened with obscurity. The Sudanese government is building a hydroelectric dam along the Nile, 600 miles upstream from the Aswan High Dam, which Egypt constructed in the 1960s, consigning much of lower Nubia to the bottom of Lake Nasser (called Lake Nubia in Sudan). By 2009, the massive Merowe Dam should be complete, and a 106-mile-long lake will flood the terrain abutting the Nile's Fourth Cataract, or rapid, including thousands of unexplored sites. For the past nine years, archaeologists have flocked to the region, furiously digging before another repository of Nubian history goes the way of Atlantis.

The ancient world was devoid of racism. At the time of Piye's historic conquest, the fact that his skin was dark was irrelevant. Artwork from ancient Egypt, Greece, and Rome shows a clear awareness of racial features and skin tone, but there is little evidence that darker skin was seen as a sign of inferiority. Only after the European powers colonized Africa in the 19th century did Western scholars pay attention to the color of the Nubians' skin, to uncharitable effect.

Explorers who arrived at the central stretch of the Nile River excitedly reported the discovery of elegant temples and pyramids—the ruins of an ancient civilization called Kush. Some, like the Italian doctor Giuseppe Ferlini—who lopped off the top of at least one Nubian pyramid, inspiring others to do the same—hoped to find treasure beneath. The Prussian archaeologist Richard Lepsius had more studious intentions, but he ended up doing damage of his own by concluding that the Kushites surely "belonged to the Caucasian race."

Even famed Harvard Egyptologist George Reisner—whose discoveries between 1916 and 1919 offered the first archaeological evidence of Nubian kings who ruled over Egypt—besmirched his own findings by insisting that black Africans could not possibly have constructed the monuments he was excavating. He believed that Nubia's leaders, including Piye, were light-skinned Egypto-Libyans who ruled over the primitive Africans, That their moment of greatness was so fleeting, he suggested, must be a consequence of the same leaders intermarrying with the "negroid elements."

For decades, many historians flip-flopped: Either the Kushite pharaohs were actually "white," or they were bumblers, their civilization a derivative offshoot of true Egyptian culture. In their 1942 history, *When Egypt Ruled the East,* highly regarded Egyptologists Keith Seele and George Steindorff summarized the Nubian pharaonic dynasty and Piye's triumphs in all of three sentences—the last one reading: "But his dominion was not for long."

The neglect of Nubian history reflected not only the bigoted worldview of the times, but also a cult-like fascination with Egypt's achievements—and a complete ignorance of Africa's past. "The first time I came to Sudan," recalls Swiss archaeologist Charles Bonnet, "people said: 'You're mad! There's no history there! It's all in Egypt!'"

That was a mere 44 years ago. Artifacts uncovered during the archaeological salvage campaigns as the waters rose at Aswan in the 1960s began changing that view. In 2003, Charles Bonnet's decades of digging near the Nile's Third Cataract at the abandoned settlement of Kerma gained international recognition with the discovery of seven large stone statues of Nubian pharaohs. Well before then, however, Bonnet's labors had revealed an older, densely occupied urban center that commanded rich fields and extensive herds, and had long profited from trade in gold, ebony, and ivory. "It was a kingdom completely free of Egypt and original, with its own construction and burial customs," Bonnet says. This powerful dynasty rose just as Egypt's Middle Kingdom declined around 1785 B.C. By 1500 B.C. the Nubian empire stretched between the Second and Fifth Cataracts.

Revisiting that golden age in the African desert does little to advance the case of Afrocentric Egyptologists, who argue that all ancient Egyptians, from King Tut to Cleopatra, were black Africans. Nonetheless, the saga of the Nubians proves that a civilization from deep in Africa not only thrived but briefly dominated in ancient times, intermingling and sometimes intermarrying with their Egyptian neighbors to the north. (King Tut's own grandmother, the 18th-dynasty Queen Tiye, is claimed by some to be of Nubian heritage.)

The Egyptians didn't like having such a powerful neighbor to the south, especially since they depended on Nubia's gold mines to bankroll their dominance of western Asia. So the pharaohs of the 18th dynasty (1539–1292 B.C.) sent armies to conquer Nubia and built garrisons along the Nile. They installed Nubian chiefs as administrators and schooled the children of favored Nubians at Thebes. Subjugated, the elite Nubians began to embrace the cultural and spiritual customs of Egypt—venerating Egyptian gods, particularly Amun, using the Egyptian language, adopting Egyptian burial styles and, later, pyramid building. The Nubians were arguably the first people to be struck by "Egyptomania."

Egyptologists of the latter 19th and early 20th centuries would interpret this as a sign of weakness. But they had it wrong: The Nubians had a gift for reading the geopolitical tea leaves. By the eighth century B.C., Egypt was riven by factions, the north ruled by Libyan chiefs who put on the trappings of pharaonic traditions to gain legitimacy. Once firmly in power, they toned down the theocratic devotion to Amun, and the priests at Karnak feared a godless outcome. Who was in a position to return Egypt to its former state of might and sanctity?

The Egyptian priests looked south and found their answer—a people who, without setting foot inside Egypt, had preserved Egypt's spiritual traditions. As archaeologist Timothy Kendall of Northeastern University puts it, the Nubians "had become more Catholic than the pope."

Under Nubian rule, Egypt became Egypt again. When Piye died in 715, his brother Shabaka solidified the 25th dynasty by taking up residence in the Egyptian capital of Memphis. Like his brother, Shabaka wed himself to the old pharaonic ways, adopting the throne name of the 6th-dynasty ruler Pepi II, just as Piye had claimed the old throne name of Thutmose III. Rather than execute his foes, Shabaka put them to work building dikes to seal off Egyptian villages from Nile floods.

Shabaka lavished Thebes and the Temple of Luxor with building projects. At Karnak he erected a pink granite statue depicting himself wearing the Kushite crown of the double uraeus—the two cobras signifying his legitimacy as Lord of the Two Lands. Through architecture as well as military might, Shabaka signaled to Egypt that the Nubians were here to stay.

To the east, the Assyrians were fast building their own empire. In 701 B.C., when they marched into Judah in present-day Israel, the Nubians decided to act. At the city of Eltekeh, the two armies met. And although the Assyrian emperor, Sennacherib, would brag lustily that he "inflicted defeat upon them," a young Nubian prince, perhaps 20, son of the great pharaoh Piye, managed to survive. That the Assyrians, whose tastes ran to wholesale slaughter, failed to kill the prince suggests their victory was anything but total.

In any event, when the Assyrians left town and massed against the gates of Jerusalem, that city's embattled leader, Hezekiah, hoped his Egyptian allies would come to the rescue. The Assyrians issued a taunting reply, immortalized in the Old Testaments Book of II Kings: "Thou trustest upon the staff of this bruised reed [of] Egypt, on which if a man lean, it will go into his hand, and pierce it: So is Pharaoh king of Egypt unto all that trust on him."

Then, according to the Scriptures and other accounts, a miracle occurred: The Assyrian army retreated. Were they struck by a plague? Or, as Henry Aubin's provocative book, *The Rescue of Jerusalem,* suggests, was it actually the alarming news that the aforementioned Nubian prince was advancing on Jerusalem? All we know for sure is that Sennacherib abandoned the siege and galloped back in disgrace to his kingdom, where he was murdered 18 years later, apparently by his own sons.

The deliverance of Jerusalem is not just another of ancient history's sidelights, Aubin asserts, but one of its pivotal events. It allowed Hebrew society and Judaism to strengthen for another crucial century—by which time the Babylonian king Nebuchadrezzar could banish the Hebrew people but not obliterate them or their faith. From Judaism, of course, would spring Christianity and Islam. Jerusalem would come to be recast, in all three major monotheistic religions, as a city of a godly significance.

It has been easy to overlook, amid these towering historical events, the dark-skinned figure at the edge of the landscape—the survivor of Eltekeh, the hard-charging prince later referred to by the Assyrians as "the one accursed by all the great gods": Piye's son Taharqa.

So sweeping was Taharqa's influence on Egypt that even his enemies could not eradicate his imprint. During his rule, to travel down the Nile from Napata to Thebes was to navigate a panorama of architectural wonderment. All over Egypt, he built monuments with busts, statues, and cartouches bearing his image or name, many of which now sit in museums around the world. He is depicted as a supplicant to gods, or in the protective presence of the ram deity Amun, or as a sphinx himself, or in a warriors posture. Most statues were defaced by his rivals. His nose is often broken off, to foreclose him returning from the dead. Shattered as well is the uraeus on his forehead, to repudiate his claim as Lord of the Two Lands. But in each remaining image, the serene self-certainty in his eyes remains for all to see.

His father, Piye, had returned the true pharaonic customs to Egypt. His uncle Shabaka had established a Nubian presence in Memphis and Thebes. But their ambitions paled before those of the 31-year-old military commander who received the crown in Memphis in 690 and presided over the combined empires of Egypt and Nubia for the next 26 years.

Taharqa had ascended at a favorable moment for the 25th dynasty. The delta warlords had been laid low. The Assyrians, after failing to best him at Jerusalem, wanted no part of the Nubian ruler. Egypt was his and his alone. The gods granted him prosperity to go with the peace. During his sixth year on the throne, the Nile swelled from rains, inundating the valleys and yielding a spectacular harvest of grain without sweeping away any villages. As Taharqa would record in four separate stelae, the high waters even exterminated all rats and snakes. Clearly the revered Amun was smiling on his chosen one.

Taharqa did not intend to sit on his profits. He believed in spending his political capital. Thus he launched the most audacious building campaign of any pharaoh since the New Kingdom (around 1500 B.C.), when Egypt had been in a period of expansion. Inevitably the two holy capitals of Thebes and Napata received the bulk of Taharqa's attention. Standing today amid the hallowed clutter of the Karnak temple complex near Thebes is a lone 62-foot-high column. That pillar had been one of ten, forming a gigantic kiosk that the Nubian pharaoh added to the Temple of Amun. He also constructed a number of chapels around the temple and erected massive statues of himself and of his beloved mother, Abar. Without defacing a single pre-existing monument, Taharqa made Thebes his.

He did the same hundreds of miles upriver, in the Nubian city of Napata. Its holy mountain Jebel Barkal—known for its striking rock-face pinnacle that calls to mind a phallic symbol of fertility—had captivated even the Egyptian pharaohs of the New Kingdom, who believed the site to be the birthplace of Amun. Seeking to present himself as heir to the New Kingdom pharaohs, Taharqa erected two temples, set into the base of the mountain, honoring the goddess consorts of Amun. On Jebel Barkal's pinnacle—partially covered in gold leaf to bedazzle wayfarers—the black pharaoh ordered his name inscribed.

Around the 15th year of his rule, amid the grandiosity of his empire-building, a touch of hubris was perhaps overtaking the Nubian ruler. "Taharqa had a very strong army and was one of the main international powers of this period," says Charles Bonnet. "I think he thought he was the king of the world. He became a bit of a megalomaniac."

The timber merchants along the coast of Lebanon had been feeding Taharqa's architectural appetite with a steady supply of juniper and cedar. When the Assyrian king Esarhaddon sought to clamp down on this trade artery, Taharqa sent troops to the southern Levant to support a revolt against the Assyrian. Esarhaddon quashed the move and retaliated by crossing into Egypt in 674 B.C. But Taharqa's army beat back its foes.

The victory clearly went to the Nubians head. Rebel states along the Mediterranean shared his giddiness and entered into an alliance against Esarhaddon. In 671 the Assyrians marched with their camels into the Sinai desert to quell the rebellion. Success was instant; now it was Esarhaddon who brimmed with bloodlust. He directed his troops toward the Nile Delta.

Taharqa and his army squared off against the Assyrians. For 15 days they fought pitched battles—"very bloody," by Esarhaddon's grudging admission. But the Nubians were pushed back all the way to Memphis. Wounded five times, Taharqa escaped with his life and abandoned Memphis. In typical Assyrian fashion, Esarhaddon slaughtered the villagers and "erected piles of their heads." Then, as the Assyrian would later write, "His queen, his harem, Ushankhuru his heir, and the rest of his sons and daughters, his property and his goods, his horses, his cattle, his sheep, in countless numbers, I carried off to Assyria. The root of Kush I tore up out of Egypt." To commemorate Taharqa's humiliation, Esarhaddon commissioned a stela showing Taharqa's son, Ushankhuru, kneeling before the Assyrian with a rope tied around his neck.

As it happened, Taharqa outlasted the victor. In 669 Esarhaddon died en route to Egypt, after learning that the Nubian had managed to retake Memphis. Under a new king, the Assyrians once again assaulted the city, this time with an army swollen with captured rebel troops. Taharqa stood no chance. He fled south to Napata and never saw Egypt again.

A measure of Taharqa's status in Nubia is that he remained in power after being routed twice from Memphis. How he spent his final years is a mystery—with the exception of one final innovative act. Like his father, Piye, Taharqa chose to be buried in a pyramid. But he eschewed the royal cemetery at El Kurru, where all previous Kushite pharaohs had been laid to rest. Instead, he chose a site at Nuri, on the opposite bank of the Nile. Perhaps, as archaeologist Timothy Kendall has theorized, Taharqa selected the location because, from the vista of Jebel Barkal, his pyramid precisely aligns with the sunrise on ancient Egypt's New Year's Day, linking him in perpetuity with the Egyptian concept of rebirth.

Just as likely, the Nubian's motive will remain obscure, like his people's history.

Critical Thinking

1. What were the major accomplishments of the Nubian "Black Pharaohs" in Egypt?

2. What is the significance of pyramids in Sudan?

3. Why are they currently threatened?

4. Provide evidence for Robert Draper's claim that "The ancient world was devoid of racism."

5. What strategies permitted the Nubians "without setting foot inside Egypt" to preserve Egypt's spiritual traditions"?

Create Central

www.mhhe.com/createcentral

Internet References

Ancient Sudan=Nubia
www.ancientsudan.org/

ROBERT DRAPER is the author of *Dead Certain: The Presidency of George W. Bush*. He recently wrote for *National Geographic* about 21st-century cowboys.

Article

Prepared by: Joseph R. Mitchell, *Howard Community College*
and Helen Buss Mitchell, *Howard Community College*

The Gold of Kush

As dam waters rise, archaeologists salvage the remains of a great kingdom.

When frequent ARCHAEOLOGY contributor Andrew Lawler reported on the construction of Sudan's massive Merowe Dam on the Nile River at Hamdab, some 220 miles north of the capital Khartoum ("Damming Sudan," November/December 2006), innumerable ancient sites were about to be flooded. The disastrous situation also posed a humanitarian crisis, as those in the water's path were systematically forced from their homes. The following year, University of Chicago archaeologist Geoff Emberling joined an international salvage effort to document sites before they disappeared. . . .

GEOFF EMBERLING

Learning Outcomes

After reading this article you will be able to:

- Discuss the effect Kush had on Egyptian history and how the building of the Merowe Dam will hinder what we can learn about its history.

I remember standing in the warm late afternoon sun on a barren hilltop in the Nubian Desert of northern Sudan in March 2008. The orange sand stretched away to the green fields and palm trees lining the Nile River in the distance. My colleagues and I had just completed a successful second dig season and we were packing finds and taking our final notes. I went for one last visit to the ancient cemetery where we had been excavating burials of people who lived on the outskirts of the early Kingdom of Kush (roughly 1700–1500 B.C.). The graves and a nearby gold-mining site, littered with ancient grinding stones, had told us a great deal about these people, including something about their kingdoms relationship with Egypt, hundreds of miles to the north.

After making an exploratory trip to Sudan in the winter of 2006, we recognized how our excavations could contribute to the emerging picture of Kush as a powerful kingdom rather than a remote Egyptian outpost, as was once thought. But we were in a race against time. The construction of the Merowe Dam, some 25 miles downstream from where we were to work, was about to flood the Fourth Cataract, a 100-mile-long stretch of the Nile that passes through a narrow valley with islands and rapids. The area had scarcely been documented before archaeological salvage work by teams from Sudan, Poland, England, Germany, and the United States started about 10 years ago. So we joined an international effort to recover what we could before the dam

was completed. Over the past decade, work by these teams in the dam area had suggested that the influence of Kush may even have reached beyond the Fourth Cataract, perhaps as many as 750 miles along the Nile—making it a worthy rival to Egypt indeed.

In just two excavation seasons—roughly 16 weeks—we gleaned a remarkable amount of information. Our excavations showed that the power of Kush rested in part on its ability to extract gold from the sands and gravels of the Nile Valley. We also unearthed evidence that has begun to illuminate the connection between Kerma (the capital of Kush) and the distant and peripheral Fourth Cataract, some 130 miles as the crow flies, across particularly harsh desert terrain.

Kush had been mentioned in ancient Egyptian texts and depicted in artistic representations as both a trade partner and enemy of the Egyptian state, beginning around 2000 B.C. In later periods, gold from Kush was sent as tribute to the pharaohs, as in the painted scenes from the walls of the tomb of Huy, the Egyptian governor of Kush during the New Kingdom (ca. 1330 B.C.).

The Kushites, like other people from Nubia, a culturally diverse region that spans what is now southern Egypt and northern Sudan, were known to the Egyptians as excellent archers and even served in the Egyptian army. Excavations at Kerma by American archaeologist George Reisner in the 1910s had revealed a town, which we now know was walled, surrounding a monumental mud-brick temple. In a royal cemetery to the east, four massive grave tumuli contained as many as several hundred human sacrificial victims. The remains were surrounded by thousands of cattle skulls, important symbols of wealth to many contemporaneous sub-Saharan people. Reisner originally proposed that Kerma was an Egyptian outpost because of the statuary and scarab seals found there.

Excavations over the past 35 years at Kerma, and over the past 10 years in the Fourth Cataract, began to suggest that the early Kingdom of Kush was larger than previously believed, and that its raids into Egypt in about 1650 B.C. were a serious threat to the capital at Thebes. Compared with other civilizations of the region, such as Mesopotamia, early Kush controlled a vast area and was able to amass significant military power. Yet Kush seemed to lack some of the characteristics of other civilizations: it had only one city of any size (Kerma), did not leave any trace of writing, and did not make extensive use of administrative tools such as seals. Only in the kingdom's latest period were inscribed Egyptian scarab seals used in administrative contexts in the region of the capital.

The expedition was a significant departure for me professionally. I had been trained in Mesopotamian archaeology and had directed excavations in Syria. More recently, I had supervised the installation of an exhibition at the University of Chicago's Oriental Institute, where I am the museum director, on ancient Nubia. I was fascinated by the beauty of the regions craft traditions, especially its extraordinary handmade pottery, which can be eggshell thin and beautifully burnished, or made in shapes imitating natural forms such as gourds, of covered with geometric designs. I was inspired to learn more about the people who made it.

Our team of about a dozen archaeologists and students traveled to the Fourth Cataract in the winter of 2007 and again in 2008, planning to work in a "concession" assigned to us by the Sudanese authorities, an area that stretched 10 miles along the right bank of the Nile and included a large island called Shirri. The group included codirector Bruce Williams, who has published nine massive volumes on the Oriental Institute's previous contribution to salvage archaeology in Nubia—the Aswan High Dam project of the 1960s—as well as students from the University of Chicago, New York University, and the University of Michigan.

It turned out, however, that out-concession was within the territory of the Manasir, one of three tribal groups living in the Fourth Cataract. The Manasir were actively resisting the Sudanese governments plans for resettling people living in the region, and refused to allow archaeologists to work in their territory. So we had to move to a backup plan, which was to work within the large concession of a Polish team from the Gdansk Archaeological Museum led by Henryk Paner (whom I came to call "Papa Henryk," not for his age, but because he was so knowledgeable about the area and so generous with that knowledge). The team had been working there for almost 10 years, documenting well over 1,000 sites and excavating sites of all periods. However, the researchers knew there were sites they would not have a chance to excavate, and so they allowed us to work within their concession.

As a Mesopotamian archaeologist, I was used to working on settlements—the large mounds called "tells" that mark ancient villages and cities. It turned out that the Gdansk team had a settlement site to offer us near the village of Hosh el-Guruf, and we went to inspect it together. By Mesopotamian standards, it was not much to look at—a small, mounded, and remarkably rocky four acres, with a scatter of pottery that extended over 25 more. I knew from

visiting other sites in the Fourth Cataract that it was a remarkably dense accumulation of cultural material by Sudanese standards, and we were happy to start working there in 2007.

After a few days of collecting pottery from the surface of the site, we began digging. Unlike Mesopotamian tells, where excavation trenches can reach a depth of 30 feet or more, Sudanese sites generally do not have deep deposits of cultural material. At Hosh el-Guruf, we dug no more than two feet before we hit the bedrock, and most of our trenches were even shallower.

We found that the site had three major occupations, in between which it had been abandoned: the later Neolithic period (ca. 4000–3000 B.C.), the early Kingdom of Kush (ca. 1700–1500 B.C.), and a smaller occupation during the early part of the Napatan period (ca. 750–600 B.C.). While we still don't have a clear understanding of the Fourth Cataract during the Neolithic period, it is possible that the people were pastoralists and were sedentary only part of the year. The Napatan period, on the other hand, marked the rise of a later dynasty of Kush that began building pyramids for elite burials and ruled Egypt as its 25th Dynasty. The most interesting single discovery from our surface collections was a clay seal impression of a Napatan queen, which suggested some level of royal contact with inhabitants of the site in that period.

We began digging trenches where we had unearthed concentrations of Kerma-period ceramics during our surface collections. Rather than the stratified remains of buildings, we excavated mostly jumbled potsherds of different periods all mixed together, and almost nothing that was clearly left in place. We may have had a fragment of one building—three stones in a kind of curving alignment—and that looked pretty good after three weeks of digging.

Yet we were fortunate to have on the team another expert from the Oriental Institute with long experience working in the area: Carol Meyer, who had directed excavations on a Roman-period gold-mining site called Bir Umm Fawakhir in the Eastern Desert of Egypt. She and Bruce Williams pointed out that there was an interesting pattern across the surface of the site—an unusually large number of big grinding stones, all broken but each originally about three feet long and several hundred pounds. As Carol looked more closely, she found that there were also clusters of smaller handheld stones used for bashing and grinding. The grinding stones were not the kind that would have been used by a family to grind grain; we unearthed fewer, much smaller stones for that purpose. Rather, they were the type discovered at sites in the Eastern Desert of Egypt and Sudan, where gold was mined. Those stones were thought to be remnants of ancient Egyptian gold mines of the New Kingdom (about 1550–1150 B.C.), but here we were amazed to have the first clear evidence that they were not Egyptian in origin, but had been used earlier by the Kingdom of Kush.

We were also lucky to have a geologist with us, James Harrell of the University of Toledo, who works on archaeological projects in Egypt and Sudan and specializes in identifying quarries. He suggested that the most likely source of gold here was Nile River gravels, worn off the bedrock formations in the middle

Nile Valley and deposited across the site during the annual floods. Support for this interpretation of the site came from the widespread knowledge of gold-mining techniques among the people living in the area today. Although gold mining is not a formal industry, we met many who knew how to mine and pan for gold in the Fourth Cataract.

As we developed the gold-working hypothesis at Hosh el-Guruf, some members of our team began excavating a contemporaneous cemetery site at Al-Widay, next to the village where we were staying, which was a two-hour drive from the nearest paved road. The villagers not only worked for the excavation, but provided fresh bread daily, delivered water for washing and cooking, and showed us genuine hospitality.

The cemetery at Al-Widay was interesting in part because it presumably contained the burials of the people who mined the gold at Hosh el-Guruf. When we returned to complete the excavation of more than 100 burials in the cemetery in the winter of 2008, we found the graves were simple pits with piles of stones on top of them. Each of the dead was buried with a standard set of three vessels—cup, bowl, and incense pot—and sometimes with additional pots and beads made of locally available carnelian, ostrich egg shell, or faience. This pattern turned out to be fairly typical of Kerma-period sites throughout the Fourth Cataract.

One thing that was striking about the cemetery was the scarcity of gold—for a community that was connected to gold mining, those who lived there did not appear to have kept much of what they found. There was one burial with 101 tiny gold beads, made from a gold sheet that was rolled and cut into small rings; another contained a single gold bead. A number of the graves had been plundered in antiquity, perhaps by people looking for gold, but others were unlooted, and there was still very little gold in those burials. In fact, very little gold has been found in any of the Fourth Cataract excavations.

At the same time, there were clearly imported items in the cemetery, such as Egyptian ceramics, scarabs, and some distinctive, polished, black-topped redware vessels with a gray band that were likely made in Kerma itself. One particularly interesting find was a scarab inscribed with the name of an Egyptian army officer, Nebsumenu, found in the burial of a young girl. We do not know how the scarab ended up in this remote area, but its presence raises questions about the connections between cultures at this time. One possibility is that Nebsumenu dropped his seal in battle or in flight from the fortress in which he served. The seal would have become part of the spoils taken by the army of Kush back to Kerma. It could then have been sent by the king of Kush as a gift to a local leader in the Fourth Cataract. Another possibility is that Nebsumenu lost his seal to the Med-jay, a well-known band of nomads, whose routes would have taken them to the Fourth Cataract region. In this scenario, the scarab would have been a symbol of success in battle.

Our research seems to have illuminated two ends of an exchange network: gold moving from the Fourth Cataract to Kerma, and a small number of objects moving from Kerma to the Fourth Cataract. It appears to have been an unequal exchange: those at the center of the kingdom were hoarding wealth, while those at the periphery were exploited. But without direct evidence that the gold was moving from this site to Kerma, it remains a hypothesis that attests to the abundance of information that still lies beneath the rocky earth.

As I stood on that hilltop, I thought about the way many of the burials had been disturbed in antiquity, apparently by looters in search of gold jewelry. In our two seasons, we carefully excavated the looters' holes first, and then investigated what remained of each original burial. At the bottom of each robbed grave, we found a stone not bigger than my fist. I imagined, at the time, that the looters ended their violation of the tombs by placing a stone at the bottom of their pits, as if to keep the spirit of the dead in its place. As I stood there, I decided that this might not be such a bad idea. So I placed a stone in each of the excavated burial pits, to honor a sense of close connection with the past, and as a sort of offering to help the dead rest in peace.

When we left Al-Widay, we dreaded the day that the dam would be completed, the area inundated, and our hosts forced (finally) to move away. And so it has happened. Our entire excavation area, so scarcely documented, is now under water.

Critical Thinking

1. How did plans for the Merowe Dam intensify archaeological exploration of Kush?
2. What did the discovery of grinding stones reveal about gold mining in the Kingdom of Kush?
3. What questions abut the "connections between cultures" were raised in the pre-dam excavation of Kush [Kerma]?

Create Central

www.mhhe.com/createcentral

Internet References

Reeder's Egypt Page
www.egyptology.com/reeder

GEOFF EMBERLING is the museum director of the University of Chicago's Oriental Institute.

From *Archaeology*, November/December 2009, pp. 55–59. Copyright © 2009 by Archaeological Institute of America. Reprinted by permission of Archaeology Magazine. www.archaeology.org

Article

Prepared by: Joseph R. Mitchell, *Howard Community College*
and Helen Buss Mitchell, *Howard Community College*

The Sacred Landscape
of Ancient Ireland

RONALD HICKS

Learning Outcomes

After reading this article, you will be able to:

• Discuss early Ireland's cosmology and its people's deep connection to the land.

Royal. The term conjures images of vast territories under the control of one monarch. And "royal site" implies a place where one might find a castle or some other form of royal residence. Early Irish manuscripts, in fact, mention four sites, each one referred to as the royal center for a province—the Hill of Tara in Meath, Dún Ailinne in Leinster in the southeast, Crúachan (referred to also as Rathcroghan) in Connacht in the west, and Emain Macha in Ulster to the north. What we actually find at each of these places is a complex of monuments that bear no resemblance to a royal residence, but that can tell us much about pre-Christian Ireland.

The monuments in each complex belong to a range of time, from the Neolithic, which began in Ireland about 4000 B.C., to the Iron Age, around 600 B.C. to A.D. 500. In each case, the focus of the complex is a very large, roughly circular earthen bank with an internal ditch, constructed on a high point of land or surrounding a hilltop. Each has a wide view in all directions. Crúachan, Dún Ailinne, and Emain Macha form an almost equilateral triangle some 80 miles on a side, with Tara near the midpoint of the north-south line connecting Emain Macha and Dún Ailinne. The significance of this arrangement is still unknown, but it is notable. Archaeological work shows that early activity at these sites may have had to do with burials, and that these enclosures were constructed during the Iron Age. Surprisingly, none of them are suitable for defense. Instead, each seems to mark off an area that only makes sense if viewed as sacred.

One of the compelling things about doing archaeological work in Ireland is that the early medieval manuscripts preserve so many tales surrounding these sites. Some stories are clearly mythological, others are pseudohistory—medieval invention—and it isn't always easy to tell them apart. Even so, they are essential in developing a full understanding of the sites. And,

in turn, by studying the sites archaeologically, we can begin to understand some of the meaning behind the myths. Collections of Old and Middle Irish stories called *dindshenchas,* literally "histories of places," were compiled between the tenth and twelfth centuries A.D. and imply a sacred geography for the pre-Christian sites in Ireland. All the places listed in these stories are connected with the old gods.

The study of Irish mythology and ancient manuscripts has been limited by a number of circumstances, beginning with a prohibition against owning Old Irish manuscripts during the Reformation in the early seventeenth century. Book burnings were common and nearly all of the early Irish material was lost. There was no scholarship conducted until the 1830s, when some manuscripts that hadn't been destroyed began to come to light. Over the years, only a very few researchers could read Old Irish, and there are still relatively few today who can. In addition, the scholars and scribes who wrote the manuscripts often used an even earlier form of the Irish language, so translations can differ. Nonetheless, the manuscripts are crucial to any understanding of pre-Christian sites in Ireland. They make it clear that in ancient Ireland the landscape itself was sacred. The royal sites were meant primarily for ceremonies connected with the kingship of each region, and for great gatherings at the time of one of the four major festivals in the agricultural and calendrical cycle of the time.

These festivals occur around the midpoints between the solstices and equinoxes, called cross-quarter days. They include Imbolc or Oimelg at the beginning of February, marking the beginning of the agricultural year and the lambing season; Beltaine in early May, when herds and flocks were driven to summer pastures; Lughnasa in August, marking the beginning of the harvest; and Samhain at the beginning of November, when the harvest ended, the herds and flocks returned, and feasting was the order of the day. Tara was associated primarily with Samhain. The other three sites were associated with Lughnasa, when a week was devoted to a festival of storytelling trading and games, mostly involving horse races. In the case of Tara, the Lughnasa assembly was held at a sister site not far north, Tailtiu. Crúachan is linked in the mythology with both Lughnasa and Samhain.

Each of the royal sites, and Tailtiu as well, was named for a woman, apparently a goddess who, according to myths or tales, died or was carried off. We are told that the festival of Lughnasa, or the games of Lugh, was founded to honor the god's foster mother, Tailtiu, who died after having the forests cleared for farming. These goddesses almost certainly represent the grain that is about to be harvested in much the same way that Persephone does in Greek and Roman stories. In those tales, Ceres (or Demeter), from whose name we get the word "cereal," saw her daughter, Persephone, carried off to the underworld, not to return until the following year.

These goddesses had a profound impact on how the Irish tribes were governed. In late Iron Age Ireland, the word for "king" actually meant something closer to "chieftain." They ruled tribal territories (*tuath*) that averaged around 120 square miles. There were nearly 300 of them, and it can be shown that their boundaries closely matched those of medieval baronies. Iron Age kings were elected from within a restricted kinship group, and, according to the few records, the inaugural ceremony for each required that the new king marry the goddess of the land. It was then his role to protect the landscape and the harvest, and, by extension, the people. If he displeased his tribe, they would remove and likely kill him. There were kings and overkings, with these relationships sorted out by way of conquest. After about A.D. 800, the concept of high king was introduced, and a word that could be likened to the modern conception of "royal" entered ancient Old Irish manuscripts.

The place known as Tech Midchuarta at the Hill of Tara is referred to in early Irish manuscripts as the House of the Women or the Great House of a Thousand Soldiers. Medieval historians tell us its long parallel earthen banks were once part of a banquet hall where the Feast of Tara, marking Samhain, was held. Modern archaeology tells us otherwise, that these earthworks were never the walls of a building but rather the boundaries of a ceremonial roadway. To trudge up this wide avenue is to follow the path of countless forgotten ritual processions.

According to the ancient stories, Tara was named for Tea, daughter of Lugaid or wife of King Eremon. The hill's namesake, according to one tale, once saw a rampart in Spain, and wanted one like it built on every hill she chose—but only the one at Tara is considered a royal site. The dindshenchas tell of over 40 places of note within the Tara complex: wells, mounds, standing stones, and gravesites of characters from legend. The monuments include three great earthen enclosures, including Ráthna Riogh, the enclosure (or fort) of kings, which has been dated to the Iron Age, within which is the Mound of the Hostages, an older earthwork dating to the Neolithic. Just to the north, adjacent to St. Patricks churchyard, where Patrick is said to have established the first church in Ireland, is the Ráth of the Synods, which has been thoroughly disturbed. A little over a century ago a group calling themselves the British Israelites became convinced that the Lost Ark of the Covenant was buried there, so they dug up the whole enclosure in search of it. Not surprisingly, they had no luck.

Almost straight north of Tara is the next royal site, Emain Macha, now called Navan Fort. Because of nearby quarrying, the full extent of the complex isn't clear. At its southern limit, it includes Mag Macha, or the Plain of Macha, where the ancient Lughnasa assembly was held. A neighboring hill to the east is Ard Macha, or Macha's High Place, now the town of Armagh. In the grounds of the Armagh Cathedral is evidence suggesting it, too, was surrounded by a bank and ditch. Like the church at Tara, its presence reflects the Christianization of the old sacred places.

The name Macha comes from the local goddess, though there are several other explanations for its source. First, we are told that it was named for the wife of Nemed, leader of the third group to settle in Ireland. In a second version of the story, Macha was the daughter of Aed the Red. In a longer version of this story, Aed was one of three kings, each of whom was to rule Ireland for seven years at a time. After Aed's death, Macha of the Ruddy Hair demanded to be allowed to take his turn. When the other two refused, she defeated them in battle and took the kingship. Thereafter she refused to share, and forced another of the defeated king's sons to dig the enclosure at Emain Macha. The third story says she was the wife of Crund, who bragged of her horse-racing prowess. Forced by King Conchobar to race while pregnant, she won and then cursed the men of Ulster so that they would suffer the pangs of labor whenever faced with a crisis. Then she gave birth to twins, died, and was buried on Ard Macha. This version also identifies her as Grian Banchure, "the Sun of the Women," suggesting she was equated with the moon and was daughter of the god Midir.

Midir also figures in the story of the next royal site, Crúachan to the southwest. It was named for Cruachu, or Cróchan Croderg, handmaiden to Étaín, second wife of Midir. Midir is said to have carried Étaín off from Tara—at a gathering he turned them both into swans, and they flew away through a hole in the roof. There is good reason to believe that Étaín was a personification of the moon, like Macha. Another source says that Cruachu was the mother of Medb, who, as queen at Crúachan, is a central character in the Irish epic *The Cattle Raid of Cooley. Tána,* or cattle raids, form a separate class of early Irish tale, and all that survive revolve around Crúachan and Samhain.

Like the other royal sites, Crúachan is a complex of earthworks and standing stones covering several square miles. The central monument is called Rathcroghan. Another is Relig na Rí, a low hill surrounded by a circular earthwork that is said to be the burial place of the kings of Connacht. A natural limestone cave nearby called Owenygat is thought to be the entrance to the underworld and the source of various otherworldly beasts. This is Síd Crúachan, one of the dwelling places of the old gods, who, according to the tales, agreed to live underground when the Gaels came to Ireland from Iberia. Dáthi's Monument, a nearby circular embankment similar to those at Tara and Emain Macha but much smaller, is said to be the burial place of the last pagan king of Ireland.

Dún Ailinne, last of the royal sites, is some 40 miles due south of Tara. From the air, it could be a twin of Emain Macha. Dún Ailinne is identified in the dindshenchas as an assembly place of warriors or young men. It received its name when

Aillenn, a daughter of Lugaid, king of Leinster and (in one version) also father of Tea, was abducted and died of shame at her captivity. Through her grave grew an apple tree, and through the grave of her lapdog, Báile, grew a yew. In another version of the story, Báile was not a dog but her lover. Hearing that she had died on the way to a liaison, he dropped dead. The same sinister messenger tells Aillenn the same thing, leading to her death. Again, it ended with an apple tree and a yew tree growing from their graves, only this time the tops of the trees were shaped like their heads. After seven years, the trees were cut down and made into "poet's tablets," upon which were written the visions, espousals, loves, and courtships of Leinster and of Ulster. Much later, the tablets were brought together at Tara at Samhain. According to legend, they sprang together and could not be pulled apart.

On a low hill immediately to the east of Dún Ailinne lie the ruins of another church said to have been founded by St. Patrick. To the west is an open range known as the Curragh, sacred to St. Brigid and thought to have been the site of a Lughnasa. Even today the Curragh is the site of one of Ireland's primary racetracks. In an uneven line northwest across the Curragh are a series of small enclosures with external banks and internal ditches, just as at the royal sites.

The namesakes of the four royal sites play very minor roles in Irish myth (except Macha), but their stories relate a great deal about early Irish kingship. For example, two are said to be named for daughters of Lugaid, a variant of Lugh, the Irish god associated with the Lughnasa festival. And all except Tara have traditions of great assemblies at that time. Another clue to the relationship between the old religion and kingship is found in the tale of Macha's race, which suggests she was a horse goddess. Horses, specifically white mares, were a symbol of kingship among the Celts. A twelfth-century account tells of an inauguration ceremony that involved the new king mating with a white mare, which was then sacrificed. The River Gabhra, at the eastern foot of the Hill of Tara, means "white mare." This association is also reflected far away in southern England, in the famous horse-shaped chalk hill figure at Uffington, which was said to have been the headquarters of the local king. The white mare even appears in an ongoing post-Christmas tradition in southwest Ireland in which a dancer dressed as a white mare tries to bite onlookers—connecting the white mare with the renewal of the year at the winter solstice.

Archaeological work at the royal sites over the past few decades has provided further evidence for their sacred or ceremonial nature. At Tara, geophysical surveys under the direction of Conor Newman, now at National University of Ireland (NUI), Galway, revealed that there are many other features on the hilltop and surrounding land that can no longer be seen, including a large post circle surrounding the Ráath of the Synods and overlapping Ráth na Riogh.

In April 2007, another major monument was found during highway construction in Lismullin, in the valley east of the hilltop adjacent to the River Gabhra. It appears to be the site of a large temple, with a surrounding post enclosure 90 yards in diameter. A funnel-shaped alignment of posts leads to the entrance of the inner structure. This site lies in a basin, forming a natural amphitheater.

During excavations at Emain Macha, a large circular mound within the enclosure was found to cover a building that had been completely filled with stones and burned shortly after its construction. This was unquestionably part of some ritual. Dendrochronology has shown that the timbers, the lower parts of which survived, dated to approximately 95 B.C. Those excavations produced another surprising find—the skeleton of a Barbary ape, a type of macaque from southern Iberia, on the Gibraltar peninsula. It was probably brought as a gift by a trader.

Geophysical surveys at Crúachan show not only that it was once surrounded by a very large circular earthwork, but also that the central mound has a more complex structure than previously believed. Little excavation has yet been done there, though the work of John Waddell of NUI Galway at Dathi's Monument indicates that it dates to about the same period as the enclosures at Tara, Emain Macha, and Dún Ailinne—the Iron Age.

Atop the hill within the Dún Ailinne enclosure, excavations carried out under the direction of Bernard Wailes of the University of Pennsylvania found a series of large circular structures with their entrances to the northeast, toward the direction of sunrise at Beltaine and Lughnasa. And as at Lismullin, there was a funnel-shaped alignment leading up to the entrance of the structures. In the center of one of the small enclosures on the Curragh, excavators found the burial of a young woman. However, it did not appear to be a typical burial. Her skeleton was lying with her hands pressed against the sides of the grave and her head ducked down. Both the excavator and a medical doctor who reexamined the records of the find some years later came to the same conclusion—she appeared to have been a dedicatory sacrifice who was buried alive. This irregular line of enclosures lies along the alignment between Dún Ailinne and Crúachan, which coincides with sunset at the summer solstice. Exactly midway between these two royal sites lies Uisneach, the traditional meeting place of the five provinces said to be the home of the Dagda, chief of the old gods, and the burial place of Lugh.

The royal sites were clearly part of a sacred landscape that we are only beginning to apprehend. By combining archaeological work with careful study of both ancient manuscripts and the spatial relationships among the monuments, we may yet come to a fuller understanding of ancient Ireland and its pre-Christian religion.

Critical Thinking

1. What can we learn from the "histories of places," compiled between the tenth and twelfth centuries of this era?
2. What festivals were celebrated at the Royal Sites and what was their significance?

3. Discuss the power and influence of the goddesses in ancient Ireland?

4. What does Ronald Hicks mean when he writes: "The Royal Sites were clearly part of a 'sacred landscape' that we are only beginning to apprehend?"

Create Central

www.mhhe.com/createcentral

Internet References

Exploring Ancient World Cultures

http://eawc.evansville.edu

RONALD HICKS is a professor of anthropology at Ball State University specializing in landscape and cognitive archaeology.

Article   Prepared by: Joseph R. Mitchell, *Howard Community College*
and Helen Buss Mitchell, *Howard Community College*

China's First Empire

Michael Loewe looks at the dynastic, administrative and intellectual background of the Qin empire, which defined how China would be run for more than 2,000 years, and at the life and achievements of the First Emperor Shi Huangdi, one of the greatest state-builders of history, whose tomb was guarded by the famous terracotta army.

MICHAEL LOEWE

Learning Outcomes

After reading this article, you will be able to:

• Discuss why Shi Huangdi was able to become China's first emperor and the effects of his reign on the course of Chinese history?

The kings of Western Zhou ruled from a small part of north-west China (present-day Shaanxi province) from 1045 BC. Their rule was long revered as a Chinese 'golden age' but in 771, overcome by dissension and subject to hostile intrusion, they were forced to forsake their original homeland and settle further east, establishing their centre at the city now known as Luoyang. Although the kings of Zhou actually survived until 256 BC, their territory and powers was severely curtailed through the rise of a number of independent leaders who could control large areas of land and style themselves with titles. As early as 777 BC, one of these leaders from Qin who, like the Zhou, came from the north-west, adopted the title of gong, often translated as duke; this title passed from father to son until 325 BC, when it was changed for the more grandiose one of king (*wang*).

This change was something more than a mere formality, and in what is known as the Warring States period (481–221 BC) six other rulers—Chu, Qi, Yan, Hann, Wei and Zhao—in different parts of China likewise adopted the title of king. The new title indicated that these men did not accept that the kings of Zhou enjoyed a position superior to their own; and it reflected the steady growth of their powers. For Qin, this process of expansion reached its culmination after 250 BC, notably in the reign of Ying Zheng (*r.* 246–210).

By 221 BC, through a combination of adroit diplomacy not necessarily bound by moral scruples, policies that looked beyond the short term gains and success in battle, Ying Zheng (259–210) emerged the triumphant conqueror of the six

coexisting kingdoms. He was by now master not only of the west but also of the northern and eastern parts of present-day China, the lush fertile lands of present-day Sichuan province and the woodlands of the north-east. In the east this area included the fields watered, and all too often flooded, by the Yellow River and the Huai River. With no remaining challengers, in 221 BC he adopted the majestic title of emperor (*Huangdi*), signifying that he claimed authority and wielded power over all lands and all peoples below the skies. He is known to history as Qin Shi Huangdi 'The First Qin Emperor', though his influence is such that he may correctly be termed China's First Emperor.

The First Qin Emperor and his advisers are credited today with having created the means of governing much of the area later known as 'China' as a unity, bequeathing a heritage on which later dynasties modelled their institutions. Even the very name 'China' as known in Western usage itself derives from Qin. The dynasty's heritage should, though, be seen in its historical context. Earlier kingdoms had already been fostering a systematic means of government conducted by trained officials chosen for their ability; and they had experimented with institutions designed to increase their own strength. By adapting such existing institutions, Qin extended their application on a far wider scale. In turn, future rulers of China looked to Qin's single empire and government as a model to which they should aspire. They followed many of Qin's practices, whether over long or short periods, over limited or wide expanses of territory.

We depend for the most part on a single source for the dynastic and political history of the Qin state, the *Records of the Historian* (*Shiji*) of Sima Tan (*d.* 110 BC) and his son Sima Qian (145–?86 BC), with no means of external verification of their content. They were officials of Qin's successor the Han dynasty, and were obliged to show that Han had been justified in eliminating Qin with what they claimed were its evil ways, so they are necessarily biased. A few highly valuable archival documents found recently verify some of the historians' statements. As the years pass, new archaeological evidence serves to validate the general picture that we have of Qin and adds to what had been known of the religious activities or mythology that formed a background to so many people's lives.

Some of the statements of the *Shiji* have been subject to question, on the grounds that they were not complete. For example, it was later alleged that Zhuangxiang Wang, king of Qin from 250–247, was not the father of Ying Zheng who succeeded him in 246 BC at the age of thirteen, but such suspicions cannot be confirmed. Ying Zheng himself fathered at least two sons but there is no record of the name of his queen or his empress; nor are there any tales, as there are for later dynasties, of the rivalries and disputes that broke out between the families of various imperial consorts, threatening the stability of the realm. Such threats arose in a different way.

The First Emperor survived perhaps three attempts at assassination, as was portrayed by artists of the succeeding empire. He achieved much. He chose officials to govern large parts of the land as provinces, rather than delegate this task to members of his family. He reorganized the system of defence lines of the north, unifying their different parts into the so-called Great Wall. This was built by conscript and convict labour but it did not follow the same line, nor was it situated in the same area, as that of the later wall of which remnants are seen north of Beijing. In a major advance that was by no means always maintained in later dynasties, the Qin empire stretched far to the south, beyond the Yangzi River; but it is difficult to estimate how effective his government was in the intemperate and unhealthy lands of the tropics, where the way of life differed markedly from that of the north.

The First Emperor died on his way back to the capital city of Xianyang (close to modern Xi'an) from a tour in the east in 210 BC. Li Si, who held the supreme office of Chancellor and was perhaps the most influential adviser at the time, suppressed news of his death, perhaps fearing that it would set off an uprising. But as happened frequently in China's history, the succession was beset by intrigue and rivalry and in this instance by violence. Fusu, son of the emperor and his named heir, was displaced and forced to commit suicide, along with Meng Tian, a military officer who under Shi Huangdi had had responsibility for the defence lines and the manning of the Great Wall and who was one of Fusu's close supporters. Huhai, a second son of the Emperor, duly took Fusu's place, to reign as the Second Emperor for a short period from 210 BC.

This outcome had been contrived by Li Si himself, in collaboration with Zhao Gao who is described as a eunuch. There is however no record of the emergence of eunuchs in the palace or government of Qin, and it is possible that it was only due to later allegations that Zhao Gao was thus named. Appointed to a senior appointment shortly after Huhai's accession, he exercised commanding powers of government, at times exciting the criticism or protests of Li Si. Clearly there was no room in Xianyang for two men each of whom wished to impose his will on the Emperor and his government, and it was Zhao Gao who emerged as the victor. Accused of disloyalty and subjected

to flogging, Li Si took his own life and by way of punishment his family was extirpated (208). Zhao Gao could now dominate the Second Emperor who, in turn, was forced to commit suicide to make way for Zhao Gao's own nominee. In the instability that followed Zhao Gao met his end in 207 BC. The Qin empire closed amid a series of uprisings and open warfare between two protagonists, Xiang Yu and Liu Bang. Claiming the title king of Han in 206, Liu Bang eliminated his rival and proclaimed himself Emperor of Han in 202. The Han empire lasted, with some interruptions, until AD 220.

Under Qin, supreme power rested in the emperor; he was advised by salaried officials many of whose titles and duties derived from earlier usage in pre-imperial Qin or the other kingdoms. At the highest level stood the Chancellor and Imperial Counsellor; ranking immediately below them nine senior ministers were responsible for duties of a specialist nature. These included ceremonial and ritual activities; security of the palace; the emperor's horse and carriages; administration of punishments; treatment of dignitaries from outside the empire; kinship relations within the imperial family; taxation; agricultural production, storage and distribution of staple foods; and products of other types, from the mountains and the lakes. There were other officials who controlled the capital city or commanded forces with which to patrol Xianyang. Others were responsible for constructing imperial buildings such as the palaces and the mausolea or for maintaining the establishments of the Empress and the Heir Apparent. Appointed directly by imperial authority, these senior officials called on the services of a large number of assistants.

In the course of creating the empire, Qin had acquired territories from the other kingdoms. To administer them these kingdoms had been formed into units known either as counties (*xian*) or as commanderies (*jun*). After 221 BC this system was applied throughout the new empire except for Xianyang itself which lay under the control of a special official, governor of the metropolitan area. Outside, there were thirty-six, or perhaps more, commanderies, each in the charge of a governor (*shou*). Junior staff carried out the task of governing an empire efficiently by maintaining order and security, promoting the production of cereal crops and hemp, as used for clothing for most persons in the land, and collecting tax.

There is nothing to show that an abstract concept of law existed in the Qin Empire, which would protect individuals from oppression, define rights and obligations, and stand above an emperor. Commands for action were issued from the emperor either as 'statutes' or as 'ordinances'; officials saw that these were implemented. Manuscripts of some of these 'laws', of 217 BC, discovered in 1975 in Hubei province, inform us of the subjects and depth of detail of these provisions. Many, which lay down approved procedures and activities and the penalties for failure to comply, concern matters such as agriculture, coinage, work of artisans, protection of government property, establishment of officials, control of travel and transmission of official documents. They may regulate the conduct of daily life to the finest detail, such as the method of stacking grain; the removal of marks made by painting, branding or incision on valuable equipment owned by the government, once this was damaged beyond repair; or the amount of lubrication allowed for wheeled vehicles.

Such documents identify crimes such as injury to other persons, robbery, murder or tax evasion, and laid down a scale of punishments ranging from the death penalty—carried out in various, sometimes grim, ways—to terms of hard labour for perhaps five or six years, mutilation by severing a foot, or payment of heavy fines. Set procedures followed arrest of an alleged criminal: interrogation to ascertain the facts; examination of the accused, perhaps after flogging; a search for corroboration; and decision of the action required by the statutes.

Officials of the kingdom of Qin had evolved several instruments to control the population, set up social distinctions, restrain criminal activity and possibly promote the farmers' work in the fields. The gift of one step in a series of eighteen 'orders of honour' conferred status on an individual; and as, with successive bestowals, an individual rose in the scale so too did his or her privileges. These included mitigation of punishment for crime; favourable terms for statutory obligations; and probably an allocation of land with which to make a living.

Provincial and local officials performed an annual task that was fundamental to government: they registered the population according to age, sex and relationship within a family, and the extent of land in various uses, for cereal crops, pasture, orchard or timber. It was on the basis of these records that officials collected taxation in its various forms. That on the land was paid in kind, a *per capita* tax in cash. Able-bodied males were obliged to serve for periods in the armed forces and also in the labour corps, being set to build a palace or a city wall, to construct a canal or perhaps pump water from one level to another; to maintain roads and bridges; and to hump grain from the fields to the designated granaries.

Another institution bore on social cohesion and the repression of crime. Five, or perhaps ten, families were formed into a group whose members were responsible for reporting suspicious activities or crimes of any one of them. A few recorded cases of the trial of a suspected criminal show how an official could require members of a responsibility group to give evidence.

Various systems of weights and measures and different types of coinage had been in use in the pre-imperial kingdoms of the fifth century BC and later. Efficient government empire wide required the collection of tax and distribution of staple products on an equitable basis. Qin therefore took steps to introduce uniformity, by issuing sets of standard weights and units of capacity, and unifying the coinage. Cast in bronze, the coins of the Qin empire were of one denomination as stated in the inscription of 'One half *liang*' (*ban liang*, 7 grams). A square hole in the centre allowed the insertion of a string to tie the coins together in units perhaps of a hundred. Probably an attempt was made to standardize the width of the carts that carried grain or other commodities, sometimes on the narrow paths up and down the hillsides or the tracks that ran between the fields and beside the waterways.

Qin needed armed forces to maintain internal security against would-be dissidents and for protection against potentially hostile peoples of the hills and pasture lands of Central Asia, such as the Xiongnu. Qin's armies drew on the conscripts whom the provincial officials assembled and perhaps to some extent on criminals, but presumably not those who had suffered punishment by mutilation. Some of these forces stood to arms in the garrisons of the north, commanded by provincial officials or officers who may be termed 'generals'. It seems unlikely that these conscripts would have been dressed and equipped as well as the soldiers buried in terracotta effigy around the tomb of the First Emperor. Such was the structure and means of government of the Qin empire and we may look at the emergence of the ideas upon which it rested. The centuries of the Warring States, before the emergence of the Qin empire, had witnessed the first flowering of China's intellectual development. Manuscripts found since the 1970s have revealed a greater diversity of the thoughts of those days than had been recognized and confirmed that these should not be classified into exclusive schools. The writers of those times were individualists quite ready to draw eclectically from the works of their contemporaries. Best known of the writers of the Warring States are those that sought the permanent principles that underlie the universe. Surviving writings known as the *Zhuangzi* and the *Daode jing* (*The Way and its Power*, ascribed to Laozi) show how these mystics saw these principles in *Dao* (the Way) and they are today categorized as Daoist. Other thinkers preferred to fasten on the lessons of the past, the means of instilling order in human activities and stability in social distinctions, and the importance of ethical values; one of these was named Kong Qiu, later known as Kongzi or Confucius (551–479 BC). For over 2,000 years he has been adopted as the model to whom Chinese rulers and officials have looked, his followers being classified by Western, but not Chinese, writers as 'Confucianist'.

But ideas of a different type lay behind Qin's growth to power. Kings and their advisers in the Warring States saw their own survival and the conquest of their enemies as their first priority. Clever men gifted with the powers of persuasion made their way from one kingdom to the next, tendering advice and offering stratagems to kings beset by danger or fired by ambition. Adopting an outlook best described as realistic, they called for measures to gather strength and govern in security. Officials capable of implementing a king's orders had to be chosen on merits rather than on the circumstances of their birth; both they and the population at large had to be trained to obey the acknowledged authority of the kingdom and disciplined to accept the burden of its demands; and kings had to be able to deploy armed forces in sufficient strength to meet emergencies.

Records such as these are ascribed to two men—Shang Yang (c.385–338) and Han Fei (c.280–c.233)—who are credited with fostering Qin's growth and categorized somewhat loosely as 'Legalists'. They both had visited other kingdoms; and both met a violent death thanks to animosities. The essays collected in the *Shangjun shu* and the *Hanfeizi* call on historical precedent and cite principle to emphasize three essential concepts: *fa*, the models of government on which orders or laws should be based; *shu*, the practical methods and expedients with which to attain a ruler's objectives; and *shi*, the visible expression of his authority.

The First Qin Emperor and his advisers took these precepts to heart, as may be evidenced in the decrees and institutions of government. In addition, his authority must be displayed, the scale of his majesty must be apparent to all. As the capital city, Xianyang housed the Emperor as the fount of all authority and the officials who implemented his orders; his palace was said to include an audience hall that could accommodate no less than 10,000 persons. Outside Xianyang the First Emperor embarked on progresses to distant parts of his realm; inscriptions on the *stelae* that he erected told of his victories over his enemies and his unification of the world under his sole authority. He proclaimed that he was the first of a line of emperors that would be numbered by the thousand. To ensure that his reputation would survive on Earth and perhaps in the hereafter, he ordered the construction of an exceptionally large tomb which would simulate the shape and features of the cosmos. Topped by a tumulus perhaps 100 meters high, the mausoleum stood out as a conspicuous reminder of the Emperor's strength. The tomb itself yet awaits excavation; around it lay buried a large number of clay warriors, drawn up in their serried ranks to guard him from his enemies.

Realistic as the outlook of the Emperor was, he was apparently not entirely disdainful of the call of religion or the force of mythology. In a search for personal immortality he sent a party of youths to put to sea to visit Penglai, a legendary isle where immortal beings live and the elixir of everlasting life may be obtained. In one of his progresses he climbed to the summit of Mount Tai, known perhaps to be the seat of unnamed powers who ruled the universe; precisely what rites the Emperor performed when there are unknown. But whatever the beliefs or hopes that inspired these undertakings, it is unlikely that they rested on a trust in heaven, the almighty power whom the kings of Zhou had worshipped and to whose gift they credited their own charge to rule the world.

Officials of Qin and their clerks wrote special documents on silk, and more routine reports, registers of land and its inhabitants and tax dues, on narrow strips of wood which were bound together to form a scroll. The clerks used a more simplified form of script than their predecessors; this had been emerging in various forms during the Warring States and was perhaps made standard by Li Si. The new form of writing served the needs of the more intensive administration of the time; it may also have helped the government to deflect attention away from the literature of earlier days, in which precepts and ethical principles could be found that might well contradict the purposes and decisions of the realistic government of imperial Qin.

Later historians voiced sharp criticisms of the steps that they said were taken by Qin to reduce attention to writings associated with the leaders and teachers of Zhou. It was claimed that, on imperial orders, copies of such books were burnt and a large number of scholars sent to their deaths; but such accounts may have been exaggerated, and it is by no means certain that these measures were as effective as was claimed.

The primary sources for the history of Qin are in general antagonistic. They therefore tended to paint Qin's government as oppressive and cruel and to blame the severity of its laws for engendering the insurgency that spelt dynastic collapse. Some of these critics of Qin may have been well aware that Han had taken over most of Qin's laws and punishments, with little mitigation of their severity. In later times when a dynasty's strength was on the ebb, an independently minded writer might occasionally press for a reversion to Qin's ways so as to restore a sense of discipline to the body politic.

Overall, by laying the foundations of empire, the First Qin Emperor introduced a radical change in China. Many of its offices and ways of government remained in force, with some adaptations, for perhaps seven centuries, until major social and economic developments required the next major changes, of the Sui (AD 589–618) and Tang (618–907) dynasties. Intellectual advance and religious practice characterized China's brilliant Song dynasty (960–1279); determined government arose with the northern, non-Chinese, emperors, and during the Ming (1368–1644) and Qing (1644–1911) dynasties; but some traces of Qin's concepts and terminology survived even until the establishment of the Republic in 1911.

Critical Thinking

1. How did the Qin Empire define "how China would be run for more than 2000 years"?

2. What were the major accomplishments of the First Emperor?

3. Why are the primary sources for the history of Qin called "antagonistic"? Explain.

Create Central

www.mhhe.com/createcentral

Internet References

Exploring Ancient World Cultures
http://eawc.evansville.edu

This article first appeared in *History Today*, September 1, 2007. Copyright © 2007 by History Today, Ltd. Reprinted by permission.

Article

Prepared by: Joseph R. Mitchell, *Howard Community College*
and Helen Buss Mitchell, *Howard Community College*

Beyond the Family Feud

After decades of debate, are younger scholars finally asking the right questions about the Olmec?

ANDREW LAWLER

Learning Outcomes

After reading this article, you will be able to:

- Discuss the differences of opinion among scholars regarding the role of Olmecs in the development of Mesoamerican civilization.

It's a drizzly autumn morning in the eastern Mexican city of Xalapa, near the heartland of what many scholars say was Mesoamerica's first civilization. At the city's elegant anthropology museum, amid one of the finest Olmec collections in the world, Yale archaeologist Michael Coe points at the giant squat stone head staring sullenly at us. "Look at this," he says enthusiastically. "When it was made, the Maya area didn't even have pottery, and the biggest sculpture from this time in Oaxaca"—an important valley to the west—"could fit in this guy's eye." The Olmec, Coe insists, "were the Sumerians of the New World."

An energetic man even at 77, he is part of an older generation of scholars who have spent a good part of their professional lives arguing among themselves over whether the Olmec birthed the rudiments of Mesoamerican civilization, or whether they were one among many contemporary peoples who contributed art, technology, and religious beliefs to the Aztec, Maya, and other cultures that Cortés and the Spanish encountered 2,500 years later. But that lingering "mother-sister" debate—often vociferous, occasionally unseemly, and sometimes downright nasty—obscures a quiet revolution in research on early Mesoamerica. While the elders bicker, a younger batch of archaeologists is pursuing other questions, asking, for example, how the ordinary Olmec lived and worked, and what they ate.

Such fundamental matters until now were largely neglected amid the academic fracas, which has focused on monumental structures, evidence of kings, and the iconography of the elite. "Everyone is flying a flag from their own valley," sighs Mary Pye, a 40-something archaeologist in Mexico City who is also in Xalapa for a conference on the Olmec. "Forget mother-sister,"

she says. "It's more complicated." The more nuanced picture emerging of early Mesoamerica does not fit that of either warring camp. Those who back the Olmec as the first civilization traditionally point to the early adoption of maize, the growth of urban centers, and the export of finished goods such as pottery throughout Mesoamerica to clinch their argument. Opponents emphasize the complexity of other cultures in different areas, such as Oaxaca. But the new research shows that during the early critical phase of urbanization the Olmec may have shunned maize, lived mostly as fishermen, and sought luxury items from distant places, while simultaneously expanding their cultural influence throughout the region.

Unlike the dry valley of Oaxaca or the chilly Basin of Mexico—home today to sprawling Mexico City—the Olmec homeland bordering the Gulf of Mexico is marshy, humid, and hot. It is also remote, and even today traveling to Olmec sites during the rainy season is treacherous. Scholars have long known of this area's famous giant stone heads—massive images of kings, chiefs, and ballplayers as heavy as 20 tons—unearthed in the nineteenth century and long considered remnants of Mesoamerica's heyday in the early centuries A.D., with its sprawling Maya cities. But it was not until the 1940s that researchers realized that the region the Aztecs called "place of wealth" was awash in pre-Maya artifacts.

It was then that, after years of investigation, the Smithsonian Institution's Matthew Stirling and Mexican art historian Miguel Covarrubias drew the startling conclusion that the Olmec heads were in fact the earliest monumental sculptures in Mesoamerica. Radiocarbon dating ultimately backed up their findings, but their further contention that the Olmec created the first Mesoamerican civilization was greeted skeptically, particularly by scholars who had long considered the highlands of the north to be the original source of urbanization.

People were undoubtedly drawn to this area by its rich aquatic resources long before the Olmec, but it was in the second millennium B.C. that the inhabitants began to live in more complex societies. They began, for example, to make pilgrimages to sacred places. Excavators at El Manatí in the 1980s found an extraordinary ritual deposit, dated about

1400 B.C., that included wooden effigies wrapped in vegetation that were preserved in thick mud, along with finely carved axes and stones of jadeite, basalt, and serpentine. They also discovered polished stones carefully laid out along the cardinal directions, and, deep under the muck, rubber balls similar to those used by the Aztec for ritual ballgames when Cortés arrived in 1519—an extraordinarily long history for a sacred sport. There is little evidence for a town at El Manatí, hinting that it was used mainly for religious purposes.

But what many consider to be Mesoamerica's first urban center emerged two centuries later just a few miles away. San Lorenzo grew up on a long ridge above a network of rivers on the marshy lowlands that feed into the Gulf of Mexico. The site was easily defended, protected from floods, and blessed with freshwater springs at its summit.

Coe and his colleagues focused on this acropolis during the 1960s, and its ten gigantic stone heads and three carved altars or thrones hint at an impressive processional way. The faces are individualized, and wear what could be leather ballplayers' helmets. Though there are no inscriptions with their identities, most scholars see the heads as representations of generations of rulers. Under the so-called Red Palace—a gravel-floored structure with painted mud walls and stone accents—is a sophisticated basalt drainage system that may have ended in a ritual bath. Stone sculptures of jaguars, serpents, and half-animal, half-human creatures provide the iconography of the Mesoamerican pantheon that reappear for millennia, from the Maya cities of the Yucatán to the Aztec capital Tenochtitlán in the north.

After a 20-year hiatus of digging at San Lorenzo, a new team led by Ann Cyphers of the National Autonomous University of Mexico is now exploring large areas off the acropolis as well, from the terraces below to the small islets surrounding San Lorenzo proper. The terraces were densely packed, mostly with simple houses with earthen floors, pole walls, and thatched roofs. Below, a wide dike or causeway a quarter-mile long was lined with houses as well. Stacey Symonds, a young researcher who is part of Cyphers's team, estimates that an average of 5,500 people may have lived in San Lorenzo proper during its heyday between 1200 and 900 B.C. And an average of 13,000 people may have lived in the city and its 155 square miles of hinterlands.

Cyphers is also exploring the various ways in which the Olmec lived around their capital. The elite resided at San Lorenzo proper and at nine surrounding sites in the immediate neighborhood. Interspersed among these larger towns were 19 smaller villages and 76 small islands built up from the marshy soil only large enough to support a single household. The villages and islands nestled within the twisting river network were ideal locations for transportation by boat and access to seafood. Above them all loomed the ridge of San Lorenzo with its magnificent monuments. Though much of Cyphers's work is yet to be published, scholars are hopeful that her finds will provide the first hard evidence of San Lorenzo's way of life outside the acropolis.

The hierarchical settlement pattern and the population—while modest compared to later Mesoamerican cities—make it clear that something unusual was taking place here. Such well-defined gradations—single households, villages, towns, city—have not yet been found elsewhere in Mesoamerica during this period. "No one can dispute that San Lorenzo is unlike anything else in Mesoamerica," says Philip Arnold, an archaeologist at Loyola University. "It belongs to a way of life that's different from contemporary culture."

Unlike traditional mother-culture advocates, who see maize as the jumpstarter for San Lorenzo, Arnold thinks that the Olmec continued to draw primarily on aquatic resources for centuries after 1200 B.C. He is part of a new vanguard in Olmec household archaeology that is quietly reexamining such long-held assumptions. "Nobody has done any comprehensive and consistent analysis of plant remains," notes Amber VanDerwarker, a 32-year-old archaeologist at Muhlenberg College in Pennsylvania. "It has been almost completely neglected." Like Arnold, she's trying to fill that gap by examining not just what people ate, but how their diet shifted over time. "The old idea is that the rise to power was linked to maize—but nobody had really analyzed remains." She also believes that while maize production was important, it wasn't the be-all and end-all, and that even during San Lorenzo's heyday locals were busy hunting and fishing as well. "It was a fairly diverse and mixed economy." Given that societies in Mesopotamia and Egypt developed as they learned to store and redistribute dry crops, the research has interesting implications for understanding civilization's emergence.

Archaeologists also are reexamining how the Olmec and other groups interacted. Coe and other backers of the mother-culture approach argue that the Olmec had wide influence throughout Mesoamerica, exporting pottery and even religion to their contemporaries. That view has been fiercely opposed by those who work in other areas of Mesoamerica, such as Kent Flannery of the University of Michigan. He and his colleague Joyce Marcus have spent decades examining the urban evolution in Oaxaca. Though they declined to talk to ARCHAEOLOGY, Flannery and Marcus insist in many publications that trade was on a reciprocal basis and that San Lorenzo was not at the center of the network.

But to a younger generation, both points of view lack the subtlety necessary to understand life in ancient Mesoamerica. Decorative cubes of ilmenite (a black iron-titanium mineral) from Chiapas and polished gray-black magnetite mirrors possibly from Oaxaca are among the luxury imports found at San Lorenzo, indicating that its rulers imported as well as exported luxury goods. At the same time, the widespread presence of Olmec pottery—from the northern Mexican highlands to Guatemala—is solid evidence that San Lorenzo was more than just another stop on the trading path.

And a good deal of that pottery was not only in the Olmec style, it was actually made in San Lorenzo. That is the surprising conclusion of a 2005 study led by Jeffrey Blomster of George Washington University that pinpointed the origin of the clay used to make pottery found from the Basin of Mexico to the north to Chiapas to the south. "We're using robust statistical techniques to get compositional data," says the 40-year-old researcher. "Before there was very little data—all we had was theory." By bringing modern analytical methods into the mix, younger scientists such as Blomster hope to provide more data to resolve debates about the Olmec.

Recent finds by David Cheetham, a Ph.D. candidate at Arizona State University, at Cantón Corralito in distant Chiapas ("The Americas' First Colony?" January/February 2006), where up to 20 percent of the pottery is Olmec in origin (including more than 4,000 pieces of San Lorenzo–style ware) underscore the extent of San Lorenzo's influence. Cantón, which covered 60 acres by the time of its demise in 1000 B.C., shows the presence of people who either were from the Olmec heartland, or had an unusually strong affinity to it. Whether they were colonists, merchants, or renegades is not known.

Both the Cantón excavations and Blomster's work, which included sherds from that site, draw fire from some researchers. Some insist that Cantón's percentage of Olmec ware is much lower, closer to five percent. And Flannery leads a group that questions Blomster's analysis of the sherds and criticizes the sampling as skewed to favor San Lorenzo wares. Flannery's group recently dismissed Blomster and his colleagues in a journal article for seeing "Meso-american civilization as the product of a kind of intelligent design." That reference to creationism—a bitter insult in the world of science—shows how vicious the debate among Mesoamerican archaeologists can be.

"There's a lot of hot air being blown over this," says Arnold. But he and other younger archaeologists are impressed by the quality and quantity of data, which could eventually clarify San Lorenzo's influence.

Another surprising piece of data published in 2006 also sets the Olmec apart from other societies of the time such as that in Oaxaca. Though the Olmec left behind the occasional intriguing symbol, it was not until after 500 B.C. that a writing system in Oaxaca and one near the Olmec heartland appear. But then a team of Mexican and U.S. scholars closely examined a 26-pound serpentine block found by locals in 1999 from a gravel quarry in a place called Cascajal, just a mile from San Lorenzo ("The Cascajal Block," January/February 2007). On one side of it are 62 carved signs. The meaning of these signs is unknown, though similar ones appear at an Olmec site in Chiapas. But given the organization of the symbols and their repetition in the inscription, the team concluded that the block conformed to all expectations of writing. Yet the script appears to have been a dead end; it bears no obvious resemblance to Isthmian, a later script found in the region, or Mayan.

Dating the block proved problematic because it was already out of context when archaeologists examined it. But given that the majority of potsherds associated with the block's original location—as stated by the locals who found it—are primarily from the end of the San Lorenzo phase, the team estimates that it was carved in 900 B.C., as the city began its decline. Some skeptics say that linking the potsherds with the block is guesswork, but even sister-culture backers such as David Grove, professor emeritus at the University of

Illinois, acknowledge that the stone provides strong evidence for Olmec writing.

Stephen Houston, a Brown University anthropologist who was part of the team that studied the Cascajal block, says future excavations could at least provide more examples of Olmec writing. For Houston, Coe, and others on the team, the inscription is yet more proof that the Olmec achieved a complexity unrivaled in Mesoamerica.

Yet the Cascajal block, the Cantón excavations, and Blomster's study aren't the only parts of the emerging picture of ancient Mesoamerica. There are also new finds that hint at the sophistication of other regions even before the appearance of the Olmec. The oldest ballcourt known today predates Olmec prominence by several centuries and is found in faraway Chiapas. Flannery and Marcus have evidence that Oaxacans built ceremonial structures and defensive palisades in the century before San Lorenzo's rise. And to the south, along the Pacific, inhabitants traded up and down the coast while producing elaborate pottery long before the kilns of San Lorenzo were fired. And excavations by Grove at Chalcatzingo, a 100-acre site between the Basin of Mexico, Oaxaca, and the Gulf lowlands, hint at massive terraces built by local people that may predate those at Olmec sites.

If ballcourts, terraces, and ceremonial structures existed in other areas, the Olmec clearly didn't invent Mesoamerican civilization. In the vibrant trade among and within the northern highlands and the southern lowlands, more than just goods were exchanged. Religious ideas, building techniques, and political systems inevitably mixed as well. Yet many younger scholars believe something special took place in San Lorenzo. "Oaxaca is isolated, the Basin is cold, and you have metals and pottery coming up the coast from the south," says Pye. "The Olmec is where it all comes together for the first time." But Pye also acknowledges the extensive trade and societal complexity elsewhere. And she notes that some areas in Mesoamerica, particularly along the Pacific coast, remain largely unexplored.

What may emerge is a broader picture of a multicenter evolution in which all the pieces fall together in one place—but that one place did not "invent" civilization as the older mother-culture folks contend.

New world archaeologists might take a page from their Old World colleagues. The latter long assumed that the Sumerians of southern Mesopotamia were the first civilization, and that great cities like Uruk, home to the legendary King Gilgamesh, brought their new way of life to their uncouth neighbors around 3000 B.C. The presence of Uruk pottery from the Iranian plateau to the Mediterranean led researchers to imagine a colonial-style system administered from Uruk.

But now, excavators in Syria and Turkey are finding that the northern end of Mesopotamia was far more advanced than scholars once thought. Though there is little doubt the Sumerians first put together all the pieces of civilization, northerners in settlements like Syria's Tell Brak were living in impressive towns with large buildings surrounded by suburbs as early as 4000 B.C. Archaeologists now understand that Mesopotamia's vastly different northern and southern regions invariably traded ideas as well as goods, no doubt increasing the tempo of creativity in both areas.

Whether the northern highlands and southern lowlands of Mesoamerica competed and cooperated in a similar way in the push toward civilization remains unproven. But there are signs that even the older generation is coming around to a more complex view than the "is not—is too" debate of the past 50 years. Grove, a respected sister-culture supporter, acknowledges that the Olmec had a large and important influence on emerging civilization in the region. "And you can't explain it all as emanating from San Lorenzo," says Richard Diehl, a University of Alabama anthropologist who worked with Coe and has long backed the mother side.

"The burning question of this generation becomes the white noise of the next," says Houston. And the new generation is already too busy looking into the day-to-day life of your average Olmec to bother with the old family feud. "When you polarize a debate, you limit the opportunities to learn," says Arnold. Studying the plant and animal remains, patterns of settlement, and pottery origin, he says, ultimately will make the old argument seem two-dimensional and obsolete. "That debate obscures who the people were," adds VanDerwarker. "And I'm interested in the people." That's an approach that ultimately may give us greater insight into the Olmec than all their magnificent, but mute, stone heads.

Critical Thinking

1. What does Andrew Lawler mean when he says, "The Olmec were the Sumerians of the New World"?

2. What is the significance of "the Cascajal Block"?

3. What might we learn from deciphering it?

4. What is the case for a "multicenter evolution" in Mesoamerica?

Create Central

www.mhhe.com/createcentral

Internet References

Civilization of the Olmecs
www.crystalinks.com/olmec.htm

ANDREW LAWLER is a staff writer for *Science* and lives in rural Maine.

Unit IV

UNIT

Prepared by: Joseph R. Mitchell, *Howard Community College*
and Helen Buss Mitchell, *Howard Community College*

The Later Civilizations to 500 CE

Life in the ancient world was likely to be short and brutal. Poor nutrition, disease, hazards of childbirth, warfare, and violence all took their toll. In the Roman Empire, for example, only one child in eight could expect to reach 40 years of age. Because value depended upon usefulness, long life was not necessarily a blessing. Women were typically subservient and mistreated, criminals and slaves were publicly slaughtered, and unwanted or imperfect children were abandoned to die. Yet, despite these harsh realities, humankind built splendid cities, formed empires, wrote history, invented sports, and created great art. Aspects of this growing diversity are explored in this section.

Athens inspired our modern ideas about government, philosophy, art, and sport. At the center of the *polis,* as these city-states were known, was the agora, a plaza ringed with civic and religious buildings. In Athens, the agora served as a meeting place for merchants and thinkers who were equally valued. Both goods and ideas were traded in this marketplace. And, atop the Acropolis stood the Parthenon, a fortress temple to the Goddess Athena that is also a marvel of engineering mastery.

As historians continue the never-ending process of revision, peoples whose contributions have been unacknowledged can receive long overdue credit. Much of science, medicine, religion, music, finance, and philosophy has its roots in Jewish culture. Despite centuries of discrimination and persecution, the Jews have outlasted all the civilizations that were once their ancient contemporaries. They have left a stunning heritage of accomplishments and courage, as the story of Masada attests.

As the Greeks and Romans created heroes and debunked the high and mighty, we see the emergence of mass entertainment as a diversion from the pressures of ordinary life. Although the gladiators were the Western world's first superstars, their lives were brutal and short. But, the cheering crowds identified for a moment with their strength and prowess, escaping for a few hours into the life of imagination. Do humans require some form of entertainment and escapism? Or is this merely a habit we began acquiring two thousand years ago?

New findings of the Roman past raise further questions about its ancient roots found in the now-vanished Etruscan civilization and its influence on the later Roman Empire. Even the end of the Roman Empire has been called into question. Perhaps, rather than "a fall," we might find a "transformation."

Article

Prepared by: Joseph R. Mitchell, *Howard Community College*
and Helen Buss Mitchell, *Howard Community College*

Unlocking Mysteries of the Parthenon

Efforts to restore the ancient temple of Athena are yielding new insights.

Evan Hadingham

Learning Outcomes

After reading this article, you will be able to:

- Determine how the restoration of the Parthenon has increased our knowledge and respect for its original builders.

During the past 2,500 years, the Parthenon—the apotheosis of ancient Greek architecture—has been rocked by earthquakes, set on fire, shattered by exploding gunpowder, looted for its stunning sculptures and defaced by misguided preservation efforts. Amazingly, the ancient Athenians built the Parthenon in just eight or nine years. Repairing it is taking a bit longer.

A restoration project funded by the Greek government and the European Union is now entering its 33rd year, as archaeologists, architects, civil engineers and craftsmen strive not simply to imitate the workmanship of the ancient Greeks but to re-create it. They have had to become forensic architects, reconstructing long-lost techniques to answer questions that archaeologists and classical scholars have debated for centuries. How did the Athenians construct their mighty temple, an icon of Western civilization, in less than a decade—apparently without an overall building plan? How did they manage to incorporate subtle visual elements into the Parthenon's layout and achieve such faultless proportions and balance? And how were the Parthenon's builders able to work at a level of precision (in some cases accurate to within a fraction of a millimeter) without the benefit of modern tools? "We're not as good as they were," Lena Lambrinou, an architect on the restoration project, observes with a sigh.

If the Parthenon represents "the supreme effort of genius in pursuit of beauty," as the 19th-century French engineer and architectural historian Auguste Choisy declared, at the moment it looks more like a construction site. Ancient masonry hides behind thickets of scaffolding, planks and steel poles. Miniature rail tracks connect sheds that house lathes, marble cutters and other power equipment. In the Parthenon's innermost sanctuary, once the home of a massive ivory-and-gold statue of Athena, a gigantic collapsible crane turns on a concrete platform.

Though heavy equipment dominated the hilltop, I also found restorers working with the delicacy of diamond cutters. In one shed, I watched a mason toiling on a fresh block of marble. He was one of some 70 craftsmen recruited for the project from Greece's sole remaining traditional marble school, located on the island of Tinos. His technique was exacting. To make the new block exactly match an old, broken one, the mason used a simple pointing device—the three-dimensional equivalent of a pantograph, which is a drafting instrument for precisely copying a sketch or blueprint—to mark and transfer every bump and hollow from the ancient stone to its counterpart surface on the fresh block. On some of the largest Parthenon blocks, which exceed ten tons, the masons use a mechanized version of the pointing device, but repairing a single block can still take more than three months. The ancient workers were no less painstaking; in many cases, the joints between the blocks are all but invisible, even under a magnifying glass.

The Parthenon was part of an ambitious building campaign on the Acropolis that began around 450 B.C. A generation before, the Athenians, as part of an alliance of Greek city-states, had led heroic victories against Persian invaders. This alliance would evolve into a de facto empire under Athenian rule, and some 150 to 200 cities across the Aegean began paying Athens huge sums of what amounted to protection money. Basking in glory, the Athenians planned their new temple complex on a lavish, unprecedented scale—with the Parthenon as the centerpiece. Surviving fragments of the financial accounts, which were inscribed in stone for public scrutiny, have prompted estimates of the construction budget that range from around 340 to 800 silver talents—a considerable sum in an age when a single talent could pay a month's wages for 170 oarsmen on a Greek warship. The Parthenon's base was 23,028 square feet (about half the size of a football field) and its 46 outer columns were some 34 feet high. A 525-foot frieze wrapped around the top of the exterior wall of the building's inner chamber. Several scholars have argued that the frieze shows a procession related to the quadrennial Great Panathenaia, or the festival "of all the Athenians." By incorporating this scene of civic celebration, the scholars suggest, the Parthenon served not merely as an imperial propaganda statement but also as an expression of Athens' burgeoning democracy—the will of the citizens who had voted to fund this exceptional monument.

When the current restoration effort began in 1975, backed by $23 million from the Greek government, the project's directors believed they could finish in ten years. But unforeseen problems arose as soon as workers started disassembling the temples. For example, the ancient Greek builders had secured the marble blocks together with iron clamps fitted in carefully carved grooves. They then poured molten lead over the joints to cushion them from seismic shocks and protect the clamps from corrosion. But when a Greek architect, Nikolas Balanos, launched an enthusiastic campaign of restorations in 1898, he installed crude iron clamps, indiscriminately fastening one block to another and neglecting to add the lead coating. Rain soon began to play havoc with the new clamps, swelling the iron and cracking the marble. Less than a century later, it was clear that parts of the Parthenon were in imminent danger of collapse.

Until September 2005, the restoration's coordinator was Manolis Korres, associate professor of architecture at the National Technical University of Athens and a leading Parthenon scholar. He has spent decades poring over every detail of the temple's construction. In a set of vivid drawings, he depicted how the ancient builders extracted some 100,000 tons of marble from a quarry 11 miles northeast of central Athens, roughly shaped the blocks, then transported them on wagons and finally hauled them up the steep slopes of the Acropolis. Yet all that grueling labor, Korres contends, was dwarfed by the time and energy lavished on fine-tuning the temple's finished appearance. Carving the long vertical grooves, or flutes, that run down each of the Parthenon's main columns was probably as costly as all the quarrying, hauling and assembly combined.

Today's restorers have been replacing damaged column segments with fresh marble. To speed up the job, engineers built a flute-carving machine. The device, however, is not precise enough for the final detailing, which must be done by hand. This smoothing of the flutes calls for an expert eye and a sensitive touch. To get the elliptical profile of the flute just right, a mason looks at the shadow cast inside the groove, then chips and rubs the stone until the outline of the shadow is a perfectly even and regular curve.

The ancients spent a lot of time on another finishing touch. After the Parthenon's exposed marble surfaces had been smoothed and polished, they added a final, subtle texture—a stippling pattern—that Korres says dulled the shine on the marble and masked its flaws. With hundreds of thousands of chisel blows, they executed this pattern in precisely ordered rows covering the base, floors, columns and most other surfaces. "This was surely one of the most demanding tasks," Korres says. "It may have taken as much as a quarter of the total construction time expended on the monument."

With such fanatical attention to detail, how could the Parthenon's architects have finished the job in a mere eight or nine years, ending somewhere between 438 and 437 B.C.? (The dates come from the inscribed financial accounts.)

One key factor may have been naval technology. Since the Athenians were the greatest naval power in the Aegean, they likely had unrivaled mastery of ropes, pulleys and wooden cranes. Such equipment would have been essential for hauling and lifting marble blocks.

Another, counterintuitive possibility is that ancient hand tools were superior to their modern counterparts. After analyzing marks left on the marble surfaces, Korres is convinced that centuries of metallurgical experimentation enabled the ancient Athenians to create chisels and axes that were sharper and more durable than those available today. (The idea is not unprecedented. Modern metallurgists have only recently figured out the secrets of the traditional samurai sword, which Japanese swordsmiths endowed with unrivaled sharpness and strength by regulating the amount of carbon in the steel and the temperature during forging and cooling.) Korres concludes that the ancient masons, with their superior tools, could carve marble at more than double the rate of speed of today's craftsmen. And the Parthenon's original laborers had the benefit of experience, drawing on a century and a half of temple-building know-how.

Moreover, the restoration team has confronted problems that their ancient Greek counterparts could never have contemplated. During the Great Turkish War in the late 17th century—when the Ottoman Empire was battling several European countries—Greece was an occupied nation. The Turks turned the Parthenon into an ammunition dump. During a Venetian attack on Athens in 1687, a cannonball set off the Turkish munitions, blowing apart the long walls of the Parthenon's inner chamber. More than 700 blocks from those walls—eroded over time—now lay strewn around the Acropolis. For five years, beginning in 1997, Cathy Paraschi, a Greek-American architect on the restoration project, struggled to fit the pieces together, hunting for clues such as the shape and depth of the cuttings in the blocks that once held the ancient clamps. Eventually, she abandoned her computer database, which proved inadequate for capturing the full complexity of the puzzle. "Some days were exhilarating," she told me, "when we finally got one piece to fit another. Other days I felt like jumping off the Acropolis." In the end, she and her co-workers managed to identify the original positions of some 500 of the blocks.

Looming over each restoration challenge is the delicate question of how far to go. Every time the workers dismantle one of Balanos' crude fixes, it is a reminder of how destructive an overzealous restorer can be. As the director of the Acropolis Restoration Project, Maria Ioannidou, explains, "we've adopted an approach of trying to restore the maximum amount of ancient masonry while applying the minimum amount of new material." That means using clamps and rods made of titanium—which won't corrode and crack the marble—and soluble white cement, so that repairs can be easily undone should future generations of restorers discover a better way.

There have been some bravura feats of engineering. The 1687 explosion had knocked one of the massive columns out of position and badly damaged its bottom segment. A serious earthquake in 1981 damaged it further, and the entire column appeared at risk of toppling. The obvious procedure was to dismantle the column, one segment after another, and replace the crumbling section. Korres, hoping to avoid "even the smallest departure from the column's perfection and authenticity of construction," designed a metal collar that exerts precisely controlled forces to grasp a column securely without harming the stone. In the early 1990s, after the careful removal of the overhead blocks and lintels, the collar was suspended by turnbuckles (adjustable connectors) inside a mounted, rectangular steel frame. By tightening the turnbuckles, the team raised the 55-ton column less than an inch. They then removed the bottom segment—which they repaired with fresh marble to an accuracy of one-twentieth of a millimeter—and slid it back into position. Finally, they lowered the rest of the column into place on top of the repaired segment. "It was a bold decision to do it this way," Korres says. "But we were young and daring then."

Perhaps none of the Parthenon's mysteries stirs more debate than the gentle curves and inclinations engineered throughout much of its design. There is hardly a straight line to be found in the temple. Experts argue over whether these refinements were added to counter optical illusions. The eye can be tricked, for instance, into seeing an unsightly sag in flat floors built under a perched roof like the Parthenon's. Possibly to correct this effect, the Athenians laid out the Parthenon's base so that the 228-by-101-foot floor bulges slightly toward the middle, curving gradually upward between 4 and 4 1/2 inches on its left and right sides, and 2 1/2 inches on its front and back. One theory holds that this slight upward bulge was built simply to drain rainwater away from the temple's interior. But that fails to explain why the same curving profile is repeated not only in the floor but in the entablature above the columns and in the (invisible) buried foundations. This graceful curve was clearly fundamental to the overall appearance and planning of the Parthenon.

And then there are the columns, which the Athenians built so that they bulged slightly outward at the center. This swelling was termed entasis, or tension, by Greek writers, perhaps because it makes the columns seem as if they are clenching, like a human muscle, under the weight of their load. Again, some scholars have long speculated that this design might compensate for another trick of the eye, since a row of tall, perfectly straight-sided pillars can appear thinner at the middle than at the ends.

No matter the motivation for these refinements, many early scholars assumed that crafting such visual elements imposed tremendous extra demands on the Parthenon's architects and masons. (One wrote of the "terrifying complications" involved.) No architectural manuals survive from the Classical Greek era, but today's experts suspect the temple builders could add curves and inclined angles with a few relatively simple surveying tricks. "If you're building without mortar, every block . . . must be trimmed by hand," notes Oxford University archaeologist Jim Coulton. "Although tilts and curvatures would require careful supervision by the architect, they don't add a lot to the workload."

Still, how could each column segment be measured so that all would fit together in a single, smoothly curving profile? The likely answer was found not in Athens but nearly 200 miles away in southwestern Turkey. In the town of Didyma rises one of the most impressive relics of the ancient world, the Temple of Apollo. Three of its 120 colossal columns still stand, each nearly twice the height of the Parthenon's. The wealthy trading city of Miletus commissioned the temple in the age of Alexander the Great, around 150 years after the Parthenon's completion. The gigantic ruins testify to a project of grandiose ambition: it was never finished despite 600 years of construction efforts. But thanks to its unfinished state, crucial evidence was preserved on temple walls that had not yet undergone their final polishing.

A few years after the Parthenon restoration began, University of Pennsylvania scholar Lothar Haselberger was on a field trip exploring the Temple of Apollo's innermost sanctuary. He noticed what seemed to be patterns of faint scratches on the marble walls. In the blinding morning sunlight the scratches are all but invisible, as I discovered to my initial frustration when I searched for them. After the sun had swung around and began grazing the surface, however, a delicate web of finely engraved lines started to emerge. Haselberger recalls, "All of a sudden I spotted a series of circles that corresponded precisely to the shape of a column base, the very one at the front of the temple." He realized he had discovered the ancient equivalent of an architect's blueprint.

Then, just above the outline of the column base, Haselberger noticed a pattern of horizontal lines with a sweeping curve inscribed along one side. Could this be related to entasis, also evident in the towering Didyma columns? After carefully plotting the pattern, the answer became clear: it was a profile view of a column with the vertical dimension—the height of the by a factor of 16. This scale drawing must have been a key reference for the masons as they carved out one column segment after another. By measuring along the horizontal lines to the edge of the curve, they would know exactly how wide each segment would have to be to create the smooth, bulging profile. Manolis Korres believes that the ancient Athenians probably relied on a carved scale drawing similar to the one at Didyma in building the columns of the Parthenon.

Haselberger also traced a labyrinth of faint scratches covering most of the temple's unfinished surfaces. The lines proved to be reference drawings for everything from the very slight inward lean of the walls to details of the lintel structure supported by the columns. There were even floor plans, drafted conveniently right on the floor. As the temple's stepped platform rose, each floor plan was copied from one layer to the next. On the topmost floor, the builders marked out the positions of columns, walls and doorways.

The discoveries at Didyma suggest that the temple builders operated on a "plan-as-you-go" basis. "Clearly, a lot of advance planning went into a building like the Parthenon," Coulton says. "But it wasn't planning in the sense that we'd recognize today. There's no evidence they relied on a single set of plans and elevations drawn to scale as a modern architect would."

Still, the Parthenon remains something of a miracle. The builders were steered by tradition, yet free to experiment. They worked to extreme precision, yet the final result was anything but rigid. A commanding building, with supple and fluid lines, emerged from a blend of improvised solutions.

But the miracle was short-lived. Only seven years after the construction of the Parthenon was completed, war broke out with Sparta. Within a generation, Athens suffered a humiliating defeat and a devastating plague. The story of the Parthenon resembles an ancient Greek tragedy, in which an exceptional figure suffers a devastating reversal of fortune. And from Korres' perspective, that calamity is all the more reason to restore the greatest remnant of Athens' golden age. "We wanted to preserve the beauty of what has survived these past 2,500 years," he says. "A reminder of man's power to create, as well as to destroy."

Critical Thinking

1. What is a "forensic architect"?
2. What skills does he or she need?
3. What is "entasis," and how did it affect the design and construction of the original columns in the Parthenon?
4. In what way does the Parthenon resemble "an ancient Greek Tragedy"?

Create Central

www.mhhe.com/createcentral

Internet References

Ancient City of Athens
www.stoa.org/athens

EVAN HADINGHAM is senior science editor of PBS's *NOVA* series. The *NOVA* program "Secrets of the Parthenon" airs January 29, 2008.

Article   Prepared by: Joseph R. Mitchell, *Howard Community College*
and Helen Buss Mitchell, *Howard Community College*

Unraveling the Etruscan Enigma

ROSSELLA LORENZI

Learning Outcomes

After reading this article, you will be able to:

- Discuss new understandings about the Etruscans made possible through archeology.

They taught the French to make wine and the Romans to build roads, and they introduced writing to Europe, but the Etruscans have long been considered one of antiquity's great enigmas. No one knew exactly where they came from. Their language was alien to their neighbors. Their religion included the practice of divination, performed by priests who examined animals' entrails to predict the future. Much of our knowledge about Etruscan civilization comes from ancient literary sources and from tomb excavations, many of which were carried out decades ago. But all across Italy, archaeologists are now creating a much richer picture of Etruscan social structure, trade relationships, economy, daily lives, religion, and language than has ever been possible. Excavations at sites including the first monumental tomb to be explored in over two decades, a rural sanctuary filled with gold artifacts, the only Etruscan house with intact walls and construction materials still preserved, and an entire seventh-century B.C. miner's town, are revealing that the Etruscans left behind more than enough evidence to show that perhaps, they aren't such a mystery after all.

When Etruscan culture began to flourish around 900 B.C., the Italian peninsula was inhabited by a variety of peoples. In addition to Greeks and Celts, there were numerous Italic tribes, all of whom spoke languages that were closely related. But the Etruscans' origins are still hotly debated, primarily because their language and religion were different from those of their neighbors. Ancient scholars had three theories about where the culture came from, each of which was based in their own biases. The fifth-century B.C. Greek historian Herodotus believed the Etruscans came from the east, fleeing a famine in Lydia, a kingdom in western Anatolia (modern Turkey). The Roman historian Livy supported a Northern European origin. And an indigenous theory was suggested by Dionysus of Halicarnassus, a Greek writer living in Rome, who argued that the Romans were really Greeks who encountered

the Etruscans when they came to Italy. The Etruscans' own mythology offered an explanation of their origins via the story of a boy, Tages, popping out of the fields of Tarquinia (the most powerful Etruscan city) with the *Etrusca Disciplina,* their religious and ritual code, in hand. In 2007, in an attempt to sort out Etruscan origins, Alberto Piazza of the University of Turin conducted a DNA study focused on three areas of Tuscany—the Casentino Valley and two towns, Volterra and Murlo. These towns are among the most archaeologically important Etruscan sites in a region also known for having Etruscan-derived place names and local dialects. The Casentino Valley sample was taken from an area bordering a region where Etruscan influence has been preserved. Scientists compared DNA samples taken from males living in Tuscany, Northern Italy, Sicily, Sardinia, the Southern Balkans, and the island of Lemnos in Greece. The Tuscan samples were taken from individuals whose families had lived in the area for at least three generations. These were then compared with data from modern Turkish, Southern Italian, European, and Middle Eastern populations. "We found that the DNA samples from individuals from Murlo and Volterra were more closely related to those of Near Eastern people than to the other Italian samples. In Murlo particularly, one genetic variant is shared only by people from Turkey," says Piazza.

But several Etruscan scholars don't accept Piazza's claim of an eastern origin for the Etruscans. "The people of Murlo are now convinced that they are genuine Etruscans, but the fact remains that there is no ancient DNA with which to compare theirs," says archaeologist Jane Whitehead of Valdosta State University.

Living in a loose confederation of towns scattered across Etruria, the land between the Tiber and the Arno rivers, the Etruscans dominated much of Italy for five centuries. Skillful seafarers and early masters of metallurgy, they exploited central Italy's rich mineral resources and traded raw copper, iron, and bronze for perfume, ivory, amber, and fine ceramics from Egypt, Greece, and Phoenicia.

When the Romans lived in what was still just a cluster of villages, Etruscan civilization had already begun to grow in wealth and power, ample evidence of which has been found in elite houses, inscribed documents, tombs filled with gold, silver, and imported luxuries dating from as early as 700 B.C. At that time, the Etruscans adopted the concept of alphabetic writing from the Phoenicians by way of the Greeks and adapted the Greek alphabet to fit their language. During the seventh century B.C., powerful Etruscan cities such as Tarquinia, Vulci, Cerveteri, Vetulonia, and Veii grew due to their favorable geographic position, which encouraged trade with the rest of the Mediterranean. By 600 B.C., their power was at its zenith and the Etruscans had become the dominant cultural and political force in Italy, expanding their reach north of the Arno into the Po Valley, south into Rome, and down into Campania.

At the beginning of the sixth century B.C., the city of Rome was still ruled by Etruscan kings. Etruscan architects oversaw the construction of some of the earliest streets, houses, and temples, and Etruscan hydraulic engineers developed a water system. But Rome's power in Italy was on the rise. Rome's last Etruscan king, Tarquinius Superbus, ascended the throne in 535 B.C. The Romans expelled him in 509 B.C. and replaced the traditional monarchy with a republican government, blaming the king's tyrannical behavior. The new Rome had emerged, forever suspicious of royal power.

During the fifth century B.C., Etruscan civilization began to decline. Their fleet was defeated by the Greeks at the battle of Cumae in the Bay of Naples in 474 B.C., and, eventually, as the Romans grew in power, they conquered and absorbed Etruscan cities. After a 10-year siege, Veii was captured in 396 B.C. and the last defeated Etruscan city, Velzna (modern Orvieto), surrendered in 265 B.C. But it is known that it wasn't only military defeats that hastened the end of Etruscan civilization, but also their failure to unite as a single, powerful state, as well as their overly rigid class system, that eventually brought an end to their dominance.

Nonetheless, long after the Romans annexed the Etruscans in the first century B.C., their culture continued to permeate Roman art, architecture, and religion. They introduced the Romans to the chariot, the toga, the idea of triumphal processions to celebrate military victories, and to the symbol of the *fasces,* an ax surrounded by a bundle of rods that became an emblem of authority for the Romans and, much later, for Mussolini and the Fascists.

Ultimately, as Rome conquered Etruscan cities and grew in prestige throughout the Mediterranean, the Etruscans became increasingly Romanized. Members of their aristocracy married into noble Roman families and adopted Roman customs, and Latin replaced Etruscan as the area's primary language. In 90 B.C., the rights of Roman citizenship were extended throughout Etruria.

Tarquinia (Tarchna or Tarchuna for the Etruscans), about 50 miles northwest of Rome, has a three-mile-long necropolis filled with more than 6,000 tombs cut into the tufa hills dating from the seventh to second centuries B.C., almost the entire span of Etruscan history. Much of what has been known about the Etruscans comes from their cemeteries, and most surviving artifacts have been grave goods from tombs. About 200 of Tarquinia's burials discovered to date feature vibrantly painted walls and vaults, and, according to Maria Cataldi, director of excavations at the necropolis, hundreds of these tombs are still buried and unexplored. Painted using a dazzling array of expensive pigments—white from calcite, red from hematite, black from charcoal, yellow from goethite, and blue from a mixture of silica, lime, copper, and alkali imported from Egypt—this hidden world populated by leaping dolphins, soaring birds, bearded snakes, jugglers, musicians, wild dancers, and joyful banquets brings one of the ancient Mediterranean's largest cities of the dead to life.

The last major tomb discovery in Tarquinia was made 25 years ago when construction for a new water line was beginning. At the time, Cataldi drilled several holes and sent a camera down into the tufa hill. "We had to make sure that the construction plan did not damage anything and we knew there were plenty of tombs there," she says. In fact, she found 29 small tombs and a large painted one. But like the majority of Tarquinia's burials, the late fifth-century B.C. underground chamber, called the Tomb of the Blue Demons after its elaborate wall paintings, was empty. Professional tomb robbers, called *tombaroli,* had discovered it decades earlier and stolen all the grave goods that had been placed there to ensure the comfort of the dead in the afterlife. Fortunately, the tombaroli left the frescoes, which contain many of the recurring themes in Etruscan art. Colorful images of contemporary life stand in stark contrast to gloomy representations of an underworld

AN ETRUSCAN TIMELINE continued

1200 B.C.	900–750 B.C.	750–600 B.C.
BEGINNINGS	**VILLANOVAN PHASE**	**ORIENTALIZING PERIOD**
Evidence of the first traces of Etruscan civilization in scattered settlements	Etruscan cities develop	Influence from the Eastern Mediterranean includes a new style of figural art shared by Greeks and Etruscans; Greek alphabet is adopted. Royal tombs filled with imported Phoenician and Greek gold, silver, and other luxury artifacts testify to the Etruscans' wealth.

populated by blue demons, images that anticipate the change in the Etruscans' view of death in their culture's final stages. Early on, the Etruscans had conceived of death in an almost relaxed way, depicting the deceased being entertained at banquets, and games, and by processions of friends and musicians. On the verge of their decline, the Etruscans adopted a vision somewhat more like that of the Greeks, of a grim underworld filled with frightening mythological creatures.

In July 2007, a team from the University of Turin led by Alessandro Mandolesi began working at the largest tomb in Tarquinia, a burial that had never been excavated due to the lack of funding for such a large project. The Queen's Tomb is 130 feet in diameter and is similar to another monumental tomb, the equally imposing King's Tomb, 600 feet away. Both date to the seventh century B.C., the Orientalizing period, so called due to the influence on the Etruscans from the eastern Mediterranean.

According to Roman tradition, Demaratus, a Greek from Corinth, landed in Tarquinia as a refugee in the seventh century B.C., bringing with him a team of painters and artisans who taught local people new artistic techniques. Demaratus then married an Etruscan noblewoman from Tarquinia, and their son, Lucumo, became the fifth king of Rome in 616 B.C., taking the name Lucius Tarquinius Priscus. The story emphasizes the acceptance of foreigners into early Etruscan society and points to Tarquinia's importance. "It was one of the most powerful cities of the Etruscan league, and a wealthy center of trade and commerce," says Mandolesi. You have to imagine people arriving from the port and seeing these two imposing mounds. They would have sensed the might of the Tarquinian rulers." Mandolesi's idea that the King's Tomb belongs to ancestors of Tarquinius Priscus is supported by the discovery of an *oinochoe* (a single-handled wine vessel) found in 1928 during excavations by the archaeologist Giuseppe Cultrera in the already heavily looted King's mound. On the bottom of the jug, an inscription bears the name Rutile Hipucartes, the Etruscanized form of the Greek name Hippocrates. According to Mandolesi, Hipucartes was most likely a Greek who settled in Tarquinia, suggesting a connection with the story of Demaratus.

The Queen's Tomb is the only known royal Etruscan tomb yet to be fully explored and the first one to be excavated since the discovery of the Tomb of the Blue Demons. So far Mandolesi's team has excavated the tomb's entrance, a large, rock-hewn stairway that faces west-northwest, where, according to the Etruscan religion, the gods of the underworld lived. The staircase descends about 20 feet into an almost 50-square-foot room made of large limestone blocks. After clearing this space, where rites and ceremonies for the deceased were performed, Mandolesi's team discovered that the walls were originally covered in a one-inch-thick layer of plaster made from gypsum that contains bright white microcrystals. The gypsum was imported from Cyprus, Egypt, and Syria, where it was used on sarcophagi, statues, and tomb walls during the same period. According to Mandolesi, the remaining traces of plaster on the tomb's walls are the first evidence for this technique having been used in Etruscan construction, and he believes that artisans from the eastern Mediterranean were employed for the job.

Mandolesi's theory that the tomb's builders came from the east is also supported by the design of the tomb itself, which is modeled after a style common in Salamis on Cyprus, where the royal necropolis dates from the eleventh century B.C. to the seventh century A.D. "It looks like the local aristocracy wanted an original design, different from all the others in Tarquinia," says Mandolesi. The Etruscans typically cut traditional tombs into the rock, and covered them with small earth mounds that are no longer preserved. But the Queen's Tomb required complex building phases—they needed to dig the burial rooms into the rock, construct the walls of the room, and finally raise the mound with layers of soil and stones.

The mound has collapsed and the now-inaccessible burial chamber is filled with earth and large rocks. But on the right side of the staircase, a streak of blood-red paint is still clearly visible, the remains of a band that once surrounded the entrance and continued across the middle of the walls. A red brush stroke outlining a semicircular form on top of a faint black image also remains. According to Mandolesi, the painting probably depicts a duck. This bird symbolized the journey into the afterlife. Mandolesi believes the Queen's Tomb predates what was thought to be Tarquinia's earliest burial, the Tomb of

AN ETRUSCAN TIMELINE continued

600–480 B.C.	480–300 B.C.	300–100 B.C.
ARCHAIC PERIOD	**CLASSICAL PERIOD**	**HELLENISTIC PERIOD**
The zenith of Etruscan power. Lucius Tarquinius Priscus becomes the first Etruscan king to rule Rome in 616 B.C. The first painted tombs at Tarquinia and the rock-cut tombs of Cerveteri appear. Bronze production reaches new heights and trade throughout the Mediterranean flourishes. The fall of the Tarquin dynasty in Rome in 509 B.C. marks the beginning of Etruscan decline.	The Greeks defeat the Etruscans at the naval battle of Cumae in 474 B.C.; after a 10-year siege, Veii, the Etruscan's most important city, is captured by Romans in 396 B.C.	The Romans gradually annex Etruscan towns. After centuries of decline, Etruscans become Roman citizens and Etruscan aristocrats join the Roman power elite.

Etruscan Daily Life

For years, excavating tombs has been the staple of Etruscan archaeology, but now, temples, seaports, roads, towns, and settlements are being explored, some for the first time. "Finally we have the chance to understand more about their daily life," says archaeologist Giovannangelo Camporeale, of the University of Florence who, for the past 30 years, has been working near Massa Marittima, on one of the largest settlements of the Archaic period ever found. The unnamed town dates from the end of the seventh and the beginning of the sixth centuries B.C. and lies at the foot of the Colline Metallifere (the "Metal Hills") near Lake dell'Accesa in Tuscany. Camporeale has found furnaces around the lake and several small mines, suggesting that it was a miners' town covering more than 75 acres where raw materials such as iron, copper, silver, and tin were extracted. The town was controlled by the powerful city of Vetulonia, which had a thriving maritime trade, and exported the metal ores to the eastern Mediterranean in exchange for high-quality ceramics.

Archaeologists have unearthed five residential quarters thus far, but given the presence of a vast necropolis, they estimate the town must have had many others. These areas are laid out on a rectangular grid, one of the first examples of this type of town planning in Italy. Many of the houses Camporeale has unearthed had sandstone foundations, walls made of sun-dried bricks, and roofs covered with locally made red terracotta tiles similar to the ones still used in Tuscany today. Each quarter contained about 10 houses and controlled one mine. There was also the industrial quarter, just 18.5 miles from the lake where the Etruscans smelted local iron. Other ores were taken elsewhere to refine. Although scholars are unsure why, its inhabitants left the settlement at the end of the sixth century B.C. "Almost all the minor centers across Etruria controlled by the great towns were abandoned at that time. Most likely, it was due to the onset of an economic crisis—possibly a decline in the profitability of the mining industry," says Camporeale. A 2009 study conducted by an international team from Denmark, Italy, and the United States suggests that industrial pollution and arsenic poisoning may also have been a cause.

Among the artifacts found in the houses, Camporeale unearthed vessels, dishes, grindstones, and tools related to wool and textile work, handicrafts usually associated with women, many of whom enjoyed an important role alongside their husbands in Etruscan society. They kept their own names instead of taking their father's and later their husband's name, as in Roman culture. Some of the most popular names inscribed on sarcophagi are Thana, Arunthia, Larthia, Ramtha, Tanaquilla, Velia, and Velka. Tomb paintings show women participating in athletic competitions, attending games, and banqueting alongside men in a way that shocked other male-dominated Mediterranean cultures.

Excavations led by Greg Warden of Southern Methodist University at a site called Poggio Colla, 22 miles northeast of Florence, have revealed that Etruscan women also participated in cult activities. Occupied from the seventh to the second centuries B.C., when it was destroyed, probably by the Romans, Poggio Colla was a northern Etruscan settlement and rural sanctuary, ideally situated to control the main passes leading to the Apennines and stretching to the Adriatic. While excavating on the acropolis, Warden's team found a tightly packed deposit of 18 objects, half of which are gold, including a set of third-century B.C. earrings, necklace pendants, and bronze rings, as well as miscellaneous objects made of metal, bone, and semiprecious stones. "It is rare to find gold jewelry outside of a tomb context, but the recovery of a whole cache in a settlement is extraordinary. I know of no other sets of jewelry that have been discovered in a similar context," says Alexis Castor of Franklin & Marshall College, an expert in ancient jewelry who works with the project.

According to Castor, the Poggio Colla deposit offers striking testimony of the use of women's jewelry in a non-funerary context. "When I saw these pairs of earrings and pendants, including a pendant with a canine tooth," says Castor, "I found it easy to imagine one or more women pulling these pieces out of their jewelry boxes and taking them to the sanctuary to be offered up." According to Castor, some sort of crisis that led to the city's abandonment may have inspired the women to leave their treasures behind, but they could also have been left by a mother asking the gods for help with a sick child, thanking them for her family's success, or some other personal scenario. "The fact that a woman donated her own pieces to the deity speaks to me of her intimate and personal religious act in a way that other mass-produced votive offerings such as terracottas or bronze figurines don't," says Castor.

Another ongoing excavation is also revealing an unprecedented view of the Etruscans' daily lives and building techniques. At the site of Poggiarello Renzetti in the Tuscan town of Vetulonia, 120 miles north of Rome, Simona Rafanelli, director of the excavation for Vetulonia's Isidoro Falchi Archaeological Museum, is digging the first intact Etruscan house to have ever been unearthed. Although it is still only partially excavated, Rafanelli has been able to date its construction to the Hellenistic period. Unlike other houses, of which only foundation stones remain, the Vetulonia house has partly standing walls and the first intact Etruscan bricks ever found. "Usually, the clay dissolves and, apart from some fragments, all that remains are red layers," says Rafanelli. The team also located small pieces of charcoal, charred wood beams, and fragments of burnt pottery, indicating that the house collapsed during a fire, probably around 79 B.C. The heat from the fire baked the bricks, likely the reason they survived.

On the spot where the owner demolished a wall to enlarge a room, the team discovered a small terracotta altar with five bronze Roman coins, probably used in a dedicatory ritual meant to ensure the good fortune of the homeowners. There were other intriguing artifacts, including two bronze door handles with nails attached at the sides, an earthenware grain storage jar standing against a storeroom wall, and more than 100 iron nails used in building a second story made from wood and clay. Raffanelli's team has also explored the basement, where foodstuffs would have been stored. The rest of the house, one of the largest in Vetulonia, will be excavated in coming seasons. The team hopes to explore the whole quarter in the future, including the remains of a staircase that lead to what may be a temple.

—R.L.

the Panthers, by some 50 years. "This suggests that decorative imagery, seen before only on pottery, was used in the necropolis much earlier than previously believed," says Mandolesi.

And the Queens Tomb held even more surprises—architectural clues point to the existence of another chamber, also once covered in gypsum. Dozens of plaster sheets that had once lined the walls lay on the ground, along with the remains of what appeared to be a stone altar. "Most likely, this was a room used for funerary rites such as the leaving of offerings, animal sacrifices, and celebrations for the deceased," says Mandolesi. Extending the excavation to the area surrounding the mound, the team also unearthed two other burials, both built in a style that indicates they are earlier than the monumental tombs and date to the first decades of the seventh century B.C. One tomb is a miniaturized version of the Queens Tomb, complete with steps, entranceway, and burial chamber at the center. This area contained what appears to be a coin (it has not yet been cleaned and conserved), some sherds of *bucchero*, a typically Etruscan black pottery, and skeletal remains that are currently being examined. The other tomb, which contains two small burial chambers with a stone entranceway, was probably intended to house two couples who might have been related to the noble buried in the great mound, since the land around the tomb belonged to the royal family, according to Mandolesi. Each room was equipped with a pair of stone benches, which resemble wooden beds. Less than 60 feet away, the team found evidence of the royal necropolis's foundation rites in a niche cut into the rock containing a broken cup from which the family may have drunk at the time the necropolis was consecrated.

While clearing the Queen's Tomb's entrance over the past three excavation seasons, Mandolesi has also found ceramic and terracotta fragments, possibly from figurines, sheets of gold, and small fragments of what may have been a finely worked bronze artifact. He hopes that during future seasons, he will be able to reach the burial chamber, which will have to be done by excavating the mound from the top down to avoid further collapse. "I think we have found traces of a lost royal treasure," says Mandolesi. "It's possible that tombaroli looted the tumulus, as they did with the King's Tomb. However, there's also a chance that the mound collapsed in antiquity, leaving the burial inaccessible and thus protected. This is an archaeologist's dream."

Critical Thinking

1. Summarize the theories of ancient scholars regarding the origins of the Etruscans.

2. How does the Etruscan "origins story" differ from those put forth by Herodotus, Livy, and Dionysus of Halicarnassus?

3. How does DNA Analysis contribute to our understanding? What is its key limitation?

4. What evidence is given for the sophistication of Etruscan Culture?

5. In addition to military defeats, what other factors hastened the end of Etruscan Civilization?

6. Which elements of Roman Culture can be attributed to Etruscan influences?

Create Central

www.mhhe.com/createcentral

Internet References

Illustrated History of the Roman Empire
www.roman-empire.net

ROSSELLA LORENZI is a freelance writer living in Italy.

Prepared by: Joseph R. Mitchell, *Howard Community College*
and Helen Buss Mitchell, *Howard Community College*

Article

Sudden Death

Gladiators Were Sport's First Superstars, Providing Thrills, Chills, and Occasional Kills

FRANZ LIDZ

Learning Outcomes

After reading this article, you will be able to:

- Determine what role gladiatorial games played and what they might tell us about Roman society.

The ruins of Carthage, that great city-state crushed by the Romans in 146 B.C., rise from the Tunisian steppes like a mouthful of bad teeth. It was from here that North Africa's Three-H Club—Hamilcar, Hasdrubal and Hannibal—invaded Europe and challenged the Roman Empire in the Punic Wars. Hulking over the few bleak tombs that still stand is El Djem, a coliseum almost as massive as the one in Rome. Few monuments better embody humanity's inhumanity. Over two centuries, El Djem provided an enormous venue for satisfying the Roman appetite for gory spectacle. From dawn until after nightfall, fatal encounters between men and men, men and beasts, and beasts and beasts were staged in this arena, whose wooden floor was covered with sand that soaked up the blood spilled in combat.

That floor is now collapsed, exposing the narrow corridors below, where an intricate rope-and-pulley system hoisted gladiators, condemned prisoners and wild animals to the surface. You can stand down there and gaze upward, much like the poor souls funneled through there once did, awaiting their fate. The extravagant butchery that was the gladiatorial games—snuff theater, if you will—seems like something out of Monty Python, a point not lost on Flying Circus alumnus Terry Jones, an Oxford don in history who cowrote and narrated a four-part series on the Crusades for the BBC and also did a documentary for the network on gladiators. While scouting locations for *Monty Python's Life of Brian* in 1978, Jones padded though El Djem's underground passageways in awed silence. "I shuddered with gleeful disgust," he recalls, "and tried to imagine how the fighters must have felt sprinting into the sunlight, surrounded by mobs baying for blood."

For seven centuries the Romans celebrated murder as public sport. "A gladiator fight was something between a modern bullfight and a prizefight," says Jones. "It was like bullfighting in

that the spectators appreciated the competitors' technique and applauded their skill and courage. It was like boxing in that you went to see people mashing each other into the ground. The games weren't decadent; they were an antidote to decadence. The Romans believed it was beneficial to watch people being slain—you learned how to meet death bravely. In the ancient city, where compassion was regarded as a moral defect, the savage killings weren't just good entertainment, but morally valuable."

The origins of the sport may lie in Etruscan slave fights, which were fought to the death to please the gods and to enhance the reputations of the slaves' owners. The Romans incorporated the tradition into their funeral ceremonies, beginning in 264 B.C. with that of Junius Brutus Pera's. Gradually, the spectacles became more lurid and more frequent—and more necessary for each ruler to provide in order to retain power and sustain the goodwill of a mostly unemployed populace. Before long, just about every Roman city had its own amphitheater. The most majestic, the Colosseum, held 50,000 spectators and offered every sort of diversion from circus acts to reenactments of historic naval battles on the flooded arena floor. Roman emperors spent vast sums on bread and circuses, entertaining the urban masses. Much like the dictators of today, emperors well understood the benefits of athletic triumphs, in propaganda and as a distraction from misery at home. The games that commemorated the emperor Trajan's victories on the Dacian frontier in 107 A.D. featured 10,000 gladiators and lasted 123 days.

Being a gladiator was a job first thought fit only for slaves, convicts or prisoners of war. But under the Republic, many freeborn citizens became gladiators, seeking a kind of macabre glamour. Under the Empire, noblemen, emperors and even women fought. As the games became more popular, criminals were sometimes remanded to gladiator schools. "In general, a sentence to the schools meant three years of training and combat in the arena followed by two years teaching in the schools," wrote Richard Watkins in *Gladiator*. Among the earliest training schools was the one near Capua from which Spartacus and 78 other gladiators made their historic escape in 73 B.C. Eluding the Roman garrison, they stole weapons, pillaged estates and freed thousands of slaves. Within a year, the bandit and his guerrilla band of 90,000 engaged the Roman legions in the Revolt of Spartacus, one of history's more forlorn campaigns. Emboldened by victories all over Southern Italy, the gladiators took on the main body of the Roman army. Its commander, Marcus Licinius Crassus, routed the rebels and cut Spartacus to pieces, celebrating his triumphal return by crucifying 6,000 of his captives along the Appian Way.

Most of the schools were run by "stable masters" who either bought and maintained gladiators for rental, or trained them for other owners. These overseers were called lanistae, which derives from the Etruscan word for butcher. Ranked and housed on the basis of experience, the four grades of trainees honed their swordmanship on straw men or fencing posts. Instructors taught them conditioning, toughness and the proper postures to assume when falling and dying. They were well-fed (barley porridge was the andro of its day) and pampered with massages and baths. In Rome, however, gladiator schools were in imperial hands. Gladiators owned by Caligula, the Empire's quintessential mad despot, supposedly trained themselves not to blink. The emperor sometimes sparred with them. "To be his partner might prove a dubious honour," wrote Anthony Barrett in *Caligula*. "It is said that when practising with a gladiator from the training school [who was armed] with [a] wooden sword, Caligula ran his partner through with a real one." (Caligula lived out every modern team owner's dream: He once ordered an entire section of gladiator fans thrown to the beasts for laughing at him.)

Every gladiator was a specialist: Spartacus was a Thracian, a class named for and outfitted in the equipment of one of Rome's vanquished enemies. Armored in shin guards and a crested helmet, and armed with a small, round shield and a dagger curved like a scythe, Thracians were generally matched against the mirmillones, who protected themselves with short Gallic swords, large oblong shields and fish-crowned helmets. The heavily armored secutor was often pitted against the practically bare-skinned retiarius, whose strategy was to entangle his opponent in a net and spear his legs with a trident. Then there were the lance-brandishing andabatae, believed to have fought on horseback in closed visors that left them more or less blind; the two-knife wielding dimachaeri; the lasso-twirling laqueari; the chariot-riding essedarii; and the befeathered Samnites, who lugged large, rectangular shields and a straight sword called a gladius, from which the word gladiator comes.

Not all gladiators were eager participants. "In Caligula's day," says Jones, "a dozen gladiators decided not to fight. They laid down their arms, figuring the emperor wouldn't want to waste 12 gladiators. It didn't work. Caligula was so infuriated by this early trade union thing that he ordered them all to be killed. Whereupon one of them jumped up, grabbed a weapon and slew all his unarmed ex-colleagues. Then Caligula stood up and said a very strange thing: 'I've never seen anything so cruel.'"

Cruelty, of course, was the sine qua non of the gladiatorial games. During a typical day out at the amphitheater, you could expect men stalking and killing beasts in the morning, execution of convicts at midday, gladiator bouts in the afternoon. The brutal truths: Mankind trumps the wild, law punishes criminality, valor vanquishes death. "The arena was . . . a symbol of the ordered world, the cosmos," Thomas Wiedemann wrote in *Emperors and Gladiators*. "It was a place where the civilized world confronted lawless nature."

Morning sessions at the Colosseum were devoted to anti-social Darwinism. In venationes, wild game was hunted amid elaborate scenery depicting, say, mountains or glades; in bestiarii, ferocious predators faced off in bizarre combinations: bears against lions, lions against leopards, leopards against crocodiles. The scale of the slaughter could be staggering. A venatio put on by Pompey in 55 B.C. included the slaughter of 20 elephants, 600 lions, 410 leopards, numerous apes and Rome's first rhinoceros. At a hunt held by Augustus, the score was 49.0 leopards, dozens of elephants, and as many as 400 bears and 300 lions—a total later matched by Nero. Roughly nine thousand animal carcasses were dragged out of the Colosseum during the opening ceremonies in 80 A.D.; 11,000 more over Trajan's four-month shindig. The Romans were so efficient at keeping their arenas stocked that entire animal populations were wiped out: Elephants disappeared from Libya, lions from Mesopotamia and hippos from Nubia. "All sorts of exotic animals were trapped in African deserts and the forests of India," Jones says. "Fans must have sat in the stands thinking, 'Ooh, what's that? I've never seen one of them before.' A lot of ostriches would come out and the hunters would chase them around a bit, and then you'd get some tigers. 'Ooh, tigers! They're interesting!' Then the tigers would be set on the ostriches. It was kind of a zoo in action."

Around noon, in an Empirical version of a halftime show, it was mankind's turn to be massacred. While spectators snacked on fried chickpeas and were misted with perfume to mask the stench of carnage, pairs of meridiani—arsonists, murderers, Christians—were sometimes subjected to what the philosopher Seneca called "sheer murder . . . , a round-robin of death." One prisoner was handed a sword and ordered to kill the other. His job complete, he was disarmed and killed by the next armed captive. This went on until the last prisoner was whacked by an arena guard. Chariots were then wheeled out beating men and women chained to posts. At a signal, trapdoors opened and leopards sprang out. In Rome, Christians really were fed to the lions. And leopards.

Still, the highlight of most games was professional gladiatorial combat. The show opened with a procession heralded by trumpets. Dressed in purple and gold cloaks, gladiators circled the arena on foot, shadowed by slaves bearing their weapons. When the combatants reached the royal box, they supposedly thrust their right arms forward and shouted, "Ave, Imperator, morituri te salutant!" (Hail, Emperor, those who are about to die salute thee!)

Supposedly, because much of what we think we know about the games is in dispute, or evolved from Hollywood sword 'n' sandal sagas. No one is quite sure if "thumbs down" meant death and "thumbs up" a reprieve. Some scholars believe spectators would turn their thumbs toward their chests as a sign for the winner to stab the loser and that those in favor of mercy turned their thumbs down as a sign for the winner to drop his sword. Which would mean the best review a fallen fighter could hope for was "one enthusiastic thumb down."

After the procession and their salutation to the emperor, weapons were tested for sharpness and combatants paired off by lot. A typical show featured between 10 and 20 bouts, each lasting about 15 minutes. A horn was blown and timid fighters were prodded into the arena with whips and red-hot brands. Each fight was supervised by two referees. Coaches stood nearby, lashing reluctant fighters with leather straps. Just like at the ballpark, the house organist would rally the betting crowd. Cries of "Verbera!" (Strike!), "Iugula!" (Slay!) and "Habet!" (That's got him!) swept the stadium. If a Roman fan yelled "Kill the umpire!" he really meant it. The first gladiator to draw blood or knock his opponent down was the victor. A beaten gladiator could appeal for clemency by casting aside his weapon and raising his left hand. His fate was left to the spectators, those early Roger Eberts. The prevailing notion that most gladiators dueled to the death is no more likely than the idea that most died in the arena. Only about one in 10 bouts were lethal, and many of those fatalities can be blamed on overzealousness. "Gladiators were very, very expensive characters," says Jones. "It cost a great deal to keep them fed and exercised and comfortable. Unless you were Caesar and wanted to impress somebody, you tended not to squander them."

When a gladiator was mortally wounded, an attendant costumed as Charon, the mythical ferryman of the River Styx, finished the job (in a pure Pythonian moment) by smashing his skull with a mallet. After the body was carried off on a stretcher, sand was raked over the bloodstained ground to ready it for the next bout. The festivities ended at sunset, although sometimes, as under Emperor Domitian (81–96 A.D.), contests were held by torchlight—night games.

Victors became instant heroes. They were crowned with a laurel wreath and given gold. Those who survived their term of service were awarded a rudis, the wooden sword signifying honorable discharge. Some so liked the gladiator life that they signed on for another tour. The Pompeiian fighter Flamma had four rudii in his trophy ease.

Gladiator sweat was considered such an aphrodisiac that it was used in the facial creams of Roman women, and top gladiators were folk heroes with nicknames, fan clubs and adoring groupies. "We think they were sex symbols," says Jones. "A piece of ancient graffito was found at the gladiatorial barracks in Rome that read SO-AND-SO MAKES THE GIRLS PANT." Gladiators were making Roman girls weakkneed until the early fourth century A.D. Christian emperor Constantine abolished the games in 325, but without much conviction, or success. In 404, the emperor Honorius banned them again after a Christian monk tried to separate two gladiators and was torn limb from limb by the angry crowd. Despite Honorius' decree, the combat may have continued for another 100 years. "The sad truth is that the Christians of Rome became good Romans and staged their own gladiatorial contests," says Jones. "Popes even hired gladiators as bodyguards. The Christians are given far too much credit—they have a lot to answer for, like being responsible for the Dark Ages."

It was the barbarian invaders who shut down the sport for good. "Whenever Goths and Vandals moved into a Roman city, the games stopped," Jones says. "The barbarians disapproved of them and found them too disgusting." And, we assume, too barbaric.

Critical Thinking

1. How was a gladiator fight like bullfighting and boxing?
2. In these ways, did it resemble the author's phrase—"Snuff Theater"?
3. What does it mean to say, "The arena was . . . a symbol of the ordered world, the cosmos"?
4. Why do you think professional gladiators were "instant heroes"? Do you agree that they were sport's first superstars?

Create Central

www.mhhe.com/createcentral

Internet References

Illustrated History of the Roman Empire
www.roman-empire.net

Article

Prepared by: Joseph R. Mitchell, *Howard Community College*
and Helen Buss Mitchell, *Howard Community College*

Apocalypse: The Great Jewish Revolt against Rome, 66–73 CE

Neil Faulkner sees the destruction of Jerusalem and fall of Masada in the 1st century as the result of a millenarian movement that sought to escape the injustices of an evil empire.

NEIL FAULKNER

Learning Outcomes

After reading this article, you will be able to:

- Discuss what Masada symbolizes for modern Jews and to what extent its lessons can be applied to other peoples.

'This is the Masada of the Palestinians', an anonymous Israeli general is supposed to have said at the height of the battle for the Jenin refugee camp on the West Bank in April 2002. New recruits to the Israeli Defence Force regularly swear an oath of allegiance at the ancient fortress of Masada, which fell to the Romans in 73 or 74 CE, and conservative Jews pray at the Wailing Wall in Jerusalem for the reconstruction of the Temple destroyed in 70 CE. The conflict in the Middle East today is fought amid the echoes of another war 2,000 years ago, in which an overwhelming military force destroyed a people's aspiration to national self-determination.

Palestine—by which I mean the southern Levant, today comprising Israel, the Occupied Territories and western Jordan—is one of the bloodiest places on earth. In antiquity, it lay on one of history's great route-ways. Caravans laden with eastern exotica destined for the Mediterranean market passed through. Waves of nomadic refugees from the desert—including the ancient Hebrews around the twelfth century BCE—were periodically washed up in 'the Land of Canaan'. And two great centres of early civilisation repeatedly met and clashed here: the Egypt of the Pharaohs and successive Mesopotamian empires ruled by Assyrians, Babylonians, Persians and others. Consequently, periods of political independence and national unity for the peoples who inhabited the region in ancient times tended to be brief. Palestine was too much a prey to periodic bouts of imperial conquest ever to remain in local hands for long.

By the first century CE, Rome was the dominant power in the Levant. The nineteenth-century view of Rome as a fount of civilisation and culture is still held in many quarters. Even though historians of latter-day monstrosities—like Hitler's Germany or Stalin's Russia—are not persuaded of their subjects' virtue by architectural monuments, Rome's roads, aqueducts and hypocausts are sometimes allowed to turn an equally monstrous system of exploitation and violence—the Roman Empire—into a model of human achievement and an object of admiration. But 'The Grandeur That Was Rome'—the towns, villas and monumental architecture, the mosaics, frescoes and sculpture, the leisured aristocratic class that enjoyed these things—was made possible only by creaming off agricultural surpluses from thousands of villages across the empire. A Jewish peasant in Palestine in the first century—after the region had been incorporated into the Roman Empire as the province of Judaea in 6 CE—would have experienced the world of Rome not as 'civilisation' but as so many parasites—the tax-gatherer, the landlord, the priest, the debt-collector, the soldier—coming to steal the fruits of his hard labour on a tiny hillside plot.

By the middle of the first century of the Common Era, society in Palestine was deeply divided. On one side stood the ordinary people, most of them Jews, living in the countryside; on the other the Romans, Greeks and the Jewish upper classes. The Romans were few in number but their authority was upheld by the power of the Imperial army. There were just a hundred or so army officers and civil servants on the staff of the procurator of Judaea and perhaps two or three thousand Roman soldiers, but there were more than ten times that number in nearby Syria, a few days' march to the north. Rome, in any case, had many friends among the population of Palestine. There were the Greeks, who occupied numerous cities on the coast and in Transjordan, forming a series of privileged urban enclaves surrounded by the mainly Jewish countryside. These cities were ruled by oligarchs who enjoyed the backing of the Roman authorities. The general population of artisans, petty traders and small farmers had a colonial mentality, jealously guarding the privileges of Greek citizenship, and capable of occasional outbursts of murderous antisemitism. The Jewish upper classes were also predominantly pro-Roman. Some were of royal blood, descendants of the old Hasmonaean kings (164–37 BCE), or of Herod the Great, the puppet king of Judea (37–4 BCE); and the latter's great-grandson, King Herod Agrippa II (50–93 CE) still ruled a string of territories on the borders of the Roman province. Others were members of the Jerusalem-based aristocracy of priests, who controlled both the Temple, supreme focus of Jewish devotion, and the Sanhedrin, a grand council which combined the roles of senate, high court and holy inquisition. The Romans looked to the high priests and the Sanhedrin for help in governing Judaea; and the Jewish elite, who were essentially big landowners living off rents, tithes and the interest on peasant debt, looked to the Romans for the protection of property and rank.

The other Palestine was the world of farms, villages and the eternal routines of life on the land. Usually we know next to nothing of such worlds. How much can we say, for example, about the peasants of eastern Britain in 61 CE, at the time of the Boudiccan Revolt? Palestine is a special case because we have several sources for the life of the people and we can therefore attempt a 'history from below' which puts the Jewish Revolt of 66–73 CE into context.

Our principal sources for the period are the works of Josephus (b. c. 37 CE), a Jewish priest and aristocrat who, as governor of Galilee, became one of the moderate leaders of the revolt in late 66. Defeated and captured some six months later by the Roman general Flavius Vespasian, Josephus was spared execution and eventually freed, becoming an interpreter and go-between in the service of his country's enemies. After the war he was well received in Rome, where his conqueror, now the emperor Vespasian, rewarded him richly for his treachery with citizenship, a grant of property and the continuing patronage of the Flavian family. Taking the name Flavius Josephus in honour of his patron, Josephus became, in effect, a court historian and propagandist for the new Flavian dynasty.

His first work, *The Jewish War*, provides a narrative outline of the political background to 66 CE and a detailed military history of the war itself. Further detail is provided in the much longer *Jewish Antiquities,* a complete history of the Jews from Adam up to the outbreak of the revolt, and *My Life,* a tendentious autobiographical essay, which deals with aspects of the author's controversial governorship of Galilee in 67. In these works Josephus describes a society in turmoil. His pages are filled with descriptions of rural bandits, sectarian radicals, urban terrorists and would-be messiahs; of riots, pogroms and communal violence; and of clashes between troops and demonstrators. He charts the mounting popular resistance, which, by the early 60s CE, had led to a breakdown in government authority.

Josephus, however, was an aristocrat and a traitor, a man blinded by class prejudice and with a new political allegiance by the time he came to write about the Jewish revolutionary movement. To him the popular leaders were simply deceivers, brigands and tyrants, their followers the victims of self-serving malice and moral depravity. He offers little sociological insight into what was, in fact, one of the most powerful anti-imperialist movements in antiquity.

Fortunately, there are other sources, and in these we seem to hear the authentic voice of revolution some 2,000 years ago. The Dead Sea Scrolls are one such source. Some 400 separate documents— complete or in fragments—have survived, mainly in the form of leather scrolls which were wrapped in linen bindings, stuffed into ceramic jars and hidden in caves around the Essene monastery at Qumran near the Dead Sea, probably to keep them safe from the Romans. They reveal the Essenes to have been a radical Jewish sect committed to the revolutionary overthrow of the Romans and their upper-class Jewish allies. The Essene vision of liberation revolved around the ancient biblical idea of the Apocalypse, imagined to be a cataclysmic period of disaster and conflict at 'the End of Days', and culminating in the intervention of heavenly armies to reinforce 'the Sons of Righteousness' in their struggle against 'the Sons of Darkness' and 'the Hordes of Belial'. The anticipated outcome was victory for God's holy forces, a cleansing of the world of its corruption, and the beginning of 'the Rule of the Saints' and 'the Kingdom of Heaven on Earth'.

Political movements with similar objectives are known from later historical periods. In his study of medieval Europe *The Pursuit of the Millennium* (1957), Norman Cohn defined a millenarian group as one which viewed salvation as something collective not personal, earth-bound not heavenly, imminent not distant in time, all-embracing not limited in scope, and involving supernatural intervention not just human action. Christopher Hill showed in *The World Turned Upside Down* (1972) that similar ideas (derived from the New Testament Apocalypse of St. John) guided the actions of some of the most radical participants in the English Revolution; and more recently, millenarianism of one form or another has sometimes been a feature of resistance to European imperialism by traditional societies. It is in the context of both the Dead Sea Scrolls and a rich body of comparative historiography, therefore, that we must interpret the turbulent society described so unsympathetically by Josephus.

Jewish tradition held that a 'messiah', or prophet-king for the end of time, would herald the coming Apocalypse and give leadership to God's people in the final battles. Josephus reported several would-be messiahs in the course of the first century, each associated with an abortive millenarian flare-up, usually involving a procession through the Wilderness, a fevered searching for signs, and an eventual bloody clash with the forces of authority. Millenarian movements require a charismatic leader to bind together disparate, unconnected people, and, by convincing them of the imminence of the Apocalypse, turn them into a revolutionary force. But the result is something highly unstable: the movement must either go forward in line with expectation, or it collapses in disappointment. So, for example, when his movement reached critical mass, Jesus— one of the several putative messiahs of his day—went to Jerusalem as prophecy required that he should, and his followers began their apocalyptic purge of the wicked, provoking the inevitable—and in this case effective—state repression.

The revolutionary message of sectarian radicals and messiahs was addressed, above all, to the poor. Josephus was explicit about the class basis of the conflict: it was, for him, a struggle between *dunatoi*—men of rank and power, the property-owning upper classes—and *stasiastai*— subversives, revolutionaries, popular leaders whose appeal was to 'the scum of the districts'. The Dead Sea Scrolls were equally explicit, though from the other side of the barricades: whereas 'the princes of Judah . . . wallowed in the ways of whoredom and wicked wealth' and 'acted arrogantly for the sake of riches and gain', the Lord would in due time deliver them 'into the hands of the poor', so as to 'humble the mighty of the peoples by the hand of those bent to the dust', and bring them 'the reward of the wicked'. Jesus, too, for whom the poor were 'the salt of the earth', had little patience with the rich:

> Beware of the scribes, who like to walk around in long robes; and to be greeted with respect in the market places, and to have the best seats in the synagogues and places of honour at banquets.

Many men had already taken the message to heart and were in revolt by the early 60s CE. Bandits were operating in much of the countryside—'social bandits' in the sense defined by Eric Hobsbawm: men whom poverty and oppression had driven to live outside the law, but who retained links with their villages, preyed only on the better-off, and were regarded by the peasants as champions of the poor. Others had become revolutionary activists—Zealots—and some of these, the *sicarii* or daggermen, were organised in underground cells to carry out selective assassinations of leading public figures. But those in the active resistance—whether millenarian radicals, social bandits or urban terrorists—were a minority, and they could not hope to defeat the Roman occupation forces without a full-scale peasant revolt. In the villages, though, they found a ready audience.

Peasant plots were commonly half or a third the size needed to support a family, and were burdened with rent, debt, tax and tithe. Many peasants must have handed over half or more of their harvest. Those who took it were from the city, rich absentee lords, people who built mansions and monuments there, who aped the manners of pagans, fawned on foreign masters, and scorned God, the Law and the Prophets. Or so it must have seemed in the villages, where men would gather in the synagogue on the Sabbath to hear itinerant preachers and debate the meaning of scripture. There was a dark mood here in the early 60s CE. Scripture, after all, gave no sanction to great estates which made a few men rich and left many with nothing. On the contrary, the peasant found enshrined in scripture ancient tribal practice designed to keep things equal. Had not the land originally been a gift of God to the Israelites—not Greeks or Romans—to be distributed in small plots for the subsistence of all? Were not debts to be cancelled and bondsmen set free every seventh year? Was not every fiftieth year intended as a Year of Jubilee, when land would be redistributed and freed of burdens? Jesus had certainly thought so. He once said, quoting from *Isaiah:*

> The Spirit of the Lord is upon me, because he has anointed me to bring good news to the poor. He has sent me to proclaim release to the captives and recovery of sight to the blind, to let the oppressed go free, to proclaim the year of the Lord's favour.

The popular movement of 66 CE amounted to a fusion of Apocalypse and Jubilee, the radical minority's vision of a revolutionary war to destroy corruption having become inextricably linked with the peasant majority's traditional aspiration for land redistribution and the removal of burdens. This was the potent mixture which exploded in an urban insurrection in Jerusalem in May 66.

The catalyst was the Roman procurator's demand for 100,000 *denarii* from the Temple treasury, probably to make up a shortfall in revenues caused by a tax strike. To enforce this demand, troops were sent into Jerusalem to disperse demonstrators, resulting in a massacre. The whole city then erupted in a fierce street battle and drove the Romans out. Jewish conservatives spent the summer attempting to restore order, first by persuasion and political manoeuvre, subsequently in an armed counterrevolution spearheaded by King Herod Agrippa's troops. With their failure, the stage was set for a full-scale invasion by the Roman army from Syria.

The revolt might have got no further. Cestius Gallus marched his army of 30,000 men all the way from Antioch to the borders of Judaea, and then inland to Jerusalem, leaving the land behind him laid waste by fire and the sword. But the Jews had mainly kept away, retreating into the hills, allowing the enemy to pass by, and watching in anger as their farms were burned. Now they came back in their thousands, closing in on the Roman communications between Jerusalem and the coast, lightly equipped irregulars armed with slings and javelins, preparing to fight not in the Roman way, in the head-on collision of pitched battle, but in the Eastern way, in the manner of skirmishers and guerrillas. Gallus found that the peasants of Judaea had risen *en masse* to his rear, and he had no choice but to call off his attack on Jerusalem and beat a retreat to the coast. Thus was the scene set for the battle of Beth-Horon.

From November 4th to 8th, 66, as the Roman column trudged back through the hills north-west of Jerusalem, it was engulfed in a hail of shot from the slopes above. Every time the Romans counter-attacked, the Jewish light infantry scurried away to safety, easily out-distancing their enemies on such broken ground. And every time, as the Romans fell back on the column, the Jews returned to resume the barrage of javelins and slingshot. Gallus eventually got his army away in the night, but he left behind 6,000 dead and all of his artillery and baggage. It was the greatest Jewish victory for 200 years, and it sounded through the villages of Palestine like a clarion call to holy war. This, surely, was God's work, the beginning of the long-awaited End of Days, the inaugural event of the Rule of the Saints.

Beth-Horon transformed an urban insurrection into a national revolution. A provisional government of high-priestly aristocrats was set up in Jerusalem; military governors were appointed to different parts of the country; coins were issued with the inscriptions 'Shekel of Israel', 'Holy Jerusalem' and 'Year One' (of the liberation, that is); and there were attempts to raise an army to defend the territory of the new Jewish proto-state. But the real strength of the revolutionary movement lay elsewhere, in the plethora of independent armed militias which now sprang up across the country. Some were established groups of bandits or terrorists, which now swelled into large guerrilla units. Others were newly formed, perhaps on the initiative of local radicals, a charismatic leader, or a would-be messiah. They varied greatly in size and readiness for war, their membership tended to fluctuate over time, and they formed unstable and shifting alliances with other groups. The government was keen either to incorporate the militias into the regular army or, where they proved unruly, to suppress them. The militias—despite the offer of government pay—generally remained aloof, reluctant to surrender their independence, and the relationship between the two parties quickly soured. The roots of this conflict were deep, and it would culminate in the revolutionary overthrow of the aristocratic regime and its replacement by a government of militia leaders in the winter of 67-68.

This revolution within a revolution has been much misunderstood, thanks largely to the almost complete absence of sociological insight in Josephus' account. The aristocratic regime had been looking in two directions. It wanted to win a strong bargaining position on the battlefield and then to negotiate peace with the Romans, perhaps involving the re-establishment of a Jewish-ruled puppet kingdom of the kind that had existed before 6 CE and briefly again in 41-44 (when the Emperor Claudius had experimented with Herodian restoration). In this way, order and the security of property could be quickly restored. For the government was also embroiled in a conflict with the militias, many of whose members were actively working for the Apocalypse and the Jubilee. Yet it was precisely the radical enthusiasm of the militias —men who believed that they were engaged in a holy war to build heaven on earth—that gave the revolution its strength. The peasant-soldiers were fighting not for kings and high priests, but for God, the overthrow of the corrupt, and for the right to land. To crush these hopes would be to kill the spirit of revolt. At root, the struggle between aristocratic *dunatoi* and popular *stasiastai*—which Josephus describes— was a struggle between those who would halt the revolution to defend property and those who favoured a 'Jacobin' policy of 'public safety', one prepared to sacrifice the interests of the rich to advance the common cause.

The fate of the aristocratic government was sealed by its defeats in 67, above all in Galilee, when Vespasian's massive army of invasion, perhaps 60,000 strong, captured a string of Jewish strongholds, including the lynchpin fortress of Jotapata, which had held out for a month under the leadership of Josephus himself. Many of the defeated were killed or enslaved, and many more slunk away; but some thousands headed for Jerusalem, determined both to settle accounts with treacherous leaders and to continue the fight in defence of the holy city. The Roman siege of Jerusalem was delayed for another two years after the radical seizure of power, however, since Rome was at war with itself over the Imperial succession in 68-69. The victor was Vespasian, so when the Romans finally came for Jerusalem, they were led by his son Titus, to whom fell the task of defeating 25,000 veteran fighters defending some of the strongest fortifications in the world.

The attackers built ramps, employed battering rams to knock down walls, and mounted massed armoured assaults through the breaches. The defenders hurled missiles from the battlements, sallied forth to burn ramps and engines, and rushed to fill the breaches and throw back the enemy's assaults. The struggle descended into an abyss of horror: men fought each other with bitter savagery; hundreds of prisoners were crucified on the hills around the city; the bodies of famine victims were tossed over the walls to rot in the sun; and as the Romans broke into the city there was mayhem and massacre. The siege was a collision of two worlds: on one side, the military imperialism of Rome guarding the power and property of the rich; on the other, the rage of land-starved peasants from whom the wealth to build 'civilisation' was stolen. There was no middle way, no possibility of compromise, and the collision of these worlds was fought with primal ferocity. The siege culminated in a three-month struggle for control of the Temple Mount, ending when, in mid-August 70, as fighting raged on the great concourse all around it, the Temple itself caught fire. In the confusion, Roman troops burst through the gates, and once inside the complex they cut down everyone they caught and looted the vast treasures stored there. Even then, resistance continued for another month in the Upper City, the remaining militiamen opting to fight on rather than surrender themselves and face a life of slavery.

The liquidation of the 'Jewish Commune' was followed by a relentless campaign to exterminate the Zealot bacillus in the province. The network of cisterns and sewers beneath Jerusalem were combed for fugitives. Some who escaped were eventually run down and destroyed as far away as Egypt and Libya. Several years of counter-insurgency drives destroyed the remaining guerrilla bases in the deserts of southern Palestine, culminating in the siege and capture of Masada in 73. Perched on a rock surrounded by cliffs in the depths of the desert, a community of 960 men, women and children had maintained their 'alternative lifestyle' for six or seven years, while the young warriors formed a guerrilla band that continued to fight for national and social liberation after all others had been defeated. Finally, though, the Romans came for them, 15,000 strong, building an impenetrable siege wall to cage the Zealots in, and then a huge siege ramp from which to bring their engines and assault troops into action. Once the walls were breached, neither victory nor flight was possible for the defenders. But when the Romans stormed the fortress, they faced no resistance and were confronted by an eerie emptiness. In a final, chilling act of revolutionary defiance, the Zealots had cheated their conquerors of the fruits of victory by destroying their possessions and committing mass suicide.

So Masada has become some sort of symbol. For some, a symbol of Israel, a nationalist icon in the predatory wars of the present; but for others—and the anonymous Israeli general at Jenin had a sense of this— it is a symbol of the oppressed fighting back, whether they be Jewish, or Arab, or anyone else, against the evils of a world dominated by greed and war.

For Further Reading

Josephus, *The Jewish War* (trans. G.A. Williamson, Penguin, 1959); G. Vermes, *The Complete Dead Sea Scrolls in English* (Penguin, 1998); J. Campbell, *Deciphering the Dead Sea Scrolls* (Fontana, 1996); H. Maccoby, *Revolution in Judaea: Jesus and the Jewish Resistance* (Ocean, 1973); I. Wilson, *Jesus: the evidence* (Pan, 1985); M. Grant, *The Jews in the Roman World* (Phoenix, 1999); P. Richardson, *Herod, King of the Jews and Friend of the Romans* (T & T Clark, 1999); Y. Yadin, *Masada, Herod's Fortress and the Zealots' Last Stand* (Weidenfeld & Nicolson, 1966).

Critical Thinking

1. Contrast the views of this time period provided by Flavius Josephus and by the Dead Sea Scrolls.

2. What does the author mean when he writes: "The popular movement of 66 CE amounted to a fusion of apocalypse and jubilee . . . which exploded in an urban insurrection in Jerusalem in May 66"?

3. In the final siege of Masada, how was it that "the Zealots had cheated their conquerors of the fruits of victory. . ."?

Create Central

www.mhhe.com/createcentral

Internet References

Masada: Desert Fortress Overlooking the Dead Sea
www.jewishvirtuallibrary.org/jsource/Archaeology/Masada1.html

Article   Prepared by: Joseph R. Mitchell, *Howard Community College*
and Helen Buss Mitchell, *Howard Community College*

The End of the Roman Empire
Did It Collapse or Was It Transformed?

BRYAN WARD-PERKINS

Learning Outcomes

After reading this article, you will be able to:

- Discuss evidence both for the fall of Rome and for its transformation.

It used to be unquestioned that the Roman empire in the West fell to violent and bloody invasion that resulted in the death of a civilization, and the start of a 'dark age', from which it would take Europe centuries to recover. Recent scholarship, however, has tended to downplay the violence, and to challenge a concept of post-Roman cultural decline. New orthodoxies are emerging: that the barbarians were peacefully 'accommodated' into the empire to serve as its defenders; and that Roman culture was quietly 'transformed' into a new guise.

In the late 1970s I worked with a team of archaeologists on the site of Luna, a Roman city in northern Italy, on the coast about halfway between Pisa and Genoa. Ancient Luna, like hundreds of other towns across the empire, enjoyed the full range of Roman urban amenities: bath-buildings with piped water; paved roads with a drainage and sewerage system beneath them; a theatre and amphitheatre; a number of imposing temples; a full complement of civic buildings including a marble-paved forum square and a basilica for commercial and political transactions; and some splendid private houses, decorated in fresco, mosaic and marble. In the searing heat of July, one of the Roman houses was particularly attractive—its main reception rooms had floors of cool marble, and opened out onto a shaded courtyard, with raised flower beds and a fountain playing at its centre. The prosperity of the city was also attested by a remarkable range of high-quality and eminently functional domestic articles. For instance, third- and fourth-century citizens were eating off glossy plates and bowls from North Africa, and even cooking in casseroles from the same region. These vessels are found in large quantities, and were clearly very widely available. Like other Roman towns, Luna's prosperity depended partly on a flourishing local agriculture, and partly on more specialized production and trade, in its case the extraction and export of the white marble now known as Carrara marble—much of imperial Rome was built in this stone.

My own interest, however, was in the history of the city in the period when the empire in the West disintegrated and disappeared. During the fifth century, Italy, after centuries of peace, faced invasion and devastation, first by armies of Goths (who sacked Rome itself in 410), and then by Vandals, raiding by sea from their north African base at the port of Carthage. The Mediterranean, which had been a peaceful commercial lake for five centuries, was contested between rival Germanic kingdoms, and became a place where raiders, as well as traders, operated. In the sixth century, Italy's troubles continued, with a long war for mastery between the Goths and the forces of the surviving east-Roman (or 'Byzantine') empire, with its capital in Constantinople. This war ended in Byzantine victory, but was followed, almost immediately, by the invasion of another Germanic people, the Lombards. The Lombards, however, failed to capture the whole of Italy, which became a divided and contested peninsula. Luna suffered directly from some of these upheavals—a large Gothic army passed through its territory in 412, and during the long Lombard-Byzantine wars it became an isolated outpost of Byzantine power, surrounded by Lombard territory. As a coastal city, it must have suffered badly from the slow decline of Mediterranean trade that has been charted by recent archaeology.

What we found had happened to the city in the fifth to seventh centuries was both striking and depressing. Sometime in the fourth or fifth centuries, the marble quarries, which were the source of much of Luna's wealth, were abandoned—and they remained closed for some 700 years thereafter. At roughly the same date, the monumental buildings of the city were progressively allowed to fall down, or were demolished, their decorative marble elements broken into pieces and used as building materials. The great basalt slabs of the Roman roadways were gradually covered over and lost under patchy gravel surfaces. The aqueduct was interrupted, piped water no longer reached the city, and its fountains fell silent, compelling the inhabitants to dig wells through the ancient monuments to the water-table beneath. The houses of the aristocracy decayed, and were buried under rubble—one of them became the site of a graveyard. Eventually, the town of Luna disappeared altogether.

The specific remains that we were excavating consisted of the scant traces of two simple wooden houses built in the sixth century A.D.—with post-holes, dry-stone footings for timber walls, and beaten earth floors. Each house was made up of two small rooms, one probably for humans, and the other for animals. These unprepossessing dwellings were built over the square of the Roman forum, the monumental heart of the ancient city. By the time they were built, all the Roman monumental buildings and shops of the forum had been abandoned and despoiled of their marble fittings, and the square itself was already covered in a deep layer of silt. These simple post-Roman houses, and the startling contrast that they presented with the imposing underlying Roman structures, seemed to point to a remarkable drop in economic and technological complexity, and in levels of material comfort. A city of mortared stone and marble, was replaced by a settlement of wood, thatch and beaten earth. Furthermore, good quality domestic goods and other indicators of sophistication and prosperity also totally disappeared: the sixth-century inhabitants of Luna, unlike their ancestors, hardly used coins at all, and almost the only pottery available to them were simple cooking-pots.

From working at Luna, and from visiting many other Roman cities with a similar history, I formed an unshakeable impression that the disappearance of the Roman world was a shattering, and negative, event in human history. But, in the very years that I was documenting this post-Roman collapse, scholars elsewhere were engineering the downfall of such conventional views. The seeds of this change had been planted in 1971, when Peter Brown published his World of Late Antiquity, a book which was to have a remarkable effect on how the end of the ancient world was viewed by historians. Brown defined and described a period, which he termed 'Late Antiquity', stretching from the third century to the eighth century A.D.; but he saw it as characterized not by the disappearance of Roman sophistication and civilization, but by lively and positive developments. Brown invited his readers to reject the old language of 'decline and fall' and to embrace instead a vision of this as a period when Roman culture was transformed and revitalized.

The spread and impact of Brown's new interpretation was slow but inexorable. He is a brilliant historian who writes beautiful prose, and he is a bewitching performer in a lecture or seminar. In the early 1970s, as an undergraduate in Oxford, I attended a course of his lectures in All Souls on early Egyptian monasticism, not because I understood much of what he was saying (I was studying later periods and his detailed arguments went way over my head), but because the way he talked, and his empathy with those tough old men of the Egyptian desert, were truly enthralling. Under his influence, the way that historians, and some archaeologists, describe the last centuries of the Western Empire and their immediate aftermath changed markedly. For instance, a massive recent research project into the fourth to eighth centuries, sponsored by the European Union, was entitled the 'Transformation of the Roman World'. The very title of this project rejects the notion of any abrupt break at the end of the Roman empire; the underlying vision is instead of a Roman World seamlessly 'transformed' into the Europe of Charlemagne. The many Germanic peoples who

entered the empire in the fifth and sixth centuries (Goths, Vandals, Franks, Burgundians, Sueves, Thuringians, Alamans, Lombards and others) are no longer seen as invaders who, wittingly or unwittingly, severely damaged the well-being of the Roman world, but as peaceful settlers in a world that continued much as before.

As a reinterpretation of the political and military history of the disintegration of the western empire, this is radical enough. But can the new upbeat thinking about the end of the Roman world be reconciled with the gloomy evidence of material collapse from Luna, and from hundreds of other similar sites across the ancient world? I think not, though efforts have been made by others to square this circle. For instance, some archaeologists have argued that one of the most striking changes at the end of the Roman period—the almost universal switch from solid stone and brick buildings, to much less permanent structures in perishable materials—was caused by cultural choice rather than economic necessity. They argue that it is possible to construct complex, sophisticated and highly decorated structures over the simple post-holes which are the only evidence we have for the buildings of post-Roman times; and that building in stone was merely a fashion—a way of expressing political and ideological allegiance to Rome—which was dropped when the empire disappeared. According to this way of thinking, the descendants and successors of the Roman aristocracy abandoned their villas, with their solid walls and floors, tiled roofs, bath-buildings, and under-floor heating, not because they were forced to, by a collapse in economic and technological sophistication, but because they actually preferred to live in wooden halls.

I find this deeply implausible: tiled roofs are, quite simply, much more durable, brick and stone floors far easier to keep clean, and stone walls more weatherproof, than their equivalents in perishable materials; and heating systems and hot baths are both effective and very pleasant indeed—much more so than a smoking open fire in the middle of a hall, and a bowl of lukewarm water. The evidence of buildings will, however, always remain controversial, because it is impossible in most cases to reconstruct with confidence, from the scant remains we find in the soil, what a post-Roman building was really like to live in. But if we look at domestic pottery, an inescapable picture emerges of technological and economic collapse at the end of the Roman period, leading to a dramatic regression in living standards. And there is little prospect of arguing it away in terms of ideological and cultural choice.

The Romans produced pottery vessels to high standards, in enormous quantities, and shipped them widely. As we have already seen, in third- and fourth-century Italy even a cooking-pot might often be imported from North Africa. Furthermore—and this is very important—good quality pottery, whether made in the region, or imported, was available at all levels of society. Fine tablewares, and imported amphorae for the storage and transport of liquids are discovered not just on the coast and in towns and rich villas, but also on inland sites and humble farmsteads.

Because pottery survives so well in the soil and because individual potsherds can be both dated and provenanced (reliably attributed to particular production sites), we know a remarkable amount about the trade in ancient pottery. We also know, from the objects themselves, that the vast majority of Roman pottery is of a quality not exceeded, in Europe, in terms of consistency and quality, before factory-made products became widely available in the eighteenth century. This judgement is based not on aesthetic considerations but on practical values. Roman pots are tough and hold liquids well; they are light and pleasant to handle; and they have smooth surfaces that are easy to clean. Furthermore, from the excavation of production sites we know a lot about the scale and levels of complexity involved in making some of the best-quality Roman wares. Excavators at a south Gaulish pottery, la Graufesenque near modern Millau, have found graffiti that record the stacking of great communal kilns, firing up to 30,000 vessels at a time. At the same site, a pit was discovered full of near-perfect vessels, discarded because they were not quite of a high enough quality; some of these pots had a hole punched through their base, in order to prevent them slipping into circulation—a remarkable testimony to Roman quality control.

Almost none of this sophistication survived into post-Roman times. In some provinces—particularly Britain—the regression was startling: even the potter's wheel, widespread in Roman times, wholly disappeared for over two hundred years. Pottery of the early Anglo-Saxon period, and also pottery of the same date from unconquered western Britain, is rare and poor in quality—of badly selected clay, hand-shaped, and fired on an open fire. The resulting vessels are porous and very friable—many would score low marks as first efforts in pottery at an infants' school. Elsewhere, the changes were slightly less dramatic and less sudden, but they were still very remarkable. On Mediterranean sites like Luna, the extraordinary and abundant range of tablewares available in Roman times became very rare in the fifth and sixth centuries, and eventually disappeared altogether; and kitchenwares, which were pretty much all that remained, became more or less restricted to a single bulbous design of pot. To explain these developments in terms of cultural change rather than of economic and technological regression, one has to work very hard indeed, perhaps imagining a culture with access to large numbers of metal vessels which replaced pottery but were all eventually recycled so they left no trace in the archaeological record!

If the archaeological evidence that points to a severe post-Roman regression cannot be squared with the historians' cheerful view of 'Late Antiquity', how has the latter come about? Partly, it is through the optimism of some archaeologists themselves, who explain all change in terms of altered cultural values. But largely it is because historians like Peter Brown examine entirely different aspects of the human condition, and therefore come to radically divergent impressions about the same periods of the past. The 'World of Late Antiquity' tends to be defined in spiritual and religious terms, as the period when Christianity became established and defined, and, slightly later, Islam emerged as the dominant religion of the southern Mediterranean. If we take these as the key things that happened in our period, then there is no problem in depicting the third to eighth centuries as a 'Golden Age' of continuous and positive development. It is certainly true that with the conversion of the Germanic kingdoms, and the eventual spread of Christianity into areas like Ireland and Scotland, far more souls were saved in these centuries than under the Roman empire.

I may be wrong to believe that the disintegration of a complex economy, and a consequent collapse of living standards mattered even more than momentous religious developments, and that they mark a decisive break in Western history—but I don't think I am. The changes that archaeologists have documented affected kings and peasants alike: palaces, as much as rural farmsteads, were far less impressive and comfortable in post-Roman times than they had been under the empire. These changes even affected God and his saints, currently the focus of much of the writing by historians on Late Antiquity. The cult of saints grew steadily through late Roman and post-Roman times, and was not slowed by the disintegration of the Roman world. But if we look at the size of the churches built for these saints, there is a dramatic shrinkage between late Roman and post-Roman times. In the fourth century, huge churches were built over the graves of the martyrs—Old St Peter's, for instance, erected by Constantine to honour Rome's premier bishop, was a massive five-aisled basilica about 100 metres long, with an atrium almost the same size again. However, by the seventh century, new churches in the West seldom exceeded 20 metres in length. Fortunately for the saints, many great churches of earlier times were still maintained—if they had had to rely on post-Roman builders, their living-conditions would have become very cramped indeed.

All the evidence suggests that most of the sophisticated features and creature-comforts that characterized Roman life, disappeared in the West in the fifth to seventh centuries, to such an extent that the change can accurately be seen as the 'end of a civilization'. Furthermore, the close coincidence of date between this collapse and the Germanic invasions of the fifth and sixth centuries suggests, beyond all reasonable doubt, that the change was caused by the disruption of war and the disintegration of the peaceful trading-world that was the Roman empire. Western Europe did eventually emerge out of the resulting slump, but it took perhaps a thousand years to regain the levels of economic activity and the high standards of living that had so impressed me in Roman Luna.

For Further Reading

Peter Brown, *The World of Late Antiquity: From Marcus Aurelius to Muhammad* (Thames and Hudson, 1971); Averil Cameron, *The Later Roman Empire,* A.D. 284–430 (Fontana, 1993) and *The Mediterranean World in Late Antiquity,* A.D. 395–600 (Routledge, 1993), Walter Goffart, Barbarians and Romans A.D. 418–584: *The Techniques of Accommodation* (Princeton University Press, 1980); J. H. W. G. Liebeschuetz, *The Decline and Fall of the Roman City* (Oxford University Press, 2001); Peter Heather, *The Fall of the Roman Empire* (Macmillan, 2005).

Critical Thinking

1. What were the findings of the research project, sponsored by the European Union, that led some historians to claim that the "Roman world seamlessly 'transformed' into the Europe of Charlemagne"?

2. As Bryan Ward-Perkins summarizes this transition, "Germanic peoples who entered the empire in the fifth and sixth centuries . . . are no longer seen as invaders who, wittingly or unwittingly, severely damaged the well-being of the Roman World, but as peaceful settlers in a world that continued much as before." What evidence does he find in Peter Brown's World of Late Antiquity (third to eighth century CE) to support this theory?

3. The "continuity" argument takes as its focus spiritual and religious developments. The "discontinuity" argument takes as its focus economic factors and living standards. Why does Bryan Ward-Perkins retain the "end of civilization" argument in the period of the fifth to seventh centuries in the West?

Create Central

www.mhhe.com/createcentral

Internet References

Illustrated History of the Roman Empire
   www.roman-empire.net

BRYAN WARD-PERKINS is Lecturer in Modern History and Fellow of Trinity College, Oxford. His book *The Fall of Rome and the End of Civilization* is published by Oxford University Press in June, 14.99 [pounds sterling].

Article

Prepared by: Joseph R. Mitchell, *Howard Community College*
and Helen Buss Mitchell, *Howard Community College*

Woman Power in the Maya World

CHRIS HARDMAN

Learning Outcomes

After reading this article, you will be able to:

- Determine what the excavation of the Maya city of Waka' reveals about its inhabitants and how these findings challenge previous assumptions about the Maya.

In Guatemala's Laguna del Tigre National Park, the dense forest hides many treasures: endangered scarlet macaws flit among the treetops, while rare jaguars hunt on the forest floor. Only recently has the world learned about one of Laguna del Tigre's greatest treasures, a 2,500-year-old city that once stood at the crossroads of the ancient Maya world. The archaeologists working on the site believe this city can answer many of the lingering questions about political events in the Petén region during the Classic Period of Maya history.

The ancient city of Waka'—known today as El Perú—first came to the attention of the modern world after oil prospectors stumbled upon it in the 1960s. Ten years later, Harvard researcher Ian Graham recorded the site's monuments, and then in 2003 two veteran archaeologists, David Freidel of Southern Methodist University (SMU) in Texas and Héctor Escobedo of the University of San Carlos in Guatemala, launched a full-scale excavation of the site.

According to the historical record, Waka' was inhabited as early as 500 BC. The city reached its political peak around 400 AD and was abandoned some four centuries later. In its heyday, Waka' was an economically and strategically important place with tens of thousands of inhabitants, four main plazas, hundreds of buildings, and impressive ceremonial centers. Researchers say the key to the city's importance was its location between two of the most powerful Maya capitals—Calakmul to the north and Tikal to the east—and that in its history Waka' switched its alliance back and forth between the two rivals. They suggest that the final choice of Calakmul may have led to the eventual demise of Waka' at the hands of a Tikal king.

"We know a great deal about the ancient inhabitants of this site from their monuments," Freidel writes in an article for *SMU Research*. "The more than 40 carved monuments, or stelae, at the site chronicle the activities of Waká's rulers, including their rise to power, their conquests in war, and their deaths." The location of Waka' right by the San Pedro Mártir River, which was navigable for 50 miles in both directions, gave it

great power as a trading center. In addition to the waterway, Freidel suggests that Waka' controlled a strategic north-south overland route that linked southern Campeche to central Petán. Freidel calls Waka' a "crossroads of conquerors in the pre-Columbian era."

One of the most intriguing people who inhabited Waka' was a woman of uncommon power and status. The discovery and excavation of her tomb in 2004 by team member José Ambrosio Díaz drew a lot of attention to the site. "We knew that we were dealing with a royal tomb right away because you could see greenstone everywhere," says David Lee, a PhD candidate at SMU who is investigating the Waka' palace complex. Greenstone is archaeologists' term for the sacred jade the ancient Maya used to signify royalty. The team found hundreds of artifacts in the tomb, which dates to sometime between 650 and 750 AD.

There were several indicators that this woman was important and powerful. Her tomb lay underneath a building on the main courtyard of the city's main palace. Her stone bed was surrounded by 23 offering vessels and hundreds of jade pieces, beads, and shell artifacts. Among the rubble, the researchers discovered a four- by two-inch jewel called a *huunal* that was worn only by kings and queens of the highest status. Typically a *huunal* was affixed to a wooden helmet called a *ko'haw* that was covered in jade plaques. Carved depictions suggest that only powerful war leaders wore these helmets. On the floor of the queen's tomb near her head, researchers found 44 square and rectangular jade plaques they believe were glued onto the wooden part of the *ko'haw*. The presence of this helmet in her tomb has led the researchers to the conclusion that this queen held a position of power not typically afforded women of the time. "She may have been more powerful than her husband, who was actually the king of El Peru," Lee concludes.

Although the presence of the helmet identifies her as a warlord, archaeologists have found no evidence of Maya women physically fighting in battles. What they have discovered are images of women as guardians of the tools of war. "The curation of the war helmet is one of the roles of royal women," says the excavation's bone expert, Jennifer Piehl. She explains that Maya iconography describes how royal women safeguarded these helmets and then presented them to their kings when they prepared for war. David Freidel says that to the Maya, war was more than just a physical act; it was also an encounter between supernaturally charged beings. Women had an active role in battle by conjuring up war gods and instilling sacred magical power in battle gear.

Other symbols of royalty were the stingray spines found in the pelvic regions of the queen's remains. Stingray spines are bloodletting implements that were used in ceremonies by Maya kings to drain blood from their genitalia. "The association between gender and power becomes blended because this person represents both kinds of power," explains Lee. "As we learn more, we are discovering that what our culture considers traditional ideas of male-female roles don't hold true for Maya royalty."

Researchers could also determine the importance of the woman by what was missing from her tomb. Some time after her burial, the tomb was opened up to remove her skull and femurs. "The cranium and crossed femurs is a very salient symbol in Maya ritual. It is the ancestor," says Piehl. The Maya would take the skull and femurs from an important ancestor and preserve them in bundles. Maya images show how these bundles were used during ceremonies or were worn on the back of the ruler's regalia. "They are literally carrying their ancestor around with them," says Lee. Researchers surmise that possession of a bundle gave legitimacy and power to the owners.

Once her status as a queen was confirmed, the question became, which queen was she? A good candidate is a woman named Lady K'abel who lived during the Late Classic period and was the daughter of the King Yuknoom Yich'aak K'ak' of Calakmul. Researchers interpret her marriage to King K'inich B'ahlan II of Waka' as a savvy political move for Calakmul, because a royal marriage could forge a permanent political bond between the two cities. Unfortunately the union would not prove to be a good political move for Waka'. Researchers suggest that it was considered an act of betrayal by Tikal, which eventually defeated Waka' in 743 AD.

A detailed portrait of Lady K'abel comes from a stela dated to 692 AD that was looted from Waka' in the late 1960s. According to Maya expert and project epigrapher Stanley Guenter, inscriptions on the front face of the stela—curated by the Cleveland Museum of Art in Ohio—clearly identify the woman as Ix Kaloomte' (lady warlord) or Lady K'abel, princess of Calakmul. "Mosaic mask pectorals formed of greenstone, shell teeth and eye whites, and obsidian pupils found in the interment are consistent with the image of Lady K'abel on Stela 34," Lee and Piehl posit in a recent paper. "These attributes clearly demonstrate the royal status of the woman and an identification with Lady K'abel." Radiocarbon dating of the queen's remains will confirm whether the woman in the tomb lived during the same time period as Lady K'abel.

Another tomb, discovered by archaeologists Michelle Rich and Jennifer Piehl in 2005, tells the story of two women from an earlier part of Waka's history, dating back to between 350 and 400 AD. The tomb contains the remains of two women between 25 and 35 years old, placed back to back, one on top of the other, with stingray spines near their groins. The bottom woman, who was pregnant, lay face down and the top woman face up. Although the tomb is tiny by royal standards—some 3 feet wide, 4 feet high and 6.5 feet long—Rich and Piehl believe that these women were high-ranking members of a royal family.

By analyzing their skeletal remains, archaeologist and osteologist Jennifer Piehl can tell a great deal about the status of these women in life. "What we can say of the bones of the two Waka' women is they were in excellent health—better than the majority of the Waka' population—which fits with them being royal," she says. In addition, the lack of dental cavities suggests that unlike ordinary Maya, these women were treated to special foods, including meat, fish, and fruit.

Further evidence of the elite status of these women comes from the seven ceramic vessels that accompanied them in death. "The first thing we saw was the cluster at [their] feet of three gorgeous, museum quality polychrome vessels," Piehl recalls. The quality of the vessels and the symbols of royalty on them indicate that the women came from a royal bloodline. Vessels of the exact stone style were also found at Tikal in a similar set of tombs containing members of a royal dynasty who were probably killed by the great fourth-century conqueror Siyaj K'ak' from Teotihuacan. According to the stone stelae from the main plazas of Waka', Siyaj K'ak' also visited that city in 378 AD on his way to conquer Tikal. "My conclusion is that these are members of the royal family that was in power before the arrival of Siyaj K'ak'," Piehl says. Freidel calls Siyaj K'ak's visit to Waka' the city's "first great experience as a crossroads of conquerors."

Rich suggests that the women were sacrificed as part of a lineage replacement, whereby one invading ruler comes in and kills the current royal family to establish his family as the only royal blood in the kingdom. "The king would have been the primary focus of sacrifice, but then the rest of the family would have to be exterminated in order to wipe out the entire ruling line," Rich says. To prove that hypothesis, the team is searching for a king from the same time period. In 2006, Héctor Escobedo and Juan Carlos Meléndez uncovered the tomb of a king under the site's main pyramid, but more research needs to be done to fully understand who that man was. Also in 2006, Rich and Varinia Mature found another ruler, but he dates to approximately 550–650, a couple of hundred years later than the women. "At this point we have two rulers and no connection to the sacrificed women," Rich says. "El Perú is a huge site, and there is so much we can learn."

Although the archaeologists involved with this project agree that further excavations of Waka' have the potential to fill in some of the gaps in the political history of the region, the future of the Waka' Archaeological Project is uncertain. Laguna del Tigre, where the Waka' archaeological site is located, is the largest nature reserve in Central America, covering some 118,600 acres of such biologically significant habitat that in 1990 it was the first site in Guatemala named to the List of Wetlands of International Importance under the Ramsar Convention on Wetlands. Despite its protected status, the forest of Laguna del Tigre is in danger due to illegal logging, slash-and-burn agriculture, and drug smuggling. Just as the forest is in peril, so is the city of Waka' and any other archaeological treasures hidden in the forest.

To ensure the protection of Waka' and the rainforest that surrounds it, Freidel developed partnerships with the government of Guatemala, the Wildlife Conservation Society, and the nongovernmental organization ProPetén to try and safeguard 230,000 acres of the forest. The group formed the K'ante'el Alliance, which means "precious forest" in Maya and refers to the mystical place where the Maya Maize God was said to be reborn and where the Maya believe their civilization began. The K'ante'el Alliance plans to protect the park by developing environmentally friendly sources of income for local communities that will celebrate the forest's resources instead of destroy them. The hope is that Waka' and Laguna del Tigre will continue to share their hidden treasures for years to come.

Critical Thinking

1. During its heyday, what accounted for Waka's economic and strategic importance?

2. What are the chief indicators that the woman buried in the royal tomb had great status and power?

3. How did the Maya ruins at this site reverse our current links between male gender and power?

Create Central

www.mhhe.com/createcentral

Internet References

Cracking the Maya Code
www.pbs.org/wgbh/nova/mayacode

CHRIS HARDMAN contributes regularly to *Américas* on archaeology, science, and conservation news.

Article

Prepared by: Joseph R. Mitchell, *Howard Community College*
and Helen Buss Mitchell, *Howard Community College*

Secrets of a Desert Metropolis
The Hidden Wonders of Petra's Ancient Engineers

Evan Hadingham

Learning Outcomes

After reading this article, you will be able to:

- Determine what evidence exists to support the claim that Petra was a thriving desert metropolis.

Today, Petra is a vast empty canyon encircled by astonishing tombs. Their magnificent facades, carved into sandstone cliffs, overlook a chaos of eroded ruins on the valley floor. Until recently, so little of the 2,000-year-old city had been explored that some scholars had branded Petra a "city of the dead" or a "tent city"—an occasional metropolis settled only seasonally by wandering peddlers and pilgrims.

Recent excavations reveal a very different city. The archaeo-logical jewel of Jordan was, in fact, a fabulously wealthy hub of merchants and traders known from Rome to China. Surrounded by a brutal desert, some 30,000 people thrived in a city that for centuries lavished precious water on public pools, baths, and fountains. Petra in its prime virtually ruled the incense trade.

The city's rulers enjoyed a reputation as canny diplomats and generals skilled in outwitting more powerful neighbors. By the first century A.D., the city boasted graceful temples, a broad avenue lined with shops, public gardens, and water brought through more than six kilometers (3.7 miles) of ceramic pipes. The canyon walls that encircled the city were crowded with more than 800 tombs that awe today's visitors as completely as they must have amazed travelers two millennia ago.

Archaeologists finally are discovering and fitting critical pieces into the abiding puzzles of Petra: How could scattered desert nomads have created so mighty a citadel? And what finally caused their prosperity to falter and their wondrous city to fade?

Investigations built on satellite imagery, aerial photography, and extensive ground surveys have banished old theories of Petra and its founders, who were known to the ancient world as Nabataeans.

Once visualized as little more than wandering, camel-borne traders, the Nabataeans are now known to have deliberately planted year-round settlements throughout the arid wilderness of southern Jordan and northern Saudi Arabia. In a region that tastes barely 10 centimeters (3.9 inches) of rain annually, these outposts were succored with the same ingeniously engineered water systems recently revealed at Petra.

And while the city's demise has been blamed on everything from the Romans to a series of devastating earthquakes, new evidence suggests a completely unexpected scenario for Petra's final centuries.

Nomadic Origins

History's first notice of the Nabataeans is in a fourth-century B.C. account by the Greek historian Hieronymus. He describes nomadic bands—wandering traders and herders of sheep and camels—who forbade the growing of grain or the construction of houses on pain of death. The archaeological picture of Nabataean origins remains obscure, although some argue their ancestors were pastoralists in the deserts of northeast Arabia.

The first Nabataean sites appear abruptly during the first century B.C. Within 100 years, they had exploded all over what is now southern Jordan and northern Saudi Arabia, including such hostile environments as the Negev and Hisma deserts.

Four centuries after Hieronymus, another Greek historian, Strabo, describes a radically different Nabataean culture. Strabo discovered a pleasure-loving people who lived in fine, stone houses and cultivated fruit and vines. The king, the historian contended, presided over lavish banquets with female singers and poured wine into his guests' golden cups. Strabo also reported that the king answered to a popular assembly.

This image of a fun-loving, populist monarchy may well be as mythical as Hieronymus' hardy, nomadic shepherds. Nonetheless, Nabataean society doubtless underwent extraordinary changes that drove its explosive growth during the first century B.C.

By that time, Nabataeans were the primary transporters of frankincense and myrrh from their sources in the southern Arabian desert. These aromatic resins were prized throughout the known world for cosmetic, medicinal, and spiritual uses, as their prominence in the Christian Nativity story implies. (Some early Christian sources suggest the Three Magi may have been Nabataean merchants.)

Camels and Caravans

The precious gums were harvested from spindly trees grown mainly in a narrow coastal region of Oman and Yemen. Petra's position at the crossroads of the incense trade produced the city's extraordinary wealth. Strabo describes caravans of as many as 2,000 camels that crossed the desert from southern Arabia to Petra and then on to Mediterranean ports or Egypt.

"These vast caravans must have needed protection from thieves and numerous stops for refreshment as they crossed the desert. There were probably lots of opportunities for Nabataean camel guides and merchants to line their pockets along the way," says University of Miami historian David Graf.

An eloquent relic of the camel-borne trade was unearthed in 1997, when archaeologists with the Petra National Trust began removing tons of sand and debris from the bottom of the Siq—a narrow gorge that provided a winding, kilometer-long (.6-mile) route into the city. There, alongside ancient paving stones that once floored the Siq, archaeologists found the stumps of larger-than-life relief sculptures carved into the cliff wall. They depict a pair of robed men, each leading a camel. One appears to be facing toward the city, while the other seems to be departing—symbols, perhaps, of the camel traffic that once echoed through this towering ravine.

If camel caravans were the bedrock of Nabataean wealth, did Petra's population live like desert nomads in roomy tents of woven camel hair, as traditional Bedouin families still do today? Little more than a decade ago, some scholars still visualized Petra as a seasonal tent city, occupied only for rituals connected with the great tombs. Such notions held as long as archaeologists mostly confined their attention to imposing tombs and temple ruins.

'Stone Tents'

Then in 1988, a joint team from Switzerland and Liechtenstein led by Rolf Stucky launched the first systematic effort to explore the urban heart of Petra. In the years since, they have discovered what Stucky describes as "a city of stone tents." The tent platforms that marked Petra's early days were replaced by substantial stone houses that were scattered informally (as tents might be) across the landscape.

In one house, excavations revealed a bowl still bearing traces of fish sauce. Another yielded a bear paw that probably came from an imported fur rug. One house even preserved traces of a multicolored wall painting from the first century A.D. It depicts architectural motifs similar to the elaborately carved tomb entrances that line the surrounding canyon.

The style of Petra was heavily influenced by the classic Greek architecture that Nabataean merchants encountered on trading visits around the Mediterranean. Local craftsmen freely adapted the Hellenistic designs to their own tastes to produce a unique blend. Both on their massive tombs and inside their homes, the people of Petra invoked the urban sophistication of the Greek and Roman world as evidence of their wealth.

High above the ruins of these prosperous homes are mountain shrines that crown the peaks around Petra. They are connected to the valley floor by broad stairways, carved in the cliff face at enormous labor by the Nabataeans. It is easy to visualize them, robed and in solemn procession, toiling slowly up these stairways to the rock-carved altars and receptacles for sacrificial blood—which at least one Nabataean inscription implies was sometimes human.

Other inscriptions—written in a precursor of today's Arabic script—identify the chief Nabataean deities as Dushara (a male god of fertility, vegetation, and everlasting life) and Al-'Uzza (a mother goddess often identified with Aphrodite of the Greeks or Isis of the Egyptians.).

Ceremonies invoking these deities occurred not only on mountaintops but also in at least four freestanding temples on either side of Petra's main street. One temple, excavated for nearly three decades by Phillip C. Hammond, was probably dedicated to Al-'Uzza or another female deity. A small, carved idol bears the tantalizing, but fragmentary inscription: "Goddess of . . ."

An Amazing Temple

One of the biggest surprises from recent work at Petra came in 1997, when Brown University archaeologists unearthed an amphitheater at the heart of a sprawling ruin dubbed the "Great Temple." The entrance to this building, erected in the first century B.C., was framed by a massive portico some 18 meters (60 feet) high, supported by four huge columns, and vividly decorated with red and white stucco and delicate floral sculptures.

The purpose of this structure in the center of the temple is a mystery. Could it be that the great temple was not really a temple at all, but the "popular assembly" mentioned by Strabo, the Greek historian?

"There are quite a few possibilities," says Martha Sharp Joukowsky, leader of the Brown team. "It could be that we're looking at a kind of temple/theater, or a law court, or a *curia*—a Roman [style] political meeting place. In future seasons, we'll search for evidence to test these various possibilities."

Barely a year after the amphitheater was found, an even more startling discovery—a true measure of Petra's extravagance—came from the area long assumed to be a marketplace. This area was, in fact, a public garden with a promenade surrounding an open-air pool, says Pennsylvania University archaeologist Leigh-Ann Bedal. A little island at the center of the pool supported a lavishly decorated structure interpreted by Bedal as a recreational pavilion.

The pool was nearly identical in size to a modern Olympic pool—50 meters (165 feet) across. An elaborate network of ceramic pipes channeled water to it from the Ain Musa gorge over six kilometers (nearly four miles) away. The pipeline carried water through the Siq to the city center, then branched off to supply the pool, the Great Temple, public baths, fountains, and other luxurious amenities.

In the middle of a blazing, barren desert, what better symbol of Petra's opulence could there be than such an extravagant use of water?

Remote Outposts

The great city was unique only in scale. Much smaller Nabataean settlements reveal traces of elaborate waterworks, temples, and bathhouses. University of Victoria archaeologist John P. Oleson, excavating a remote outpost called Humeima in southern Jordan, found a roofed, stone aqueduct 27 kilometers (17 miles) long—a remarkable feat of planning and construction.

Oleson believes that Petra's first-century monarchs actively encouraged the spread of a more settled way of life throughout their realm, building water channels and bathhouses even in the parched canyons of the Hisma desert. "We're not sure what lay behind this wide-scale settlement planning," Oleson says, "but one idea is that new villages and towns helped discourage attacks by desert nomads on the caravan routes. Also, the Nabataean kings probably wanted to encourage the growth of a new economy in case the incense trade faltered."

The classic tale of Petra's demise begins with the city's annexation by the Romans in A.D. 106. The Romans, in this telling, gradually drained Petra's wealth by diverting caravans northward to new centers, notably Palmyra in Syria. Then, in A.D. 363, a devastating earthquake supposedly finished off the impoverished Nabataeans.

New work by David Graf and others, however, indicates that Nabataean sites and the old caravan routes still prospered well into the Roman era. Petra, in fact, was given the Roman title *metropolis,* while the governor of Rome's Arabian province chose to be buried in one of Petra's fanciest tombs.

Petra's Demise

The spectacular discovery in 1993 of the Petra scrolls proves that as late as the sixth century A.D., when these papyrus records were compiled, Petra's traditional systems of land ownership and irrigation were still in place. Indeed, fragments of old Nabataean beliefs and values may well have lingered until the coming of Islam in A.D. 631.

Skillfully exploiting their position as middlemen on the fringes of the classical world, the Nabataeans blended the comforts and style of Greece and Rome with their Arabian roots. This exotic cultural mixture captivates both researchers and visitors to Petra. Yet even more remarkable was the Nabataeans' command of water, a mastery that enabled them to colonize the desert and protect the caravans that had brought them so much wealth and greatness.

Critical Thinking

1. What surprises about the ancient city of Petra in Jordan have been revealed through modern archaeological excavations?

2. "Petra in its prime virtually ruled the incense trade," we are told. What were some of the common uses for incense in the ancient world?

3. Why was a pool in a public garden so extraordinary? How was it sustained?

Create Central

www.mhhe.com/createcentral

Internet References

Masada: Desert Fortress Overlooking the Dead Sea
   www.jewishvirtuallibrary.org/jsource/Archaeology/Masada1.html

---

Evan Hadingham is Science Editor of NOVA, the PBS science series, and author of *Lines to the Mountain Gods* and other books on prehistory.

Unit V

UNIT   Prepared by: Joseph R. Mitchell, *Howard Community College*
and Helen Buss Mitchell, *Howard Community College*

The Great Religions

According to the World Almanac, there are approximately 2.1 billion Christians, 1.4 billion Muslims, 900 million Hindus, 375 million Buddhists, and 14 million Jews in the world. Zoroastrians number less than 200,000, though they were once more numerous. More than two thirds of the world's population affirms a religious affiliation. As shapers of values, history, loyalties, and daily life, the world's religions have played a powerful role in world history. At times, religion is a source of conflict, as it currently is between Jews and Muslims in the Middle East, or between Hindus and Muslims in Kashmir. At the same time, religion is a potent force for binding people together and creating a shared identity.

Religion and culture have a reciprocal relationship—each shapes and is shaped by the other. Since religions tell a story, that narrative is often bound up with the history of a civilization. Because the great world religions have their origins in premodern times, understanding the stories they tell can shed light on the development and evolution of world cultures. Common themes in world religions include the moral codes that determine the relationship between one person and another, and the larger question of the relationship between humans and a greater entity—either a personal deity or an impersonal force. Indian civilization, the world's oldest, produced Hinduism, Buddhism, Jainism, and Sikhism. The Buddha grew up as a Hindu, but centuries after his enlightenment Buddhism crossed the Himalayas into China and, ultimately, into the wider world. Globalization has carried all these faiths around the world through immigration, and many in the United States have become attracted to Buddhism as converts.

Since the 1949 Communist Revolution, China has been officially atheistic. So, the number of Confucians and Taoists is vastly underrepresented. Confucianism, however, has spread throughout the Pacific Rim, shaping the conduct of business and government, and Taoism has offered a quiet way of living for millions who feel pressured by the stresses of modern life. The translation of ancient texts, begun in earnest in the West during the nineteenth century, has made the wisdom of ancient faiths accessible to a worldwide audience.

The monotheisms of Judaism, Christianity, and Islam rest on revealed truth. For followers of these faiths, sacred texts often have enormous authority. Although there is a shared heritage among these religions through the spiritual "fatherhood" of Abraham, there are also substantive differences. In Jerusalem, sites sacred to all three traditions stand within yards of one another—the Wailing Wall, what remains of the now-destroyed Jewish Temple; the site of Jesus' crucifixion and burial, sacred to Christians; and the Dome of the Rock, from which Muslims believe the Prophet Muhammad rose into heaven to converse with God. Little wonder, then, that disputes over control of these holy places can lead to war.

Scholarly analysis of sacred texts can be threatening to orthodox believers. Muslims hold the Qur'an/Koran unchanged from God's original speaking through the Prophet; yet, textual comparisons reveal subtleties of interpretation and context. In Christianity, the discovery of ancient Gospels, once honored but excluded from the New Testament canon, has revealed the active participation of women in early Christianity—as disciples, prophets, preachers, and teachers. Suppressed for centuries, these texts allow us to recover a lost heritage of equality between women and men. Recent attempts on the parts of Jews, Christians, and Muslims to rediscover their common inheritance as the children of Abraham offer some hope for expanded interfaith dialogue. Even in officially secular nations, such as France and the United States, where religious freedom and the separation of church and state prevail, religion remains a permeating influence. Immigrant populations have sometimes brought fervent belief systems that clash with a more secular dominant culture. There is often tension over how law ought to operate. As we evaluate human history, the role of religion in human culture has been and continues to be a vital one.

Article

Prepared by: Joseph R. Mitchell, *Howard Community College*
and Helen Buss Mitchell, *Howard Community College*

Ancient Jewel

From early Greece to the modern civil rights movement, Indian thought and philosophy have had a wide-ranging influence on Western culture.

T. R. (JOE) SUNDARAM

Learning Outcomes

After reading this article, you will be able to:

- Determine what contributions ancient India has made to human history and how these contributions are still relevant today.

The very word *India* conjures up exotic images in one's mind. Yet this name for the south Asian subcontinent is of Western making, mediated by the Persians and the Arabs. The name used in ancient Sanskrit texts is *Bharat* (for the land of Bharatha, a legendary king), which is also the official name of the modern republic. Other familiar Western words such as *Hindu, caste,* and *curry* are also totally foreign to India. The general knowledge that exists in the West about India, its early history, philosophy, and culture is, at best, superficial. Nevertheless, since it would be impossible in a brief article to do justice to even one of these topics, I shall provide a brief, accurate glimpse into each.

India covers about 1.2 million square miles and is home to a population of 895 million; in comparison, the United States covers 3.6 million square miles and has 258 million residents. Thus, the population density of India is nearly 10 times that of the United States. (The size of classical India—which includes modern-day India, Pakistan, Bangladesh, and parts of Afghanistan—is about two-thirds that of the continental United States.)

But statistics about India can be misleading. For example, while only about one-quarter of the population is "literate," able to read and write, this has to be viewed in light of the strong oral traditions present in India since antiquity. Therefore, while a "literate" American may often be unaware of the collective name of the first 10 amendments to the U.S. Constitution, an "illiterate" Indian peasant would be aware of the history of his ancestors from antiquity to the present day.

Not only is India one of the oldest civilizations in the world, being more than 6,000 years old, but also it may be the oldest continuing civilization in existence; that is, one without any major "gaps" in its history. As the renowned historian A. L. Basham has pointed out,

> Until the advent of archeologists, the peasant of Egypt or Iraq had no knowledge of the culture of his forefathers, and it is doubtful whether his Greek counterpart had any but the vaguest ideas about the glory of Periclean Athens. In each case there had been an almost complete break with the past. On the other hand, the earliest Europeans to visit India found a culture fully conscious of its own antiquity.

Crucible of Learning

- India's may be the oldest continuing civilization in existence.
- To avoid misunderstanding India, it is essential to appreciate three central tenets of Indian thinking: assimilating ideas and experiences, a belief in cycles, and the coexistence of opposites.
- India has made numerous contributions to contemporary Western understanding of mathematics, science, and philosophy.

India is a land of many ancient "living" cities, such as, for example, Varanasi. Even at sites like Delhi, many successive cities have been built over thousands of years. Among old buried cities that have been unearthed in modern times by archaeologists are Mohenjo-Daro and Harappa.

Of these cities, the renowned archaeologist Sir John Marshall writes that they establish the existence

> in the fourth and third millennium B.C., of a highly developed city life; and the presence in many houses, of wells and bathrooms as well as an elaborate drainage system, betoken a social condition of the citizens at least equal to that found in Sumer, and superior to that prevailing in contemporary Babylonia and Egypt.

Thus, India was the "jewel of the world" long before the Greek and Roman civilizations.

Figure 1 Continuous civilization: Excavations at Mohenjo-Daro and Harappa reveal well-planned towns and a sophisticated urban culture dating back to 2500 B.C.

Note: Embassy of India.

Nor was classical India isolated from developing civilizations in other parts of the world. Clay seals from Mohenjo-Daro have been found in Babylonia and vice versa. Ancient Indian artifacts such as beads and bangles have been found in many parts of the Middle East and Africa. India and Indian culture were known to the Greeks even before the time of Alexander the Great. The Greek historian Herodotus wrote extensively about India during the sixth century B.C. Also, during this period many Greeks, including Pythagoras, are known to have traveled to India.

Sixth century B.C. was a period of great religious and philosophical upheaval in India. Hinduism was already an established, "old" religion, and reform movements were beginning to appear, such as one by a prince known as Siddhartha Gautama, who later came to be known as the Buddha. The religion that was founded based on his teachings spread not only throughout Asia but also to many parts of the world, including Greece, and it helped spread Indian culture in the process.

In Alexander the Great's campaign to conquer the world, his ultimate goal was India; he died without achieving that objective. When Seleucus Nicator, Alexander's successor, tried to follow in Alexander's footsteps, he was soundly defeated by Indian emperor Chandragupta Maurya. A peace treaty was signed between the two, and Seleucus sent an ambassador, Megasthenes, to the court of Chandragupta. Megasthenes sent glowing reports back to Greece about India, and he pronounced Indian culture to be equal or superior to

his own, a high compliment indeed, since Greece was then near its zenith.

For the next 1,500 years or so, India—rich in material wealth, scientific knowledge, and spiritual wisdom—enjoyed the reputation of being at the pinnacle of world civilizations. Arab writers of the Middle Ages routinely referred to mathematics as *hindsat,* the "Indian science."

And as is well known now, it was Columbus' desire to reach India that led to the discovery of America. Indeed, the explorer died thinking that he had discovered a new sea route to India, while he had merely landed on a Caribbean island. Columbus' mistake also led to the mislabeling of the natives of the land as "Indians," a label that survived even after the mistake had been discovered.

The Upanishads

Indian philosophy is almost as old as Indian civilization, and its zenith was reached nearly 3,000 years ago with the compilation, by unknown sages, of 108 ancient philosophical texts known as the Upanishads. These texts reflect even older wisdom, which was passed down from generation to generation through oral transmission. A Western commentator has remarked that in the Upanishads the Indian mind moved from cosmology to psychology, and that while most other contemporary civilizations were still asking the question "What am I?" the Indian mind was already asking, "Who am I?"

Figure 2 A terra-cotta toy cow: Ancient Indian civilizations featured highly talented artisans and craftsmen.
Note: Embassy of India.

Figure 3 Indian music has influenced Western artists, particularly in modern times. The beat of the tabla can be heard in pop music ranging from the Beatles to Michael Jackson.
Note: Khorrum Omer/The World & I.

When translations of the Upanishads first became available in the West in the nineteenth century, the impact on European philosophers such as Goethe and Schopenhauer and on American writers such as Emerson and Whitman was profound. "In the whole world," wrote Schopenhauer emotionally, "there is no study as beneficial and as elevating as the Upanishads." Emerson wrote poems based on the texts.

One of the principal underlying themes in the Upanishads is the quest for a "personal reality." This quest began with the conviction that the limitations of our sensory perceptions give us an imperfect model to comprehend the real world around us; this is known as the concept of *maya*. Since individual perceptions can be different, different people can also have different "realities."

For example, a happy event for one individual may be an unhappy one for another. Recognition and perfection of our personal reality is the quintessential goal of Indian philosophy and is also the basic principle behind yoga. Indeed, the literal meaning of the Sanskrit word *yoga* is "union," and the union that is sought is not with any external entity but with one's self. This is, of course, also the principal tenet of modern psychoanalysis.

From a Western perspective, to avoid misunderstanding India in general, and Indian philosophy in particular, it is essential to appreciate three central tenets of the Indian way of thinking. These are:

Assimilation. In the Indian way of thinking, new experiences and ideas never replace old ones but are simply absorbed into, and made a part of, old experiences. Although some have characterized such thinking as static, in reality such thinking is both dynamic and conservative, since old experiences are preserved and new experiences are continually accumulated.

Belief in cycles. Another central tenet of the Indian character is the belief that all changes in the world take place through cycles, there being cycles superimposed on other cycles, cycles within cycles, and so on. Inherent in the concept of cycles is alternation, and the Upanishads speak of the two alternating states of all things being "potentiality" and "expression."

Acceptance of the coexistence of opposites. Early Western readers of the Upanishads were puzzled by the apparent inherent ability of the Indian mind to accept the coexistence of seemingly diametrically opposite concepts. Belief in, and acceptance of, contradictory ideas is a natural part of the Indian way of life, and the logical complement to the tenets already mentioned. It is an indisputable fact that birth (creation) must necessarily be eventually followed by death (destruction). Creation and destruction are inseparable alternations. Even concepts such as "good" and "evil" are complementary, as each of us may have within us the most lofty and divine qualities and at the same time the basest qualities. We ourselves and the whole world can be whatever we want to make of them.

These three tenets are responsible for the amazing continuity of the Indian civilization, its reverence for the elderly, and the acceptance of the aging process without a morbid fear of death.

Ironically, the culture that taught of the need to renounce materialistic desires also produced some of the most pleasurable things in life. The intricacies and highly developed nature

Figure 4 Melodic inspiration: Performing traditional dance and music in Orissa.
Note: Khorrum Omer/The World & I.

of Indian art, music, dance, and cuisine are examples. And the *Kama Sutra* is perhaps the oldest, and best known, manual on the pleasures of love and sex.

From Pythagoras to King

Throughout history, India's contributions to the Western world have been considerable, albeit during the Middle Ages they were often felt only indirectly, having been mediated by the Middle Eastern cultures.

After the early contacts between Greece and India in the sixth and fifth centuries B.C., many concepts that had been in use in India centuries earlier made their appearance in Greek literature, although no source was ever acknowledged. For example, consider the so-called Pythagorean theorem of a right triangle and the Pythagorean school's theory of the "transmigration of souls"; the former was in use in India (for temple construction) centuries earlier, and the latter is merely "reincarnation," a concept of Vedic antiquity. There was also a flourishing trade between the Roman Empire and the kingdoms in southern India, through which not only Indian goods but also ideas made their journey westward.

During the Middle Ages, the Arabs translated many classical Indian works into Arabic, and the ideas contained in them eventually made their way to Europe. A principal mission of the "House of Wisdom" that was established by the caliph in Baghdad in the eighth century was the translation of Indian works.

Among the major Indian ideas that entered Europe through the Arabs are the mathematical concept of zero (for which there was no equivalent in Greek or Roman mathematics) and the modern numerical system we use today. Until the twelfth century, Europe was shackled by the unwieldy Roman numerals. The famous French mathematician Laplace has written: "It is India that gave us the ingenious method of expressing all numbers by ten symbols, each receiving a value of position as well as an absolute value, a profound and important idea which appears so simple to us now that we ignore its true merit."

India's contributions to other areas of science and mathematics were equally important. The seventh-century Syrian astronomer Severus Sebokht wrote that "the subtle theories" of Indian astronomers were "even more ingenious than those of the Greeks and the Babylonians."

The scientific approach permeated other aspects of Indian life as well. For example, classical Indian music has a highly mathematical structure, based on divisions of musical scales into tones and microtones.

In modern times, Indian music has had a considerable influence on Western music. Starting in the 1960s, the famous Indian sitar virtuoso Ravi Shankar popularized sitar music in the West, and now the melodic strains of the sitar, as well as the beat of the Indian drum known as tabla, can be heard in the works of many pop-music artists, ranging from the Beatles to Michael Jackson. The movies of the Indian filmmaker Satyajit Ray have also made a significant impact on the West.

The contributions of many modern Indian scientists have been important to the overall development of Western science. The mathematical genius Srinivasa Ramanujan, who died in 1920, has been called "the greatest mathematician of the century" and "the man who knew infinity." The discovery by the Nobel Prize–winning Indian physicist Chandrasekhara Venkata Raman of the effect (which bears his name) by which light diffusing through a transparent material changes in wavelength has revolutionized laser technology. The theoretical predictions by the Nobel Prize–winning astrophysicist Subrahmanyan Chandrasekhar on the life and death of white-dwarf stars led to the concept of "black holes."

In the literary area, the poetry of Nobel laureate Rabindranath Tagore and the philosophical interpretations of the scholar (and a former president of India) Sarvepalli Radhakrishnan have inspired the West. Albert Einstein was one of the admirers of the former and corresponded with him on the meaning of "truth."

In terms of our daily dietary habits, many vegetables such as cucumber, eggplant, okra, squash, carrots, many types of beans, and lentils were first domesticated in India. Rice, sugarcane, and tea, as well as fruits such as bananas and oranges, are of Indian origin. The name *orange* is derived from the Sanskrit word *narangi*. Chicken and cattle were also first domesticated in India, albeit the latter for milk production and not for meat consumption. Cotton was first domesticated in India. The process of dying fabrics also was invented in India. Indian fabrics (both cotton and silk) have been world renowned for their quality since antiquity. The game of chess was invented in India, and the name itself derives from the Sanskrit name Chaturanga.

India's most popular modern exports have been yoga and meditation. Hatha yoga, the exercise system that is a part of yoga, is now taught widely in America, in institutions ranging from colleges to hospitals. Many scientific studies on the beneficial effects of yoga practice are now under way. A similar state of affairs is true of Indian meditation techniques, which people under stress use for mental relaxation.

Finally the Rev. Martin Luther King, Jr., repeatedly acknowledged his debt to Mahatma Gandhi for the technique of nonviolent civil disobedience, which he used in the civil rights movement. For all India's material contributions to the world, it is its spiritual legacy that has had the widest impact. The ancient sages who wrote the Upanishads would have been pleased.

Additional Reading

A. L. Basham, *The Wonder That Was India,* Grove Press, New York, 1959.

———, *Ancient India: Land of Mystery,* Time-Life Books, Alexandria, Virginia, 1994.

Will Durant, *The Story of Civilization: Part I, Our Oriental Heritage,* Simon and Schuster, New York, 1954.

Critical Thinking

1. What qualified India to be called "Jewel of the World" long before the civilizations in Greece and Rome?

2. What is meant by this statement: ". . . in the Upanishads, the Indian mind moved from cosmology to psychology"?

3. How do you suppose an acceptance of the coexistence of opposites has influenced Indian life?

Create Central

www.mhhe.com/createcentral

Internet References

Cultural India
www.culturalindia.net

T. R. (JOE) SUNDARAM is the owner of an engineering research firm in Columbia, Maryland, and has written extensively on Indian history, culture, and science.

Prepared by: Joseph R. Mitchell, *Howard Community College*
and Helen Buss Mitchell, *Howard Community College*

Article

The Shrine of Islam's Tragic Divisions

CORINNE ATKINS

Learning Outcomes

After reading this article, you will be able to:

- Discuss the effect of the Sunni-Shia division within Islam today and whether it can be mended.

On August 29th, 2003, a huge car bomb went off in the central Iraqi town of Najav, killing more than 100 people, including the Shi'ite cleric Ayatollah Mohammed Baqr al-Hakim. Coming hard on the heels of an equally devastating explosion at the UN headquarters in Baghdad, it emphasised the dangers inherent in the reconstruction of Iraq, and the tensions within the country, many of them derived from the country's political and religious past.

It was in this region, then known as Mesopotamia, that some of the most significant and tragic events of early Islam occurred. The three towns of Kufa, Najav and Kerbala, which all lay relatively close to each other, south of Baghdad, became pivotal to what is now known as the Shia branch of Islam.

The Sunni-Shia schism in Islam can be traced back to the issues that arose over the leadership of the Muslim community shortly after the death of the Prophet Mohammed in AD 632.

Since Mohammed's only daughter, Fatima, could not step into her father's shoes, three caliphs (deputies) assumed control for the brief period AD 632–656. Some, however, refused to recognise them. Known as the Shias, they were followers of Mohammed's charismatic son-in-law, Ali ibn Abi Talib (AD 600–661).

The word 'Shia' is an abbreviation of the phrase 'Shiat Ali', meaning the 'partisans of Ali'. Arguing that only the blood line could be the recipient of Mohammed's divine guidance, they believed the Prophet had designated Ali as his political successor and had imparted to him the power of interpreting religious knowledge. Ali and his descendants were therefore the only rightful successors of the Prophet.

Their opponents, the Sunnis, supported the view that the Prophet's legitimate successor could be chosen by man and should be an elected member of the Prophet's own tribe.

In AD 656, after the assassination of Uthman, the third caliph, Ali ascended to the caliphate. Seven months after taking charge, he moved the capital of the caliphate from Medina in Arabia to Mesopotamia.

Apart from Mecca and Medina themselves, the most important urban centres of the empire at this time were Basra and Kufa in Mesopotamia, and Damascus in Syria.

Mecca was not an option for the new capital: a volunteer army of 3,000 warriors had been raised there to oppose Ali. This army then captured and occupied Basra in southern Mesopotamia, a city which had originally acknowledged Ali's authority. Damascus too became a centre of strong opposition to Ali.

Ali would not choose Medina for his capital, fearing that the City of the Prophet, which already had been plunged into a storm of civil strife, would be plundered, its people massacred and its government would collapse. He also wanted it to be saved from destruction or desecration in future wars. If Islam was to remain in pristine condition, then Medina, the fountain head of the teachings of the Koran, needed to remain a spiritual capital only. In any case, although Medina had pledged allegiance to his cause, support for Ali there was minimal.

In Kufa, though, on the western bank of the Euphrates, about 170 km from Baghdad, Ali had a strong following. His choice of this city as the new capital was in particular a recognition of the efforts made by the people of Kufa in restoring law and order to the region and for their success in recapturing Basra after sending reinforcements at a critical time in Ali's career. As a result, he took an unpretentious residence there in 657, transferring his government from Medina to Kufa. Kufa now became the new capital of Islam.

Yet his actions in abandoning the Prophet's city for Kufa were called into question. Ali proposed to Muawiyah, his rival in Damascus, a compromise solution for the succession, to which the latter appeared to agree. The two leaders would each nominate a suitable successor, who would subsequently resign to leave room for a third man, acceptable to both sides. Ali's nominee resigned, but Muawiyah refused to withdraw his own nominee for the caliphate. Then Muawiyah instigated the murder of Ali, who was stabbed to death while praying at a mosque in Kufa. In this, the second-oldest mosque in Iraq, can still be seen the pulpit where Ali was murdered.

Following their master's instructions for his burial place, Ali's followers tied his body to a camel and let it roam in the desert until it finally rested 11 kilometres north-east of Kufa, in Najav.

Here Ali was buried and a shrine erected. It was to become one of the most famous in the Muslim world. The town, today with a population of about 560,000, has been a pilgrimage centre ever since.

The divide between the Sunnis and Shias was to amplify between Ali's second son, Hussein, and Muawiyah's son, Yazid I, who succeeded his father in AD 680. Hussein refused to swear allegiance to Yazid. To Hussein, Yazid, the son of his father's assassin, could never represent Islam as it would have been blasphemous to accept a situation arising from the power of brute force. This scenario threatened to jeopardise the survival of the whole religion. Recognising that Islamic unity was at stake, Hussein decided to confront Yazid's army. Expecting to gather support for his views, he trekked across the desert with seventy or so followers until he came across Yazid's 4,000 supporters near Kerbala. After attempting to force him to surrender and cutting him off from water, Hussein and his followers were killed by Yazid's men.

Hussein, defiant to the end, died with a sword in one hand and a Koran in the other. According to tradition, his decapitated body was buried in a spot near the battlefield. There is also a sanctuary in honour of one of Hussein's followers, Abbas, who attempted to breech the enemy and fetch water.

To Shi'ite Muslims, the battle at Kerbala exemplifies the clash of good and evil, the virtuous battling against the wicked. Hussein exposed and challenged the illicit means of gaining power in the empire but he did this at the expense of his life.

Each year, in the Muslim month of Muharran, large numbers of pilgrims gather at the Kerbala shrine and perform processions, passion plays and other commemorations of Hussein's martyrdom.

Shias therefore regard Sunnis as secular usurpers whilst Sunnis see Shias as heretics.

Today, the Shia towns of Iraq remain a huge magnet for pilgrims flocking from all over the world; and they remain flashpoints, tragic reminders of the past.

Critical Thinking

1. What was the basis for the Shi'a/Sunni split in Islam that followed the death of the Prophet Muhammad?
2. How was Ali's burial place decided?
3. What was built on that spot?
4. For Shi'ite Muslims what does the Battle at Kerbala, during which Ali's second son, Hussein died, exemplify?

Create Central

www.mhhe.com/createcentral

Internet References

Major World Religions
www.omsakthi.org/religions.html
Religion Search Engines: Islam, Hinduism, Buddhism and Baha'I
www.suite101.com/article.cfm/search_engines/14603

Article

Prepared by: Joseph R. Mitchell, *Howard Community College*
and Helen Buss Mitchell, *Howard Community College*

The Dome of the Rock: Jerusalem's Epicenter

WALID KHALIDI

Learning Outcomes

After reading this article, you will be able to:

- Determine why Jerusalem is so central to the monotheistic religions of the Middle East and how the Dome of the Rock reflects this centrality.

Islam is the third great monotheistic religion of the world. Its followers, about a billion people, constitute the majority of the population in some 50 countries. Like Judaism and Christianity, Islam has rich and deep associations with the city of Jerusalem.

Islam is an Arabic word which means "submission"; in its religious context it means submission to the will of God alone. The message of Islam was delivered by the Prophet Muhammad, who was born in Makkah, in present-day Saudi Arabia, in the year 570 and died in 632. Such was the power of the divine message he preached that, within 100 years of his death in Madinah, Islam had spread across North Africa, into Spain and across the borders of France in the West, and to the borders of India and China in the East. (See *Aramco World*, November/December 1991.)

Very early in this period—in 637—the forces of Islam won Jerusalem from the Byzantine Empire, whose capital was in Constantinople, signing a treaty by which the holy city was surrendered to 'Umar ibn al-Khattab, the second caliph, or successor, of Muhammad. For the following 1280 years, except for the period between 1109 and 1187, during the Crusades, Jerusalem remained in Muslim hands: In 1917, during World War I, the British took control of the city Muslims call al-Quds, "The Holy."

To understand Jerusalem's position in Islam, we need to look at how Islam sees itself in relation to Judaism and Christianity, to which of course Jerusalem is also sacred.

Islamic doctrine states that God has, since creation, revealed His teachings repeatedly to humankind through a succession of prophets and scriptures. The first of this line was the prophet Noah, according to many Muslim scholars; others believe Adam must be considered the first. But in this line of succession, Muhammad is the last, or "seal" of the prophets, and the teachings revealed to him are the culmination of all the previous messages. Muslims believe that the Qur'an, the literal word of God revealed to Muhammad, follows the Torah and the Gospels as God's final revelation. Thus the Qur'an accords great reverence to the Hebrew prophets, patriarchs and kings who received revelations from God and are associated with Jerusalem. Similarly, Jesus Christ is revered as one of God's most dedicated messengers, and Jerusalem, as the locus of much of his teaching, is further blessed by that association.

To Islam, then, Jerusalem is sacred for many of the reasons it is sacred to Judaism and Christianity, but in addition, it is sacred for specifically Muslim reasons. The most important of these is the Prophet Muhammad's miraculous nocturnal journey, or *isra'*, to *Bayt al-Maqdis*, "the house of holiness," in Jerusalem and his ascent from there to heaven—the *mi'raj*. These events are mentioned in a number of verses of the Qur'an, most clearly in the first verse of Chapter 17, titled *Al-Isra'*. Accounts of the Prophet's life supply the details. Led by the angel Gabriel, Muhammad traveled in one night from Makkah to the site of *al-masjid al-aqsa*, "the furthest mosque," on Mount Moriah, called the Temple Mount, in Jerusalem. The site derives its name from the temples and houses of worship built there over the millennia, including the temple of the prophet Solomon, the temple of Jupiter, the Herodian temple and the al-Aqsa Mosque.

There, Muhammad led Abraham, Moses, Jesus and other prophets in prayer. Then, from a rock on the Temple Mount, Muhammad was taken by Gabriel to heaven itself, to "within two bowlengths" of the very throne of God.

The spot from which the Prophet's ascent began was sanctified in the eyes of Muslims by the *mi'raj;* the Qur'an refers to the prayer site as *al-masjid al-aqsa*. From Muhammad's journey evolved a vast body of Muslim devotional literature, some authentic and some uncanonical, that places Jerusalem at the center of Muslim beliefs concerning life beyond the grave. This literature is in circulation in all the diverse languages spoken by the world's one billion Muslims, most of whom to this day celebrate the anniversary of the *mi'raj*.

Jerusalem is also uniquely linked to one of the "pillars" of the Muslim faith, the five daily prayers. The earliest Muslims,

Figure 1   The noble sanctuary.   The editors are grateful for the valuable help they received in compiling this map and checking it for accuracy. Thanks to architectural photographer Saïd Nuseibeh, whose book *The Dome of the Rock,* was published by Rizzoli (1996); to Jeff Spurr of the Aga Khan Program for Islamic Architecture and the Visual Collections of the Fine Arts Library at Harvard University; to Ahmad Nabal of the Aga Khan Visual Archives, Rotch Visual Collection, Massachusetts Institute of Technology; and to Dr. Walid Khalidi.

Note: Watercolor by Tom McNeff. Copyright © 1996 ARAMCO Services Company.

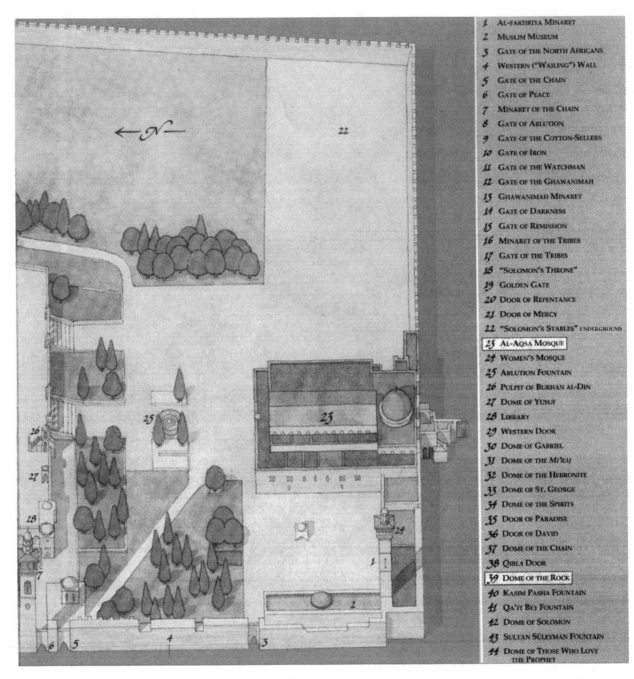

1   AL-FAKHRIYA MINARET
2   MUSLIM MUSEUM
3   GATE OF THE NORTH AFRICANS
4   WESTERN ("WAILING") WALL
5   GATE OF THE CHAIN
6   GATE OF PEACE
7   MINARET OF THE CHAIN
8   GATE OF ABLUTION
9   GATE OF THE COTTON-SELLERS
10 GATE OF IRON
11 GATE OF THE WATCHMAN
12 GATE OF THE GHAWANIMAH
13 GHAWANIMAH MINARET
14 GATE OF DARKNESS
15 GATE OF REMISSION
16 MINARET OF THE TRIBES
17 GATE OF THE TRIBES
18 "SOLOMON'S THRONE"
19 GOLDEN GATE
20 DOOR OF REPENTANCE
21 DOOR OF MERCY
22 "SOLOMON'S STABLES" UNDERGROUND
23 AL-AQSA MOSQUE
24 WOMEN'S MOSQUE
25 ABLUTION FOUNTAIN
26 PULPIT OF BURHAN AL-DIN
27 DOME OF YUSUF
28 LIBRARY
29 WESTERN DOOR
30 DOME OF GABRIEL
31 DOME OF THE MI'RAJ
32 DOME OF THE HEBRONITE
33 DOME OF ST. GEORGE
34 DOME OF THE SPIRITS
35 DOOR OF PARADISE
36 DOOR OF DAVID
37 DOME OF THE CHAIN
38 QIBLA DOOR
39 DOME OF THE ROCK
40 KASIM PASHA FOUNTAIN
41 QA'IT BEY FOUNTAIN
42 DOME OF SOLOMON
43 SULTAN SÜLEYMAN FOUNTAIN
44 DOME OF THOSE WHO LOVE
    THE PROPHET

Figure 1   *(continued)*

for a time, turned toward Jerusalem to pray. A later revelation transferred the *qibla,* the direction of prayer, to Makkah, but to this day Jerusalem is known as "the first of the two *qiblas.*" And according to Muhammad's teachings, it was during the *mi'raj* that Muslims were ordered by God to pray, and that the number of the daily prayers was fixed at five.

The center of Muslim power shifted, through the centuries, from one great capital to the next: from Madinah to Umayyad Damascus to Abbasid Baghdad to Mamluk Cairo and to Ottoman Constantinople. But after Jerusalem became part of the Muslim state in 637, whichever dynasty was in control of that city lavished it with care and attention in the form of public monuments: mosques, colleges for the study of the Qur'an and the traditions of the Prophet, hospitals, hospices, fountains, orphanages, caravansarais, baths, convents for mystics, pools and mausolea. This is why Jerusalem's Old City, within the 16th-century walls built by the Ottoman sultan Süleyman, strikes the modern-day visitor with its predominantly Muslim character.

Caliph 'Umar personally came to Jerusalem to accept the city's surrender from the Byzantines, and visited the site of *al-Masjid al-aqsa,* known to some Muslims today as *al-Haram al-Maqdisi al-Sharif,* "the Noble Sanctuary of Jerusalem," or simply *al-Haram al-Sharif.* The site lay vacant and in ruins; 'Umar ordered it cleaned, and, tradition says, took part in the work himself, carrying dirt in his own robe. When the site had been cleansed and sprinkled with scent, 'Umar and his followers prayed there, near the rough rock from which Muhammad had ascended to heaven.

Two generations later, about 691, the Umayyad caliph 'Abd al-Malik ibn Marwan's Syrian craftsmen built in the same location the earliest masterpiece of Islamic architecture, the Dome of the Rock *(Qubbat al Sakhra)*—the octagonal sanctuary, centered on the rock, whose golden dome still dominates the skyline of Old Jerusalem. 'Abd al-Malik's son al-Walid, who ruled from 705 to 715, built the second major monument, the al-Aqsa Mosque, also on the Temple Mount.

The octagonal plan of the Dome of the Rock may not have been accidental. Cyril Glassé, in his *Concise Encyclopedia of Islam,* points out that "the octagon is a step in the mathematical series going from square, symbolizing the fixity of earthly manifestation, to circle, the natural symbol for the perfection of heaven. . . . In traditional Islamic architecture this configuration symbolizes the link between earth . . . and heaven. . . ." Nor is it coincidence that the elegant calligraphy that encircles the structure inside and out—240 meters, or 785 feet, of it—includes all the Qur'anic verses about the prophet Jesus. "The calligraphic inscriptions," writes Glassé, "recall the relationship between Jerusalem and Jesus . . . and the architecture, above all the octagonal form supporting a dome, is symbolic of the . . . ascent to heaven by the Prophet, and thus by man." Mount Moriah, with the Dome of the Rock at its center, is thus "the place where man, as man, is joined once more to God. . . ."

History, tradition and symbolism intersect in this building, whose presence suffuses Jerusalem.

Critical Thinking

1. Why is Muhammad called the "seal of the prophets"?
2. What does this mean?
3. For what specifically Muslim reason is the city of Jerusalem sacred to Muslims?
4. What is the symbolic meaning of the octagonal plan of the Dome of the Rock?

Create Central

www.mhhe.com/createcentral

Internet References

Major World Religions
   www.omsakthi.org/religions.html
Religion Search Engines: Islam, Hinduism, Buddhism and Baha'I
   www.suite101.com/article.cfm/search_engines/14603

Dr. Walid Khalidi was educated in London and Oxford and has taught at Oxford University, the American University of Beirut and Harvard University. Since 1982, he has been a senior research fellow at Harvard's Center for Middle Eastern Studies. Members of his family have served Jerusalem as scholars, judges, diplomats and members of parliament since the late 12th century.

From *Aramco World,* September/October 1996, pp. 20–35. Copyright © 1996 by SaudiAramco World. Reprinted by permission.

Article

Prepared by: Joseph R. Mitchell, *Howard Community College*
and Helen Buss Mitchell, *Howard Community College*

Zoroastrians Keep the Faith, and Keep Dwindling

LAURIE GOODSTEIN

Learning Outcomes

After reading this article, you will be able to:

- Discuss the key beliefs and practices of Zoroastrianism.

In his day job, Kersey H. Antia is a psychologist who specializes in panic disorders. In his private life, Mr. Antia dons a long white robe, slips a veil over his face and goes to work as a Zoroastrian priest, performing rituals passed down through a patrilineal chain of priests stretching back to ancient Persia.

After a service for the dead in which priests fed sticks of sandalwood and pinches of frankincense into a blazing urn, Mr. Antia surveyed the Zoroastrian faithful of the Midwest— about 80 people in saris, suits and blue jeans.

"We were once at least 40, 50 million—can you imagine?" said Mr. Antia, senior priest at the fire temple here in suburban Chicago. "At one point we had reached the pinnacle of glory of the Persian Empire and had a beautiful religious philosophy that governed the Persian kings.

"Where are we now? Completely wiped out," he said. "It pains me to say, in 100 years we won't have many Zoroastrians."

There is a palpable panic among Zoroastrians today—not only in the United States, but also around the world—that they are fighting the extinction of their faith, a monotheistic religion that most scholars say is at least 3,000 years old.

Zoroastrianism predates Christianity and Islam, and many historians say it influenced those faiths and cross-fertilized Judaism as well, with its doctrines of one God, a dualistic universe of good and evil and a final day of judgment.

While Zoroastrians once dominated an area stretching from what is now Rome and Greece to India and Russia, their global population has dwindled to 190,000 at most, and perhaps as few as 124,000, according to a survey in 2004 by *Fezana Journal*, published quarterly by the Federation of Zoroastrian Associations of North America. The number is imprecise because of wildly diverging counts in Iran, once known as Persia—the incubator of the faith.

"Survival has become a community obsession," said Dina McIntyre, an Indian-American lawyer in Chesapeake, Va., who has written and lectured widely on her religion.

The Zoroastrians' mobility and adaptability has contributed to their demographic crisis. They assimilate and intermarry, virtually disappearing into their adopted cultures. And since the faith encourages opportunities for women, many Zoroastrian women are working professionals who, like many other professional women, have few children or none.

Despite their shrinking numbers, Zoroastrians—who follow the Prophet Zarathustra (Zoroaster in Greek)—are divided over whether to accept intermarried families and converts and what defines a Zoroastrian. An effort to create a global organizing body fell apart two years ago after some priests accused the organizers of embracing "fake converts" and diluting traditions.

"They feel that the religion is not universal and is ethnic in nature, and that it should be kept within the tribe," said Jehan Bagli, a retired chemist in Toronto who is a priest, or mobed, and president of the North American Mobed Council, which includes about 100 priests. "This is a tendency that to me sometimes appears suicidal. And they are prepared to make that sacrifice."

In South Africa, the last Zoroastrian priest recently died, and there is no one left to officiate at ceremonies, said Rohinton Rivetna, a Zoroastrian leader in Chicago who, with his wife, Roshan, was a principal mover behind the failed effort to organize a global body. But they have not given up.

"We have to be working together if we are going to survive," Mr. Rivetna said.

Although the collective picture is bleak, most individual Zoroastrians appear to be thriving. They are well-educated and well-traveled professionals, earning incomes that place them in the middle and upper classes of the countries where they or their families settled after leaving their homelands in Iran and India. About 11,000 Zoroastrians live in the United States, 6,000 in Canada, 5,000 in England, 2,700 in Australia and 2,200 in the Persian Gulf nations, according to the *Fezana Journal* survey.

This is the second major exodus in Zoroastrian history. In Iran, after Muslims rose to power in the seventh century A.D., historians say the Zoroastrian population was decimated by massacres, persecution and conversions to Islam. Seven boat-loads of Zoroastrian refugees fled Iran and landed on the coast of India in 936. Their descendants, known as Parsis, built Mumbai, formerly Bombay, into the world capital of Zoroastrianism.

The Zoroastrian magazine *Parsiana* publishes charts each month tracking births, deaths and marriages. Leaders fret over the reports from Mumbai, where deaths outnumber births six to one. The intermarriage rate there has risen to about one in three. The picture in North America is more hopeful: about 1.5 births for one death. But the intermarriage rate in North America is now nearly 50 percent.

Soli Dastur, an exuberant priest who lives in Florida, is among the first generation of immigrants who started the trend. Mr. Dastur grew up in a village outside Mumbai, where his father was a priest, the fire temple was the center of town and his whole world was Zoroastrian.

He arrived in Evanston, Ill., in 1960, where he knew of no other Zoroastrians, to attend college on a scholarship provided by one of the Parsi endowments in Mumbai, which have since provided scholarships to many others. He earned a Ph.D., worked as a chemical engineer and married an American Roman Catholic he met on a blind date 40 years ago.

Mr. Dastur is a priest in much demand to perform ceremonies because of his melodic chanting of the prayers. He and his wife, Jo Ann, have two grown daughters. Neither married a Zoroastrian.

"They're good human beings," Mr. Dastur said. "That's more important to me."

The very tenets of Zoroastrianism could be feeding its demise, many adherents said in interviews. Zoroastrians believe in free will, so in matters of religion they do not believe in compulsion. They do not proselytize. They can pray at home instead of going to a temple. While there are priests, there is no hierarchy to set policy. And their basic doctrine is a universal ethical precept: "good thoughts, good words, good deeds."

"That's what I take away from Zoroastrianism," said Tenaz Dubash, a filmmaker in New York City who is making a documentary about the future of her faith, "that I'm a cerebral, thinking human being, and I need to think for myself."

Ferzin Patel, who runs a support group for 20 intermarried couples in New York, said that while the Zoroastrians in the group adored their faith and wanted to teach it to their children, they in no way wanted to compel their spouses to convert.

"In the intermarriage group, I don't think anyone feels that someone should forfeit their religion just for Zoroastrianism," Ms. Patel said.

Despite, or because of, the high intermarriage rate, some Zoroastrian priests refuse to accept converts or to perform initiation ceremonies for adopted children or the children of intermarried couples, especially when the father is not Zoroastrian. The ban on these practices is far stronger in India and Iran than in North America.

"As soon as you do it, you start diluting your ethnicity, and one generation has an intermarriage, and the next generation has more dilution and the customs become all fuzzy and they eventually disappear," said Jal N. Birdy, a priest in Corona, Calif., who will not perform weddings of mixed couples. "That would destroy my community, which is why I won't do it."

The North American Mobed Council is so divided on the issue of accepting intermarried spouses and children that it has been unable to take a position, said Mr. Bagli, the council's president. He supports accepting converts because he said he can find no ban in Zoroastrian texts, but he estimated that as many as 40 percent of the priests in his group were opposed.

The peril and the hope for Zoroastrianism are embodied in a child of the diaspora, Rohena Elavia Ullal, 27, a physical therapist in suburban Chicago.

Ms. Ullal knew from an early age that her parents wanted her to marry another Zoroastrian. Her mother, a former board president of the Chicago temple, helped organize Sunday school classes once a month there, enticing teenagers with weekend sleepovers and roller-skating trips.

The result was a core group of close friends who felt more like cousins, Ms. Ullal said recently over breakfast.

Both of her brothers found mates at Zoroastrian youth congresses, and one is already married. Ms. Ullal stayed on the lookout.

"There were so few," she said. "I guess you're lucky if you find somebody. That would be the ideal."

Ms. Ullal's college boyfriend is also the child of Indian immigrants to the United States, but he is Hindu. [They married on Saturday and had two ceremonies—one Hindu, one Zoroastrian.] But Ms. Ullal says that before they even became engaged, they talked about her desire to raise their children as Zoroastrians.

"It's scary; we're dipping down in numbers," she said. "I don't want to hurt his parents, but he doesn't have the kind of responsibility, whereas I do."

Critical Thinking

1. In what ways has Zoroastrianism influenced Christianity and Islam?
2. What are the chief factors in the so-called "demographic crisis" that has led to "dwindling numbers"?
3. In what ways are modern Zoroastrians "thriving"?
4. ". . . Their basic doctrine is a universal ethical precept: 'Good thoughts, Good words, Good deeds.' " Explain the implications of having this as a central belief.

Create Central

www.mhhe.com/createcentral

Internet References

Major World Religions
www.omsakthi.org/religions.html

Article

Prepared by: Joseph R. Mitchell, *Howard Community College*
and Helen Buss Mitchell, *Howard Community College*

First Churches of the Jesus Cult

Andrew Lawler

Learning Outcomes

After reading this article, you will be able to:

- Describe the contents of recently excavated, ancient Christian churches and understand what they tell us about how well early Christianity was tolerated by its neighbors.

As dusk approaches, Korean pilgrims in white baseball caps blow horns and sing hymns atop Tel Megiddo. This crossroads in northern Israel—also known as Armageddon—is where the New Testament says the final battle pitting good against evil will begin. Below the huge mound, tour buses idle, throngs of visitors buy postcards, and a nearby McDonalds does a thriving business at its drive-through window.

On the opposite side of the busy highway are the grim brick walls and coiled barbed wire of a high-security prison. It is an awkward place for an important archaeological site. Unlike at the mound, visitors are not welcome here. Even archaeologists must apply well in advance for access—something I wasn't granted—so I am left standing outside the gates with Yotam Tepper of the Israel Antiquities Authority. The mosaic floor that he and a team of inmates discovered under the prison yard may mark one of the earliest known places of Christian worship.

Although the site may date to a full century before the Roman emperor Constantine issued the Edict of Milan transforming Christianity from a disparate group of Jesus-worshipping cults to a powerful state religion in A.D. 313, these early followers of the controversial faith weren't hiding their beliefs. "There were Samaritans and Jews and Romans and Christians all living together in just this small place," says Tepper. A Roman soldier paid for the mosaics, and members of the congregation may even have baked bread for Rome's sixth legion, stationed nearby.

The find at Megiddo is a key piece of evidence in a radical rethinking of how Christianity evolved during its first three centuries, before it was backed by the might of empire. Until recently, scholars had to rely on ancient texts that emphasize the vicious persecution of the church—think lions dining on martyrs in Rome's Colosseum. A growing body of archaeological data, however, paints a more diverse and surprising picture

in which Christians thrived alongside Jews and the Roman military. These finds make this "a definitive time in our field" since they appear to contradict the literary sources on which historians have long depended, says Eric Meyers, a biblical archaeologist at Duke University.

Megiddo is only the latest in a series of recent digs in the Near East revealing a more complex history of the early Christian era. Near the Red Sea in the Jordanian city of Aqaba, archaeologists have uncovered what the dig director, Thomas Parker of North Carolina State University, argues is a pre-Constantinian prayer hall. At Capernaum, just an hour's drive from Megiddo, Franciscan monks believe they have excavated a pilgrimage site dating to as early as the first century A.D. on the shores of the Sea of Galilee. Such discoveries are unusual; the only undisputed early Christian worship site is at Dura Europas, on the Euphrates River in modern Syria, which was excavated in the 1920s and '30s by French and American teams. How the most recently discovered sites were used and dated, however, is hotly contested.

Formal churches were rare before A.D. 325, when Constantine convened the Council of Nicea formalizing many church practices, and embarked on a building campaign that used the Roman basilica—a spacious rectangular enclosed space, typically with an apse and an altar on one end—as the model for Christian places of worship. The basilica became the standard still used for churches around the world.

Before that innovation, however, Christians gathered in *domus ecclesiae,* or house churches. Eager to keep a low profile during uncertain times, many Christian communities met in homes throughout the first centuries to celebrate rituals such as the Eucharist, which used wine and bread to recall Christ's sacrifice and to bind the community of believers together. In a letter to the Romans, St. Paul mentions "the church that is in their house," and numerous other early writers cite homes where congregations met. "This type of architecture was quite private, so it was not visibly a Christian building," says Joan Taylor, a historian at University College in London. "Otherwise, it might get smashed and you might get killed."

That was a legitimate fear. The Jewish high council, according to the New Testament, ordered the death of the first Christian martyr, Stephen. Christians—who still were seen as a Jewish sect—refused to join Jews in the Bar Kokhba revolt against the Romans in A.D. 132–135. Judged as traitors by the

Jewish community, they were killed in retribution. After the revolt, however, the decimated Jewish population posed far less of a threat than the Romans. Nero had already scapegoated Christians for burning Rome in A.D. 64; Emperor Decius (A.D. 249–251) had pursued lay Christians as well as clergy; and Diocletian and Galerius had infamously persecuted Christians at the end of the third and beginning of the fourth centuries A.D. There is little doubt Christians suffered terribly during the religions early days. But the evidence from Near Eastern digs, combined with new thinking about the Roman Empire, demonstrates that there were substantial periods when Christians were tolerated, accepted, and even embraced by their tormentors.

This is indisputably the case at Dura Europas, a formidable city and Roman garrison that guarded the eastern frontier of the empire. Excavations in the 1930s revealed a domus ecclesia that includes an inscription dating it to A.D. 231—the only Christian house church which scholars agree predates Constantine. The house church was located near the city gate where Roman soldiers would have been stationed. "There's no way the Romans didn't know about the Christians," says Simon James, an archaeologist at the University of Leicester.

For decades the house church has remained an archaeological oddity. New clues, however, have been emerging far to the south, at Capernaum along the Sea of Galilee in Israel, where Franciscan scholars have been excavating a site for the past century. They believe it was the house of Peter and other apostles; Jesus is said to have lived here and taught at the local synagogue. Today, a squat and ugly modern concrete church hovers above the house. Visiting Italian nuns and Nigerian pilgrims peer down through the church's glass floor at the foundations of the octagonal shrine built a century or so after Constantine legalized Christianity. The octagon was a typical shape for shrines and places of importance, from Roman tombs to the Dome of the Rock. Below the Capernaum structure, the excavators found 11 floors, layered one on top of the other, dating from the second century B.C. through the fourth century A.D., says Michele Piccirillo, a Franciscan archaeologist.

Piccirillo's office is a high-ceilinged room just off the Via Dolorosa in Jerusalem, with a bare bulb illuminating religious paintings and stacks of books. He makes strong and bitter coffee as he lays out the case for Capernaum as one of Christianity's most ancient places of worship. Digging through his papers, he points out the evolution of the house. He notes that the early layers include lamps and cooking pots, while from the second century A.D. on, they have only found lamps—circumstantial evidence that the site may have been transformed from a private home into a place of pilgrimage or worship. And some bits of plaster in the central room show graffiti by Christians, including the name Peter and references to "Christ" and "Lord" in Aramaic, Greek, Latin, and Syriac. "There is continuity—this house eventually was used as a church," he says. He believes the domus ecclesia dates from at least the third century.

"There is no doubt that the graffiti suggests early Christian pilgrims venerated the site," Meyers says. "The excavators have been very, very responsible—they're not making this up."

Other archaeologists disagree with this interpretation. Taylor, who closely examined the data, believes the site was not used for worship until the fourth century. But Meyers is impressed with the evidence. "There is no doubt that the graffiti suggests early Christian pilgrims venerated the site," he says. "The excavators have been very, very responsible—they're not making this up." But he adds that Franciscans like Piccirillo "have a vested interest in proving the antiquity of holy sites." What is not in dispute, however, is the existence of an elaborate synagogue across the street, dating to the same time as the octagonal building. The Franciscans believe it was built on the foundation of an earlier Jewish house of worship dating to the first century A.D.—and possibly the same one in which Jesus is said to have preached. Whether or not the monks have found Peter's house, it is clear that Jews and Christians coexisted peacefully here.

Further to the south, in Jordan, the team led by Parker uncovered another candidate for a pre-Constantinian church in the late 1990s. Located just a short walk from the Red Sea in the port of Aqaba, the small site is today surrounded by busy streets and hotels in this popular seaside resort. Like Dura Europas, the city in Roman times was a thriving center of trade at the edge of the empire—and an important military post. Unlike a scattering of other archaeological sites in this city, there are no signs yet explaining the potential significance of the mud-brick structure that lies crumbling in the sun, protected by a short wire fence. More than 100 coins, the latest dating to the last decade in the reign of Constantinius II (A.D. 337–361), were found in the building, which measures 85 by 53 feet. Based on the coins and pottery, Parker estimates that the building was constructed in the late third or early fourth century A.D.—though he says a post-325 date is not out of the question.

Given the east-west orientation, basilica-like plan, glass oil-lamp fragments, and a cross found in a grave in a nearby cemetery, he argues that the building was a formal church rather than a domus ecclesia. The theory has yet to win many supporters, but scholars are eager to see his final publication of the find, which should be out this year. "I am skeptical," says Jodi Magness, an archaeologist at the University of North Carolina at Chapel Hill who specializes in the period and is digging just across the border in Israel," I haven't seen anything yet that persuades me."

Magness has her own potential candidate for a pre-Constantine church in southern Israel at a site called Yotvata, a Roman fort that was built around A.D. 300. In 2006, her team found a semicircular niche cut into the fort's wall flanked by two pilasters and an inscription that may be a Christian prayer.

The niche was likely built in the early fourth century but a more precise date will require further excavation—including the removal of a British police station that was built over it in the 1930s.

The controversy surrounding the church at Megiddo began in 2003, when prisoners were assigned to expand the buildings housing Christian and Muslim Palestinian prisoners. When the crew working in the interior yard hit archaeological remains, prison officials alerted the Israel Antiquities Authority, which put Tepper, a graduate student at Tel Aviv University, in charge of the salvage effort. He conducted the work primarily with a team made up of 70 prisoners.

Like Dura Europas and Aqaba, Megiddo was full of Roman soldiers. And like Capernaum, it was primarily a Jewish town. Situated on a strategic spot between the Mediterranean coast and the Sea of Galilee, its bloody future as the site of the last battle between good and evil forecast by the New Testament's Book of Revelation reflects its past: here, battles raged involving Egyptians, Canaanites, Assyrians, Greeks, Romans, Turks, and British. But during Roman times, it was the site of a Jewish village called Kefar 'Othnay, a Roman legion camp, and eventually a Byzantine city called Maximianopolis.

"It was a small village with nothing special," says Tepper. The settlement, likely founded by Jews or Samaritans in the second half of the first century, covered about 15 acres and was located next to a Roman legion base. In late 2005, as he was wrapping up the dig, Tepper came across the remains of a building on the edge of the village closest to the Roman camp. The building had four wings, an exterior courtyard with bread ovens, and a series of rooms opening onto an interior courtyard. In the western wing Tepper's team uncovered a hall measuring 5 by 10 yards and oriented north to south. In the middle of the hall, they found four mosaic panels with inscriptions surrounding a podium. Two panels are decorated with simple geometric patterns; a third is slightly larger with Greek inscriptions on each end. The fourth shows two flopping fish—a tuna and a sea bass—circled by squares, triangles, and diamonds with a large inscription on one end.

Tepper faxed images of the mosaics to Leah di Segni, an epigrapher at Hebrew University who was working from her third-floor walk-up apartment in West Jerusalem. At first she says she assumed the mosaics were part of a temple to Mithras, a Persian god popular with Roman troops from the empire's eastern frontier to Scotland. Di Segni translated one inscription as "Gaianus, also called Porphyrius, centurion, our brother, has made the pavement at his own expense as an act of liberality. Brutius has carried out the work." A second inscription is a memorial to four women with common Greek names. But the third inscription was the stunner: "The god-loving Akeptous has offered the table to God Jesus Christ as a memorial."

She immediately phoned Tepper and told him to look for Roman pottery. He promptly found sherds and coins that he says date the site to the early third century. They found more than 100 coins in the complex, one-third of which date to the second and third centuries A.D. and the remaining two-thirds to

the fourth century. Almost all of the early coins come from the hall, including several in pristine condition from the reigns of emperors Elagabalus (A.D. 218–222) and Severus Alexander (A.D. 222–235)."These coins," Tepper says, "should probably be associated with the founding of the building." The latest one, he notes, is dated to Diocletian's reign in the late third century. The absence of any post-Diocletian coins may mean that the building was abandoned in the fourth century, says Tepper. He also says he has Roman pottery that confirms his conclusion.

Most of the jar fragments in the complex appear to be from the third century A.D., with the latest dating to the early fourth century. Pottery fragments found alongside and below the mosaic floor are no later than the third century, he adds. Two stone stamps that were used by the bakers of the Roman legions to mark the bread they made were found in the complex, another sign that soldiers may have been Christians at a time when the faith was officially outlawed.

Tepper's conclusions have been greeted skeptically by senior archaeologists, such as Magness and Piccirillo. "There are a lot of early coins—so what?" says Magness, who notes that the area under the mosaic floor, which might yield critical dating material, has yet to be excavated. "I don't think they have convincing evidence," she adds. Piccirillo agrees. An expert in Byzantine mosaics, he believes their style indicates they could be as late as the fifth century.

Others are more intrigued. "I'm open to Megiddo as a third-century site," says Taylor. "It's idiosyncratic," she adds, since it does not fit the model of Christian churches during and after the time of Constantine. Those structures are easily recognizable by their basilica shape with an altar on the east end and main entrance to the west. "This is a time before all the dictates come from above," says Taylor. And Meyers, a pottery expert, says that while everyone is awaiting a final publication, he is convinced that the sherds are distinctively mid-Roman rather than from a later era.

If Megiddo does prove to be an early prayer hall, then it will lend strength to the growing view among scholars that the early Church in the Holy Land was highly diverse during the two centuries between the death of Jesus and Constantine's edict. "The traditional view was that early Christianity was not licensed, that it had to hide," says Taylor. "That's shifting to a recognition that there were periods of persecution followed by periods of peace." And those well-documented periods of persecution might have had spotty results. Decrees issued from Rome, Taylor says, might have little impact at the fringes of a vast empire, at places like Megiddo and Dura Europas.

Meyers agrees. He also believes the Megiddo site is evidence that scholars need to rethink the idea that the Holy Land was largely devoid of Christians after the Roman destruction of Jerusalem and subsequent Jewish revolts. According to Meyers, the archaeological evidence points to a complex and closer relationship between early Christians and Jews. Despite Byzantine decrees persecuting Jews, he notes that impressive synagogues sprang up around the empire at places like Capernaum. "The two sister religions have an often robust and positive" relationship, says Meyers. He believes the excavations show that it goes back to Christianity's early days.

How Roman soldiers influenced the evolution of early Christianity remains an open question. Though the Roman army was often the weapon used to smash Christian places of worship, soldiers were also drawn to a host of eastern cults such as Mithraism and Christianity. "A lot of soldiers regarded it as sensible to get on the right side of the local deities," says James.

Meanwhile, work at the Megiddo site has stopped. Israeli officials would like to move the prison, but there is no budget to do so. There are not even funds to finish the excavations and conserve the site. The idea of turning the area into a major tourist destination—the nearby Tel Megiddo already draws hundreds of pilgrims each day—appears to be on indefinite hold. Standing outside the prison gate, Tepper says that the money and jobs involved make moving the prison difficult. He is currently busy with other salvage excavations around the Sea of Galilee. By now the sun is setting and the tourist buses have all left Tel Megiddo. Tepper gives the prison walls one last glance and climbs in his battered jeep as the gate opens briefly—but only to let in a new batch of prisoners.

Critical Thinking

1. What are the key features of Christianity during its first three centuries, "before it was backed by the might of Empire"?
2. Where did Christians meet for worship before basilicas were built after Constantine legalized Christianity?
3. In what ways was Christianity shaped by its popularity in the Greco-Roman world?
4. How might Christianity have been different if it had remained in the Middle East?

Create Central

www.mhhe.com/createcentral

Internet References

Religion Search Engines: Christianity and Judaism
www.suite101.com/article.cfm/search_engines/13501

ANDREW LAWLER is a staff writer for *Science* magazine.

Article   Prepared by: Joseph R. Mitchell, *Howard Community College*
and Helen Buss Mitchell, *Howard Community College*

Women in Ancient Christianity
The New Discoveries

KAREN L. KING

Learning Outcomes

After reading this article, you will be able to:

- Understand the evidence that is offered to prove that women actively participated in the life of the early Christian faith as well as its relevance for our contemporary world.

In the last twenty years, the history of women in ancient Christianity has been almost completely revised. As women historians entered the field in record numbers, they brought with them new questions, developed new methods, and sought for evidence of women's presence in neglected texts and exciting new findings. For example, only a few names of women were widely known: Mary, the mother of Jesus; Mary Magdalene, his disciple and the first witness to the resurrection; Mary and Martha, the sisters who offered him hospitality in Bethany. Now we are learning more of the many women who contributed to the formation of Christianity in its earliest years.

Perhaps most surprising, however, is that the stories of women we thought we knew well are changing in dramatic ways. Chief among these is Mary Magdalene, a woman infamous in Western Christianity as an adulteress and repentant whore. Discoveries of new texts from the dry sands of Egypt, along with sharpened critical insight, have now proven that this portrait of Mary is entirely inaccurate. She was indeed an influential figure, but as a prominent disciple and leader of one wing of the early Christian movement that promoted women's leadership.

Certainly, the New Testament Gospels, written toward the last quarter of the first century CE [Christian Era], acknowledge that women were among Jesus' earliest followers. From the beginning, Jewish women disciples, including Mary Magdalene, Joanna, and Susanna, had accompanied Jesus during his ministry and supported him out of their private means (Luke 8:1–3). He spoke to women both in public and private, and indeed he learned from them. According to one story, an unnamed Gentile woman taught Jesus that the ministry of God is not limited to particular groups and persons, but belongs to all who have faith (Mark 7:24–30; Matthew 15:21–28). A Jewish woman honored him with the extraordinary hospitality of washing his feet with perfume. Jesus was a frequent visitor at the home of Mary and Martha, and was in the habit of teaching and eating meals with women as well as men. When Jesus was arrested, women remained firm, even when his male disciples are said to have fled, and they accompanied him to the foot of the cross. It was women who were reported as the first witnesses to the resurrection, chief among them again Mary Magdalene. Although the details of these gospel stories may be questioned, in general they reflect the prominent historical roles women played in Jesus' ministry as disciples.

Women in the First Century of Christianity

After the death of Jesus, women continued to play prominent roles in the early movement. Some scholars have even suggested that the majority of Christians in the first century may have been women.

The letters of Paul—dated to the middle of the first century CE—and his casual greetings to acquaintances offer fascinating and solid information about many Jewish and Gentile women who were prominent in the movement. His letters provide vivid clues about the kind of activities in which women engaged more generally. He greets Prisca, Junia, Julia, and Nereus' sister, who worked and traveled as missionaries in pairs with their husbands or brothers (Romans 16:3, 7, 15). He tells us that Prisca and her husband risked their lives to save his. He praises Junia as a prominent apostle, who had been imprisoned for her labor. Mary and Persis are commended for their hard work (Romans 16:6, 12). Euodia and Syntyche are called his fellow-workers in the gospel (Philippians 4:2–3). Here is clear evidence of women apostles active in the earliest work of spreading the Christian message.

Paul's letters also offer some important glimpses into the inner workings of ancient Christian churches. These groups did not own church buildings but met in homes, no doubt due in part to the fact that Christianity was not legal in the Roman world of its day and in part because of the enormous expense to such fledgling societies. Such homes were a domain in which women played key roles. It is not surprising then to see women taking leadership roles in house churches. Paul tells of women who were the leaders of such house churches (Apphia in Philemon 2; Prisca in I Corinthians 16:19). This practice is confirmed by other texts that also mention women who headed churches in their homes, such as Lydia of Thyatira (Acts 16:15) and Nympha of Laodicea (Colossians 4:15). Women held offices and played significant roles in group worship. Paul, for example, greets a deacon named Phoebe (Romans 16:1) and assumes that women are praying and prophesying during worship (I Corinthians 11). As prophets, women's roles would have included not only ecstatic public speech, but preaching, teaching, leading prayer, and perhaps even performing the eucharist meal. (A later first century work, called the Didache, assumes that this duty fell regularly to Christian prophets.)

Mary Magdalene: A Truer Portrait

Later texts support these early portraits of women, both in exemplifying their prominence and confirming their leadership roles (Acts 17:4, 12). Certainly the most prominent among these in the ancient church was Mary Magdalene. A series of spectacular 19th and 20th century discoveries of Christian texts in Egypt dating to the second and third century have yielded a treasury of new information. It was already known from the New Testament gospels that Mary was a Jewish woman who followed Jesus of Nazareth. Apparently of independent means, she accompanied Jesus during his ministry and supported him out of her own resources (Mark 15:40–41; Matthew 27:55–56; Luke 8:1–3; John 19:25).

Although other information about her is more fantastic, she is repeatedly portrayed as a visionary and leader of the early movement. (Mark 16:1–9; Matthew 28:1–10; Luke 24:1–10; John 20:1, 11–18; Gospel of Peter). In the Gospel of John, the risen Jesus gives her special teaching and commissions her as an apostle to the apostles to bring them the good news. She obeys and is thus the first to announce the resurrection and to play the role of an apostle, although the term is not specifically used of her. Later tradition, however, will herald her as "the apostle to the apostles." The strength of this literary tradition makes it possible to suggest that historically Mary was a prophetic visionary and leader within one sector of the early Christian movement after the death of Jesus.

The newly discovered Egyptian writings elaborate this portrait of Mary as a favored disciple. Her role as "apostle to the apostles" is frequently explored, especially in considering her faith in contrast to that of the male disciples who refuse to believe her testimony. She is most often portrayed in texts that claim to record dialogues of Jesus with his disciples, both before and after the resurrection. In the Dialogue of the Savior, for example, Mary is named along with Judas (Thomas) and Matthew in the course of an extended dialogue with Jesus. During the discussion, Mary addresses several questions to the Savior as a representative of the disciples as a group. She thus appears as a prominent member of the disciple group and is the only woman named. Moreover, in response to a particularly insightful question, the Lord says of her, "You make clear the abundance of the

revealer!" (140.17–19). At another point, after Mary has spoken, the narrator states, "She uttered this as a woman who had understood completely" (139.11–13). These affirmations make it clear that Mary is to be counted among the disciples who fully comprehended the Lord's teaching (142.11–13).

In another text, the Sophia of Jesus Christ, Mary also plays a clear role among those whom Jesus teaches. She is one of the seven women and twelve men gathered to hear the Savior after the resurrection, but before his ascension. Of these only five are named and speak, including Mary. At the end of his discourse, he tells them, "I have given you authority over all things as children of light," and they go forth in joy to preach the gospel. Here again Mary is included among those special disciples to whom Jesus entrusted his most elevated teaching, and she takes a role in the preaching of the gospel.

In the Gospel of Philip, Mary Magdalene is mentioned as one of three Marys "who always walked with the Lord" and as his companion (59.6–11). The work also says that Lord loved her more than all the disciples, and used to kiss her often (63.34–36). The importance of this portrayal is that yet again the work affirms the special relationship of Mary Magdalene to Jesus based on her spiritual perfection.

In the Pistis Sophia, Mary again is preeminent among the disciples, especially in the first three of the four books. She asks more questions than all the rest of the disciples together, and the Savior acknowledges that: "Your heart is directed to the Kingdom of Heaven more than all your brothers" (26:17–20). Indeed, Mary steps in when the other disciples are despairing in order to intercede for them to the Savior (218:10–219:2). Her complete spiritual comprehension is repeatedly stressed.

She is, however, most prominent in the early second century Gospel of Mary, which is ascribed pseudonymously to her. More than any other early Christian text, the Gospel of Mary presents an unflinchingly favorable portrait of Mary Magdalene as a woman leader among the disciples. The Lord himself says she is blessed for not wavering when he appears to her in a vision. When all the other disciples are weeping and frightened, she alone remains steadfast in her faith because she has grasped and appropriated the salvation offered in Jesus' teachings. Mary models the ideal disciple: she steps into the role of the Savior at his departure, comforts, and instructs the other disciples. Peter asks her to tell any words of the Savior which she might know but that the other disciples have not heard. His request acknowledges that Mary was preeminent among women in Jesus' esteem, and the question itself suggests that Jesus gave her private instruction. Mary agrees and gives an account of "secret" teaching she received from the Lord in a vision. The vision is given in the form of a dialogue between the Lord and Mary; it is an extensive account that takes up seven out of the eighteen pages of the work. At the conclusion of the work, Levi confirms that indeed the Saviour loved her more than the rest of the disciples (18.14–15). While her teachings do not go unchallenged, in the end the Gospel of Mary affirms both the truth of her teachings and her authority to teach the male disciples. She is portrayed as a prophetic visionary and as a leader among the disciples.

Other Christian Women

Other women appear in later literature as well. One of the most famous woman apostles was Thecla, a virgin-martyr converted by Paul. She cut her hair, donned men's clothing, and took up the duties of a missionary apostle. Threatened with rape, prostitution, and twice put in the ring as a martyr, she persevered in her faith and her chastity. Her lively and somewhat fabulous story is recorded in the second century Acts of Thecla. From very early, an order of women who were widows served formal roles of ministry in some churches (I Timothy 5:9–10). The most numerous clear cases of women's leadership, however, are offered by prophets: Mary Magdalene, the Corinthian women, Philip's daughters, Ammia of Philadelphia, Philumene, the visionary martyr Perpetua, Maximilla, Priscilla (Prisca), and Quintilla. There were many others whose names are lost to us. The African church father Tertullian, for example, describes an unnamed woman prophet in his congregation who not only had ecstatic visions during church services, but who also served as a counselor and healer (On the Soul 9.4). A remarkable collection of oracles from another unnamed woman prophet was discovered in Egypt in 1945. She speaks in the first person as the feminine voice of God: Thunder, Perfect Mind. The prophets Prisca and Quintilla inspired a Christian movement in second century Asia Minor (called the New Prophecy or Montanism) that spread around the Mediterranean and lasted for at least four centuries. Their oracles were collected and published, including the account of a vision in which Christ appeared to the prophet in the form of a woman and "put wisdom" in her (Epiphanius, Panarion 49.1). Montanist Christians ordained women as presbyters and bishops, and women held the title of prophet. The third century African bishop Cyprian also tells of an ecstatic woman prophet from Asia Minor who celebrated the eucharist and performed baptisms (Epistle 74.10). In the early second century, the Roman governor Pliny tells of two slave women he tortured who were deacons (Letter to Trajan 10.96). Other women were ordained as priests in fifth century Italy and Sicily (Gelasius, Epistle 14.26).

Women were also prominent as martyrs and suffered violently from torture and painful execution by wild animals and paid gladiators. In fact, the earliest writing definitely by a woman is the prison diary of Perpetua, a relatively wealthy matron and nursing mother who was put to death in Carthage at the beginning of the third century on the charge of being a Christian. In it, she records her testimony before the local Roman ruler and her defiance of her father's pleas that she recant. She tells of the support and fellowship among the confessors in prison, including other women. But above all, she records her prophetic visions. Through them, she was not merely reconciled passively to her fate, but claimed the power to define the meaning of her own death. In a situation where Romans sought to use their violence against her body as a witness to their power and justice, and where the Christian editor of her story sought to turn her death into a witness to the truth of Christianity, her own writing lets us see the human being caught up in these political struggles. She actively relinquishes her female roles as mother, daughter, and sister in favor of defining her identity solely in spiritual terms.

However horrifying or heroic her behavior may seem, her brief diary offers an intimate look at one early Christian woman's spiritual journey.

Early Christian Women's Theology

Study of works by and about women is making it possible to begin to reconstruct some of the theological views of early Christian women. Although they are a diverse group, certain reoccurring elements appear to be common to women's theology-making. By placing the teaching of the Gospel of Mary side-by-side with the theology of the Corinthian women prophets, the Montanist women's oracles, Thunder Perfect Mind, and Perpetua's prison diary, it is possible to discern shared views about teaching and practice that may exemplify some of the contents of women's theology:

- Jesus was understood primarily as a teacher and mediator of wisdom rather than as ruler and judge.
- Theological reflection centered on the experience of the person of the risen Christ more than the crucified savior. Interestingly enough, this is true even in the case of the martyr Perpetua. One might expect her to identify with the suffering Christ, but it is the risen Christ she encounters in her vision.
- Direct access to God is possible for all through receiving the Spirit.
- In Christian community, the unity, power, and perfection of the Spirit are present now, not just in some future time.
- Those who are more spiritually advanced give what they have freely to all without claim to a fixed, hierarchical ordering of power.
- An ethics of freedom and spiritual development is emphasized over an ethics of order and control.
- A woman's identity and spirituality could be developed apart from her roles as wife and mother (or slave), whether she actually withdrew from those roles or not. Gender is itself contested as a "natural" category in the face of the power of God's Spirit at work in the community and the world. This meant that potentially women (and men) could exercise leadership on the basis of spiritual achievement apart from gender status and without conformity to established social gender roles.
- Overcoming social injustice and human suffering are seen to be integral to spiritual life.

Women were also actively engaged in reinterpreting the texts of their tradition. For example, another new text, the Hypostasis of the Archons, contains a retelling of the Genesis story ascribed to Eve's daughter Norea, in which her mother Eve appears as the instructor of Adam and his healer.

The new texts also contain an unexpected wealth of Christian imagination of the divine as feminine. The long version of the Apocryphon of John, for example, concludes with a hymn about the descent of divine Wisdom, a feminine figure here called the Pronoia of God. She enters into the lower world and the body in order to awaken the innermost spiritual being of the soul to the truth of its power and freedom, to awaken the spiritual power it needs to escape the counterfeit powers that enslave the soul in ignorance, poverty, and the drunken sleep of spiritual deadness, and to overcome illegitimate political and sexual domination. The oracle collection Thunder Perfect Mind also adds crucial evidence to women's prophetic theology-making. This prophet speaks powerfully to women, emphasizing the presence of women in her audience and insisting upon their identity with the feminine voice of the Divine. Her speech lets the hearers transverse the distance between political exploitation and empowerment, between the experience of degradation and the knowledge of infinite self-worth, between despair and peace. It overcomes the fragmentation of the self by naming it, cherishing it, insisting upon the multiplicity of self-hood and experience.

These elements may not be unique to women's religious thought or always result in women's leadership, but as a constellation they point toward one type of theologizing that was meaningful to some early Christian women, that had a place for women's legitimate exercise of leadership, and to whose construction women contributed. If we look to these elements, we are able to discern important contributions of women to early Christian theology and praxis. These elements also provide an important location for discussing some aspects of early Christian women's spiritual lives: their exercise of leadership, their ideals, their attraction to Christianity, and what gave meaning to their self-identity as Christians.

Undermining Women's Prominence

Women's prominence did not, however, go unchallenged. Every variety of ancient Christianity that advocated the legitimacy of women's leadership was eventually declared heretical, and evidence of women's early leadership roles was erased or suppressed.

This erasure has taken many forms. Collections of prophetic oracles were destroyed. Texts were changed. For example, at least one woman's place in history was obscured by turning her into a man! In Romans 16:7, the apostle Paul sends greetings to a woman named Junia. He says of her and her male partner Andronicus that they are "my kin and my fellow prisoners, prominent among the apostles and they were in Christ before me." Concluding that women could not be apostles, textual editors and translators transformed Junia into Junias, a man.

Or women's stories could be rewritten and alternative traditions could be invented. In the case of Mary Magdalene, starting in the fourth century, Christian theologians in the Latin West associated Mary Magdalene with the unnamed sinner who anointed Jesus' feet in Luke 7:36–50. The confusion began by conflating the account in John 12:1–8, in which Mary (of Bethany) anoints Jesus, with the anointing by the unnamed

woman sinner in the accounts of Luke. Once this initial, erroneous identification was secured, Mary Magdalene could be associated with every unnamed sinful woman in the gospels, including the adulteress in John 8:1–11 and the Syro-phoenician woman with her five and more "husbands" in John 4:7–30. Mary the apostle, prophet, and teacher had become Mary the repentant whore. This fiction was invented at least in part to undermine her influence and with it the appeal to her apostolic authority to support women in roles of leadership.

Until recently the texts that survived have shown only the side that won. The new texts are therefore crucial in constructing a fuller and more accurate portrait. The Gospel of Mary, for example, argued that leadership should be based on spiritual maturity, regardless of whether one is male or female. This Gospel lets us hear an alternative voice to the one dominant in canonized works like I Timothy, which tried to silence women and insist that their salvation lies in bearing children. We can now hear the other side of the controversy over women's leadership and see what arguments were given in favor of it.

It needs to be emphasized that the formal elimination of women from official roles of institutional leadership did not eliminate women's actual presence and importance to the Christian tradition, although it certainly seriously damaged their capacity to contribute fully. What is remarkable is how much evidence has survived systematic attempts to erase women from history, and with them the warrants and models for women's leadership. The evidence presented here is but the tip of an iceberg.

Critical Thinking

1. How is the "story" of Mary Magdalene being rewritten in the light of new discoveries?
2. What do the recently discovered Egyptian writings tell us about the prominent roles of women in early Christianity?
3. How was women's early prominence undermined?
4. What does Karen L. King mean when she writes that the evidence in her article supporting models for women's leadership is "but the tip of the iceberg"?

Create Central

www.mhhe.com/createcentral

Internet References

Religion Search Engines: Christianity and Judaism
www.suite101.com/article.cfm/search_engines/13501

KAREN L. KING is Professor of New Testament Studies and the History of Ancient Christianity at Harvard University in the Divinity School. She has published widely in the areas of Gnosticism, ancient Christianity, and Women's Studies.

From *Frontline Report: Jesus to Christ: The First Christians*, April 6, 1998. Copyright © 1998 by Karen King. Reprinted by permission of the author.

Unit VI

UNIT

Prepared by: Joseph R. Mitchell, *Howard Community College*
and Helen Buss Mitchell, *Howard Community College*

The World of the Middle Ages, 500–1500

World historians have some difficulty with this period of time. In the history of Europe, the Middle Ages, or the medieval period, is a time of retreat after the fall of Rome. This thousand year span covers feudalism, the growth of national states, the bubonic plague (called the Black Death), reestablishment of long-distance trade, the domination of the Roman Catholic church, and the emergence of Western civilization. For world historians, Western developments during this period of time are important for the future, but they pale in comparison with the achievements of Islamic civilization and with the changes that people elsewhere in the world were experiencing.

Lifespan and comfort for most European and West Asian people in the year 1000 were little improved from conditions in the previous years, during the reign of the Roman Empire. In Mesoamerica, however, the Maya had created a sophisticated culture that, at its zenith, rivaled that of ancient Egypt. And, the Anasazi, in the North American Southwest, flourished for centuries before disappearing.

In the New World, civilization evolved later than it did in the Old World. Perhaps this was due to the pattern of migration to the Western Hemisphere and the later development of agriculture in that part of the world. The Maya, nonetheless, constructed magnificent stone cities and developed complex social and economic institutions. Classics from the Maya culture, such as the *Popol Vuh,* have given scholars access to myths and rituals that gave life meaning. Unfortunately, much of this sophisticated New World civilization was destroyed in the Spanish conquest. And, the diseases brought by Europeans wreaked havoc among populations that had no exposure, and therefore no immunity, to measles, chickenpox, or scarlet fever.

Meanwhile, this period of time represents a golden age for Islamic power and culture. The Arabs preserved Greek writings, studying and commenting on the dialogues and treatises of Plato and Aristotle that were lost to the Western world. They also became interested in astronomy, and impressed the world with their architecture and advanced medicine. People in the Middle East established the first hospitals and pharmacies, as well as the first universities.

By the 5th century CE, the Roman Empire had established a durable Eastern capital in Constantinople—at the intersection of Europe and Asia—that would survive barbarian attacks and last another thousand years. The Holy Roman Empire, created when Charlemagne was crowned by Pope Leo III on Christmas Day, 800, symbolized an enduring European ideal of unity. This might explain the valiant defense of Constantinople in the face of overwhelming force, before it fell to the Ottoman Turks in 1453.

Explanations for the fall of the Roman Empire have occupied historians for centuries, with internal decay and barbarian invasions being most often-cited as causes. What is certain, however, is that Rome did weaken and eventually disappear. At least, this is true for the Western Roman Empire. Although the Eastern Empire today is no longer a world power, its former capital city (Constantinople, now Istanbul), in the heart of Muslim Turkey, remains the seat of Orthodox Christianity.

Toward the end of this period, farming improved in the West and nations formed. In England, the first halting step toward civil liberties was taken with the signing of the Magna Carta.

Article

Prepared by: Joseph R. Mitchell, *Howard Community College*
and Helen Buss Mitchell, *Howard Community College*

The Survival of the Eastern Roman Empire

Stephen Williams and Gerard Friell analyse why Constantinople survived the barbarian onslaughts in the fifth century, whereas Rome fell.

STEPHEN WILLIAMS AND GERARD FRIELL

Learning Outcomes

After reading this article, you will be able to:

- Determine why the Eastern Roman Empire survived more than a thousand years longer than its Western counterpart and what effect this had on the history of both empires.

The old attitude still prevails in some quarters that what we know of as the Roman Empire was dismembered in the fifth century, and that what survived in the East was something different—Byzantium, Greek and Christian; fascinating, no doubt, but no longer the real Rome. This quite misleading picture is often accompanied by another: that the survival of the Eastern half in the terrible fifth century, when the West went under, was a more or less natural development—even unconsciously anticipated by Constantine's wise foundation of his new capital in the wealthier, more urbanised East.

The reality of course was very different. Despite the administrative division into East and West, which predated Constantine, the empire was everywhere seen as one and indivisible. At the beginnings of the fifth century both halves faced similar chronic problems: immature or inept emperors, rebellious armies, external barbarian invaders and the large and dangerous settlements of barbarian 'allies' within imperial territories. By difficult expedients and innovations the East was eventually able to overcome these problems, while the West was not. After several attempts, Constantinople accepted that it had not the strength to save the West, but it still treated it as a group of temporarily lost provinces to be recovered when the situation permitted—a view that the emperor Justinian in the sixth century took entirely literally.

After the disastrous defeat by the immigrant Visigoths at Adrianople (Edirne) in 378, the new Eastern emperor, Theodosius, was eventually able to fight and manoeuvre them into signing a treaty in 382, settling them in the Balkans as 'allies'

(*foederati*), since they could not possibly be expelled. They were obliged to support the emperor, militarily, on request, but this was nonetheless a radically new departure in foreign policy, the result of Roman weakness. Instead of mere farmer-settlers under Roman administration, this was an entire armed Germanic nation established deep within Roman territory under its own tribal leaders. It could not help but be a precedent for other land-hungry barbarians. Theodosius, however, had no option but to hope that in time the Goths could be assimilated as others had been.

After Theodosius's death in 395, his two young sons, Arcadius (377–408) and Honorius (384–423), inherited the thrones of East and West respectively. Both boy-emperors were immature and incapable (Honorius was practically retarded), and although strong loyalty to the dynasty kept them on their thrones, they were entirely managed by individuals or factions within the two courts. Instead of the cooperation that was badly needed, the two governments of East and West intrigued and manoeuvred against each other like hostile states for over ten years, with damaging consequences.

On Theodosius's death the Visigoths immediately broke out of their assigned territories and ravaged the Eastern provinces, under their leader Alaric, who now declared himself king. Temporarily without their main army, the Eastern government, dominated by the eunuch chamberlain Eutropius, was able to deflect Alaric westwards by granting him a top military command in Illyricum (Yugoslavia). The combined status of Roman general and tribal warlord created yet another dangerous precedent. Alaric was able to exploit the deep hostility between the two governments, becoming a destabilising force over the next fifteen years.

In the West, real power was legitimately in the hands of the commander-in-chief Stilicho, of Vandal origin, who had been appointed guardian of the boy-emperor Honorius. He was resented and feared by the ruling circles at Constantinople, who had him declared a public enemy. Stilicho, hoping in vain to force Alaric back into his former alliance, was able to defeat him several times but not destroy him. He had to crush a revolt in Africa (encouraged by Constantinople) and then defeat an Ostrogothic invasion of Italy itself. He was by now forced to buy barbarian fighting men from any source and on any terms, often with personal promises, and even grants of land.

To defend Italy, Stilicho had to strip Britain and the Rhine frontier of troops, and at New Year 407 multiple barbarian invaders crossed the frozen Rhine into Gaul virtually unopposed, never to be expelled again. For this, Stilicho's political enemies in the Senate contrived to have him condemned and executed on the weak emperor's orders, whereupon thousands of his loyal barbarian troops, fearing for themselves and their families, fled over to join Alaric. With Stilicho removed, nothing could prevent Alaric from besieging and finally sacking Rome in 410.

The East had rid itself of the menace of Alaric by propelling him westwards, but this did not free it from other barbarian dangers. What Alaric's Visigoths could do, others could imitate. A new revolt broke out in 399 among the recently-settled Ostrogothic federates. Gainas, the general sent to suppress it, mistrusted the government and was himself of Gothic origin and the commander of other Gothic federate troops. The two Gothic groups joined forces, marched on Constantinople and occupied it, with Gainas dictating his terms to the emperor. However, he was met by a violent anti-Gothic, popular backlash and total hostility from the civil government. Having achieved nothing, he attempted a clumsy withdrawal from the capital in which many Goths and their families were massacred by the mob. Those that escaped were later defeated by loyal units (also commanded by a Goth).

These events had a profound effect on the civilian ruling circles in Constantinople. Henceforth they were determined to keep a firm grip on imperial power and curb ambitious generals, especially those of Gothic origin, even though many were entirely loyal. For several years Goths were excluded from top commands, armies were thinned in numbers, and care was taken to avoid any new settlements of barbarian federates. The Praetorian Prefect, Anthemius, the acknowledged leader of the state, invested instead in strengthening the defences on the Danube frontier, building a new and massive belt of land walls to protect Constantinople, its emperor and government, from both barbarian invasions and its own potentially dangerous armies.

The exclusion of Gothic generals did not last long. With the federate crises past, and a growing external threat from the Huns, able professional commanders such as Plinta, Aspar and Areobindus once again rose to the top *Magister* posts. The fact that they were divorced from any federate or tribal power base (unlike Alaric and Gainas) made them acceptable. They remained what they had been in the previous century—loyal members of the Roman ruling class.

The really farsighted achievement of the Eastern empire during this period was not so much the weakening of the power of the army, as the institutionalising of it within a central ruling establishment at Constantinople, which included the palace and civil bureaucracy. The Eastern field army, about 100,000 strong, was already divided into five regional mobile groups,

and the commands carefully balanced between men of Gothic and Roman origin. Two of these groups—the Praesental armies—were stationed in the vicinity of Constantinople and their commanders, of whatever background, were senior members of the senate and members of the emperor's inner council of state, the Consistory.

Any successful, ambitious general was faced with a choice and a temptation. He could use external military violence to try to dominate the emperor at Constantinople, perhaps even making himself emperor, or at least military dictator. Or he could use the army's indispensability and natural leverage within the legitimate, established power structure where there was a place for him at the top table.

Gainas had attempted the first option and had been ruined. Other military leaders overwhelmingly chose the second. Though politically powerful, the army was only one of several competing, but also interlocking, forces around the throne. To break out of this careful web of power risked losing everything. Certainly, there were bitter conflicts within the Constantinople establishment. For many years the deficiencies of the pious and bookish emperor Theodosius II (408–450) were heavily compensated by his dominating sister Pulcheria, who did everything possible to keep power within the palace and the imperial family rather than the civil ministers and generals. But even she had to negotiate with these other power centres.

The solidarity of the inner establishment was strikingly demonstrated when confronted by the end of an imperial dynasty, when all the old threats of factional coup, military violence and even civil war reared their heads in the struggle to place a new emperor on the throne. Aware of what each stood to lose, palace, bureaucracy, army and, later, church found ways to fight their conflicts behind closed doors and then present an agreed imperial choice to be acclaimed by the senate, the troops, the people and the wider world.

This orderly transmission of imperial power was achieved in the elevation of Marcian in 450, Leo in 457 and Anastasius in 491, all of them dynastic breaks. Through these precedents, buttressed by an increasingly elaborate ceremony of emperor-making, violent coups and civil wars became the exception. Even if a declared rebel succeeded in gaining wide support outside, he still had to cash in his imperial claims in the capital itself, in the face of the central establishment and the city's virtually impregnable defences: if he did not already enjoy powerful allies within the city this was a daunting task.

Thus, an important factor in the durability of the establishment was simply the acknowledged geographical concentration of power and authority in a single capital, Constantinople, which was in every sense what Rome had once been. The emergence of a viable, rival power base was made very difficult, and this, as much as the city's strategic position and fortifications, contributed heavily to the stability and survival of the Eastern state.

Of all the elements in the establishment, stability was most steadfastly provided by the civil bureaucracy, which provided experience, statecraft and continuity. They kept the impersonal, administrative machine functioning even during violent conflicts within the palace, or purges of this or that faction. These

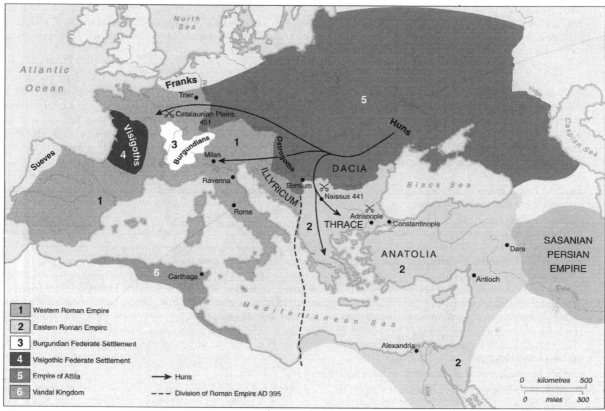

Figure 1   By 450, the Western empire was already a patchwork of barbarian settlements whereas the East retained its integrity.

senatorial mandarins, in fact, represented a new service aristocracy created by Constantine. Frequently of modest origins, they owed their power and status not to birth or landed wealth, but entirely to government service. Consequently, regardless of whether a particular emperor was strong or weak, they took great care to uphold and strengthen the imperial authority itself, since their careers, and hence their prosperity, completely depended on it.

In contrast, the great Western senatorial clans such as the Anicii and Scipiones were only concerned to husband their already huge accumulated family wealth, and treated high state positions as no more than honorific perquisites. Part of the East's undoubtedly greater financial muscle, therefore, was due not just to its inherently greater wealth but also to these mandarins' more honest management of the tax machine, even when it bore on their own aspiring social order.

In the West, the response to the problem of a weak unmilitary emperor was quite different. Real power was concentrated in a military strongman such as Stilicho who ruled on his behalf and enjoyed extraordinary authority, making appointments and issuing laws in the emperor's name. The long reign of the feeble Honorius, the multiple military emergencies and the need to raise and move armies rapidly made this new ruling figure indispensable. After a few years of turmoil the general Constantius stepped into this new position, now vaguely designated

'Patrician' and perhaps better described as military dictator or *generalissimo*. After him came Aetius. Both were patriotic and energetic rulers but had no legally acknowledged position beyond their monopoly of military force, and no regular way of transferring their power to a successor. Each had to intrigue or fight his way to dominant power, which was destructive and destabilising.

Inevitably they came to depend more on their personal popularity and prestige among the troops, whom they recruited and paid. A gulf steadily grew up between the real power of the warlord with his army, and the symbolic, legal authority with the emperor in his palace. During the invasion of Italy, Stilicho had persuaded Honorius to shift the imperial capital from Milan to the safe refuge of Ravenna, creating a geographical split in addition to the political one.

Constantius achieved a degree of stability in the West, but at enormous cost. Visigoths, Burgundians, Franks, Suevi and Vandals were all settled as federates on large tracts of Gaul and Spain, and were evolving into Germanic kingdoms under only the most nominal Roman overlordship. Constantius and Aetius skilfully exploited their rivalries to maintain some ascendancy. But having relinquished control of so much taxable land and its populations, the regular Roman armies were only one force among many, and no responsible leader could do more than hold the balance, and avoid risking this force if possible.

The Hun menace took on an entirely new dimension with Attila, who had unified them under a single king and subjected all the remaining tribes to Hun rule. His object was not land to settle, but plunder, tribute and glory, and once again the blow fell initially on the East. His hordes ravaged the Balkans three times in the 440s, sacking and ruining many major cities and enslaving their populations. The Roman armies that met him in the field were repeatedly beaten by his cavalry, but he was always deterred by Constantinople whose defences he could not storm. After each invasion he had to be bought off by an increasingly ignominious 'treaty' and larger annual payments, involving heavier taxation of the senatorial classes. In all, the East paid him about nine tons of gold, until the new emperor Marcian finally tore up the treaties and defied him.

Yet here, the two great resources of the East came to the rescue: the impassable fortifications of Constantinople and the enormous taxable wealth of the Asiatic provinces—Anatolia, Syria, Palestine, Egypt. So long as this great land gate was kept shut and so long as these provinces remained secure—meaning peaceful relations with Persia—Attila could always be bought off and much of the Balkan territories temporarily lost without mortal damage to the empire.

Relations with Persia were always a crucial consideration if the empire was to avoid the perils of fighting on two frontiers simultaneously. Unlike other potential enemies, Persia was a centralised, sophisticated state, and both empires were continually involved in a chess game of military and diplomatic manoeuvres which at intervals broke down into open war. In set battle the Romans could usually win, but at quite huge logistical costs. The 1,400-mile frontier zone along the Euphrates was already the most expensive in terms of providing troops and resources. The danger was not so much that Persia would conquer the Roman provinces, as that they would disrupt the whole delicate defensive system of Arab alliances and force the empire to a great commitment of forces, imperilling other frontiers.

But, although Persia tried to take advantage of the empire's difficulties elsewhere, its war aims were limited and it was usually amenable to negotiation. After nearly twenty years of peace, a brief Persian attack in 441 was halted and led to a new treaty involving Roman payments. At the same time, Persia's ambitions were severely checked by pressure from their own northern enemies, the Ephthalite horse peoples, akin to the Huns, who were tacitly encouraged by Constantinople. Whatever martial propaganda they still broadcast to their peoples, the two empires gradually came to accept the advantages of avoiding costly and unrewarding wars, and sought if possible to resolve conflicts by other means. As a result, a mature and structured diplomacy became as important as the military strategy.

Finally, after suffering heavier casualties in battle for diminishing returns of plunder, Attila decided to cut his losses and invade westward. Here Aetius, with all his carefully cultivated barbarian friendships, performed a diplomatic miracle in uniting and commanding the mutually hostile Germanic kingdoms in a great coalition to stop Attila in 451. After a huge and bloody battle on the Catalaunian plains of northern Gaul, Attila was forced for the first time to retreat. The next year he mounted an abortive invasion of Italy. Soon afterwards, he died suddenly in a drunken stupor. Within a short time his always personal and charismatic 'empire' collapsed.

In the West, Aetius was immediately concerned to disperse the more numerous and powerful Germanic armies as quickly as possible. But now that the main barbarian threat seemed removed, he was treacherously murdered by the emperor Valentinian III (425–455) who had long hated him. In revenge, Aetius's partisans assassinated Valentinian shortly afterwards, ending the Theodosian dynasty.

The next *generalissimo* figure, Ricimer, was himself a barbarian and naturally well-qualified to deal with the overwhelmingly barbarian army and allies. He was related both to the Visigoth and Sueve royal houses, and very willing to allow more federate settlements. Ricimer was a leader spanning two worlds. He saw the Roman empire more as a prestigious, unifying symbol than a political reality, and he set up and deposed puppet emperors at will. In the end it was only logical that a barbarian king should step into the ruling role of patrician and *generalissimo*. When that happened there was no need to retain even a figurehead emperor in the West. In 476 the barbarian king Odovacer forced the emperor Romulus Augustulus to abdicate, and sent an embassy to Constantinople declaring that he would henceforth rule as the viceroy of the Eastern emperor. The fiction of a single united Roman empire was still retained.

The East had tried, and partially succeeded, in arranging the fragments of Attila's old empire to its advantage, but it had been forced to accept two large blocs of Ostrogoths, formerly subjects of Attila, as federates in Illyricum (Yugoslavia) and Thrace (Bulgaria-Romania). These were a destabilising element, each too strong to be defeated by a single Roman field army. In the confused reign of Zeno (474–491) all the dangerous elements erupted again: open conflict in the imperial family, civil wars for the throne, rebellion by the Gothic federates. At one point there was fighting within the capital itself. There seemed a real danger that the Ostrogoths would carve out permanent kingdoms for themselves in the way this had happened in the West.

For a time, the central establishment lost control, but they had several strong advantages. There was always a strong core of regular Roman troops to balance the federates, and they continued to be steadily recruited. All the soldiers, Roman or federate, could only be paid from the central treasuries, which were a potent lever in negotiations, as were timely bribes of gold. The Goths also suffered periodic food shortages which the imperial government, with its network of cities and supply depots, naturally exploited. The two Gothic blocs were often in competition and could easily be played off against each other. Their aims were opportunistic and their long-term goals uncertain. One king, Theoderic (471–526), wanted larger, more secure territories for his people, while the other, Strabo, aimed at a top Roman command and a seat at the centre of government.

By the time Zeno had managed to crush or conciliate his other domestic enemies, by adroit and unscrupulous manoeuvring, Strabo was dead and all the Goths followed Theoderic. In 488, with only one king to deal with, Zeno played the masterstroke. Instead of poor and precarious lands in the Balkans, he invited Theoderic to take Italy from Odovacer. Theoderic did so, finally freeing the East of the federate problem.

It was left to the next emperor Anastasius (491–518) to consolidate these gains. Himself a civil bureaucrat who knew the government machinery intimately, he overhauled and improved the entire fiscal system to produce considerably greater sums for the treasury without injuring the mass of taxpayers. With these funds he expanded the armies by raising pay, built new defences, revived and repopulated much of the Balkans, and fought a successful war against Persia, still leaving a healthy surplus. It was with these great resources that Justinian was soon to embark on his ambitious schemes of reconquest.

The East had certain long-term advantages: a strategically placed capital, shorter vulnerable frontiers, a wealthier agricultural base. But it demanded a high order of statecraft to overcome all the external and internal threats of the fifth century. Individually, its leaders were no more skilful than their Western counterparts, but they managed to evolve institutions and practices which applied these skills and perpetuated them. The Constantinople establishment; the constitutional rituals of imperial succession; the integration of the top army commands; the opposition to federate settlements; the centralised pool of administrative, fiscal and diplomatic experience—all these enabled the East to avoid the unravelling process of diminishing control which occurred in the West.

For Further Reading

A.H.M. Jones, *The Later Roman Empire* (2 vols, Oxford University Press, 1990); J.B. Bury, *History of The Later Roman Empire*, (Dover paperbacks, 1958); R.C. Blockley, *East Roman Foreign Policy* (ARCA, 1992); J.H.W.G. Liebeschuetz, *From Diocletian to the Arab Conquest,* (Oxford University Press, 1990); J.H. W.G. Liebeschuetz, *Barbarians and Bishops: Army, Church and State in the Age of Arcadius and Chrysostom* (Oxford University Press, 1991); C. Mango, *Byzantium. The Empire of New Rome* (London, 1980).

Critical Thinking

1. How did institutionalizing the army create stability in the Eastern Roman Empire?

2. How did the "impossible fortifications of Constantinople and the enormous taxable wealth of the Asiatic provinces" protect the Eastern Empire against Attila the Hun?

3. How did a "mature and structured diplomacy" help Constantinople reach a stalemate with Persia?

Create Central

www.mhhe.com/createcentral

Internet References

Labyrinth Home Page to Medieval Studies
    www.georgetown.edu/labyrinth/
WWW Medieval Resources
    http://ebbs.english.vt.edu/medieval/medieval.ebbs.html

STEPHEN WILLIAMS and GERARD FRIELL are also the authors of *Theodosius: the Empire at Bay* (Batsford, 1994).

Article

Prepared by: Joseph R. Mitchell, *Howard Community College*
and Helen Buss Mitchell, *Howard Community College*

Trophy Skulls and Beer

Unearthing the Source of an Andean Empire's Power

ANDREW CURRY

Learning Outcomes

After reading this article, you will be able to:

- Discuss what accounted for the rise to power of the Wari Empire and what contributed to its demise.

In the clear Peruvian mountain air, the view from the sun-baked summit of Cerro Baúl stretches 50 miles or more. The vista is dominated by dozens of arid valleys and distant Andean peaks. A thousand years ago, a person on this 2,600-foot mountain would have been standing at the southern frontier of the Wari Empire, which dominated much of what is now Peru from A.D. 600 until it disappeared around 400 years later, a period archaeologists call the Middle Horizon. The Wari likely thought of Cerro Baúl as sacred; even now, the ground here is littered with carefully arranged pebbles in the shape of houses or farms and the occasional empty bottle of liquor, left behind by locals as offerings to the spirit of the mountain. But archaeological evidence shows the mountaintop was much more than a holy place on the fringes of an empire. It may be the key to understanding how the Wari managed to control a state that stretched some 800 miles to the north.

To me, the hilltop looks like a lifeless jumble of tan boulders. But Donna Nash, an archaeologist from Chicago's Field Museum and codirector of the Cerro Baúl Archaeological Project, sees something quite different. Striding across the bleak surface, pointing to the outlines of walls and corridors that have long since collapsed or been blown away, she conjures a vision of what once stood here—a palace complex of colorful two-story buildings. At one time, she says, hundreds of people lived up here. Everything they needed—water, food, precious stones for crafting beads, clay for making pots, and corn for brewing beer—had to be carried to the top. In what was once the courtyard of the central palace, archaeologists found three tree stumps, evidence of a garden that must have been nourished with water brought up in jars.

Living on top of a mountain was a tremendous display of power and wealth. And mountaintop temples would have had great views of other peaks, perhaps an important element of Wari rituals. "It's not an economically efficient production site," Ryan Williams, the dig codirector and Nash's husband, tells me later. "But you impress the neighbors by living closer to the gods."

And, perhaps, by showing them a good time. The most critical building at Cerro Baúl may have been the brewery. A four-room structure about 2,500 square feet, it had all the equipment needed to make *chicha,* a corn-based beer still popular in the Andes. The first step was drying the corn, then it was soaked until it sprouted and ground to a mash. One room in the brewery had five grindstones, all brought to the mountaintop from another peak three and a half miles away. "In the plaster floor, you could see where the knees of the women grinding were," Nash says. The mash was then boiled in one of eight ceramic vats. The last step was fermentation; 12 huge jars, each holding 40 gallons, or enough to brew 1,800 pints of chicha, were set into the floor of the brewery's central patio.

As we stand among the ruins, Nash tells me the Wari—usually thought of as a fairly bloodthirsty bunch, based on pottery painted with images of warriors, beheadings, and bound captives—may have actually wooed local leaders with a potent mix of corn beer and hallucinogens. Mountaintop palaces might have functioned like embassies, and could have played a role in a soft-power effort to impress the neighbors with great parties.

"Alcohol is a part of our politics, but we don't think about it. Beer was a tool of state back then, just like it's a tool now," Nash says. "You get more flies with honey. I think the Wari figured that out and were really, really good at it."

Despite decades of research into their culture, the Wari are still remarkably enigmatic. Initially, archaeologists mistook their carefully planned cities for Inca ruins. Later scholars wondered if the distinctive, military-themed pottery was made by a people who were an offshoot of the Tiwanaku, a culture whose state centered around Lake Titicaca and had borders that came to within just a few miles from

Cerro Baúl. "Wari is an interesting phenomenon because it was missed," says William Isbell, an archaeologist at Binghamton University. "Nobody recognized the Wari until the late, 40s."

A distinct Wari culture emerged around A.D. 600, from a group who archaeologists call the Huarpa, located near Ayacucho, in the mountains of central Peru. Within a century, the Wari pushed out of the Ayacucho region and planted colonies as far north as modern-day Lima and beyond, and south all the way to Cerro Baúl. There are as many opinions on how and why they were able to spread so far, so quickly as there are archaeologists who study the Wari. Even less is known about what brought the empire to an end.

In the early 1970s, Isbell began a major excavation of Huari, the empire's capital near Ayacucho. Only then could archaeologists appreciate the scale and complexity of the Wari culture. Isbell's initial survey work revealed a huge, complex city. Tightly packed, multistory buildings and a well-organized, uniform architectural style set it apart from the more free-form architecture of Tiwanaku. The city's scale was overwhelming: three miles on each side, the urban core alone covered more than 6,000 acres.

Archaeologists' initial impressions of Wari culture were grim. Pottery—often in the form of large cups, or keros—was decorated not just with warriors and bound captives but with fierce-looking supernatural creatures, deities with serpents projecting from their heads and long, sharp teeth. Skeletal remains showed evidence of human sacrifice. And the monumental architecture found at the capital showed evidence of sharp class distinctions—the elite lived in their own neighborhoods, for example.

But the sheer size of the site made getting a clear picture impossible. "You'd need millions of dollars and many archaeologists' lifetimes to make sense of it," says Catholic University archaeologist Anita Cook. As it turned out, archaeologists were given less than a decade. Modern-day politics intervened just as work at Huari was beginning to yield tantalizing data on Wari architecture and ceremonial practices. In 1980, the Communist guerilla group called the Sendero Luminoso, or Shining Path, began a campaign of terror in the Peruvian countryside, blowing up government buildings and fighting with the Peruvian military. The Ayacucho area was one of the movement's strongholds.

The impact on archaeology was immediate. The violence in and around Ayacucho made excavation impossible, and many local museums, including the one at Huari itself, were ransacked, obliterating years of research. However, the Shining Path rampage in and around Ayacucho had an unexpected silver lining for archaeologists.

Unable to work in the Wari heartland, researchers looked farther afield, excavating far-flung Wari settlements along the Peruvian coast, in the southern highlands, and in the mountains near Cuzco. "The Sendero Luminoso brought archaeology to a screeching halt in the central highlands for a decade," says Mary Glowacki, an archaeologist for the Florida Bureau of Archaeological Research who works on Wari sites in the mountains near Cuzco. "Because Ayacucho couldn't be studied, professors started sending students out to provincial cities. That's when we began to see evidence for what was perceived as imperial expansion."

Wari outposts all over Peru gave scholars new insights into how Wari culture ticked. At site after provincial site, the architecture was nearly identical, down to the measurements of the walls. The implication was that a single political entity—an empire—had built outposts all over, and all at once. "There's an architectural pattern that was clearly Wari," Cook says. One of the most dramatic examples was found near Cuzco.

Called Pikillacta (the name means "flea town" in the local Quechua language), the site resembles a sheet of graph paper when seen from the air: row after row of perfectly square rooms stretch across nearly 500 acres, all contained within a wall 40 feet high. "The architecture just knocks your socks off," Isbell says. "But we don't know how Pikillacta worked." Even basic architectural details, like how people moved from room to room inside the complex, are unclear.

The more archaeologists explored the Wari hinterlands, the more it looked like the Wari created an extensive Andean empire. What no one could agree on was how. Pikillacta only deepened the mystery. "The architectural remains are very cryptic," says Isbell. "We thought that there were going to be barracks and institutional sites for soldiers, but our work indicates they were never finished. They were multistoried constructions, and all we have are the foundations. It may not be that accurate a picture." Were the formidable sites barracks for Wari armies? Or something else entirely? Suggestions have ranged from temple complexes to mausoleums filled with mummies to administrative centers full of bureaucrats.

Because of the warlike images on Wari pottery and the rigid planning of their settlements, many scholars assumed they were violent, totalitarian conquerors. But finds such as the brewery atop Cerro Baúl have begun to change the way archaeologists see the Wari. "We're all walking on eggshells now because so much new data is coming out," says Cook. Rather than a rigid, one-dimensional empire governed by fear and violence, a more complex picture is emerging, of a flexible culture that could have included everything from ritual executions of foreign leaders to drug-fueled parties in its repertoire. (Stylized images of the hallucinogenic plant *Anadenanthera colubrina* are often found on urns used to brew beer, a clue that the Wari may have added a special kick to their chicha.)

But Cook says violence still played an important role. Since 1999, she and Isbell have been excavating a site called Conchopata, a Wari town not far from the capital of Huari. It has been a rich source of data on Wari architecture, giving researchers in the provinces something to compare their sites to. It's also yielded concrete evidence that violence was sometimes employed as a part of Wari rituals. Archaeologists uncovered several buildings thought to be temples or ritual spaces. Inside, mingled with the bones of slaughtered llama and smashed pots painted with scenes of warriors and gods, were 31 severed human heads.

Vanderbilt University bioarchaeologist Tiffiny Tung says the heads are proof that the vivid pictures of violence and military might the Wari painted on their pottery reflected reality. "There's a hole drilled in the top for a carrying cord, and cut marks indicate that they were fresh skulls," defleshed with care, Tung says. "Specialists were processing these skulls to transform them [into trophies]." About a quarter of the skulls belonged to children.

Even more important, perhaps, is that stable isotope analysis of the skulls showed the majority came not from Conchopata but from the fringes of the Wari Empire. "A portion of the heads are coming from distant locations," she says. "It's possible that Wari military agents were traveling, taking captives back to Conchopata, ritually sacrificing them and transforming them into trophy heads." The captives could have been beheaded and their skulls stripped on the spot, then carried back as trophies to the heartland. But the Wari often painted people tied up alongside severed heads. "There's clearly a connection between bound captives and trophy heads," Tung says.

Trophy heads have been found in the Wari hinterlands, too. In 2007, Glowacki found an elaborately prepared trophy head at a Wari cemetery site called Cotocotuyoc, near Cuzco. Defleshed and carved in a way that resembles the ones Tung studied at Conchopata, the Cotocotuyoc skull was suitable for use as a drinking vessel. An alignment of gold tacks on the skull suggests that someone attached artificial hair to it, perhaps to make it more lifelike. "It's very unusual, the only one we've ever recovered," says Patricia Knobloch, a member of the Institute of Andean Studies based in San Diego, California. "But the imagery is everywhere. Trophy skulls were rather common."

Nash and Williams have a different story to tell at Cerro Baúl. Among thousands of Tiwanaku remains found just a few miles away, none has any indications of violent death—surprising for the neighbors of a supposedly bloodthirsty empire. When I ask Nash about the ample violence depicted on Wari pottery, she mischievously suggests it might just be propaganda. "If we based our understanding of the United States on imagery, we'd think everybody walks around in bikinis and is blonde," she says. "We need to analyze human remains, figure out who's who and look for evidence of violence." Nash argues that even the trophy heads might not be conclusive evidence for warfare or human sacrifice—they could be signs of ancestor worship, unimaginably gruesome to us but not unknown in ethnological research from tribes further north, in the Amazon.

So far, only a few sets of human remains have been found at Cerro Baúl and the digs Nash has done lower on the mountainside. That in itself is surprising. University of Florida archaeologist Michael Moseley was the first to identify the site in 1980s. He dubbed it the "Masada of the Andes," after the plateau where a few hundred Jews held off Roman legions for two months.

This close to the edge of an empire, it made sense for Wari warriors to build a mountaintop castle for protection against invaders. But look closer, Williams says, and the idea of Cerro Baúl as an impregnable fortress crumbles. The plateau is forbidding, but it's also dry as a bone. "I always thought it would

be a strange place for a military fort because there's no source of water," says Williams. In a prolonged siege, the lack of water would be a profound weakness.

So what inspired the Wari to locate a settlement on such an unlikely perch? This close to the Tiwanaku, the palace and temples atop the mountain were like an advertisement for Wari superiority and a diplomatic mission all rolled into one. Nash has found evidence that the Tiwanaku and Wari mingled all the way up the slopes of the mountain. "Maybe the Tiwanaku people were living on the flanks of Cerro Baúl because the Wari threw better parties," Nash says.

Even though their architecture may have been rigid and uniform, it doesn't mean the Wari ran foreign policy the same way. Katharina Schreiber, an archaeologist at the University of California, Santa Barbara, uses the term "mosaic of control" to describe the patchwork strategies the Wari might have used to subdue, eliminate, buy off, or charm local leaders. "The Wari were an early experiment in empire-building. They had no history of prior empires, no precedent to look back on," Schreiber says. "They found it takes very different strategies to control different places."

What worked at the southern end of the empire at Cerro Baúl may not have been the right strategy in the distant north. Flexibility may have been the secret to Wari success. "Intimidation is a powerful imperial tool, and it's hard to intimidate if you don't show your power at least once," Nash says. "But successful empires allow diversity and take advantage of it."

Before we leave the mountaintop, Nash leads me back to the remains of the palace to show me what might be one of the most tangible links to the Wari ambassadors. Around A.D. 850, someone was buried here in a corner of the courtyard. The tomb was looted long ago—Nash and Williams found human teeth embedded in the wall of the tomb, though the rest of the body had been removed—but whoever was buried here must have been important. After the burial, there was a tremendous feast that included guinea pigs, llama, Andean hare, and seven different kinds of fish from the ocean 40 miles away. Dozens of pots and cups were smashed on top of the tomb, just before the palace itself was torn down.

Nash and Williams have evidence for another momentous feast that took place two centuries after the palace was dismantled. After brewing nearly 2,000 pints of beer over the course of more than a week, it seems the Wari held one last drunken blowout at Cerro Baúl. Two dozen or more lords, each raising a uniquely decorated kero, toasted one last time, then smashed the ceramic drinking vessels on the floor of the brewery. Then they lit the building on fire and left the mountaintop forever.

Not long after Cerro Baúl was abandoned, the Wari experiment with empire ran its course. The end remains as mysterious as the beginning. There were no great upheavals, no invasions from neighboring powers. Small villages were abandoned in favor of larger settlements and cities, and then the cities themselves emptied out. It would be centuries before the Inca stepped into the vacuum the Wari left behind, once again uniting what is now Peru through a familiar mixture of intimidation, coercion, and attraction.

Nash is effusive about the things she and Williams have found on this mountaintop. But she's under no illusions that Cerro Baúl is a typical Wari site. Looking out over the arid landscape below, she draws an unexpected analogy. "Cerro Baúl is essentially London in the Roman Empire," she says. Like London to the Romans, Cerro Baúl was on the edge of the world. And like London, archaeology has shown that Cerro Baúl was connected to a well-organized, smoothly functioning political system, one that needed the Middle Horizon equivalents of ambassadors and provincial governors and diplomatic receptions out on the frontier. "How did they do it? How did they control an area 300 miles south of their capital for 400 years?" Nash asks me as we get ready to descend. "And what did people feel like who got sent out to Cerro Baúl?" One thing is for certain—they could count on a kero of chicha.

Critical Thinking

1. What does Donna Nash mean when she says, "Beer was a tool of state back then, just like it's a tool now. You get more flies with honey."?

2. What does Katharine Schreiber mean when she uses the phrase "mosaic of control" to describe Wari Empire Building?

3. What does Donna Nash mean when she says, "Cerro Baul is essentially London in the Roman Empire"?

Create Central

www.mhhe.com/createcentral

Internet References

Lords of the Earth: Maya/Aztec/Inca Exchange
www.mayalords.org/

ANDREW CURRY is a contributing editor at ARCHAEOLOGY

From *Archaeology*, January/February 2010, pp. 38–43. Copyright © 2010 by Archaeological Institute of America. Reprinted by permission of *Archaeology Magazine*. www.archaeology.org

Article

Prepared by: Joseph R. Mitchell, *Howard Community College*
and Helen Buss Mitchell, *Howard Community College*

The Ideal of Unity

Russell Chamberlin examines the origins and development of Europe's persistent vision of unity from the birth of the Holy Roman Empire to its fall.

RUSSELL CHAMBERLIN

Learning Outcomes

After reading this article, you will be able to:

- Discuss why the medieval Holy Roman Emperors were unable to unify Europe and understand why the ideal of unity still rings clear for many Europeans today.

Neither holy, nor Roman, nor an empire'. Voltaire's gibe about the Holy Roman Empire was literally true but, like all such glib gibes missed the essential point. For a thousand years people believed it existed or thought it ought to exist. For a thousand years, as they tore at each other in fratricidal wars, Europeans nevertheless nursed the idea of a unity that would bind, not destroy, their racial identities. The Treaty of Rome of 1957, which established the European Economic Community, might lack the drama of the events of Christmas Day, 800, but it shared the same dynamic, and the Treaty may yet prove more durable than the crown.

On that day, Karl der Grosse, King of the Franks, King of the Lombards, Patrician of Rome, better known to English and French posterity as Charlemagne, had bent in prayer in the basilica of St Peter's in Rome. He was startled (some said later) when, without warning, Pope Leo III advanced and placed a circlet of gold on his head. The congregation, in a well-rehearsed chorus, acclaimed him as Roman law prescribed, 'To Carolus Augustus, crowned by God, mighty and pacific emperor, be life and victory'.

The giant silver-haired Frank rose to his feet, towering above the slighter-built Latins and, according to his biographer, Einhard, protested—just a little too much, in the view of posterity. His counsellor, the Englishman Alcuin, who had wide contacts in Rome, must have been well aware of the tide moving in Rome and had surely informed his master of the plans to revive the Roman empire with him at its head. Indeed, after the acclamation the rituals of coronation went smoothly, suggesting that all had been prepared long beforehand. And whatever his private thoughts, the new Emperor voluntarily took part in the ceremonies that followed.

Whoever stage-managed the event in St Peter's had done his work well by arranging that 'acclamation' by the Roman people and clergy. Even in the most dictatorial and tyrannical days of the classical empire the emperor was in theory chosen—acclaimed—by the army and the people, and the idea that the Roman empire was a *res publica* had never been abandoned, even when it had become a formality.

Charlemagne's protests were diplomatic and political: he was objecting to the time and manner of Leo's act and its heavy symbolism. Moreover, he realised that the man who bestowed a crown could take it back. Charlemagne was having none of that. When, eleven years later, he made his last surviving son Louis co-emperor it was he who, personally, placed the crown on the young man's head. Centuries later, Napoleon took the hint and, in making himself 'emperor' of the French, took care to crown himself.

There was another reason for Charlemagne to protest: Leo's action was illegal. There could be only one *imperator* on earth and he (or, to be exact, she, Irene) was already reigning in Constantinople. Strictly speaking, the Roman Empire—the empire of Augustus, Nero, Virgil and Tacitus—endured until 1453 when the last true Roman emperor fell beneath Turkish swords. Leo's act began the long degradation of the once awesome title, so that, in due course, there would emerge an 'emperor' of Austria, an 'emperor' of Mexico, of Haiti, and, ultimate absurdity, the British style, 'king-emperor', adopted after the acquisition of the Indian Empire even as, ironically, the mighty empire itself would dwindle down to a 'loose federation of German princes under the presidency of the House of Habsburg'.

The Byzantines derided the coronation of Charlemagne. To them he was simply another barbarian general with ideas above his station. Indeed, he took care never to style himself *Imperator Romanorum*. His jurists, dredging through the detritus of empire, came up with a title which met with his approval: *Romanum gubernas imperium* 'Governing the Roman Empire'. The resounding title of this first of the post-classical Western Emperors was 'Charles, Most Serene Augustus, crowned by God, great and merciful Emperor, governing the Roman empire and by the mercy of God, King of the Lombards and the Franks'.

Although illegal, the coronation and acclamation were perhaps inevitable. In the Western world, the rule of law had broken down. Alcuin, a stickler for law and conventions, gave his opinion:

> Upon you alone reposes the whole salvation of the Churches of Christ. You are the avenger of crime, the guide of the wanderers, the comforter of the mourners, the exaltation of the righteous.

A thousand years later, James Bryce, the great historian of the Holy Roman Empire, agreed that a vacuum had been created in Europe by the rise of Byzantium. The coronation of Charlemagne 'was the revolt of the ancient Western capital against a daughter who had become a mistress, an exercise of the sacred right of insurrection justified by the weakness and wickedness of the Byzantine'. That wickedness had plumbed new depths a few years earlier when the reigning emperor Constantine had been blinded and, deposed by his mother who claimed to reign as 'emperor': to Western apologists, the Byzantine throne was vacant and the Frankish monarch was merely taking up the sceptre laid down by the Latin Caesars. One of the great myths of history is the portrayal of the 'Fall of the Roman Empire' as a Hollywood-type scenario in which shaggy, skin-clad Germanic 'barbarians' hurl themselves upon elegant, toga-clad 'Romans', raping, murdering, destroying what they could not eat, wear or carry off. In reality the 'barbarians' were inferior only in culture, not intelligence. They could, and did, respond to the majesty of the Empire. For a people without written records, that Empire must have seemed, quite literally, eternal: an almost supernatural structure around which the world always had and always would revolve. But they realised that behind this outward show was a hugely complex human system that had brought stability out of chaos. In the early 5th century, the Visigothic chieftain, Arhalhauf, spoke for most of his fellow barbarians:

> It was at first my wish to destroy the Roman name and erect in its place a Gothic empire. But when experience taught me that the untameable barbarism of the Goths would not suffer them to live under the sway of law I chose the glory of renewing and maintaining by Gothic strength the fame of Rome.

The Franks themselves had entered history fighting alongside the Roman army at one of its last great battles, that of Chalons in 451 A.D. when it turned back the invasion of Attila the Hun. The captain of the Frankish host was Merovech, who founded the first Frankish dynasty, the Merovings, but they were gradually shouldered aside by their own Mayors of the Palace. The dynasty ended bloodlessly in 751, when Charlemagne's father Pippin appealed to Rome, asking, in effect, who should wear the crown: he who was the puppet or he who truly ruled? Pope Zarachias came down in Pippin's favour. He thus began that link between pope and Germanic king that was to dominate the notion of the Western Christian empire for centuries.

Meanwhile, a debt had been contracted and four years later the papacy sent Pippin the bill. In January 754 Pope Stephen and a small entourage braved the Alps in mid-winter to throw himself at the feet of Pippin and plead for help against Aistulf, King of the Lombards, who had dared to seize the property of the Church. Pippin avoided the tricky business of precedence between pope and monarch by sending his fourteen-year-old son to escort Stephen to the palace, thus providing posterity with its first glimpse of the future Charlemagne.

The historiography of Charlemagne is tantalising. Later, he had his own biographer, in his devoted secretary and architect Einhard. But though Einhard declared he would record nothing through hearsay, he also glossed over facts unfavourable to his hero. The surviving evidence of the development of the relationship between the papal and Frankish courts is one-sided, for while all the popes' letters survived in the Frankish archives, the letters from Pippin and his sons have disappeared from the Vatican, probably looted on the orders of Napoleon.

After Charlemagne's debut, little is heard of him directly until the death of his father in 768. He emerged on the European stage with his capture of the Lombard capital of Pavia in 774, thereby acquiring the Iron Crown of the Lombards and establishing the Frankish control beyond the Alps. The young king began to lay the foundations of what was to become an imperial regime and which, eventually, would provide a blueprint for Europe for centuries.

Distance and communication were the greatest problems he faced, as for all medieval monarchs. He tackled these by establishing *missi domini,* trusted counsellors with delegated powers who penetrated every part of his enormous realm, which ran from the Elbe to the Tiber, conveying his will in documents known as 'capitularies'. These provide a means for historians to follow the thought processes by which he governed his expanding realm. Named after the articles or capitula into which they were divided, each was nominally concerned with a specific subject but tended to be wide-ranging, as though the King were saying, 'Oh, yes that reminds me . . .'. Nothing was too small: the provision of a dowry for a young girl; the number and type of tools to be kept in a manor. Nothing was too large: the composition of the Host in the mass; the conduct of priests.

The deeply religious Charlemagne, through his relationship with a succession of six popes, strove to advance the ideal of a theocratic state governed by a priest and a king in harmony. But there was no doubt as to which he considered the dominant partner. When Pope Leo III announced that a vial of the Precious Blood had been found in Mantua the sceptical King ordered an enquiry. Nothing more was heard of the miraculous substance. His restless, questing, creative mind stimulated the so-called Carolingian renaissance, that sudden flowering of learning which was doomed to disappear after his death. But it left its permanent mark, in the form of the Carolingian miniscule script, which replaced the ugly, spiky Merovingian script, and was adopted by the humanist Poggio Bracciolini in the fifteenth century and through him became the model for all fonts of print.

The King's transmutation into Emperor made little personal difference to him. He did not fall into the trap of trying to pass himself off as a Roman and in so doing losing contact with his roots. Only twice did he wear the robes of the Patrician, both times by direct request of the pope. He dressed and acted in a manner indistinguishable from his subjects. He took literally the precept 'where the emperor is, there is Rome' and his beloved city of Aachen became the Rome of the North.

Charlemagne's imprint on Aachen remains evident over a thousand years later. The city's *rathaus* is built on the foundations of his palace, making it the world's longest occupied seat of administration. Even more astonishing is his chapel, designed by Einhard on the basis of the mystic octagon. Nothing has changed in its interior. The Emperor Frederick Barbarossa (r. 1152–90) provided an immense candelabra to celebrate Charlemagne's canonisation in 1165: the Emperor Henry II (r. 1002–24) provided the golden front of the altar, but nothing else has been added. The mezzanine gallery, on which the throne is placed, is approached by a flight of stairs which could be in a modest town church. The throne itself, composed of plain slabs of stone, is unchanged; Thirty emperors have been crowned in it: each resisted the temptation to add his symbols to its simple expression of majesty.

With the death of Charlemagne in 814, cracks in the state opened up in the Empire, as warlords struggled for dominance. Yet the memory continued of that compact made on Christmas Day 800, and those boasting Carolingian blood, no matter how remote or illegitimate, advanced their claims over the rest. But without effect. It seemed that the Empire was at an end before it had started.

It was revived only by bizarre events in Rome in the mid-tenth century. By this time, Rome was on the edge of collapse. The aqueducts had long since failed, forcing the population, now shrunk to less than 20,000, to huddle in the unhealthy lower areas. Bandit families holed up in the once-great buildings, fighting each other and preying on the populace. The Donation of Constantine, an eighth-century forgery according to which the first Christian Emperor had supposedly granted the Church vast territories in central Italy, had turned the papacy into a territorial monarchy, to be fought for as any other secular prize. The papacy itself was in a state of grotesque degradation, with popes murdering or being murdered, placed on the throne by their paramours, hurled off it by their rivals. Two extraordinary women ruled both the city and the papacy, Theodora and her daughter Marozia, the probable model for the later legend of Pope Joan. The sober papal historian, Cardinal Baronius, writing in the sixteenth century, labelled this period the 'Pornocracy'. In 961 the Apostolic throne was occupied by Marozia's grandson, a dissolute twenty-year-old called John XII. Threatened by a Lombard warlord, Berengar, he summoned a Germanic monarch, the Saxon Otto I, to his aid, promising that crown of empire which—it was now believed—only a pope could bestow.

Like Charlemagne before his own imperial coronation, Otto was already a figure of European stature. At Lechfeld (955) near Augsburg, his army had destroyed an immense army of Magyars, true barbarians as murderous as the Huns. It was claimed that his warriors hailed him as *imperator* after the battle: inherently unlikely but testament to how he was seen.

Otto came at John's summons but he had no illusions about the fickle, violent Romans. He instructed his sword-bearer, Ansfried:

> When I kneel today at the grave of the Apostle, stand behind me with the sword. I know only too well what my ancestors have experienced from these faithless Romans.

But all passed smoothly. John listened contritely to the lecture on morals by the pious Saxon, and made specious promises. Yet the moment Otto withdrew from Rome to commence the campaign against Berengar, John offered the crown of empire—to Berengar. That failing, he peddled it round, with no takers. It is difficult to interpret John's lunatic actions. It is possible that he wanted to show that he could make and unmake an emperor at will. It is possible that he was mentally unbalanced. Even his *curia* revolted. Otto convened a synod to which the pope was summoned to account for himself. John dashed off a contemptuous response ignoring the emperor: 'To all the bishops. We hear that you wish to make another pope. If you do, I excommunicate you by almighty God and you have no power to ordain no one or celebrate mass'. Ponderously humorous, Otto urged him to improve his morals and his grammar: 'We thought that two negatives made a positive' but followed this with a threat: unless the pope presented himself, he would be deposed. This too was ignored. At the synod a catalogue of John's crimes was presented, ranging from rape to sacrilege.

On December 1st, Pope John XII was formally deposed and a nominee of Otto's took his place. John ignored this too. In Otto's absence he returned to Rome and took bloody revenge on those who had testified against him and who had remained in the city. How the matter might have ended, with a Roman-born pope calling on the support of a Roman mob, is difficult to speculate—but a cuckold caught the Holy Father *in flagrante* and, enraged, cudgelled him to death.

The blows of the cudgel might have ended the theological debate but it did nothing to resolve the secular one. The Romans had seen their bishop, their prince, deposed by a German; and they rose in revolt. The papal crown was the symbol of Roman sovereignty and, to gain control of that symbol, emperor and city were now prepared to destroy each other and themselves. Otto subjected Rome to a terrible vengeance; but it rose again. Again he smashed it down. Again it rose. And again. The Emperor died and his son Otto II continued to pour out German blood and wealth seeking the double goal of a purified papacy and a Roman crown.

With the approach of the millennium, there was a pause in the cycle of violence. The pope was the pious and learned Sylvester, reputed to be a magician, so versed was he in the sciences. The emperor was his pupil, the youthful Otto III (r. 983–1002) who, with his pope, swore to restore the splendours of the Roman empire infused with Christian belief. He built himself a palace on the Aventine, dressed in the toga, cast a medal with the legend 'Otto Imperator Augustus' and on the reverse the proud claim *Renovatio Imperii Romanorum*. But the Romans rose against him, drove him and his pope out of the city, and reverted to murderous anarchy. He died outside the city in January 1002, not quite twenty-two years of age. Sylvester survived his brilliant but erratic protégé by barely sixteen months. His epitaph summed up the sorrow that afflicted all thoughtful men at the ending of a splendid vision:

> The world, on the brink of triumph, its peace now departed, grew contorted in grief and the reeling Church forgot her rest.

The failure of Otto III and Sylvester marked the effective end of the medieval dream of a single state in which an emperor ruled over the bodies of all Christian men, and a pope over their souls. At Canossa in 1077 Pope Gregory VII avenged the deposition of John XII when the Emperor Henry IV was forced to beg for forgiveness in the snow. In 1300 Pope Boniface VIII displayed himself to pilgrims robed in imperial trappings, calling out 'I, I am the emperor'. But he, too, was eventually destroyed.

Looking down through the long perspective of the Holy Roman Empire is a melancholy experience of watching the dream fall apart. The Italians fought endless civic wars under the banner of Guelph or Ghibelline, Pope or Empire, but they were little more than pretexts for strife. Yet as the actual power of the emperor waned, the ideal of the universal monarch increased so that the imperial nadir coincided with its most able apologia, Dante's *De Monarchia*. Henry VII (r. 1312–13) came in 1310 in answer to Dante's summons to resolve the conflict, but became trapped in the complexities of Italian politics and died shamefully.

Dante's call for the risen majesty of empire became its requiem. Nevertheless, in 1354 a Germanic emperor was again summoned to Italy to take the crown and bring peace to a tortured land—but where Henry had come in majesty, the progress of his son Charles IV 'was more as a merchant going to Mass than an emperor going to his throne', as the Florentine merchant Villani observed sardonically. Petrarch, who had implored him to come, joined Villani in condemning him. 'Emperor of the Romans but in name, thou art in truth no more than the king of Bohemia'. But Petrarch was looking back to a mythical Golden Age, while Charles accepted he was living in an Age of Iron. Shrugging off the criticism he returned home and promulgated his Golden Bull, which effectively turned the crown of empire into a German crown.

The last word is perhaps best left to the sardonic Edward Gibbon:

> It is the duty of a patriot to prefer and promote the exclusive interest and glory of his native country; but a philosopher may be permitted to enlarge his views and to consider Europe as one great Republic.

For Further Reading

In 1965, Aachen put on an exhibition, embodied in four volumes edited by Wolfgang Braunfells, *Karl der Grosse: Lebenswerk und Nachleben*, D.A. Bullough, *Age of Charlemagne* (1965); James Bryce, *The Holy Roman Empire,* (8th ed. 1887); Russell Chamberlin, *Charlemagne, Emperor of the Western World.* (2nd ed. 2003); F.L. Ganshof, *Frankish Insitutions under Charlemagne:* trans S. Bruce and Mary Lyon. (1968); Gregorovius, Ferdinand *History of the City of Rome in the Middle Ages,* trans. Annie Hamilton. (1912); Thomas Hodgkin, *Italy and Her Invaders* (1899); Friedrich Heer, *The Holy Roman Empire* (Phoenix, 2003); Horace K. Mann, *The Lives of the Popes in the Early Middle Ages* (1902–32); W. Ullman, *Medieval Papalism* (1949).

Critical Thinking

1. List several reasons behind Charlemagne's objections to being crowned Holy Roman Emperor by Pope Leo III.
2. How did Charlemagne solve the problem of "distance and communication"?
3. What does Russell Chamberlin mean when he writes: "Looking down the long perspective of the Holy Roman Empire is a melancholy experience of watching the dream [of unity] fall apart"?

Create Central

www.mhhe.com/createcentral

Internet References

Labyrinth Home Page to Medieval Studies
www.georgetown.edu/labyrinth/
WWW Medieval Resources
http://ebbs.english.vt.edu/medieval/medieval.ebbs.html

RUSSELL CHAMBERLIN is the author of some thirty books on European travel and history. He has been awarded an honorary degree by the University of Surrey.

This article first appeared in *History Today,* November 2003, pp. 56–63. Copyright © 2003 by History Today, Ltd. Reprinted by permission.

Article

Prepared by: Joseph R. Mitchell, *Howard Community College*
and Helen Buss Mitchell, *Howard Community College*

Who Were the Anasazi?

The Navajo stake a controversial claim to an ancient legacy.

KEITH KLOOR

Learning Outcomes

After reading this article, you will be able to:

• Determine what differences exist among theories of the origins of the Anasazi and which theory makes the strongest case.

"Welcome to the dark side of the moon," says Taft Blackhorse. He and fellow Navajo Nation archaeologist John Stein are showing me the desolate and windswept site of Kin Klizhin, or "Black Charcoal" in Navajo. The lonely, multistory masonry structure, or "great house," is our first stop in Chaco Culture National Historical Park in northwestern New Mexico. The two have brought me here to explain the origins of the ancient people known as the Anasazi, a sophisticated culture that thrived in the Four Corners region from about A.D. 500 to 1300. Blackhorse and Stein tell a story about Chaco Canyons dozens of great houses that you won't find in any archaeology textbooks. It's also a story that today's Pueblo people, including the Hopi—who claim the Anasazi legacy as their own and have historically strained relations with the Navajo—reject out of hand.

"This is the barbecue pit," says Blackhorse, pointing to the foot of a well-preserved, two-story building that archaeologists have interpreted as a rare, above-ground religious chamber known as a tower kiva. Unlike most Navajo who have strong taboos against dealing with the deceased, Blackhorse is not afraid of burials or places associated with the dead, such as ancient sites like Kin Klizhin.

"Yep," agrees Stein. "They be cooking up some stuff here." He walks carefully around the tower kiva's perimeter as if he were examining it for the first time. A beanpole with a droopy mustache, Stein is an Anglo who has spent the better part of his life safeguarding archaeological sites for the Navajo Nation. He has put in 40 years studying Chaco alone and is the supervisory archaeologist for the Chaco Sites Protection Program, which represents Navajo interests in the management of sites associated with the canyon.

Both are well regarded in Southwestern archaeological circles, but I'm confused by their talk of cookouts. The National Park Service (NPS) signpost at the path's entrance vaguely describes Kin Klizhin as a place of "ceremonial function." But Blackhorse explains that the kiva served as a human sacrificial altar and a center for ritual cannibalism. His story, like everything else about Chaco according to Navajo belief, is about the Gambler, an evil magician with a hooked, crooked nose who enslaved the ancient Navajo and forced them to build the great houses of Chaco.

According to Blackhorse, the Gambler rode out to Kin Klizhin on a large reptile that was his guardian. His priests sacrificed humans at the site, and the Gambler, says Blackhorse, came here "to swallow their souls."

This is not the tale the NPS tells visitors to Chaco.

Much of Chaco's history remains shrouded in mystery, but the orthodox interpretation is that by 1050, it had become a ceremonial, administrative, and economic center. The massive great houses, the largest of which stood more than three stories tall, were connected by roads linking 150 of them in the Four Corners region.

Most scholars agree Chaco served as a special gathering place, where many Pueblo peoples and clans converged to share their ceremonies and traditions.

But Blackhorse and Stein disagree with this benign view of Chaco. They also don't think that the modern Hopi of Arizona and the Rio Grande Pueblo groups of New Mexico are the sole heirs to Chaco's cultural heritage. Instead, the two contend that Chaco was a melting pot of various Native American groups, and argue that Navajo cosmology, oral tradition, and Chaco's building design all point to a strong link between the Navajo and the Anasazi. Blackhorse's master narrative is straight out of Navajo oral history: Chaco was designed and built by the Navajo at the behest of the Gambler, a Lex Luthor-type villain who came from the south and enslaved the Navajo after beating them at games. He then used Chaco's dark energy to gain control over nature and build a sprawling empire in the Four Corners. According to the Navajo legend, the Gambler also enslaved the Pueblo people.

But the evidence for this story in the archaeological record is slight. When I ask NPS archaeologist Roger Moore if he knows anything about Kin Klizhin being used for human sacrifice and cannibalism, he tells me the site hasn't been officially excavated. "There's no way of knowing," he says. "From an archaeological standpoint, we can't substantiate it and we can't deny it."

Stein concedes the theory that the Navajo descend from the Anasazi is "incredibly unpopular" among Southwestern archaeologists. (The very word Anasazi, a Navajo noun Blackhorse translates as "ancient ones," is controversial.) The NPS, despite its Pueblo-centric narrative, is more receptive. Prompted by the 1990 Native American Graves Protection and Repatriation Act (NAGPRA), the NPS ruled in 1999 that the Navajo—along with 18 modern-day Pueblo tribes—had ancestral affiliation to Chaco Canyon, which borders the Navajo reservation. The decision came after federal researchers completed an exhaustive inventory of Chaco's collection of human remains and ceremonial objects.

But no archaeological evidence for the Navajo's prehistoric ties to Chaco was cited in the decision. Rather, the NPS relied largely on Navajo oral history. The story of the Gambler, and its significance in Navajo culture, was cited specifically.

The decision stunned the archaeological world. The scientific consensus is that the Navajo belong to the Athabascan language group, whose members are found mainly in Alaska and Canada (the Apache are also Athabascan). It's thought that the ancestors of the modern Navajo didn't even enter the Four Corners until about the 1500s, almost 300 years after Chaco was abandoned. Archaeologists believe the Navajo adopted some Pueblo traits after their arrival in the Southwest. Following the Pueblo Revolt against the Spaniards in 1680, some Pueblo groups sought refuge with the Navajo. The two groups intermarried and their cultures became entwined to a certain extent.

"The Navajo weren't Navajo until they started integrating Pueblo traits," contends Michael Yeatts, an archaeologist with the Hopi tribe. As an example, he points to the Navajo Yeibechi healing ceremony, which he says resembles certain Hopi rituals.

There are other intriguing cultural similarities between the Navajo and Pueblo tribes. The Acoma, a Pueblo tribe in New Mexico, have a similar Gambler story that explains the ruins of Chaco, but omits the Navajo. Additionally, numerous mythological characters, including the Hero Twins, also found in Mesoamerican lore, figure prominently in both Navajo and Pueblo origin stories.

Unsurprisingly, the Navajo chafe at the notion that they co-opted Pueblo history as their own. "We have always been here," says Blackhorse, referring to the Four Corners area.

After the NPS's 1999 decision on Chaco, which legitimized the Navajo claims to prehistoric links to Chaco, Blackhorse became intent on shoring up the evidence to cement the Navajo's standing. One of the projects he's working on now is connecting place names in Chaco to significant Navajo events and ceremonies. The Navajo named many sites in Chaco, such as Kin Klizhin, and are known to have periodically occupied the canyon since the 1700s. But Blackhorse insists that some Navajo ceremonies can be traced much farther back to show that his people have Anasazi lineage.

The NPS, for its part, has been forced to walk a tightrope between science and respect for Navajo traditions, whatever their origins may be. But, Moore says, "Archaeologically, it's hard to see their argument."

Stein and Blackhorse concede Navajo legends aren't well represented in the archaeological record, but they counter by pointing out that there is a dearth of data on Navajo sites in general before the 1700s. So the Navajo say that plenty of earlier sites may be there; they just haven't been found yet. But that is no longer true.

The massive Fruitland gas-drilling project that's been underway since the late 1980s just outside Farmington, New Mexico, has uncovered thousands of new Navajo sites. Richard Wilshusen, now an adjunct curator at the University of Colorado's Natural History Museum in Boulder, was part of a research team investigating hundreds of these sites in the 1990s. In a forthcoming study, he argues that a wealth of new archaeological data, combined with other lines of evidence, show that the Navajo didn't emerge as a distinct cultural group until between 1600 and 1650, at least 100 years after scholars once thought.

During his surveys of the scrubby desert outside of Farmington, Wilshusen started noticing remains of early Navajo dwellings, brush-covered structures called wikiups, and earth-covered homes known as hogans. Twenty years later, Wilshusen still marvels at his good fortune. "It was an accident. I was looking for Pueblo I sites," he explains, referring to the A.D. 700–900 era of Pueblo culture. Instead, he may have found the genesis of the Navajo.

Wilshusen says that southern Athabascan speakers ancestral to the Navajo and Apache arrived in the Southwest around 1450. They spread into southern Colorado, and northern and eastern New Mexico—areas that were largely depopulated after the abandonment of Pueblo sites in the Four Corners around 1350. These Athabascan people kept their nomadic hunter-gatherer lifestyle for the next 100 years, living in wikiups. By 1525, they separated into Plains and Mountain groups. It was only sometime between 1600 and 1650, Wilshusen argues, "that a distinct Navajo culture emerged in the uplands and the early Apache on the plains."

It is the new archaeological data that makes Wilshusen certain he is on to something. "We had nothing like the dates we got from the Fruit-land project," he says, alluding to the sparse record of early Navajo sites. This partly owes to the difficulty of recognizing those ancestral Navajo sites. "They're very subtle," he explains, and very hard to see. "All that might remain of a small wikiup or hogan is a scattering of charred timbers. With sweat lodges, only piles of stone are left. "But we've gotten really good at seeing them," Wilshusen says.

Out of thousands of sites identified during the Fruitland project, hundreds have been radiocarbon and tree-ring dated. Wilshusen is able to use these dates to trace the development of Navajo culture. He notes an "architectural shift afoot" by 1600, when residential structures became bigger. The most striking changes after 1650, he says, are the clustering of residential timber structures called forked-stick hogans, and the appearance of fortresslike pueblitos and a new polychrome pottery. It's at this point, Wilshusen concludes, that the Navajo emerged as a distinct group.

Ironically, Wilshusen uses the Navajo's own oral history to buttress his case, particularly one famous legend known as the

Gathering of the Clans, which tells how different clans joined together and traditional Navajo social and cultural mores developed, such as rules about marriage and treatment of spouses. Wilshusen has linked accounts about the Gathering of the Clans to incidents recorded in 17th- and 18th-century Spanish documents. These include a massive famine that caused the partial abandonment of many other pueblos. According to oral history, this event resulted in new Navajo clans. In addition to matching the calendar dates of new clans with mentions of them in Spanish records, Wilshusen was able to reconstruct enough history to determine that local architecture, language, clothing, weaponry, farming practices, and pottery become distinctly "Navajo" between 1605 and 1645.

As late afternoon storm clouds cast Chaco Canyon in a steely gray hue, Blackhorse, Stein, and I drive seven miles northeast of Kin Klizhin to Chaco's most prominent landmark, the great house known as Pueblo Bonito. The dark forces of Kin Klizhin originate there, say Blackhorse and Stein.

Some Chaco scholars have come to believe that Bonito was where the Anasazi elites dwelled. "That's bullshit," says Stein when we arrive at the D-shaped great house, which once stood as high as five stories and contained up to 600 rooms. "This place is astronomical," he says. "The alignments that we're seeing out there all converge on this building." He points to the network of narrow "roads" out on the stark desert landscape that have been the focus of much debate in recent years. Some scholars think that the roads served as a transportation network connecting outlying communities for trade purposes. Others believe them to be ceremonial passageways.

Stein sees the alignments and architecture as part of the same "cosmological timepiece." When I ask to what end, Blackhorse responds in a low whisper, "Controlling the elements. It's always about controlling the elements."

In terms of their astronomical perspective, Stein and Blackhorse are not that different from other scholars who have come to interpret Chaco Canyon as a ritual landscape infused with astronomical meaning: an ancient metropolis organized around sun and moon cycles.

NPS interpreters at Chaco sometimes speculate as much, too, but they will attribute the arrangement to ancient Pueblo cosmology, which, of course, bears some similarities to Navajo cosmology.

What sets Blackhorse and Stein apart from their peers is not so much their embrace of archaeoastronomy, which long ago muscled its way into scholarly debates about Chaco. It's that they tie the celestial theory of Chaco's construction to Navajo oral history to tell a Navajo story. But, as Wilshusen delicately points out, they're missing one piece of crucial evidence. "I'd be very interested to see the archaeology," he says. "There just isn't evidence that Athabascans were there."

The NPS, forced to accentuate the positive when asked about the Navajo connection to Chaco, has little choice but to be officially polite. Says Russell Bodnar, chief of interpretation at Chaco, "The work [Blackhorse and Stein] are doing is very interesting and adds to our knowledge and to our perspective about what happened at Chaco."

When the NPS recognized the Navajo's prehistoric links to Chaco, it stepped into an epic debate over ethnic and cultural origins. But as Wendy Bustard, curator at Chaco, recalls, even at the time an NPS lawyer was astute enough to realize the decision might have larger political implications: "He recognized that our decision under NAGPRA could be used to address other matters of dispute between the Hopi and Navajo."

The Hopi and Navajo have a contentious history. The reservation boundaries for the Hopi Tribe and Navajo Nation have been in dispute ever since the original U.S. treaties and executive orders that created them in the late 19th century. The lines have been redrawn multiple times, owing, in part, to arbitrary Congressional decisions as well as input from tribal oral histories. The resulting arrangement has since led to a steady succession of court battles between the two tribes over water rights and land use issues. It also left the Hopi landlocked within the Navajo Nation, the largest Indian reservation in the country at 25,000 square miles.

Given this backdrop, it's easy to see how NAGPRA has become a proxy battleground for grievances that have nothing to do with burials. After all, if a group's historic land claims are legally enshrined by NAGPRA, they could have greater standing in a court of law. Bustard acknowledges this potential, but is quick to add, "One would think that the court might recognize evidence used for NAGPRA is pretty weak. It's a pretty loose standard."

Nonetheless, each tribe is maneuvering to exploit NAGPRA for its own advantage. For example, the Navajo Nation Historic Preservation Department requests a statement acknowledging the nation's affiliation to Anasazi sites be included in official reports of research done on Navajo land.

The Hopi, for their part, often put the squeeze on Southwestern archaeologists to publicly criticize the Navajo claims of links to Pueblo sites. This makes archaeologists, who are still trying to repair their historically tense relations with Native Americans, deeply uncomfortable. Either way, it seems, scholars get caught in the crossfire. University of Colorado at Boulder archaeologist and ARCHAEOLOGY contributing editor Stephen H. Lekson, who has spent many years working at Chaco, is still singed by his experience on the hot seat at an NPS-sponsored "Four Corners Affiliation Conference" at Fort Lewis College in Durango, Colorado. At one session, "I was literally in the middle of it, sitting in a chair with the Navajo on one side and Hopi on the other," he says. "I became the surrogate for punch-counter-punch arguments between the tribes. Instead of going after each other, both sides went after me. I was asked to come down on one side and I wouldn't."

Even Blackhorse and Stein don't agree on everything. I found it interesting that they emphasized different opinions when I asked them about what caused the collapse of Chaco. Stein referred to drought as probably being one of the triggers that led to the abandonment of the area. Black-horse, meanwhile, finished telling me the Gambler story, how the Hero Twins defeated the Gambler to free all the Chaco slaves. According to Navajo oral history, all the tribes left the area except the Navajo, who agreed to stay behind as the guardians of Chaco to prevent its power from being exploited again. "We have a ceremony related to this event," Blackhorse says. "It's called 'Speaking it back into the ground to never let it rise again.'"

Critical Thinking

1. What do the Navajo say is the role of "the gambler" in establishing Chaco Canyon?
2. Why do Stein and Blackhorse insist, "the place is astronomical . . . controlling the elements. It's always about controlling the elements."?
3. What is the chief basis for the dispute between the Hopi and the Navajos?

Create Central

www.mhhe.com/createcentral

Internet References

Lords of the Earth: Maya/Aztec/Inca Exchange
www.mayalords.org/

KEITH KLOOR is a freelance journalist who writes frequently about the archaeology of the Southwest for Science and other publications.

From *Archaeology*, November/December 2009, pp. 18, 60, 62, 68–69. Copyright © 2009 by Archaeological Institute of America. Reprinted by permission of *Archaeology Magazine*. www.archaeology.org

Article

Prepared by: Joseph R. Mitchell, *Howard Community College*
and Helen Buss Mitchell, *Howard Community College*

The Age of the Vikings

Norse seafarers plundered, traded, and settled from Canada to Russia.

A.D. 793 was a particularly nasty year along the northeastern coast of England. First came the "fierce, foreboding omens," and the "wretchedly terrified" populace watched fiery dragons dance across the sky. A great famine struck. And then "the ravaging of heathen men destroyed God's church at Lindisfarne through brutal robbery and slaughter." And so began the Age of the Vikings.

ARNE EMIL CHRISTENSEN

Learning Outcomes

After reading this article, you will be able to:

- Understand the traditional interpretation of the Vikings' role in European history and how this interpretation has been modified in recent years.

This *Anglo-Saxon Chronicle* description of the first major Viking raid is typical of contemporary accounts of the Norsemen. In a remarkably violent time, the Vikings were feared above all others in Europe. Yet they were much more than brutal warriors. The Norse proved themselves to be colonizers, city-builders, law-givers, architects, explorers, and merchants.

For 250 years, from about A.D. 800 until 1050, people of Denmark, Sweden, and Norway played a potent role in European history far out of proportion to the size and population of their mother countries. They plundered, traded, and settled from deep into Russia all the way to Newfoundland on the edge of the New World. They terrorized powerful, established kingdoms like France and England.

The Norse sailed up the rivers of France and Spain, laid siege to Paris, and attacked coastal towns in Italy. In the east, they traded with Arab merchants at Bulgar on the Volga and raided as far east as the Caspian Sea. From Kiev, they traveled downriver to the Black Sea and attempted an attack on the Byzantine capital of Constantinople.

The Vikings' Reach

From Scandinavia, Norse seafarers carried raids, trade, and colonies throughout their expanding world. They swept the coasts of Europe, followed rivers deep into Russia, and crossed the seas to settle Iceland, Greenland, and (briefly) North America.

Norse Graves Reveal the Paradox of War and Peace
Burying Vikings

An Arab traveling through Russia nearly 1,200 years ago happened upon an extraordinary sight: the fiery burial of a Viking chieftain.

The leader's great ship was hauled ashore and his valuables loaded aboard it. The body was dressed in fine clothes and placed on the ship. A slave woman who had chosen to follow her master into the afterlife was killed and her body was placed aboard. Then the chieftain's horse and dog were sacrificed for the grave. Finally, the ship was set ablaze and a mound built over the ashes of the funeral pyre.

Ibn Fadlans described the ninth-century A.D. scene in his journal—the only eyewitness account of a Viking burial. Fortunately for archaeologists, not all Norse funerals involved burning the remains; sometimes whole ships were buried with their owners and property, offering a remarkable glimpse into the life and times of the Norsemen.

The graves give mute testimony to the violence of the Viking age. Nearly all males were buried with weapons. A warrior fully equipped for the next world was interred with his sword, ax, and spear, and often with a bow and arrows. A wooden shield with a central iron boss was the usual protection. The helmets and armor seen on modern representations are extremely rare, and the horned helmet of cartoon Vikings has never been seen in a real Norse grave.

The graves also reveal the paradox of the Vikings: Alongside the fearsome set of arms, the accouterments of peace are also found. Craftsmen were buried with their tools, blacksmiths with their hammer, tongs, and files. Farmers had their hoe, scythe, and sickle; and along the coasts, the dead were often buried with their boats and fishing equipment. Women took with them their personal jewelry, as well as textiles and kitchen tools.

Only metal objects survive the centuries in most graves, but conditions at a few, especially beneath the blue clay on the Oslo Fjord, preserved even wood, leather, and textiles. The clay and tightly stacked turf used in some of the burials produced graves as well sealed as hermetic jars. Everything sacrificed in such graves has been preserved in the moist, oxygen-free conditions.

The preserved contents of three extremely rich ship graves— from *Oseberg, Gokstad,* and *Tune*—are among Norway's national treasures. At the time of the burial, the ships were pulled ashore on rollers and placed in a pit dug into the ground. A burial chamber was built on board to hold the body and provisions needed for a life after death. Then a huge mound was built over the grave.

The remains of a man were found in the *Gokstad* grave, and the *Tune* ship probably also held a male. But the *Oseberg* grave was the resting place for two women, one 50 to 60 years old and the other in her 20s. The *Oseberg* and *Gokstad* graves had been robbed, so the fine weapons and jewelry that must have been among the original grave goods were not found. Articles of wood, leather, and textiles, however, did not interest the robbers and have survived.

UDO Archives/courtesy of Smithsonian Institution.
The most famous of Viking ships came from the Oseberg Burial Mound, shown here during excavations in 1904. The impermeable blue clay of the mound in the Oslo Fjord protected the ship and its contents for more than 1,000 years.

It is unclear which of the *Oseberg* women was the recipient of the grave, and which was the after-death companion. Women often held high status in Norse society, and the *Oseberg* grave belonged to a high-ranking woman.

Her grave held the evidence of her role as the main administrator of a manor. Even after death, she was equipped to spin and weave and supervise milking, cheese-making, and work in the fields. For land travel, she had three sleds and a wagon complete with sacrificed horses and two tents. Cooking equipment, wooden troughs and buckets, a cauldron, a frying pan, and a carving knife were at hand, as were two oxen, grain, apples, and blueberries.

Objects such as the wagon and several finely carved wooden animal heads probably were religious icons, suggesting the woman may have been both a political and religious leader. The many decorated wooden objects seem to be the work of several different woodcarvers. Except for this grave, our knowledge of Viking art is based mainly on preserved metalwork that generally is smaller than the wooden objects. But whether metal or wood, the artistic goal was the same: to create a carpet of inter-twined, fantastic animals.

The number of different artisans represented suggests the "Oseberg queen" was a patron of the arts who assembled the best wood-carvers and weavers at her court. The woodcarvings prove that some Vikings were as handy with chisel and knife as with sword and spear.

Scandinavian Ships Drove the Vikings' Fierce Amphibious Warfare
The Perfect War Machine

Viking warships were fearsome works of art. The sight of that curved prow suddenly cresting the horizon could send whole cities into panic a millennium ago.

The Scandinavian shipbuilders who created these unique and pioneering craft were quite possibly the most important factor in establishing Norse military supremacy and creating a far-flung web of trade and colonization. A leading Swedish archaeologist, Bertil Almgren, called Viking ships the only ocean-going landing craft ever devised—which would explain how small bands of warriors could terrorize settled societies.

Early accounts of Norse attacks demonstrate the military value of these unique craft and the shattering amphibious tactics they permitted. The ships—light, flexible, and free to maneuver in shallow water—had no need of harbors. They could be easily beached by their crews, who then transformed themselves from oarsmen to fierce shock troops who swarmed over their terrified targets.

A surprise amphibious attack could hit almost anywhere along Europe's coasts and rivers. Then after a quick and bloody battle, the Norsemen were gone—far out to sea again before a counterattack could be mounted. The Vikings learned early how to tack their ships against the wind, allowing immediate escape even with the wind at their faces. At a time when civilized armies were supposed to march overland, the amphibious tactics of the Norsemen were devastating.

The Viking ship, that near-perfect war machine of its day, was the culmination of a long Scandinavian shipbuilding tradition that dates back to at least 350 B.C. Many of the techniques developed by Norse shipbuilders are still used for small boats today, so 1,000-year-old problems can be answered by living boatbuilders.

The sail came rather late to Viking ships, probably not until early in the eighth century. But the new sailing ships were perfected through four generations to serve raiders and traders alike.

Even with a full crew, the *Gokstad* could float in one meter (just over three feet) of water. She could be beached by the crew and was well suited for surprise attacks on foreign shores.

The Viking ships were clinker built: Long planks were overlapped and fastened together with iron rivets to form the hull. This planking shell was built first, then the ribs inserted afterwards for strength and stability. This method produces

much lighter, more flexible ships than those that began with the stout interior frame to which outer planking was added.

Norse shipbuilders gained even more flexibility by lashing the ship's ribs and planking together. The backbone of keel and stems fore and aft increased strength. Most ships were built of oak; pine was also used.

As society changed during the Viking Age, different kinds of ships were developed. Warships were long and slender, built for speed with large crews who could man the oars. Cargo ships were much wider and slower and relied more on sails than did the warships. Busy trade routes from Western Norway to Iceland and Greenland required seaworthy ships.

Much of what we know about Viking shipbuilding comes from the Norse practice of burying important personages in their ships. Three especially notable excavated ship burials come from Oseberg, Gokstad and Tune in Norway. All three are exhibited in the Viking Ship Museum at Bygdoy in Oslo.

Norway's National Museum recently used tree-ring analysis to date these three pristine ships. The *Oseberg* was built between A.D. 815 and 820, the other two in the A.D. 890s. The *Oseberg* is 22 meters (72 feet) long and could be rowed by 30 men. The *Gokstad* stretches 24 meters (78 feet) with room for 32 oarsmen, while the *Tune* was probably about 20 meters (65 feet) long.

All three had a mast amidships, with the sail of *Gokstad* estimated at about 120 square meters (1,300 square feet). Sails were made of wool, and the task of collecting wool, and sorting, spinning, weaving, and sewing such a sail must have been a greater task than building the ship.

The *Oseberg* was less seaworthy than the later *Gokstad* and *Tune* ships, but still well-suited for trips across the North Sea in summer. It is probably typical of the warship used for the early raids. The seaworthiness of the *Gokstad* has been proved by the three replicas which have crossed the North Atlantic in modern times, yet the ship could float freely in as little as one meter (just over three feet) of water.

Most of the routes taken by Viking Age seafarers were in coastal waters or across fairly short stretches of open sea. Navigation was based on landmarks; and in coastal waters, it was usual to find a good harbor for the night and camp on the shore. Only on the long stretches of open water from Western Norway to Iceland and Greenland would sailors be out of sight of land for several days.

Men from the sea. Scandinavia was hardly unknown to the rest of Europe when the surprise raids began. Archaeological evidence shows cultural contacts dating back several millennia, but the distant Nordic area was of little import to the rest of Europe.

That changed suddenly in A.D. 793, when "men from the sea" plundered Lindisfarne monastery on Northumberland Island. Within a few years, every summer brought a wave of attacks on Ireland, England, France, and the North Sea's Frisian Islands.

Some of the Viking raiders stayed behind to build well-planned cities like Dublin and Kiev or take over existing ones like York. Others came with family and livestock to settle as farmers in England, Scotland, Normandy, and Russia. For 200 years, their ships sailed all the known waters of Europe and ventured where ships had never been.

Great ventures under famous chiefs often involved men from throughout Scandinavia, but the three countries divided their world into distinct spheres of interest.

The Swedes sailed mainly to the east, trading and settling along the Russian rivers and settling in towns as far south as Kiev. They must have played a role in creating the Russian state, although the importance of the role is debated. The Norsemen's eastern expansion was less warlike than the move against Western Europe. Trade was key in the east, and the enormous quantities of ancient Arab coins found in Sweden demonstrate how far the trade networks reached.

Sweeping across Europe the Danes sailed south to Friesland (in northern Europe), France, and southern England, occasionally reaching even Spain and Italy. Much of England became known as the "danelaw." In France, the embattled king invited Rollo, a Norse chieftain, to settle in Normandy as a French duke—in exchange for keeping other Vikings at bay.

Norway held sway in the west and northwest. Norwegian settlements on Orkney and Shetland may predate the Viking Age, when Norway drilled deep roots into northern England, Scotland, and Ireland. Scandinavian jewelry recovered from English graves tell of whole families emigrating, while Celtic names in Iceland suggest some settlers came from Ireland with Irish wives.

Farther west, the settlers came upon virgin land: the Faroe Islands, Iceland, and Greenland. The settlement of Iceland intensified around A.D. 900, when Norwegian kings strengthened their central government, according to a unique source, *Land-namabok,* which tells the story of the settlement and names many of the settlers.

Chiefs often preferred to emigrate rather than submit to higher authority; family and friends usually followed. Some settlers had no choice after being outlawed at home. The man who led the colonization of Greenland, Eirik the Red, was expelled from Iceland for killing and other mayhem.

New world colony. Sailing still farther westward, the Norse reached North America and launched a settlement around A.D. 1000. Conflicts with the original inhabitants of the New World doomed the colony, however, and the settlers returned to Greenland.

The location—and even the existence—of the Norsemen's North American settlement has been hotly debated for more than a century, with suggestions ranging from Labrador to Manhattan. Unassailable proof was discovered in the 1960s by Helge and Anne Stine Ingstad with their excavations at L'Anse aux Meadows on northern Newfoundland. Houses like those excavated on Iceland and Greenland, Viking artifacts, and radiocarbon dates of about A.D. 1000 proved this to be a site built and used by Norse people.

What accounts for this rapid, violent expansion? Well-organized states such as France and the Anglo-Saxon kingdoms of England were taken by complete surprise and were rarely able to resist the amphibious attacks.

Written accounts from the time, which were hardly objective, paint the Vikings as merciless pirates, robbers, and brigands.

And, indeed, they no doubt were. But these were violent times. Accounts from Ireland state that the Irish themselves plundered about as many monasteries and churches as the Vikings. The Frankish Empire grew via long and bloody wars, and the Anglo-Saxon kingdoms fought one another repeatedly. The Vikings may well have been just the most efficient raiders of their day.

But they were more than warriors. Some of their leaders not only won great battles, but founded kingdoms in conquered lands, planned cities, and gave laws that are still in force. The remains of fortresses that could house an army have been found in Denmark. Dating to the end of the Viking Age, the circular forts are laid out with a precision that impresses modern surveyors. The forts testify to an advanced knowledge of geometry and surveying.

Farmers and blacksmiths in their homelands, the Norse mostly were farmers and stockbreeders who supplemented their larder by fishing and hunting. Barley, oats, and some wheat were cultivated; and cattle, horses, sheep, goats, and pigs were raised. Iron-making was an important resource in Sweden and in Norway, with bog ore to supply the iron and ample wood to fuel the furnace pits. Some areas quarried steatite for cooking vessels and slate for whetstones.

The farmers were generally self-reliant, although luxury goods and such necessities as salt formed the basis of thriving trade. Steatite items survive the centuries well and turn up in excavations outside Scandinavia; but such perishable goods as furs, ropes of seal and walrus skins, and dried fish must also have been important trade items. Many Arab coins have been found in Scandinavia, and although we do not know what was purchased with the coins, iron and slaves are possibilities.

Warfare was rarely allowed to interfere with trade. As Alfred of Wessex fought desperately to block a Viking invasion, he was visited by Ottar, a Norwegian merchant. Ottar's story was written down and survives as the only contemporary report on Viking society by a Viking. Ottar lived in the far north of Norway and collected his trade goods as taxes paid by nearby indigenous people, the Saami. He mentions furs, eiderdown, and skin ropes, as well as walrus teeth—the "ivory of the Arctic."

A source of warriors. One force driving Norse expansion may have been the *odel,* which seems to extend back to Viking times. The *odel* dictated that a farm should not be divided but inherited intact by the oldest son. Younger sons and daughters received far less and likely had to clear new land or go abroad to acquire a farm. Landless younger sons may have given chieftains the manpower they needed to raid Europe.

Although West European sources tell a grim story of the Vikings, archaeological excavations paint a much more varied picture. Excavated farms and graves reveal artifacts from a peaceful life centered on the rhythm of a year that revolved around agriculture. Piles of stones tell of careful clearing of the land, and we have found the furrows left by a plowing 1,100 years ago.

Roland Hejdström.

This oval brooch from Sweden's Gotland Island was made in Karelia, Russia.

As the years progressed, Norse society changed. Fewer chieftains controlled more and more resources, forming the basis of kingdoms until each of the three countries united into a central kingdom along roughly the same borders as today. Marketplaces grew into towns with well-planned streets and plots for homes.

From Staraya Ladoga and Kiev in Russia to Dublin in Ireland, we find evidence of townspeople basing their life on trade and handicraft. Garbage disposal was not a high priority, and the thick layers of ancient refuse are now gold mines for archaeologists. Excavations illuminate everything from changing fashions to the kinds of lice that bedeviled the townspeople.

Christian Vikings. The Viking age ended in the eleventh century, as Scandinavian kingdoms adopted Christianity. The raids gradually ended, and the pantheon of warrior gods faded. Viking gods lived on as our days of the week: Tuesday, Wednesday, Thursday and Friday. Ty and Thor were war gods; Wotan (or Odin) was the chief god with power over life, death, and poetry; Frey and his sister Freya were the gods of fertility. We know little of Viking religion, as written sources are late and colored by Christian belief. The gods demanded sacrifice, and temples and holy forests were probably dedicated to these deities. Like their Greek and Roman counterparts, the Viking gods had human traits.

The northern countries, once the scourge of a continent, became a regular part of Christian Europe and great changes ensued. But for the people of the Norselands, life went on. They continued to sow and reap, and herd and hunt as they had for generations beyond counting.

Critical Thinking

1. In addition to being plunderers and seafarers, what new skills are the Vikings now credited with having?
2. How do Norse graves capture "the paradox of war and peace"?
3. Why was the Viking ship a "near perfect war machine"?
4. How did the *odel* supply manpower for the Vikings to raid Europe?

Create Central

www.mhhe.com/createcentral

Internet References

NOVA Online: The Vikings
www.pbs.org/wgbh/nova/vikings/

ARNE EMIL CHRISTENSEN, of the University Museum of National Antiquities in Oslo, specializes in shipbuilding history and craftsmanship in the Iron Age and Viking period.

From *Scientific American Discovering Archaeology*, September/October 2000, pp. 40–47. Copyright © 2000 by Arne Emil Christensen. Reprinted by permission of the author.

Article

Prepared by: Joseph R. Mitchell, *Howard Community College*
and Helen Buss Mitchell, *Howard Community College*

The Fall of Constantinople

Judith Herrin tells the dramatic story of the final moments of Byzantine control of the imperial capital.

JUDITH HERRIN

Learning Outcomes

After reading this article, you will be able to:

- Determine what factors contributed to the fall of Constantinople to the Turks in 1453 and what effect this had on both eastern and western worlds.

"At this moment of confusion, which happened at sunrise, our omnipotent God came to His most bitter decision and decided to fulfil all the prophecies, as I have said, and at sunrise the Turks entered the city near San Romano, where the walls had been razed to the ground by their cannon . . . anyone they found was put to the scimitar, women and men, old and young, of any conditions. This butchery lasted from sunrise, when the Turks entered the city, until midday . . . The Turks made eagerly for the piazza five miles from the point where they made their entrance at San Romano, and when they reached it at once some of them climbed up a tower where the flags of Saint Mark and the Most Serene Emperor were flying, and they cut down the flag of Saint Mark and took away the flag of the Most Serene Emperor and then on the same tower they raised the flag of the Sultan . . . When their flag was raised and ours cut down, we saw that the whole city was taken, and that there was no further hope of recovering from this."

With these words, and much longer descriptions of the slaughter that followed, the Venetian Nicolo Barbaro recorded the fall of Constantinople to the Ottoman Turks. His eyewitness account describes the progressive stranglehold devised by the Turks and the sense of fatalism that developed within the city. As the major trading partner of the empire, Venice had strong links with Constantinople and its citizens fought bravely in its defence. Barbaro's account of their loyalty is impressive. Although he is less favourably inclined to the Genoese, who also played a leading role in the defence of the city, his account has the immediacy of one who lived through the siege.

There is no shortage of records of the fall, although some were concocted long after the event and claim a presence that turns out to be quite inauthentic. Greeks, Italians, Slavs, Turks and Russians all composed their own versions; they cannot possibly be reconciled. But those written closer to the date, May 29th, 1453, and by people involved in some capacity all share a sense of the disaster they documented. Taking account of many of their variations and contradictions, they permit a basic outline of events to be constructed.

The leaders of what became such a mythic battle were both younger sons who had never expected to become rulers. The Ottoman sultan Mehmet II, born in 1432, was made sole heir at the age of eleven by the death of his two elder brothers; Constantine XI, born in 1404, was the fourth of six sons of Manuel II, whose imperial authority was inherited by the eldest John VIII. When John died in 1448, the Empress-Mother Helena insisted that Constantine should be crowned in a disputed succession. His two younger brothers, Demetrios and Thomas, were appointed Despots in the Morea (southern Greece), and took no interest in the fate of Constantinople. In 1453 the Sultan was twenty-one years old, the Emperor forty-nine, and the Ottomans far out-numbered the Christian forces who undertook the defence of the city.

The imperial capital dedicated by Constantine I in AD 330 had resisted siege on numerous occasions. The triple line of fortifications constructed on the land side in the fifth century had held off attacks by Goths, Persians, Avars, Bulgars, Russians, and especially Arabs. Even today they make an impressive sight. Over the centuries new aqueducts and cisterns were built to ensure an ample water supply, and the imperial granaries stored plentiful amounts of grain.

From the first attempt by the Arabs to capture the city in 674–78, Muslim forces aimed to make Constantinople their own capital. Using this ancient foundation as their base, they hoped to extend their power across Thrace and the Balkans into Europe, in the same irresistible way that they advanced across North Africa into Spain. Frustrated in these efforts, the centre of their operations was moved to Baghdad, and they occupied the Fertile Crescent and vast areas further east. In the eleventh century these same ambitions were taken up by Turkish tribes from central Asia, who constantly harried the empire. First Seljuks and later Ottomans maintained pressure on Constantinople, hoping to take a symbol of unconquered strength and great strategic importance.

Their aim was not merely political and military. For centuries Constantinople was the largest metropolis in the known world, the impregnable core of a great empire, served by a deep-water port that gave access to the sea. Known as New Rome and the Queen City, it had been built to impress, its magnificent public monuments, decorated with statuary set in an elegant classical urban landscape. Its apparent invincibility and famous reputation made it a great prize. The city was also reputed to be hugely wealthy. While the Turks had no interest in its famous collection of Christian relics, the fact that many were made of solid gold and silver, decorated with huge gems and ancient cameos, was of importance. Their existence added weight to the rumour that Constantinople contained vast stores of gold, a claim which cannot have been true by 1453. By the early fifteenth century the city had lost all its provinces to Turkish occupation and was totally isolated. The surviving Greek territories of Trebizond and the Morea were similarly surrounded and made no effort to assist the ancient capital.

It is notoriously difficult to reconstruct the early history of the Ottoman Turks from the sparse sources that survive. They seem to have been a tribe of *ghazi* warriors (men devoted to holy war) who gradually adopted a more organised monarchy. Their leader Osman (1288–1326) gave his name to the group, which is now associated with one of the most successful empires of all time. During the fourteenth century these Ottoman Turks took full advantage of the civil war in Byzantium. From his capital at Nikomedia Sultan Orhan offered assistance to John VI, claimant to the throne, and married his daughter Theodora, thus setting up an excellent excuse for invading the empire.

At the same time, he was able to exploit unexpected developments at Gallipoli when an earthquake shook the castle fortifications so violently that they collapsed in 1354. Orhan ferried an entire army across the Dardanelles and opened a bridgehead on the European shore. The conquest of Thrace, the last province loyal to the empire, and the capture of Adrianople, which became the Ottoman capital as Edirne, meant that the Turks were now in a position to threaten the capital from the west. Once they could mount an attack by land as well as by sea, Constantinople was totally surrounded. This stranglehold on the empire was symbolised by the treaty of 1373, which reduced the emperor to the status of a Turkish vassal. John V agreed to pay Sultan Murad an annual tribute, to provide military aid whenever it was required, and to allow his son Manuel to accompany the Turks back to their court as a hostage.

Despite a surprising defeat by the Mongols in 1402, Ottoman attempts to capture Constantinople continued. In preparation for the campaign of 1452–53, Sultan Mehmet II ordered the blockade of the city. Since the southern entrance to the Bosphorus from the Aegean at the Dardanelles was already in Ottoman hands, he concentrated on the northern entrance from the Black

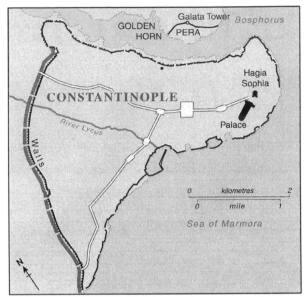

Figure 1

Sea. Two castles were constructed close to the mouth of the Bosphorus on the Asian and European shores, to prevent any aid arriving from the Black Sea. Barbaro gives a vivid description of how the garrison at Rumeli Hisar on the European shore tried to control shipping by firing on any galleys entering the Bosphorus until they lowered their sails:

> From the walls of the castle, the Turks began to shout 'Lower your sails, Captain' . . . and when they saw that he was unwilling to lower them, they began to fire their cannon and many guns and a great number of arrows, so that they killed many men . . . After he had lowered his sails, the Turks stopped firing, and then the current carried the galleys towards Constantinople. And when they had passed the castle and the Turks could not reach them any longer with their cannon, the captain quickly raised his sails and got through safely.

Ships also carried oars so that sailors could row with the current in order to avoid the blockade.

Byzantine rulers had made too many appeals to Western powers to come to the aid of their Christian city. The crusading movement had been exhausted by numerous military disasters. After the failure of the crusade of 1396 at Nicopolis on the Danube, the young emperor Manuel II made a long tour of western capital cities between 1399 and 1403 in the hope of gaining financial and above all military support for the defence of the city. In Paris he noticed a fine tapestry hanging in the palace of the Louvre and wrote a letter to his old tutor describing its beauty. In London he was invited to the Christmas dinner hosted by Henry IV at the palace of Eltham. Manuel's attempts to obtain aid were enhanced, as so many times before, by a promise to unite the Latin and Greek churches.

In this respect Manuel and his son John VIII proved that they could achieve the desired ecclesiastical union. At the Council of Ferrara-Florence in 1438–39 the union of the churches was finally realised. But even after this major compromise, help from the papacy, the Italian city republics and the monarchs who had received Manuel during his trip was slow to materialise. In the autumn of 1452, the papal legate Cardinal Isidore and Bishop Leonard of Chios arrived in the city with a body of archers recruited and paid for by the papacy. The Cardinal then celebrated the official union of the Latin and Greek churches in the cathedral of Hagia Sophia on December 12th.

As Bishop Leonard of Chios reports the event:

> Through the diligence and honesty of the said Cardinal, Isidore of Kiev, and with the assent (if it was not insincere) of the emperor and the senate, the holy union was sanctioned and solemnly celebrated on December 12th, the feast of Saint Spiridon, the bishop.

But even with the union in place, Western promises to assist the last great Christian centre in the East Mediterranean proved empty, while a large portion of the Greek population of Constantinople remained obstinately opposed to it.

Among those who joined the Greek inhabitants in the city to defend it against the expected siege, were numerous representatives of the Italian republics of Venice and Genoa. Both enjoyed commercial privileges from trading in Constantinople but were staunch rivals. Some of those who fought had been residents for many years, had adopted Byzantine citizenship and married Greek wives. A significant number of Armenians were present and the resident Catalan traders took part under their consul. Prince Orhan, pretender to the Ottoman throne, who had lived for years as a guest of the Byzantine court, offered his services with his Turkish companions. Ships from Ancona, Provence and Castile added to the naval forces, and a group of Greeks from Crete elected to remain in the city. When they saw what would happen, though, on February 26th, 1453, six of their ships slipped away with one Venetian.

The inhabitants were greatly cheered by the arrival in January 1453 of the Genoese *condottieri,* who braved the Turkish blockade and got through with his two ships and about 700 men. This was Giovanni Giustiniani Longo, identified in many sources as Justinian, a friend of the emperor, whose determination to assist the city was greatly appreciated. Constantine XI put him in charge of the weakest part of the land walls, the section by the Gate of Romanos, and, as Nestor-Iskander says:

> . . . he invigorated and even instructed the people so that they would not lose hope and maintain unswerving trust in God . . . All people admired and obeyed him in all things.

After masterminding the defence Justinian was hit on the chest during the last days of the assault. The Genoese managed to get him out of the city on one of the first ships to leave after the capture but he died at Chios. His disappearance lowered the spirits of the Christian forces.

Also among the defenders was a young man called Nestor, who had been taken captive by a Turkish regiment in Moldavia, southern Russia, forcibly converted to Islam and enrolled in the unit. Since he had some education, Nestor, renamed Iskander, was employed in military administration and learned about

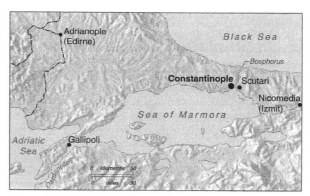

Figure 2

Turkish artillery practices. He accompanied the unit on its march to Constantinople and then ran away, 'that I might not die in this wretched faith'. His account of the siege may have been written many years later when he was a monk in a Greek monastery, but it has the quality of a lived experience, a first-hand account of what he witnessed as a noncombatant. It has been suggested that he was attached to Giustiniani's forces at the Romanos Gate and helped them to identify the Ottoman commanders and their weaponry.

Siege warfare was revolutionised in the fifteenth century by the invention of cannon. In the 1420s when the Byzantines had their first experience of bombardment by cannon, they reduced the effectiveness of the new weapon by suspending bales of material, wood and anything that might absorb and diffuse its impact. But the fifth-century fortifications of Constantinople presented an easy target. Now Byzantium needed new technology as well as new warriors to match the enemy. Appreciating this vital combination, in 1451 Constantine XI employed a Christian engineer, a Hungarian named Urban, to assist with the first, while he sent numerous appeals to the West for extra soldiers. But when he failed to pay Urban adequately, the cannon expert offered his skills to the Turkish side. The former allies of the Empire, meanwhile, sent little or no assistance.

It was undoubtedly Byzantine inability to invest in this technology of warfare that sealed the fate of the city. Once Urban was in the employ of the Sultan, who was happy to pay what he asked, the Hungarian cast the largest cannon ever produced, a 29 foot-long bore which fired enormous stones variously identified as weighing 1,200–1,300 lbs. This was called Imperial (*Basilica*) and was so heavy that a team of sixty oxen had to haul it from Edirne. It could only be fired seven times a day because it overheated so greatly. But once correctly positioned opposite the Gate of Romanos and fired, it brought down the ancient walls and created the historic breach through which the Ottoman forces entered the city on the morning of May 29th.

Against this monster weapon, the defenders set up their own much smaller cannon. But when fired they caused more damage to the ancient structures of the city than to the enemy. All the regular techniques of siege warfare were employed: the attackers dug tunnels under the walls, and built tall siege towers which they rolled up to the walls, in order to fix their scaling ladders. The defenders dug counter tunnels and threw burning material into those of the invaders; they poured hot pitch from the walls and set fire to anything wooden set against them. The smoke of fires, as well as cannon, meant that the combatants fought without seeing clearly what was around them.

In 1453 Easter was celebrated on Sunday April 1st, and the next day the Emperor ordered the boom which protected the city's harbour on the Golden Horn to be set in place. Once it was stretched between Constantinople and the Genoese colony of Pera it prevented ships from entering the harbour. As they watched the Turks bringing up their forces, the inhabitants must have realised that battle was about to commence. From April 11th, the cannon bombardment began and the following day the full Turkish fleet of 145 ships anchored two miles off from Constantinople. Fighting occurred on land and sea, with a major onslaught on the walls on April 18th, and a notable naval engagement on April 20th. After the land battle Constantine XI ordered the clergy and monks to gather up the dead and bury them: a total of 1,740 Greeks and 700 Franks (i.e. Westerners) and Armenians, against 18,000 Turks. This duty was repeated on April 25th, when 5,700 defenders were slain, and 35,000 enemy. While the figures (which vary from source to source) are not reliable, the sense of loss and disaster permeates all accounts. Constantinople had been under siege in effect for many years. In 1453 the actual conquest took forty-six days.

Towards the middle of May after stalwart resistance, the Sultan sent an envoy into the city to discuss a possible solution. Mehmet still wished to take the city, but he announced that he would lift the siege if the Emperor paid an annual tribute of 100,000 gold bezants. Alternatively, all the citizens could leave with their possessions and no one would be harmed. The Emperor summoned his council to discuss the proposal. No one seriously believed that such a huge sum could be raised as tribute, nor were they prepared to abandon the city. As in many earlier meetings he had with Cardinal Isidore and the clergy of Hagia Sophia, the Emperor refused to consider flight. Further discussion on the issue was useless. He had embraced his heroic role.

One aspect of the siege emphasised by many authors is the immense din of battle. The Turks made their dawn prayers and then advanced with castanets, tambourines, cymbals and terrifying war cries. Fifes, trumpets, pipes and lutes also accompanied the troops. Three centuries later this manifestation of Turkish military music inspired Mozart to some of his most exciting compositions. In response to the Turks' percussive noise, the Emperor ordered the bells of the city to be rung, and from the numerous churches the tolling of bells inspired the Christians to greater zeal. Trumpets blared at the arrival of troops in support of the city. Nestor-Iskander records how the sound of church bells summoned the non-combatants, priests, monks, women and children to collect the crosses and holy icons and bring them out to bless the city. He also says that women fought among the men and even children threw bricks and paving stones at the Turks once they were inside the city. His account reminds us of the long clash of Muslim and Christian forces which can still be heard today.

George Sprantzes, Constantine XI's loyal secretary, recorded the outcome of the final battle and the way the last emperor of Byzantium conducted himself:

> On Tuesday May 29th, early in the day, the sultan took possession of our City; in this time of capture my late master and emperor, Lord Constantine, was killed. I was not at his side at that hour but had been inspecting another part of the City according to his orders . . . What did my late lord the emperor not do publicly and privately in his efforts to gain some aid for his house, for the Christians and for his own life? Did he ever think that it was possible and easy for him to abandon the City, if something happened? . . . Who knew of our emperor's fastings and prayers, both his own and those of priests whom he paid to do so; of his services to the poor and of his increased pledges to God, in the hope of saving his subjects from the Turkish yoke? Nevertheless, God ignored his offerings, I know not why or for what sins, and men disregarded his efforts, as each individual spoke against him as he pleased.

In many respects the city of Constantinople which had for so long eluded the Arabs and Turks was no longer the great Queen of Cities it had once been. That city had already been destroyed in 1204 by Western forces of the Fourth Crusade who had plundered its wealth and then occupied it for fifty-seven years. When the Byzantines reconquered their capital in 1261, they attempted to restore its past glory but could never recreate its former strength. As the Ottomans closed in on their prize, Constantinople became the last outpost of Christian faith in the Middle East, and its inhabitants had to face their historic destiny. The battle between Christianity and Islam was joined around the city.

Constantine XI was the first to realise this and his disappearance during the last day of fighting heightened the myth of 1453. Although a head was solemnly presented to Sultan Mehmet and a corpse given to the Greeks for formal burial, Constantine's body was never found. As a result many stories of his escape and survival circulated. The idea that he had found shelter within the walls of the city and would emerge to triumph over the Muslims is typical. The prolonged resistance and bravery of the defenders made heroes of them all. And within a few years, to have been present in the city on May 29th, 1453, became a badge of honour, claimed by many who had been elsewhere. By the same token Sultan Mehmet would have delighted in the nickname which recognised his role in the fall: from the late fifteenth century onwards, and even today, 550 years later, he is still known as Mehmet the Conqueror.

For Further Reading

J. R. Melville Jones, *The Fall of Constantinople 1453: Seven Contemporary Accounts* (Amsterdam 1972); J. R. Jones, *Nicolo Barbaro: A Diary of the Siege of Constantinople 1453* (New York 1969); Nestor-Iskander, *The Tale of Constantinople (of Its Origin and Capture by the Turks in the Year 1453)*, translated and annotated by Walter K. Hanak and Marios

Philippides (New Rochelle NY and Athens 1998);
M. Philippides, *The Fall of the Byzantine Empire: A Chronicle by George Sphrantzes 1401–1477* (Amherst, 1980); Steven Runciman, *The Fall of Constantinople 1453* (Cambridge 1965); Mark Bartusis, *The Late Byzantine Army: Arms and Society, 1204–1453* (Philadelphia, 1992)

Critical Thinking

1. In the mythic battle that gave the Turks victory over Constantinople in 1453, what is the significance of the fact that the leaders on both sides "never expected to become rulers"?
2. What strategies led to Sultan Mechmet II's ultimate success?
3. What were some of the reasons that Western powers were unable or unwilling to respond to Byzantine pleas to "come to the aid of their Christian City"?
4. Do you agree that it was Byzantine inability "to invest in this technology of warfare [cannons]" that sealed the fate of the city?

Create Central

www.mhhe.com/createcentral

Internet References

Labyrinth Home Page to Medieval Studies
www.georgetown.edu/labyrinth/
WWW Medieval Resources
http://ebbs.english.vt.edu/medieval/medieval.ebbs.html

JUDITH HERRIN is Professor of Late Antique and Byzantine Studies at King's College London. Her most recent book is *Women in Purple. Rulers of Medieval Byzantium* (Weidenfeld and Nicolson, 2002).

Unit VII

UNIT

Prepared by:Joseph R. Mitchell, *Howard Community College*
and Helen Buss Mitchell, *Howard Community College*

1500: The Era of Global Expansion

It might be argued that the most important event in the formation of the modern world is the industrial revolution. In that case, textbooks should divide at that point. A date of 1800 could roughly mark the start not only of the industrial revolution, but also the liberal, political revolts in France, the United States, and Latin America. Yet, 1500 is the time of the Reformation, the Renaissance, and the great global explorations. This is the start of the Western domination of the world that continues into the present. Therefore, most world historians accept 1500 as a suitable breaking point for teaching purposes. So it is with the two volumes of *Annual Editions: World History.*

In global exploration, the Scandinavians might have led the way with their colonies in Iceland, Greenland, and Nova Scotia. But, their attempt failed for ecological reasons. The Chinese also might have led the way if it had not been for indifference, internal economic problems, politics, and perhaps, arrogance. Zheng He, a court eunuch and Muslim, directed a powerful fleet westward on successful explorations that carried him to India and the eastern coast of Africa. But, the Chinese government stopped the voyages and destroyed the ships. Like those of the Vikings, the Chinese discoveries were left unexploited.

Subsequent explorations were left to the Europeans, who, led by the Italian Marco Polo, had the ambition as well as the technology to undertake them. The Portuguese sailed southward around Africa, while Christopher Columbus headed westward. His encounter with a new world changed the course of history and paved the way for other Europeans to follow and share in the exploitation of lands and peoples. The quincentenary of his 1492 voyage brought unprecedented criticism from native activist groups, who see Columbus as the symbol of their subsequent oppression.

Another group of people left Spain the day before Columbus sailed toward the Americas. Jews and Muslims who refused to convert to Christianity were expelled from Spain by the Catholic monarchs Ferdinand and Isabella. Cordoba, Spain had been a seat of Islamic culture during the classical period of Islamic civilization, while the rest of Europe was immersed in the so-called Dark Ages. During this *reconquista* or reconquest of Spain, the king and queen engaged in an early form of ethnic cleansing.

Global expansion led rapidly to Western world dominance. Non-Western cultures after 1500 were progressively less able to preserve their own cultural and political autonomy, and thousands if not millions perished through the spread of European diseases. Driven by a combination of greed and religious fervor, Europeans explored the world. The search for spices drove the Portuguese to India, and a competitive spirit led Magellan to circumnavigate the globe, a feat accomplished by no other civilization.

Through these voyages, Europeans were able to bypass the Middle East and open up new trade lanes. That marked the beginning of a global shift in commerce. Time and technology were on the side of the West.

Article

Prepared by: Joseph R. Mitchell, *Howard Community College*
and Helen Buss Mitchell, *Howard Community College*

The Explorer Marco Polo

PAUL LUNDE

Learning Outcomes

After reading this article, you will be able to:

- Discuss Marco Polo's contributions to world history and correlate his accomplishments to subsequent events.

M arco Polo died in 1324, the year before Ibn Battuta set off, at age 21, from his native Tangier. Though they never met, Ibn Battuta almost certainly encountered people in his Indian Ocean travels who had seen Marco Polo and his entourage, for in 1292 Marco Polo sailed through the China Sea, the Malacca Strait and the Indian Ocean on his way home to Venice. His mission, on behalf of Yuan ruler Khubilai Khan, was to escort and deliver a bride for the Mongol Ilkhanid sultan Argun, then ruling the Islamic heartlands.

The number of islands in the Indian Ocean, Marco Polo wrote, is 12,700, "as shown by the maps and writings of the practiced seamen who ply in these waters." He added the disclaimer: "There is no man in all the world who could tell the truth about all the islands of the Indies." His account of the major ports, products and trade routes is remarkably accurate, despite some understandable geographical confusion and unreliable estimates of distances. Above all, he conveys a sense of wonder and enthusiasm for this world in which "everything is different"—a phrase he repeats frequently. He is alive to human, linguistic and zoological diversity, and this explains the great charm of his book.

He is also perhaps the first European writer since classical times to mention the monsoon: "I must tell you that it takes a full year to complete the voyage, setting out in winter and returning in summer. For only two winds blow in these seas, one that wafts them out and one that brings them back; and the former blows in winter, the latter in summer."

His voyage began with a sailing from Zaitun (Quanzhou) to the kingdom of Champa in South Vietnam, a distance he estimates at 2400 kilometers (1500 mi). Champa was a main source of aloeswood, 'ud in Arabic, much sought after throughout Islamic lands to this day as an aromatic, and ebony, used for making chessmen and pencases.

Although he did not visit Java, he mentions it is "the biggest island in the world, . . . a very rich island, producing pepper, nutmegs, spikenard, galingale, cubebs and cloves and all the precious spices. . . . It is visited by great numbers of ships and merchants who buy a great range of merchandise, reaping handsome profits and rich returns. . . . It is from this island that the merchants of Zaitun and Manzi [southern China] in general have derived and continue to derive a great part of their wealth, and this is the source of most of the spice that comes into the world's markets."

Java did not, of course, produce all the spices he lists: the cloves and nutmegs came from the Moluccas; the pepper may have been imported from Malabar. But all were available in its markets.

Marco Polo says Khubilai Khan had never been able to conquer Java. In fact, he attacked the year after Marco's visit, following attempts against Burma, Champa and Annam. The Yuan sought to impose their power at sea as well as on land, but they were dogged by failure, beginning with the destruction of the great fleet sent against Japan in 1274. Their persistent and costly attempts at naval domination nevertheless show their determination to control not only the overland routes to China, but the maritime ones as well—an ambition encouraged by Muslim traders in the Yuan empire, who would have welcomed the elimination of non-Muslim competition in Japan and South and Southeast Asia.

Marco Polo sailed from South Vietnam to the Malay Peninsula, where "gold is so plentiful that no one who did not see it could believe it. There are elephants and wild game in profusion." There was also brazilwood, which produced a red dye for the textile industry and which Marco tried, unsuccessfully, to transplant to Venice.

He then sailed through the Strait of Malacca, which he is the first to describe, to Sumatra, which he calls "Java the Lesser." This was, he wrote, divided into eight kingdoms, each with its own language. One of the kingdoms was "Ferlec"—probably Periak in northern Sumatra. There, he says, the people used to be Hindus, but have converted to Islam through contact with Muslim merchants. He adds that this was true only of the inhabitants of the city, the mountain people being cannibals. The process of Islamization—at the hands of traders from India and mainland Southeast Asia, rather than from Arabia—was just beginning: This is the earliest reference to a Muslim sultanate in the Indonesian archipelago. He spent five months in Samudra waiting for the northeast monsoon so he could continue his voyage west to Sri Lanka.

He estimates the circumference of Sri Lanka at 2400 miles, adding that it was once much bigger, measuring 3500, "as

Figure 1 Venice in the late 13th or early 14th century, where Marco Polo grew up in a merchant family.

appears in the mariners' charts of this sea." He explains, "The north wind blows so strongly in these parts that it has submerged a great part of this island under the sea." The reference to marine charts is reason to believe that they were used by Indian Ocean sailors; however, none have survived.

Then as now Sri Lanka was famous for precious stones, in particular rubies. The king owned a ruby the length of a man's palm and the thickness of his arm, flawless "and glowing red like fire." This royal ruby is also mentioned in the seventh voyage of Sindbad; Marco Polo says Khubilai Khan sent an embassy to purchase it, but the king would not part with it.

Sumatran city-dwellers, Marco Polo wrote, used to be Hindus, but had converted to Islam through contact with Muslim merchants from India and mainland Southeast Asia.

Marco Polo landed from Sri Lanka on the southeastern, or Coromandel, coast of India, and his long account of the country is filled with information on local customs, religion, dress and diet. He describes the pearl-fishing industry in the Gulf of Manaar and the importation of Arabian horses from Hormuz, Kais, Dhufar, Shihr and Aden. The king of Coromandel purchased an average of 2000 horses a year, paying a bit less than 250 grams of gold (about 8 oz) for the finest. As they did not survive long in the climate, the demand was constant.

Marco Polo had much to say about the thriving trade in ports like Kayal, Comorin, Quilon, Thana, Somnath and Cambay, all of which he visited. For several he gives the latitude by indicating the height of the Pole Star above the horizon, the same method used by Ahmad ibn Majid. These ports were linked to both China and the Mediterranean:

There is great abundance of pepper and also of ginger, besides cinnamon in plenty and other spices, turbit and coconuts. Buckrams are made here of the loveliest and most delicate texture in the world. In return, when merchants come

Figure 2   So important a trading center was Hormuz in the late 12th century that Marco Polo passed through it twice, once on his overland journey to China and again on his sea voyage home.

here from overseas, they load their ships with brass, which they use as ballast, cloth of gold and silk, sandal, gold, silver, cloves, spikenard and other such spices that are not produced here. . . . Goods are exported to many parts. Those that go to Aden are carried thence to Alexandria.

To the northwest, in Gujarat, Marco Polo notes the region's independence and its own form of Indo-Aryan speech; he is one of the few medieval travelers to remark on linguistic diversity. He mentions the famous cotton of Gujarat and the export of leather goods to Arabia and other countries: "Suffice it to say that in this kingdom are produced leather goods of more consummate workmanship than anywhere in the world and of higher value." The ships that called at Cambay brought gold, silver and brass, exchanging them for leather goods, cotton textiles and indigo.

He then crossed the Indian Ocean to the island of Socotra, a Nestorian outpost off the coast of southern Arabia that still had an archbishop appointed from Baghdad. Socotra was famed in the Middle Ages for the export of "dragon's blood," an astringent resin used for treating wounds. The island also exported ambergris, salt fish and fine cotton cloth. Ships bound for Aden called here to trade and reprovision.

Immediately after describing Socotra, Marco Polo gives a hearsay account of Madagascar, beyond which no one sails, he says, because of the strong southern current. (This was the current that led the Arab geographers too to believe that ships that sailed beyond Madagascar would be unable to return.) There, he says, ships come with cloth of gold and silks, trading for ivory and ambergris and other local products. Madagascar, he says, is also the home of the gryphon, and he says he talked to men who had actually seen it. It was not, as Europeans believed, a blend of bird and lion, but a true bird of colossal size: "They report that they are so huge and bulky that one of them can pounce on an elephant and carry it up to a great height in the air. Then it lets go, so that the elephant drops to earth and is smashed to pulp, whereupon the gryphon bird perches on the carcass and feeds at its ease." He then says that the islanders call this bird the *rukh*—an old friend from the tales of the voyages of Sindbad.

Like any good businessman, Marco Polo noted the products of each place he visited, the port traffic, the relative values of goods and the trade relationships that existed.

After this excursus on East Africa, Marco Polo proceeded to Aden, "the port to which all the ships from India come." He describes how ships transfer their cargoes to smaller boats in the harbor, "sail for seven days along a river" (presumably the Red Sea), and then transfer the goods to camel-back and send them overland on a 30-day trip to the Nile and thence to Alexandria and the Mediterranean.

He describes three other flourishing Arabian ports—Shihr, Dhufar and Qalhat, all exporting fine horses to India; Shihr and Dhufar also exported frankincense. He then crossed the Gulf to Hormuz, not the "New Hormuz" that Ibn Battuta saw on the island of Jarun, but the mainland town. Marco describes the system of ventilators (*badgir*) that funneled cool air into the interior of the houses and made life bearable.

A number of other European travelers and missionaries took advantage of the *pax mongolica* to travel to the Far East in the early 14th century. Several of them, including Odoric of Pordenone, Fray Jordan Catalán de Sévérac and Fray Pascual de Vitoria, sailed home through the Indian Ocean. They wrote short accounts of their travels that supplement, but do not eclipse, Marco Polo's.

Nicolò dei Conti voyaged widely in the Indian Ocean between 1414 and 1439. His itinerary is remarkable: Baghdad–Hormuz–Qalhat–Cambay–Malabar–Madras–Malapur–Sumatra–Burma–Ava–Pegu–Java–Borneo–Champa–Quilon–Cochin–Calicut–Cambay again–Aden–Berbera–Jiddah–Makkah–Cairo–Venice. He spent nine months in Borneo and learned from traders of the existence of the far-off Moluccas, the Spice Islands that the early Arab geographers had known only as *bilad manbit al-'atar,* "the country where the spices grow." He is the first author to refer to the bird of paradise, species of which live only in New Guinea and adjacent islands and whose feathers were much prized by the Chinese and Ottoman Turks.

On his return to Europe, his caravan crossed with that of a Christian knight, Pero Tafur, near Mount Sinai. Nicolò told Pero Tafur that he had left home at 18, lost his inheritance, spent a year at the court of Tamerlane in Samarkand, then set off for India. In India, Nicolò claimed, he had been received by Prester John, "very graciously and [he] showed me many favors, and married me to the woman I now have with me, and she bore me these children." Prester John, he said, was a great lord with 25 kings in his service, and he had sent two unsuccessful expeditions in search of the sources of the Nile.

On his return to Italy, Nicolò dictated his travels to the papal secretary and learned humanist Poggio Bracciolini, to whom we owe the survival of so many key works. He toned down his account, producing a short, informative report of his travels. Much of his geographical information was recorded by the Venetian Fra Mauro on his wonderful map of 1459, a map which, incidentally, clearly shows Africa as a peninsula. Yet Nicolò's conversation in the desert with Pero Tafur shows the medieval side of this remarkable man, whose obsession with Prester John and the sources of the Nile was shared by the Portuguese and spurred them to undertake their punishing voyages.

Nicolò had been able to travel freely while Tamerlane was alive, but when Tamerlane's empire crumbled after his death in 1404, the overland routes were no longer safe, and Nicolò was forced to return to Italy by sea. He was not the only one inconvenienced by the death of the Central Asian conqueror, nor was he the only one to turn to the sea.

Critical Thinking

1. What would you list as some of the most useful information Marco Polo brought back from his voyages to aid future travelers?

2. What was the purpose of Ibn Battuta's "mission"?

3. Of all the "news" about places and peoples he encountered on his voyages, which of Marco Polo's revelations do you imagine were the most interesting to stay-at-home readers?

Create Central

www.mhhe.com/createcentral

Internet References

Gander Academy's European Explorers Resources on the World Wide Web

www.stemnet.nf.ca/CITE/explorer.htm

Magellan's Voyage Around the World

www.fordham.edu/halsall/mod/1519magellan.html

Article

Prepared by: Joseph R. Mitchell, *Howard Community College*
and Helen Buss Mitchell, *Howard Community College*

1492: The Prequel

Decades before Columbus, Zheng He sailed from China with 300 ships and 28,000 men. His fleet got as far as Africa and could have easily reached America, but the Chinese turned back. What happened?

NICHOLAS D. KRISTOF

Learning Outcomes

After reading this article, you will be able to:

- Understand the extent to which the 15th-century Chinese fleet could have been a deterrent to western expansion in Asia and why the Chinese scuttled their fleet later in the century.

From the sea, the tiny East African island of Pate, just off the Kenyan coast, looks much as it must have in the 15th century: an impenetrable shore of endless mangrove trees. As my little boat bounced along the waves in the gray dawn, I could see no antennae or buildings or even gaps where trees had been cut down, no sign of human habitation, nothing but a dense and mysterious jungle.

The village's inhabitants, much lighter-skinned than people on the Kenyan mainland, emerged barefoot to stare at me with the same curiosity with which I was studying them. These were people I had come halfway around the world to see, in the hope of solving an ancient historical puzzle.

The boatman drew as close as he could to a narrow black-sand beach, and I splashed ashore. My local Swahili interpreter led the way through the forest, along a winding trail scattered with mangoes, coconuts and occasional seashells deposited by high tides. The tropical sun was firmly overhead when we finally came upon a village of stone houses with thatched roofs, its dirt paths sheltered by palm trees. The village's inhabitants, much lighter-skinned than people on the Kenyan mainland, emerged barefoot to stare at me with the same curiosity with which I was studying them. These were people I had come

halfway around the world to see, in the hope of solving an ancient historical puzzle.

"Tell me," I asked the first group I encountered, "where did the people here come from? Long ago, did foreign sailors ever settle here?"

The answer was a series of shrugs. "I've never heard about that," one said. "You'll have to ask the elders."

I tried several old men and women without success. Finally the villagers led me to the patriarch of the village, Bwana Mkuu Al-Bauri, the keeper of oral traditions. He was a frail old man with gray stubble on his cheeks, head and chest. He wore a yellow sarong around his waist; his ribs pressed through the taut skin on his bare torso. Al-Bauri hobbled out of his bed, resting on a cane and the arm of a grandson. He claimed to be 121 years old; a pineapple-size tumor jutted from the left side of his chest.

"I know this from my grandfather, who himself was the keeper of history here," the patriarch told me in an unexpectedly clear voice. "Many, many years ago, there was a ship from China that wrecked on the rocks off the coast near here. The sailors swam ashore near the village of Shanga—my ancestors were there and saw it themselves. The Chinese were visitors, so we helped those Chinese men and gave them food and shelter, and then they married our women. Although they do not live in this village, I believe their descendants still can be found somewhere else on this island."

I almost felt like hugging Bwana Al-Bauri. For months I had been poking around obscure documents and research reports, trying to track down a legend of an ancient Chinese shipwreck that had led to a settlement on the African coast. My interest arose from a fascination with what to me is a central enigma of the millennium: why did the West triumph over the East?

For most of the last several thousand years, it would have seemed far likelier that Chinese or Indians, not Europeans, would dominate the world by the year 2000, and that America and Australia would be settled by Chinese rather than by the inhabitants of a backward island called Britain. The reversal of fortunes of East and West strikes me as the biggest news story of the millennium, and one of its most unexpected as well.

As a resident of Asia for most of the past 13 years, I've been searching for an explanation. It has always seemed to me that the turning point came in the early 1400's, when Admiral Zheng He sailed from China to conquer the world. Zheng He (pronounced JUNG HUH) was an improbable commander of a great Chinese fleet, in that he was a Muslim from a rebel family and had been seized by the Chinese Army when he was still a boy. Like many other prisoners of the time, he was castrated—his sexual organs completely hacked off, a process that killed many of those who suffered it. But he was a brilliant and tenacious boy who grew up to be physically imposing. A natural leader, he had the good fortune to be assigned, as a houseboy, to the household of a great prince, Zhu Di.

In time, the prince and Zheng He grew close, and they conspired to overthrow the prince's nephew, the Emperor of China. With Zheng He as one of the prince's military commanders, the revolt succeeded and the prince became China's Yongle Emperor. One of the emperor's first acts (after torturing to death those who had opposed him) was to reward Zheng He with the command of a great fleet that was to sail off and assert China's pre-eminence in the world.

Between 1405 and 1433, Zheng He led seven major expeditions, commanding the largest armada the world would see for the next five centuries. Not until World War I did the West mount anything comparable. Zheng He's fleet included 28,000 sailors on 300 ships, the longest of which were 400 feet. By comparison, Columbus in 1492 had 90 sailors on three ships, the biggest of which was 85 feet long. Zheng He's ships also had advanced design elements that would not be introduced in Europe for another 350 years, including balanced rudders and watertight bulwark compartments.

The sophistication of Zheng He's fleet underscores just how far ahead of the West the East once was. Indeed, except for the period of the Roman Empire, China had been wealthier, more advanced and more cosmopolitan than any place in Europe for several thousand years. Hangzhou, for example, had a population in excess of a million during the time it was China's capital (in the 12th century), and records suggest that as early as the 7th century, the city of Guangzhou had 200,000 foreign residents: Arabs, Persians, Malays, Indians, Africans and Turks. By contrast, the largest city in Europe in 1400 was probably Paris, with a total population of slightly more than 100,000.

A half-century before Columbus, Zheng He had reached East Africa and learned about Europe from Arab traders. The Chinese could easily have continued around the Cape of Good Hope and established direct trade with Europe. But as they saw it, Europe was a backward region, and China had little interest in the wool, beads and wine Europe had to trade. Africa had what China wanted—ivory, medicines, spices, exotic woods, even specimens of native wildlife.

In Zheng He's time, China and India together accounted for more than half of the world's gross national product, as they have for most of human history. Even as recently as 1820, China accounted for 29 percent of the global economy and India another 16 percent, according to the calculations of Angus Maddison, a leading British economic historian.

Asia's retreat into relative isolation after the expeditions of Zheng He amounted to a catastrophic missed opportunity, one that laid the groundwork for the rise of Europe and, eventually, America. Westerners often attribute their economic advantage today to the intelligence, democratic habits or hard work of their forebears, but a more important reason may well have been the folly of 15th-century Chinese rulers. That is why I came to be fascinated with Zheng He and set out earlier this year to retrace his journeys. I wanted to see what legacy, if any, remained of his achievement, and to figure out why his travels did not remake the world in the way that Columbus's did.

> **Westerners often attribute their economic advantage today to the intelligence or hard work of their forebears, but a more important reason may well have been the folly of the 15th-century Chinese rulers who dismantled Zheng He's fleet.**

Zheng He lived in Nanjing, the old capital, where I arrived one day in February. Nanjing is a grimy metropolis on the Yangtze River in the heart of China. It has been five centuries since Zheng He's death, and his marks on the city have grown faint. The shipyards that built his fleet are still busy, and the courtyard of what had been his splendid 72-room mansion is now the Zheng He Memorial Park, where children roller-skate and old couples totter around for exercise. But though the park has a small Zheng He museum, it was closed—for renovation, a caretaker told me, though he knew of no plans to reopen it.

I'd heard that Zheng He's tomb is on a hillside outside the city, and I set out to find it. It wasn't long before the road petered out, from asphalt to gravel to dirt to nothing. No tomb was in sight, so I approached an old man weeding a vegetable garden behind his house. Tang Yiming, 72, was still lithe and strong. His hair was gray and ragged where he had cut it himself, disastrously, in front of a mirror. Evidently lonely, he was delighted to talk, and offered to show me the path to the tomb. As we walked, I mentioned that I had read that there used to be an old Ming Dynasty tablet on Zheng He's grave.

"Oh, yeah, the old tablet," he said nonchalantly. "When I was a boy, there was a Ming Dynasty tablet here. When it disappeared, the Government offered a huge reward to anyone who would return it—a reward big enough to build a new house. Seemed like a lot of money. But the problem was that we couldn't give it back. People around here are poor. We'd smashed it up to use as building materials."

A second mystery concerned what, if anything, is actually buried in Zheng He's tomb, since he is believed to have died on his last voyage and been buried at sea. So I said in passing that I'd heard tell the tomb is empty, and let my voice trail off.

"Oh, there's nothing in there," Tang said, a bit sadly. "No bones, nothing. That's for sure."

"How do you know?"

"In 1962, people dug up the grave, looking for anything to sell. We dug up the ground to one and a half times the height of a man. But there was absolutely nothing in there. It's empty."

The absence of impressive monuments to Zheng He in China today should probably come as no surprise, since his achievement was ultimately renounced. Curiously, it is not in China but in Indonesia where his memory has been most actively kept alive. Zheng He's expeditions led directly to the wave of Chinese immigration to Southeast Asia, and in some countries he is regarded today as a deity. In the Indonesia city of Semarang, for example, there is a large temple honoring Zheng He, located near a cave where he once nursed a sick friend. Indonesians still pray to Zheng He for a cure or good luck.

Not so in his native land. Zheng He was viewed with deep suspicion by China's traditional elite, the Confucian scholars, who made sure to destroy the archives of his journey. Even so, it is possible to learn something about his story from Chinese sources—from imperial archives and even the memoirs of crewmen. The historical record makes clear, for example, that it was not some sudden impulse of extroversion that led to Zheng He's achievement. It grew, rather, out of a long sailing tradition. Chinese accounts suggest that in the fifth century, a Chinese monk sailed to a mysterious "far east country" that sounds very much like Mayan Mexico, and Mayan art at that time suddenly began to include Buddhist symbols. By the 13th century, Chinese ships regularly traveled to India and occasionally to East Africa.

Zheng He's armada was far grander, of course, than anything that came before. His grandest vessels were the "treasure ships," 400 feet long and 160 feet wide, with nine masts raising red silk sails to the wind, as well as multiple decks and luxury cabins with balconies. His armada included supply ships to carry horses, troop transports, warships, patrol boats and as many as 20 tankers to carry fresh water. The full contingent of 28,000 crew members included interpreters for Arabic and other languages, astrologers to forecast the weather, astronomers to study the stars, pharmacologists to collect medicinal plants, ship-repair specialists, doctors and even two protocol officers to help organize official receptions.

In the aftermath of such an incredible undertaking, you somehow expect to find a deeper mark on Chinese history, a greater legacy. But perhaps the faintness of Zheng He's trace in contemporary China is itself a lesson. In the end, an explorer makes history but does not necessarily change it, for his impact depends less on the trail he blazes than on the willingness of others to follow. The daring of a great expedition ultimately is hostage to the national will of those who remain behind.

In February I traveled to Calicut, a port town in southwestern India that was (and still is) the pepper capital of the world. The evening I arrived, I went down to the beach in the center of town to look at the coastline where Zheng He once had berthed his ships. In the 14th and 15th centuries, Calicut was one of the world's great ports, known to the Chinese as "the great country of the Western ocean." In the early 15th century, the sight of Zheng He's fleet riding anchor in Calicut harbor symbolized the strength of the world's two greatest powers, China and India.

On this sultry evening, the beach, framed by long piers jutting out to sea, was crowded with young lovers and ice-cream vendors. Those piers are all that remain of the port of Calicut, and you can see at a glance that they are no longer usable. The following day I visited the port offices, musty with handwritten ledgers of ship visits dating back nearly a century. The administrator of the port, Captain E. G. Mohanan, explained matter-of-factly what had happened. "The piers got old and no proper maintenance was ever carried out," he said, as a ceiling fan whirred tiredly overhead. "By the time we thought of it, it was not economical to fix it up." So in 1989, trade was halted, and one of the great ports of the world became no port at all.

The disappearance of a great Chinese fleet from a great Indian port symbolized one of history's biggest lost opportunities—Asia's failure to dominate the second half of this millennium. So how did this happen?

While Zheng He was crossing the Indian Ocean, the Confucian scholar-officials who dominated the upper echelons of the Chinese Government were at political war with the eunuchs, a group they regarded as corrupt and immoral. The eunuchs' role at court involved looking after the concubines, but they also served as palace administrators, often doling out contracts in exchange for kickbacks. Partly as a result of their legendary greed, they promoted commerce. Unlike the scholars—who owed their position to their mastery of 2,000-year-old eunuchs, lacking any such roots in a classical past, were sometimes outward-looking and progressive. Indeed, one can argue that it was the virtuous, incorruptible scholars who in the mid-15th century set China on its disastrous course.

After the Yongle Emperor died in 1424, China endured a series of brutal power struggles; a successor emperor died under suspicious circumstances and ultimately the scholars emerged triumphant. They ended the voyages of Zheng He's successors, halted construction of new ships and imposed curbs on private shipping. To prevent any backsliding, they destroyed Zheng He's sailing records and, with the backing of the new emperor, set about dismantling China's navy.

By 1500 the Government had made it a capital offense to build a boat with more than two masts, and in 1525 the Government ordered the destruction of all oceangoing ships. The greatest navy in history, which a century earlier had 3,500 ships (by comparison, the United States Navy today has 324), had been extinguished, and China set a course for itself that would lead to poverty, defeat and decline.

Still, it was not the outcome of a single power struggle in the 1440's that cost China its worldly influence. Historians offer a host of reasons for why Asia eventually lost its way economically and was late to industrialize; two and a half reasons seem most convincing.

The first is that Asia was simply not greedy enough. The dominant social ethos in ancient China was Confucianism and in India it was caste, with the result that the elites in both nations looked down their noses at business. Ancient China cared about many things—prestige, honor, culture, arts, education, ancestors, religion, filial piety—but making money came far down the list. Confucius had specifically declared that it was wrong for a man to make a distant voyage while his parents were alive, and he had condemned profit as the concern of "a little man." As it was, Zheng He's ships were built on such a grand scale and carried such lavish gifts to foreign leaders that the voyages were not the huge money spinners they could have been.

In contrast to Asia, Europe was consumed with greed. Portugal led the age of discovery in the 15th century largely because it wanted spices, a precious commodity; it was the hope of profits that drove its ships steadily farther down the African coast and eventually around the Horn to Asia. The profits of this trade could be vast: Magellan's crew once sold a cargo of 26 tons of cloves for 10,000 times the cost.

A second reason for Asia's economic stagnation is more difficult to articulate but has to do with what might be called a culture of complacency. China and India shared a tendency to look inward, a devotion to past ideals and methods, a respect for authority and a suspicion of new ideas. David S. Landes, a Harvard economist, has written of ancient China's "intellectual xenophobia"; the former Indian Prime Minister Jawaharlal Nehru referred to the "petrification of classes" and the "static nature" of Indian society. These are all different ways of describing the same economic and intellectual complacency.

Chinese elites regarded their country as the "Middle Kingdom" and believed they had nothing to learn from barbarians abroad. India exhibited much of the same self-satisfaction. "Indians didn't go to Portugal not because they couldn't but because they didn't want to," mused M. P. Sridharan, a historian, as we sat talking on the porch of his home in Calicut.

The 15th-century Portuguese were the opposite. Because of its coastline and fishing industry, Portugal always looked to the sea, yet rivalries with Spain and other countries shut it out of the Mediterranean trade. So the only way for Portugal to get at the wealth of the East was by conquering the oceans.

The half reason is simply that China was a single nation while Europe was many. When the Confucian scholars reasserted control in Beijing and banned shipping, their policy mistake condemned all of China. In contrast, European countries committed economic suicide selectively. So when Portugal slipped into a quasi-Chinese mind-set in the 16th century, slaughtering Jews and burning heretics and driving astronomers and scientists abroad, Holland and England were free to take up the slack.

When I first began researching Zheng He, I never thought I'd be traveling all the way to Africa to look for traces of his voyages. Then I came across a few intriguing references to the possibility of an ancient Chinese shipwreck that might have left some Chinese stranded on the island of Pate (pronounced PAH-tay). One was a skeptical reference in a scholarly journal, another was a casual conversation with a Kenyan I met a few years ago and the third was the epilogue of Louise Levathes's wonderful 1994 book about China's maritime adventures, "When China Ruled the Seas." Levathes had traveled to Kenya and found people who believed they were descended from survivors of a Chinese shipwreck. So, on a whim and an expense account, I flew to Lamu, an island off northern Kenya, and hired a boat and an interpreter to go to Pate and see for myself.

Pate is off in its own world, without electricity or roads or vehicles. Mostly jungle, it has been shielded from the 20th century largely because it is accessible from the Kenyan mainland only by taking a boat through a narrow tidal channel that is passable only at high tide. Initially I was disappointed by what I found there. In the first villages I visited, I saw people who were light-skinned and had hair that was not tightly curled, but they could have been part Arab or European rather than part Chinese. The remote villages of Chundwa and Faza were more promising, for there I found people whose eyes, hair and complexion hinted at Asian ancestry, though their background was ambiguous.

And then on a still and sweltering afternoon I strolled through the coconut palms into the village of Siyu, where I met a fisherman in his 40's named Abdullah Mohammed Badui. I stopped and stared at the man in astonishment, for he had light skin and narrow eyes. Fortunately, he was as rude as I was, and we stared at each other in mutual surprise before venturing a word. Eventually I asked him about his background and appearance.

"I am in the Famao clan," he said. "There are 50 or 100 of us Famao left here. Legend has it that we are descended from Chinese and others.

"A Chinese ship was coming along and it hit rocks and wrecked," Badui continued. "The sailors swam ashore to the village that we now call Shanga, and they married the local women, and that is why we Famao look so different."

Another Famao, with the same light complexion and vaguely Asian features, approached to listen. His name was Athman Mohammed Mzee, and he, too, told of hearing of the Chinese shipwreck from the elders. He volunteered an intriguing detail: the Africans had given giraffes to the Chinese.

Salim Bonaheri, a 55-year-old Famao man I met the next day, proudly declared, "My ancestors were Chinese or Vietnamese or something like that." I asked how they had got to Pate.

"I don't know," Bonaheri said with a shrug. Most of my conversations were like that, intriguing but frustrating dead ends. I was surrounded by people whose appearance seemed tantalizingly Asian, but who had only the vaguest notions of why that might be. I kept at it, though, and eventually found people like Khalifa Mohammed Omar, a 55-year-old Famao fisherman who looked somewhat Chinese and who also clearly remembered the stories passed down by his grandfather. From him and others, a tale emerged.

Countless generations ago, they said, Chinese sailors traded with local African kings. The local kings gave them giraffes to take back to China. One of the Chinese ships struck rocks off the eastern coast of Pate, and the sailors swam ashore, carrying with them porcelain and other goods from the ship. In time they married local women, converted to Islam and named the village Shanga, after Shanghai. Later, fighting erupted among Pate's clans, Shanga was destroyed and the Famao fled, some to the mainland, others to the village of Siyu.

Every time I heard the story about the giraffes my pulse began to race. Chinese records indicate that Zheng He had brought the first giraffes to China, a fact that is not widely known. The giraffe caused an enormous stir in China because it was believed to be the mythical *qilin,* or Chinese unicorn. It is difficult to imagine how African villagers on an island as remote as Pate would know about the giraffes unless the tale had been handed down to them by the Chinese sailors.

Chinese ceramics are found in many places along the east African coast, and their presence on Pate could be the result of purchases from Arab traders. But the porcelain on Pate was overwhelmingly concentrated among the Famao clan, which could mean that it had been inherited rather than purchased. I also visited some ancient Famao graves that looked less like traditional Kenyan graves than what the Chinese call "turtle-shell graves," with rounded tops.

Researchers have turned up other equally tantalizing clues. Craftsmen on Pate and the other islands of Lamu practice a kind of basket-weaving that is common in southern China but unknown on the Kenyan mainland. On Pate, drums are more often played in the Chinese than the African style, and the local dialect has a few words that may be Chinese in origin. More startling, in 1569 a Portuguese priest named Monclaro wrote that Pate had a flourishing silk-making industry—Pate, and no other place in the region. Elders in several villages on Pate confirmed to me that their island had produced silk until about half a century ago.

When I asked my boatman, Bakari Muhaji Ali, if he thought it was possible that a ship could have wrecked off the coast near Shanga, he laughed. "There are undersea rocks all over there," he said. "If you don't know exactly where you're going, you'll wreck your ship for sure."

If indeed there was a Chinese shipwreck off Pate, there is reason to think it happened in Zheng He's time. For if the shipwreck had predated him, surviving sailors would not have passed down stories of the giraffes. And if the wreck didn't occur until after Zheng He, its survivors could not have settled in Shanga, since British archeological digs indicate that the village was sacked, burned and abandoned in about 1440—very soon after Zheng He's last voyage.

Still, there is no hard proof for the shipwreck theory, and there are plenty of holes in it. No ancient Chinese characters have been found on tombs in Pate, no nautical instruments have ever turned up on the island and there are no Chinese accounts of an African shipwreck. This last lacuna might be explained by the destruction of the fleet's records. Yet if one of Zheng He's ships did founder on the rocks off Pate, then why didn't some other ships in the fleet come to the sailors' rescue?

As I made my way back through the jungle for the return trip, I pondered the significance of what I'd seen on Pate. In the faces of the Famao, in those bits of pottery and tantalizing hints of Chinese culture, I felt as though I'd glimpsed the shadowy outlines of one of the greatest might-have-beens of the millennium now ending. I thought about the Columbian Exchange, the swap of animals, plants, genes, germs, weapons and peoples that utterly remade both the New World and the Old, and I couldn't help wondering about another exchange—Zheng He's—that never took place, yet could have.

If ancient China had been greedier and more outward-looking, if other traders had followed in Zheng He's wake and then continued on, Asia might well have dominated Africa and even Europe. Chinese might have settled in not only Malaysia and Singapore, but also in East Africa, the Pacific Islands, even in America. Perhaps the Famao show us what the mestizos of such a world might have looked liked, the children of a hybrid culture that was never born. What I'd glimpsed in Pate was the high-water mark of an Asian push that simply stopped—not for want of ships or know-how, but strictly for want of national will.

All this might seem fanciful, and yet in Zheng He's time the prospect of a New World settled by the Spanish or English would have seemed infinitely more remote than a New World made by the Chinese. How different would history have been had Zheng He continued on to America? The mind rebels; the ramifications are almost too overwhelming to contemplate. So consider just one: this magazine would have been published in Chinese.

Critical Thinking

1. Why does Nicholas Kristof write: "For most of the last several thousand years, it would have seemed far likelier that Chinese or Indians, not Europeans, would dominate the world by the year 2000"?

2. In what ways was Zheng He "an improbable commander of a great Chinese fleet"?

3. Do you agree that "the folly of 15th-century Chinese rulers" laid the groundwork for the rise of Europe and, eventually America?

Create Central

www.mhhe.com/createcentral

Internet References

The Great Chinese Mariner Zheng He
www.chinapage.com/zhenghe.html

NICHOLAS D. KRISTOF is the Tokyo bureau chief of *The New York Times.* He is the author, with Sheryl WuDunn, of "China Wakes."

Article

Prepared by: Joseph R. Mitchell, *Howard Community College*
and Helen Buss Mitchell, *Howard Community College*

The Other 1492: Jews and Muslims in Columbus's Spain

Fouad Ajami

Learning Outcomes

After reading this article, you will be able to:

- Determine why Jews and Muslims were being expelled from Spain in 1492 at the same time as Columbus's ships were leaving.

The Edict of Expulsion issued by Ferdinand and Isabella on March 31, 1492, had the Jews quitting Spain on the last day of July of the same year. All Don Isaac Abravanel could do for his people was secure them a two-day stay of execution. Abravanel, one of the great figures of Iberian Jewry, had given Ferdinand and Isabella eight years of service: he had organized the chaotic finances of Castile and Aragon and helped the sovereigns in their final push against the Muslim stronghold of Granada. The work of the Reconquista against Muslim Spain completed, Don Isaac was suddenly thrown into the supreme challenge of his life.

Fragments survive of Abravanel's futile pleas to the Spanish sovereigns. There is the narrative by Don Isaac himself recorded in exile: "Thrice on my knees I besought the King. 'Regard us, O king, use not thy subjects so cruelly.' But as the adder closes its ear with dust against the voice of the charmer, so the King hardened his heart against entreaties of his supplicants."

Ferdinand and Isabella offered Don Isaac the chance to stay in Spain with his wealth and position intact—the edict had prohibited the Jews from taking any gold, coins, or silver with them. In return, he would of course have to undergo baptism and conversion. Abravanel chose dispossession and exile. There were lands where the life of the faith could be lived—the Italian city-states, Portugal, the Netherlands, the Muslim domains of the Ottoman Sultan, the Barbary states of Tunis, Algiers, and Tripoli, and there was a haven in Egypt.

Thanks to the two-day extension secured by Abravanel the last ships that took the Jews to these lands left Spain on the second of August. "This fleet of woe and misery," says one chronicler, was to sail parallel to a fleet of high promise. Christopher Columbus's fleet was ready for sea on the second of August: the men received their communion at the Church of St. George

in Palos on that day. The Captain General set sail in the early hours of the third day of August.

Months earlier there had been another departure: Boabdil, the last Muslim king of Granada, took to the road. History and grief and yearning have touched and ennobled that story. On the last ridge, overlooking Granada, the storytellers say, Boabdil paused to catch a final glimpse of his realm. The ridge came to be known as El Ultimo Sospiro del Moro, the Moor's last sigh. Boabdil's unsentimental mother is said to have taunted him during his moment of grief. "You should weep like a woman for the land you could not defend like a man." In truth, there was not much that Boabdil could have done. Granada was living on borrowed time. Boabdil cut the best possible deal with the Spanish: an estate for himself, a pledge of safety for the people of his city, safe passage for those who could not bear to live under Christian rule. The victors made another promise: Muslims who stayed behind were not to be molested; their religious rights were to be honored. That pledge would be violated. The remaining Muslims would face, a decade hence, the same choice offered the Jews: conversion or exile. A century later the Moriscos—the Moorish converts to Christianity—were also expelled.

Men invent and reinvent the past. In the legend of Moorish Spain, the Jews of Toledo opened the gates of the city to the Muslim conquerors when they came in 711. They were eager to welcome the Muslim armies that had overrun the Visigothic kingdom. The legend is groundless. In the war between the Goths and the Muslim armies, the Jews were, for the most part, quiet spectators. To be sure, they were glad to see the defeat of the Goths. The same must have been true of the Ibero-Roman natives of the peninsula. The Goths had been severe rulers. They had not allowed the Jews to sing their Psalms, to celebrate Passover, to testify in court against Christians, or to observe their dietary laws. Forced baptisms of Jews was a recurring phenomenon under Visigothic rule. Centuries later Montesquieu was to observe that "all the laws of the Inquisition had been part of the Visigothic code" that regulated the conduct of the Jews in seventh-century Spain.

It was a polyglot world that the Muslims came to rule in the Iberian peninsula. There were Arabs, Berbers, Jews, and blacks,

Muslims of native Spanish stock, native Christians. Islam was overextended in Spain; it thus made its accommodation with its habitat, ruled with a light touch. At its zenith in the tenth and eleventh centuries, it was to fashion a society of tranquillity and brilliance. Its cities thrived. Cordoba's population approximated a quarter million people; it was unmatched by any European city of the time. Its only rivals were the cities of Baghdad and Constantinople. The economy of Muslim Spain boomed, tied as it was to the larger Muslim economy. The Jews came into their own during these two centuries of prosperity. Literacy spread; Jewish academies opened in Cordoba, Granada, Toledo, Barcelona. Hispano-Arabic culture thrived in the cities of the south. A rich body of Judeo-Arabic philosophy was to become the distinctive gift of this age. Spanish Jewry declared its intellectual independence from the religious authority of the Iraqi academies that had been pre-eminent down through the ages. The Arabs had prided themselves on their poetry and literature; the Jews were to run a close race.

This was a world in flux, an ideal setting for a community of outsiders. There was room for talent; it was easy for Jews to find their way into all walks of public life. "No office, except that of the ruler, seemed to be out of the reach of a talented and ambitious Jew," Norman Stillman writes in his historical survey, *The Jews in Arab Lands*. Success at court was not without its hazards though. It called forth its steady companion—the wrath of the crowd. A Jew by the name of Samuel ben Naghrela was the ruler's minister in the Berber kingdom of Granada until his death in 1056. Ten years later his son, Joseph, was crucified by a mob on the city's main gate in an anti-Jewish riot. The father had risen on his own: he knew the hazards of success. The son had taken success for granted. He was, says one chronicle, "proud to his own hurt and the Berber princes were jealous of him." This riot was the first massacre of Jews in Muslim Spain. The date was December 30, 1066. About 1,500 families perished in that riot.

No measure of cultural brilliance would compensate for the political fragility of the edifice. A Muslim poet of Granada may have intuited the weakness underneath the cultural glitter when he wrote that he had "the fault of rising in the West." The Muslims had conquered the plains and the Mediterranean coast. The mountains in the north, the poorer regions of old Castile, were in Christian hands. This set the stage for a bloody and long struggle.

Trouble came to paradise as the eleventh century drew to a close. The Jews were caught between the pressures of the Reconquista and a Muslim society awakening to a new sense of vulnerability—and intolerance. Moses Ben Maimon, better known as Maimonides (1131–1204), the great figure of medieval Jewish life, quit his native birthplace in Cordoba and sought shelter in Cairo. (Maimonides became a luminary in the life of Cairo; he rose to become the physician of Saladin.) A yearning for Zion, for life in the land of Israel, was to find its way into the poetry of the time. The "Golden Age" of the Jews of Muslim Spain had drawn to a close. Small messianic Jewish movements made their appearance—an expression of the malaise of the Jews as the Andalusian cocoon was to be torn asunder.

Little was to remain of the Moorish realms in the peninsula. Toledo had been lost in 1085; Cordoba itself in 1236, Valencia in 1238, Seville two years later. By 1264 all that remained were Granada and its surroundings. That Muslim foothold was spared because the warring kingdoms to its north—Castile, Aragon, Navarre, Portugal—had been busy with their own feuds. Reconquista remained in abeyance, while Granada became a veritable protectorate of Castile. The loss of Constantinople to the Ottoman Turks in 1453 would help focus the attention of Christendom on Granada. Granada would now become a matter of faith rather than realpolitik. The unification of Castile and Aragon under Ferdinand and Isabella sealed Granada's fate.

Hope had deluded the Jews in the domains of Ferdinand and Isabella. The Crown, traditionally the protector of the Jews against the Church and townsmen, would be more audacious now. The Jews would be dispossessed and fed to the mob in the service of royal absolutism.

Pick up the trail a good century before the Inquisition and Edict of Expulsion: over the course of that pivotal century the place of the Jews in Spain had become untenable. The Jews farmed the taxes of the state; they were the ideal scapegoat for all the disgruntled. The mob and the priests who led the mob in intermittent outbursts against the Jews saw a Jewish conspiracy behind every cruel turn of fate. Jewish physicians were carrying poison under their fingernails, Jewish sorcerers were everywhere, a Jewish cabal was out to undo Christianity.

The Jewish world was hit with great ferocity in a wave of massacres that took place in 1391. The troubles began in Seville and spread to Cordoba, Valencia, and Barcelona. Before the great terror subsided, some 25,000 may have been killed. A new law was passed in 1412: the so-called "Ordinance on the Enclosure of the Jews and Moors" at Valladolid. The Jews were now to wear a distinctive yellow garment; Jews and Moors were banned from serving as spice dealers, tax farmers, moneylenders, physicians, or surgeons; they were to live in separate enclosures locked and guarded at night. A massive wave of conversion was to take place in 1412–15.

Baptism bought time for those who chose it. But now a new crisis threatened. Where they had been a people apart, the sin of the Jews was separation. Now it was their assimilation that agitated their enemies. The Grand Inquisitor doing his work in the 1480s would claim that he was hunting crypto-Jews among the conversos. We know better now, thanks to the able work of the Israeli historian Benzion Netanyahu. In a book titled *The Marranos of Spain* Netanyahu turns the story inside out. Conversion had worked, it had depleted the Jewish world and increased the self-confidence of the conversos. They were no longer a minority who had gone astray; they now outnumbered the Jews of the realm.

Mobility denied the Jews was now theirs. They flocked into professions from which they had been excluded: the law, the army, the universities, the church. One rabbi, Solomon Levi, christened as Paul de Santa Maria, rose to become bishop of Burgos. The Talmudist Joshua Halorqi left Judaism for the Church, took the name Jeronimo de Santa Fe, and became a zealous advocate of his new faith. By 1480 half the important offices in the court of Aragon were occupied by conversos or their children. The great energy of the conversos rankled the Jews, increasing numbers of whom dispensed with the cherished notion that the conversos were *anusim* (forced ones) who were destined to return to the faith. More important, though, it galvanized the forces that sought the eradication of the Jewish presence in Spain. If the Jews had slipped through the gate as converts, they had to be banished and destroyed. The line had to be redrawn. Tomas de Torquemada, the priest who was the evil genius of the Inquisition, knew where he was heading. The conversos and those who remained true to the Jewish faith may have taken two separate paths. In one swift, terrible decade, Torquemada would bring them together. The Inquisition in 1481 against the conversos, the Edict of Expulsion in 1492.

A tale of dubious authenticity has the Ottoman Sultan Bayezid II (1481–1512) wondering about Ferdinand and about the folly of his expulsion of the Jews: "Do they call this Ferdinand a wise prince who impoverishes his kingdom and thereby enriches mine?" The tale aside, the lands of Islam provided safe havens for the Jews. The gates of many Muslim realms were opened before the Sephardim. The new lands were eager to accommodate them, as they brought with them new skills in the making of weaponry and gunpowder, in printing and medicine. They knew the languages of Europe. In the great struggle of the age between Islam and Christendom the Jews found a reprieve. For the rulers of the Ottoman Empire the Jews were ideal subjects.

By the standards of Europe in the High Middle Ages, the world of Islam was, on the whole, a tolerant world. It was not an "interfaith utopia" (to borrow the words of the distinguished historian of Islam Bernard Lewis). The life the Jews led was circumscribed. It was a life without illusions. There was a clear division of labor; political power, careers in the bureaucracy and the military were off limits. There was a body of discriminatory law: houses of worship could not be built higher than mosques; Jews and Christians were often required to wear distinctive garb. They could not bear arms or ride horses. They had to pay higher taxes than those paid by Muslims.

And some Muslim realms were harder than others. Morocco stood out in the degradation it heaped upon the Jews. Here Islam was frontier Islam, embittered by wars against Portugal and Spain. The Jews were the only non-Muslim community in Morocco. The limits imposed upon them—enclosed ghettos that functioned like the Juderias of Aragon and Castile—recalled the degradations of Europe. The Jews of Morocco lived at the mercy of the elements. It was feast or famine. Merciful sultans alternated with cruel ones. What the sultans gave, the preachers and the crowd frequently took away. The protection the rulers offered in this wild and anarchic realm could never withstand what one historian described as the three miseries of Morocco: plague, famine, and civil war.

It was easier in other Muslim lands. The private domain Islamic rule conceded, the freedom from forced conversions must have seemed particularly generous when compared with what prevailed in medieval Europe. A Jew writing to his co-religionists in Europe described Turkey as a land where "every man may dwell at peace under his own vine and fig tree." The Jews were a people on the run. The tolerance in the new surroundings seemed wondrous. A converso who made a new life in Turkey and returned to the faith spoke of Turkey in nearly messianic terms, described it as "a broad expansive sea which our Lord has opened with the rod of his mercy. Here the gates of liberty are wide open for you that you may fully practice your Judaism."

Jewish centers of learning and commerce sprouted throughout the Muslim world. Salonika, conquered by the Turks early in the 1400s, was to become, for all practical purposes, a Jewish city. Jews became the city's overwhelming majority. They dominated the life of the city until its loss to the Greeks in 1912. A substantial Jewish colony laid roots in Istanbul. The town of Safed, in Palestine, attracted Jewish textile makers and scholars, and became a famous center of learning. Close by there was a protected niche for the Jews in the life of Egypt. Baghdad's Jewry was perhaps in a league by itself. It had its academies, a vigorous mercantile elite with far-flung commercial operations.

Then the world of the Jews of Islam closed up. It happened over a long period of time. The civilization of Islam itself went into eclipse, its Ottoman standard-bearers were overtaken by Europe in the seventeenth century. The Jews who had done well by civilization in the midst of a surge were to suffer its demise. Increasingly the Christian European powers set the terms of the traffic with Islamic lands. For intermediaries these European powers preferred the local Christian communities—Greeks, Armenians, Christian Arabs. And these local Christians were sworn enemies of the Jews, bent on cutting them out of international commerce and diplomacy. The knowledge—of foreign languages, of science and medicine—that Jews had brought with them from Europe had receded and been rendered obsolete. European missions were busy at work shoring up the skills and the privileges of the Christians of the "east." On the defensive, the Islamic order itself was growing increasingly xenophobic and intolerant. The submission to Europe had to be hidden under displays of chauvinism. The Jews of Islam headed into a long night. The center of the Jewish world had long shifted westward. Lewis sums up the closing of that Jewish world in the east in his book *The Jews of Islam:*

"The growing segregation, the dwindling tolerance, the diminished participation, the worsening poverty, both material and intellectual, of the Jewish communities under Muslim rule."

From this long slumber the Jews of the east were awakened by a movement fashioned by their kinsmen in the west: modern Zionism. It came calling on them, summoned them to a new undertaking. The Jews of Islam had been spared both the gift of modern European history (the Enlightenment, the bourgeois age, the emancipation) and then the horrors visited on European Jewry. Zionism had been spun with European thread. But the Jews of the east took to it. To be sure, there were many who had wanted to sit out the fight between Arab and Jew in Palestine and to avert their gaze. Some of the leading figures of Egyptian Jewry the chief Rabbi Haim

Nahum, the head of the community, a banker by the name of Joseph Aslan de Cattaoui Pasha whose family had presided over the community since the mid-nineteenth century—were men "devoted to king and country" who had wanted nothing to do with Zionism. But the ground burned in Egypt. Fascist doctrines of nationalism and a new Islamic militancy were sweeping through the place. Palestine and the struggle between Arab and Jew were too close: the world of Egyptian Jewry couldn't withstand all of this.

It was now past living those circumscribed lives. Modern nationalism—in its Arab and Jewish variants—blew away the world of the Arab Jews. The braver and younger souls among the Jews of Arab lands didn't care to live the quiet and worried lives of their elders. When the first Arab-Israeli war of 1948–49 opened, there were some 800,000 Jews in the Arab world; some 6 percent of world Jewry. A decade or so later, Harat al Yahud (the Jewish quarter) in Muslim cities belonged to memory. The large Jewish communities in Morocco, Algeria, Egypt, Iraq, packed up and left. There was a new and altered geography of Jewish life; the center of gravity had shifted again, toward two poles: the New World and Israel.

Setting sail to the New World, Columbus had had little to say about that "parallel fleet of woe and misery" that carried the Jews out of Spain. He was careful to note, though, that he wanted the Jews excluded from the lands he would discover and claim for Spain. Fate mocked him.

It came to pass that in the midst of the retrospects and the celebration and the rampant revisionism of the quincentennial of Columbus's voyage of discovery, Arabs and Jews at an impasse came together in Madrid in October 1991. (Benjamin Netanyahu, Israel's deputy foreign minister, went to Madrid; his father, the distinguished historian Benzion Netanyahu, had chronicled the heartbreak of the Jews of Spain and the shattering of their world.) It was a "good venue," the innocent said of Madrid, the right place for Muslims and Jews to come together. Perhaps it was. The Spanish certainly thought so; the great irony would have been too much for them to ponder. Beyond the tumult of the conference and its utterances, those in the know, though, could have sworn that they could hear both the Moor's last sigh and the parting words of hurt and pride of Don Isaac Abravanel, and that plea that fell on deaf ears.

Critical Thinking

1. Do you find it ironic that Jews and Muslims who failed to convert to Christianity were expelled from Spain one day before Columbus and his men set sail for Ferdinand and Isabella in 1492?

2. In what sense was it "a polyglot world" that Muslims came to rule in the Iberian Peninsula?

3. In what sense was it true that "trouble came to paradise" for Jews in Spain at the close of the 11th century?

4. In what sense was it true that "by the standards of Europe in the High Middle Ages, the world of Islam was, on the whole, a tolerant world"?

Create Central

www.mhhe.com/createcentral

Internet References

Gander Academy's European Explorers Resources on the World Wide Web
www.stemnet.nf.ca/CITE/explorer.htm

FOUAD AJAMI is professor of Middle East Studies at the School of Advanced Studies, Johns Hopkins University.

Fouad Ajami. From *The New Republic*, April 6, 1992, pp. 22–25. Copyright © 1992 by TNR II, LLC. Reprinted by permission.

Article

Prepared by: Joseph R. Mitchell, *Howard Community College*
and Helen Buss Mitchell, *Howard Community College*

A Taste of Adventure

Kerala, India, and the Molucca Islands, Indonesia

The history of spices is the history of trade.

Learning Outcomes

After reading this article, you will be able to:

- Discuss why spices were a desired commodity and how the Portuguese were able to dominate the trade in spices.

Soon after dawn on May 21st, 1498, Vasco da Gama and his crew arrived at Calicut after the first direct sea voyage from Europe to Asia. If history's modern age has a beginning, this is it. Europe's ignorance of, and isolation from, the cosmopolitan intellectual and commercial life of Asia were ended forever. With ships, weaponry and a willingness to use them both, the countries of Europe were about to colonise the rest of the world. To support this expansion, its merchant classes would invent new forms of commercial credit and the first great corporations, vital parts of capitalism's operating system, and spread their trading networks across the seven seas. And what did the men shout as they came ashore? "For Christ and spices!"

And what did the men shout as they came ashore? "For Christ and spices!"

The proselytising part turned out to be disappointingly unnecessary: there were already plenty of Christians living on the Malabar coast, following the arrival of a Syrian contingent many centuries earlier. But as far as spice went, Da Gama and his crew were right on the money. Then, as now, Calicut was a gateway to the world's greatest pepper-growing region—indeed this was why the Syrians had moved there in the first place. As such it was at the heart of the spice trade, a network of sea routes and entrepots in the making for millennia: the world economy's oldest, deepest, most aromatic roots.

For thousands of years before Da Gama and hundreds of years afterwards, the secret of the spice trade was simple: great demand and highly controlled supply. Some of that control was enforced through political power or contrived through mercantile guile. Some was simply a gift from the gods of climate and botany. Legend has it that, before leaving, Da Gama dared to ask the zamorin of Calicut whether he could take a pepper stalk with him for re-planting. His courtiers were outraged, but the potentate stayed calm. "You can take our pepper, but you will never be able to take our rains." He knew how important the region's unusual twin monsoon, both phases of which bring heavy rain, was to its fickle crop. To this day, though regions elsewhere grow pepper, Kerala reigns supreme in its quality, dominating the high end of the market.

If those vital downpours have not washed away what passes for the road, a few days travel into Kerala's rolling Western Ghats, where waterfalls roar and herds of wild elephants loom from soft mist, brings you to the ancestral home of *Piper nigrum*. High up in the middle of nowhere, Iddicki produces the finest pepper in the world, its peppercorns always dark and heavy, bursting with flavour. Its vines wind their way around almost every tree in sight, climbing ten metres or more into the sky.

After such a journey you might expect Iddicki to be a sleepy backwater. In its own idyllic way, though, it is a boomtown worthy of the Wild West. Fancy jeeps clog the narrow streets; shops overflow with the latest necessities of rural life, like washing machines and stereos. Giant satellite dishes shove their expensive snouts at the heavens from every other house. One of the world's largest stashes of gold is in rural India, and to judge by its glittering jewellery shops this town has considerably more than its fair share. "Black gold," explains one pepper farmer with a broad grin, is fetching top prices on the world market.

Until you talk to them about that world market, Iddicki's residents seem much like farmers anywhere else in the developing world—scraping a living at the margins of the market economy. Thomas Thomas, one of the several hundred thousand smallholders who grow Kerala's pepper, is a good example. A humble man of the earth, he speaks softly and still wears his *dhothi*, a traditional loincloth, when he tills his soil. But with a little prompting he will give you an analysis of the pepper market sophisticated enough to make a Chicago commodities trader blush: current prices, the direction of the futures market, the costs versus benefits of holding stocks. A local spice dealer explains over a feast of fiery snapper and spiced tapioca at his spacious bungalow that "there is full price-discovery in this market." The farmers who sell their crops to him (for resale at the big market in Jewtown, which has replaced Calicut as the hub of Kerala's pepper trade) do so with the latest New York and Rotterdam prices in hand. One particularly sharp farmer, he moans, is cutting out the middlemen altogether and shipping his stocks directly to Europe.

The global aspect of the dealer's trade is nothing new. As far back as 2600 BC, there are records of the Egyptians feeding spices obtained from Asia to labourers building the great pyramid of Cheops, to give them strength. Archeological evidence suggests that cloves were quite popular in Syria not long after, despite the fact that, like nutmeg and mace, they came only from the spice islands of what is now Indonesia. Long before the 6th century BC, when Confucius advocated the use of ginger, the Chinese were obtaining spices from the tropics. Europe imported them before Rome was founded.

Today spices are chiefly flavourings for food, but a hundred other uses have contributed to the demand through history. In ancient Egypt cassia and cinnamon fetched a high price because they were essential for embalming; so too were anise, marjoram and cumin, used to rinse out the innards of the worthy dead. Hammurabi's legal code, which called for severe punishment of sloppy or unsuccessful surgeons, did much to encourage the use of medicinal spices in Sumeria.

Particularly in Europe, though, food came to matter most. Spices preserve, and they also make the poorly preserved palatable, masking the appetite-killing stench of decay. After bad harvests and in cold winters the only thing that kept starvation at bay was heavily salted meat—with pepper. And there was never enough of it. Thus pepper began the association with gold it still has in the streets of Iddicki, often at a one-to-one exchange rate. In order to call off their siege of Rome in 408 AD, the Visigoths demanded a bounty in gold, silver and pepper. In the Middle Ages plague added to the demand for medicinal spices; a German price table from the 14th century sets the value of a pound of nutmeg at seven fat oxen. At the same time "peppercorn rents" were a serious way of doing business. When the *Mary Rose,* an English ship that sank in 1545, was raised from the ocean floor in the 1980s, nearly every sailor was found with a bunch of pepper-corns on his person—the most portable store of value available.

The great beneficiaries of Europe's need were the Arabs. Spices could change hands a dozen times between their source and Europe, soaring in value with each transaction, and the Arabs were the greatest of the middlemen. Keen to keep it that way, they did everything possible to confuse consumers about the spices' origins. As early as the 5th century BC an Arab cover story fooled Herodotus into believing that cinnamon was found only on a mountain range somewhere in Arabia. The spices were jealously guarded by vicious birds of prey, he wrote, which made their nests of the stuff on steep mountain slopes. Arabs would leave out large chunks of fresh donkey meat for the birds to take back to their nests, which would crash to the ground under the weight. The brave Arabs then grabbed the nests, from under the talons of their previous owners.

Nto everyone was fooled. In the 1st century AD the Roman historian Pliny grew concerned at the way the empire's gold flowed ever to the east, and set out to expose the truth and undercut the Arab monopolists who he reckoned to be selling pepper at prices a hundred times what they paid for it in India. It did not help that the gluttonous Romans were, in the words of Frederic Rosengarten, a spice historian, "the most extravagant users of aromatics in history". They used spices in every imaginable combination for their foods, wines and fragrances. Legionaries headed off to battle wearing perfume. The rich slept on pillows of saffron in the belief that it would cure hangovers.

Resentment against the Arab stranglehold had led Rome to launch an invasion of Arabia in 24 BC, an ill-fated expedition that ended in humiliation. But where military means failed, market intelligence prevailed. In 40 AD, Hippalus, a Greek merchant, discovered something the Arabs had long tried to obscure: that the monsoons which nourish India's pepper vines reverse direction mid-year, and that trips from Egypt's Red Sea coast to India and back could thus be shorter and safer than the empire had imagined. Roman trade with India boomed: the Arab monopoly broke.

Early in the 7th century, an obscure spice merchant named Muhammad re-established Arab dominance of the spice trade by introducing an aggressive, expansionary Islam to the world. When the muslims took Alexandria in 641 AD, they killed the trade which had long flourished between Rome and India. As they tightened their grip on the business over the next few centuries, prices in Europe rose dramatically. During the Middle Ages, spices became a luxury that only a few in Europe could afford. This was bad news for the poor and good news for Venice. Its shrewd merchants struck a deal with the Arabs that made them the trade's preferred—indeed almost exclusive—European distributors. Even during the crusades, the relationship bought wealth to all concerned.

The rest of Europe did not care at all for the Muslim Curtain, as the Islamic empire separating west from east came to be called, or for the Venetians. The final blow came in 1453 when the Ottoman Turks took Constantinople, shutting down the small overland trade that had previously evaded the Arab-Venetian monopoly. The Egyptians, gate-keepers of the trade with Venice, felt confident enough to impose a tariff amounting to a third of the value of spices passing through their fingers.

Salvation for the palates and exchequers of Europe's kings lay in finding a sea route to the Indies. In particular, the hunt was on for Malacca, the most important entrepôt in the spice trade and the fabled gateway to the Spice Islands. Spain and Portugal financed dozens of exploration parties in its general direction; half would never make it back home. The rationale for this expense and danger was simple: "He who is lord of Malacca has his hand on the throat of Venice."

He who is lord of Malacca has his hand on the throat of Venice.

It was as part of Portugal's *Drang nach Osten* that Vasco da Gama rounded Africa's Cape of Good Hope to reach India in 1498. As waves of Portuguese explorers returned to Lisbon with their loads of spices, the Venetians and the Egyptians were stunned: the price of pepper in Lisbon fell to one-fifth that in Venice.

The Spaniards, too, were less than happy. They had sent Christopher Columbus to find a route to the Indies via the west, but he had failed, hitting upon the previously unknown Americas instead. In his zeal to convince his paymasters and himself that he had succeeded, he named the new world's natives as Indians and their sacred *chiles* "red" pepper—two unpardonable obfuscations that have confused people to this day.

Pope Alexander IV was drafted in to keep the two expansionist powers apart; the result was the treaty of Tordesillas, which granted all discoveries west of a mid-Atlantic meridian to Spain, and those east of it to Portugal. But the Spanish clung to the possibility of a western end-run to the Spice Islands, and financed Ferdinand Magellan on what would become the first circumnavigation of the earth. Magellan himself was killed in the Philippines, but his sidekick, Sebastian del Cano, completed the momentous journey—with a landfall at the Spice Islands en route. In 1522 his *Victoria* returned to Europe with a tonne of spices on board. The king awarded him a coat of arms embellished with two cinnamon sticks, three nutmegs and twelve cloves.

But the Portuguese had pipped Spain to the post. They had captured the vibrant free-trading port of Malacca, in what is now Malaysia, in 1511. Using the intelligence they gathered there, they made it to the promised land: the tiny Banda Islands, the world's only source of nutmeg and mace, which they reached the following year. Nutmeg is the pit of the nutmeg tree's fruit, and mace, which commanded and still commands a higher price, is the delicate red aril which comes between the pit and the fruit's husky exterior. Chaucer extolled "nutemuge put in ale . . ." and it remains an essential part of Coca-Cola's secret formula.

After filling their holds, the Portuguese began their return. One ship ran aground, stranding its crew on a remote island. Hearing of a strange race of white men in his parts, the sultan of Ternate, the most powerful of the clove isles, sent for them—and so the Europeans found the last secret source of spice.

Look out from the expansive verandah of the sultan's palace in Ternate and one of history's great microcosms lies before you. Dominating one side is Gamalama, the island's temperamental volcano. Opposite it stands its equally fickle twin on the island of Tidore. The two spits of land, not a mile apart, are now almost unknown beyond their immediate vicinity. But five centuries ago their names were uttered with breathless excitement across Europe as their rulers, ancient rivals, played the new great powers off against each other with promises of limitless wealth.

Dark, husky aromas swirl through the palace as incense made specially of local spices finds its way into the thick tropical air. The place is overflowing with gifts from distant customers: priceless Chinese vases, exquisitely carved Indian daggers, fine Venetian glassware, all of them evidence of the influence these rulers once wielded. Ask politely, and you might be allowed to gaze—from a respectful distance, and only after

much ceremony—at the sultan's magical crown, its hundred sparkling gem-stones hanging heavy like ripe peaches. You are not the first impressionable tourist here. Francis Drake gushed about the palace, especially its 400-strong harem. And it seems that it's still good to be the king: one of the gifts on display is an enormous modern settee, helpfully labelled "Lazy chair: for the sultan to take naps."

For much of the 16th century, Spain and Portugal tried to win control of the trade in cloves that made such a lifestyle possible. This meant entangling themselves in the long-running rivalry between the rulers of the two islands, who were in-laws. The European powers would build alliances and forts in one place and then the other, only to find themselves kicked out or caught up in endless intrigues and feuds. After decades of this Machiavellian palaver the Portuguese emerged as the top European player in the clove market, but they never really made it a monopoly. Indeed, they allowed the Dutch, who were growing increasingly anxious for a piece of the action, to be their chief distributors in the north and west of Europe. After Spain gobbled up Portugal in 1580, though, the trade changed again. The Spanish tightened control of the market to which they now had exclusive access, cutting the Dutch out of the picture and raising prices across the continent.

Convinced that they had to find a way to control the source of the spices, the Dutch got their act together. In 1602 they formed the Dutch East India Company (the *Vereenigde Oost-Indische Compagnie,* VOC), an association of merchants meant to reduce competition, share risk and realise economies of scale. Other European countries also formed East India companies—everyone from Portugal to Sweden to Austria had a go—but none was ever as successful in the spice trade as the VOC. By 1670 it was the richest corporation in the world, paying its shareholders an annual dividend of 40% on their investment despite financing 50,000 employees, 30,000 fighting men and 200 ships, many of them armed. The secret of this success was simple. They had no scruples whatsoever.

The secret of this success was simple. The Dutch had no scruples whatsoever.

The VOC's first conquest was the Banda archipelago. Unlike the sultans of the clove islands, who relished the attention lavished upon them by their European suitors and the opportunities for mischief that came with it, the fiercely independent Islamic merchants of the Bandas had never allowed Spain or Portugal to build forts on their islands: they insisted on their freedom to trade with all nations. This independence proved their undoing, since it encouraged the VOC to put the nutmeg trade first on its order of business.

For a taste of Banda's romance nothing beats a trip to Run, an explosion of nutmeg trees in the middle of a turquoise sea. Reaching it after a night aboard ship is a magical experience; scores of dolphins dart about your bow-wave as the first glints of sunrise streak across the sky. It feels much as it must have done when English adventurers first claimed the place, making it the country's first colony anywhere. Not much of a colony, it must be said: the island is so small that even a modest fishing vessel can come ashore only at high tide. Yet this seemingly insignificant toe-hold in nutmeg-land so exercised the Dutch that they traded away a promising young colony on the other side of the world to secure it. That island was New Amsterdam, now better known as Manhattan.

The purchase of Run demonstrates the VOC's persistence; it does not do justice to the company's cruelty (normally, but not exclusively, meted out to non-Europeans). Its most successful head, Jan Pieterszoon Coen, had earlier convinced the reluctant Bandanese of his firm's God-given right to monopolise the nutmeg trade in a more typical style: he had had every single male over the age of fifteen that he could get his hands on butchered. Coen brought in Japanese mercenaries to torture, quarter and decapitate village leaders, displaying their heads on long poles. The population of the isles was 15,000 before the VOC arrived; 15 years later it was 600.

When they turned to the clove trade the Dutch had no time for the squabbling politics of Ternate and Tidore. The VOC uprooted all the Sultans' clove trees and concentrated production on Ambon, an island where its grip was tight. By 1681, it had destroyed three-quarters of all nutmeg trees in unwanted areas and reorganised farming into plantations. It imposed the death penalty on anyone caught growing, stealing or possessing nutmeg or clove plants without authorisation. It drenched every nutmeg with lime before export, to ensure that not one fertile seed escaped its clutches. Yet high on its hillside Afo lives to tell its tale.

Climb through the dense, aromatic forests that cover the steep slopes of Ternate's volcano, and you will find this living testament to the ultimate futility of monopoly. Nearly 40 metres tall and over 4 metres round, Afo is the world's oldest clove tree, planted in defiance of the Dutch ban nearly four centuries ago. Despite the VOC's extreme precautions, Afo's sister seedlings, stolen in 1770 by an intrepid Frenchman (curiously, named Poivre), ended up flourishing on the Seychelles, Réunion and especially Zanzibar, which later became the world's largest producer of cloves. By the end of the 18th century the emergence of these rivals had broken the Dutch monopoly for good.

By that time the VOC was already a hollow mockery of its original ghastly self. As early as the end of the 17th century, careful analysis of the books shows that its volume of trade was reducing every year. Even a monopoly so ruthlessly enforced could not help but leak, and the VOC's overheads were huge—tens of thousands of employees, garrisons, warships. Decades of easy rents had created a corrupt and inefficient beast. By 1735, dwindling spice income had been overtaken by textiles in the company's profit column. In 1799, the most vicious robber baron of them all met its final end. The VOC went bankrupt.

The demise of the VOC was not just a pleasing comeuppance. It was evidence that, in just two centuries, Europeans had changed the spice trade forever. The spices that were once limited to tiny islands in hidden archipelagoes were being grown around the world and in large quantities. Trade routes that spanned oceans were becoming commonplace and, as such, competitive. The Dutch did their best to buck the trend, destroying their stocks so blatantly that, according to one observer, the streets of Amsterdam were "flooded with nutmeg butter". But it was all in vain. Spices were no longer that hard to come by. Monopolies gave way to markets.

Those markets remained rich in romance; the allure of the trade, its role as a cultural crossroads, its many rival players, its uncertainties and its opportunities for smuggling (even relatively cheap spices carry a lot of value for a given weight) kept the spice bazaars of Kerala, Ambon and Rotterdam fascinating. And lucrative, too; though no one could control the overall flow of spice any more, information could still be rushed ahead fast enough—or sequestered behind long enough—for people in the know to make a killing. Now, though, the information itself has started to flow freely. "There just aren't so many secrets any more," reflects a spice trader in Rotterdam. "The farmers in Vietnam are walking around with mobile phones. They know the market price as soon as I do."

Such traders are now caught in a trap. Their space for bargaining and trade, opened up with the end of monopoly production, is being hemmed in by ever more powerful purchasers—the food giants and spice multinationals. In an age of free-flowing information these buyers can bypass the markets and go directly to the source. From Jew-town, still the key pepper entrepôt, to Rotterdam, London and New York, the main international markets, spice traders are a dying breed. One industry veteran reckons that only a fifth of the trading concerns that flourished 30 years ago are still in business.

Their problems stem from men like Al Goetze. Meet him in his office near Baltimore, at the staid headquarters of McCormick, the world's largest spice firm, and his conservative suit and dry manner might lead you to mistake him for a stuffy corporate type. But to his admiring colleagues he is "a modern day Marco Polo."

Procurement managers at food-processing firms were once content to purchase spices through brokers, never leaving the comfort of their air-conditioned offices. Mr Goetze hits the road. He and his men have travelled to nearly every country on earth that grows spices, again and again. McCormick has set up joint-ventures or wholly owned subsidiaries in over a dozen key spice-producing countries in recent years.

Once the reason for going to the source was price. Now, Mr Goetze says, quality is what matters. Both American and European regulators, prompted by increasing consumer awareness of food safety, have been cracking down hard on impurities. Mr Goetze points to an unlikely assortment of objects in a display case: stones, rusty nails, giant cockroaches, plastic beach sandals. All were crammed into bursting burlap bags and sold to McCormick with its spice. Big processing firms and marketers, frightened that such stuff—or, worse, microscopic impurities that come with it—might make it to the dinner plates of litigious customers, are going straight to the source to clean things up.

Hot Chile

"Oh Blessed Incomparable Chile, ruler of all things . . . I give thee thanks for my digestive health, I give thee thanks for my very life!" Thus the Transcendental Capsaicinophilic Society, one of the worrying number of cults devoted to *capsicum:* chiles or "red" pepper.

If it sounds as if they are on drugs then so, in a way, they are. Paul Bosland of the Chile Pepper Institute in New Mexico reckons they and all chile-heads are high on endorphins, painkillers released by the body to block the sting of the capsaicin which gives chiles their bite.

The addicts are spread all over the world. Travelling on the back of the European spice trade, America's chiles have since colonised every corner of the earth so thoroughly that everyone thinks they have always been around. Even the top man at the Indian Spices Board refuses to accept that chiles are an import, pulling dubious sanskrit references from the Vedas to bolster his point. His clinching argument? "Indians can go months without touching black pepper, but not a day goes by that we don't eat chile peppers."

This is fast becoming true everywhere else, too. Americans' consumption of chile has doubled over the past two decades; they now use the spice in almost everything. Salsa now outsells ketchup as America's top condiment. But black pepper still gets all the glory as the world's most important traded spice. Unlike its fickle namesake, red pepper grows like mad all over the place. So though there may be a great demand for it, no one makes much money out of trading it. Bad news for traders, good news for foodies.

Stones, rusty nails, giant cockroaches, plastic beach sandals, all crammed into bursting burlap bags and sold with the spice.

Alfons van Gulick, the head of Rotterdam's Man Producten, the world's biggest and most influential spice-trading firm, is understandably unimpressed: "McCormick should stick to polishing its brand and selling, rather than telling countries how to produce spice." But the people for whose products McCormick and Man Producten compete have an interest in Mr Goetze's strategy. The Indian Spices Board is already helping members improve standards and obtain seals of approval such as ISO certification. The hope is that, over time, producers can go downstream and capture more of the fat margins that come with the "value-added" processing now done in rich countries.

Industry analysts are sceptical about vertical integration. In other commodities it has not been much of a success. Cutting out the middleman may pose unexpected problems for conservative multinationals, unfamiliar with the culture and risks involved in going upstream. And then there is volatility, on which middlemen thrive and which farmers and multinationals dislike. Asked whether the trade has lost its mystery, one animated trader replies "Mystery? I experience it every day when I try to figure out what is going on with prices in this market!"

Producers hate this, and have made various attempts to iron out the market's ups and downs. The International Pepper Community—which includes India, Indonesia and Brazil among its members—has tried for decades to form a producers' cartel to boost prices, without any success. Price fixing by vanilla growers in Madagascar succeeded for a while, but then Uganda flooded the market with cheaper beans. Indonesia and Grenada, the top producers of nutmeg, managed to boost prices for a few years by limiting supply, but cheating quickly scuppered the arrangement. Quiet talks are underway between top cardamom producers in India and Guatemala, who produce nearly all the world's output, to restrict supply; it may work for a while, but not for long.

Every decade or so, an ambitious individual trader tries to do with money what the producers cannot do by agreement. To corner the pepper market would offer huge riches, and so people regularly have a go. Half a century ago, it was an Armenian; a decade ago, an American. Now it appears that a shadowy Indonesian tycoon may be making a play for at least the white pepper market. But history teaches that such grandiose efforts at monopoly face an uphill struggle. And though it may be possible to milk them for a while, the modern day economics of the trade ensure that they cannot last. The spice trade, once the stuff of legends, has become a market much like any other. And a taste of luxury beyond the dreams of almost every human in history is available to almost everyone, almost everywhere.

Critical Thinking

1. For thousands of years "the secret of the spice trade was simple: great demand and highly controlled supply." Explain.
2. Why was it true that "the great beneficiaries of Europe's need (for spices) were the Arabs"?
3. Why was the Dutch East India Company ultimately successful in the spice trade?

Create Central

www.mhhe.com/createcentral

Internet References

Gander Academy's European Explorers Resources on the World Wide Web
www.stemnet.nf.ca/CITE/explorer.htm

Article

Prepared by: Joseph R. Mitchell, *Howard Community College*
and Helen Buss Mitchell, *Howard Community College*

The Significance of Lepanto

GREGORY MELLEUISH

Learning Outcomes

After reading this article, you will be able to:

- Determine the immediate results of the Battle of Lepanto, as well as its long-term implications.

Since September 11, 2001, there has been quite an outpouring of books dealing with the historical relationship between Islam and the Christian West. This has included a number of surveys of the history of that relationship, some emphasising conflict and bloodshed and others the sometimes harmonious association that at times existed between the two civilisations. New studies of the Crusades have emerged, including the first complete history of the movement since Runciman's classic work, in the shape of Christopher Tyerman's *God's War.*

The Battle of Lepanto has a major place in the symbolism of the Western-Islamic relationship, and Niccolò Capponi's recently published *Victory of the West: The Story of the Battle of Lepanto* treats the battle as a major encounter between the Islamic Ottoman empire and the forces of Western Christendom.

Lepanto was the last great battle that could be described as a simple clash between Christendom and Islam. Fought on October 7, 1571, it saw the fleet of the Ottoman empire pitted against an alliance of Spain, Venice and various other minor players to form a Holy League under the leadership of Don Juan of Austria, the illegitimate half-brother of Philip II of Spain.

The battle was the response of the Christian powers to the invasion of the Venetian possession of Cyprus. At stake was control of the Mediterranean. If the Ottomans had won then there was a real possibility that an invasion of Italy could have followed so that the Ottoman sultan, already claiming to be emperor of the Romans, would have been in possession of both New and Old Rome. The Pope could have become as much a tool of the Ottoman sultan as his Orthodox counterpart the Patriarch of Constantinople already was.

Yet, as Capponi points out, the Holy League was hardly a model of Christian solidarity. The Spanish and the Venetians had different strategic objectives—the Spanish were concerned primarily with Italy, North Africa and the Western Mediterranean, while Venice was anxious to recover Cyprus and protect its interests in the eastern Mediterranean. The Spanish were not keen for a battle that might lose them precious resources, particularly as

Philip II, with interests as well in northern Europe, was usually on the verge of bankruptcy. The Spanish were also concerned that the Venetians were in the process of cutting a deal with the Ottomans. Just a few days before the battle there was a conflict between the Spanish and Venetians that almost tore the fleet apart. Nevertheless the alliance held and the League fleet scored a stunning success.

The League's victory, as one might expect, did not translate into Christian hegemony of the Mediterranean. The Ottomans soon repaired their losses and the Venetians, heavily dependent on trade with the Ottoman empire, soon sued for peace, including paying an indemnity. If anything the Battle of Lepanto confirmed the status quo in the Mediterranean. The Ottomans had reached the limit of their power with only a few small territorial gains, such as Crete conquered from the Venetians in the mid-seventeenth century, waiting to be made. The cultural shape of the lands around the Mediterranean was confirmed with a largely Islamic East and South staring across the waters at a Christian North and West. The Ottoman empire, like the ancient Roman empire and the Byzantine empire before it, was left with the task of defending its ever diminishing borders over the next three centuries. When it did finally "fall" after the First World War the ramifications were enormous, and we are still attempting to cope with them from Bosnia to Iraq.

> **For the people of Western Europe the Battle of Lepanto was an enormous psychological boost because it demonstrated that the "Turk" could be beaten.**

For the people of Western Europe the Battle of Lepanto was an enormous psychological boost because it demonstrated that the "Turk" could be beaten. The aura of invincibility surrounding the Ottoman empire was broken. Lepanto was very easy to interpret in terms of Christendom versus Islam because it was one of those rare occasions when the religious division of the combatants was so clear-cut. Of course, in the wider world of strategic alliances the situation was far more complex. The French often supported the Ottomans against the Spanish and Hapsburgs, while the Orthodox Christians of the Eastern

Mediterranean generally preferred the tolerant rule of the Ottomans to attempts by the Venetians to impose Catholic bishops on them.

But there are other ways of considering Lepanto. One is to interpret it in terms of a dynamic innovative West pitted against the "stagnant" East. The League won because it used innovative tactics. The usual form that galley warfare took was to ram the enemy ships and then take them by storm. The Venetian ships attempted a new and different tactic. Using a larger and modified form of galley known as galleasses, they filled these ships with cannons and attempted to blow as many of the Ottoman galleys as possible out of the water. League ships carried many more cannon and its troops made much greater use of firearms. Many of the Ottoman troops preferred to use bows, although these were not necessarily inferior to the clumsy arquebus of that time. Capponi has a very good grasp of the military dimensions of Lepanto, and although this is sometimes tedious for those with little interest in strictly military matters, a grasp of such matters is crucial if the battle is to be understood.

If the League had kept to the established "rules" of naval warfare of the time they would probably have lost the battle. In the sixteenth century the Ottoman empire was much more powerful than its rivals in Western Europe but its power was founded on the adaptation of the traditional institutions of Islamic civilisation. This meant in particular the janissaries, the use of slave soldiers and slave administrators as the core of the Sultan's power. This gave the Sultan a loyal and efficient bureaucratic-military machine, although the cost was that this machine tended to behave like the praetorian guard of the Roman empire and to push the Sultan into war to satisfy its desire for plunder.

The state machinery of much of the West was much more ramshackle and less centralised. They relied heavily on Italian bankers and on the wealth of Italy. Nevertheless both the Emperor Charles V and his successor Philip II of Spain had to deal with the constant threat of bankruptcy.

In the longer term, however, the future belonged to the new commercial instruments of the West rather than to the bureaucratic machinery of the Ottomans. In her study of seventeenth-century Crete, *A Shared World,* Molly Green demonstrates that the commercial techniques and practices used by the Venetians were much more sophisticated and developed than those of the Ottoman regime that replaced them in mid-century. It was also the case that the Ottomans were slow to take to make use of printing, with the "printing revolution" that swept the West in the sixteenth century not really taking off in the Islamic world until the nineteenth century.

Even if the Ottomans had won it was unlikely that they would have established hegemony over Western Europe. True, they would have dominated the Mediterranean in the short term and it is likely that they would have been able to conquer Southern Italy and even take Rome. But the history of Byzantium from Justinian onwards suggests that this would have been the limit of their conquests. The Ottomans failed to take Vienna in both the 1520s and the 1680s partly because the supply lines into Central Europe were too long.

In any case it is clear that by the 1570s the dynamic that had driven the earlier Ottoman conquests had largely exhausted itself. Despite defeat at Lepanto they remained in control of Cyprus but that was the extent of Sultan Selim's conquests. In the seventeenth century they were able to wrest Crete from the Venetians but that was the last of their European conquests.

This suggests that Lepanto is better understood in terms of the dynamics of imperial expansion than some desire by Islam to subdue and conquer the world. The Ottoman empire came into being because of the decaying state of the Byzantine empire in the Balkans and Anatolia, a decadence aggravated by the conquest of Constantinople in 1204 during the Fourth Crusade. The Ottomans succeeded because they defeated their possible rivals, such as the Serbs, in battle.

They did so because they possessed what Ibn Khaldun in his *Muqaddimah* called *asabiya* or a strong sense of social solidarity. According to Ibn Khaldun, barbarians are able to conquer an established settled civilisation because they have a strong sense of their social solidarity that is grounded in the harshness and necessity of nomadic life. However, having conquered a settled society the invaders in turn are conquered by the comfort and soft living of that society until, with their *asabiya* decaying they, in turn, are conquered by another group of uncorrupted barbarians.

Linking social solidarity to imperial success was not limited to Islamic theorists. In his explanation of the worldly success of the Roman empire in book five of the *City of God,* Augustine, drawing on Sallust's *War with Catilene,* argued that empire had shifted to the West and Rome because the Romans possessed a high level of virtue. By virtue he meant the capacity to place the common good above personal gain, a virtue that he saw was destroyed particularly by the sin of avarice.

Sallust emphasised the simple lives of the uncorrupted Romans, and attributed their success to the "eminent merit of a few citizens" before "the state had become demoralised by extravagance and sloth". These ideas were to form the basis of the Western ideal of republicanism and republican virtue that still resonates in our contemporary world.

Now this analysis of history made enormous sense in both Asia and Europe for a long time. Rome, and the Roman empire, had to face an almost continuous set of threats, beginning with the Celts, then moving through to the Germans, Huns, Avars, Arabs and Turks. The Ottoman Turks simply delivered the *coup de grâce* to what had become little more than a living corpse. China built its "great wall" to protect itself from nomadic predators, while the damage inflicted by the Mongols on the settled Islamic world, including the sack of Baghdad, was staggering.

The argument that it was a strong sense of social solidarity that grows out of what could be described as a lifestyle founded on poverty has, I believe, powerful explanatory power. A settled civilisation, by creating a measure of comfort and a settled way of life, makes itself a target for those living outside their boundaries who are drawn by what it has to offer.

In his recent study *War & Peace & War,* Peter Turchin has built on the idea of *asabiya* to emphasise the importance of social co-operation as means of building strong states. He quotes a number of examples of small determined bands being able to overthrow political entities that, on paper, looked far more powerful. Alexander the Great and his superbly drilled Macedonian phalanx is perhaps the best known of these examples.

For Turchin, co-operation rather than competition is the key to success for any state. Moreover, Turchin maintains, it is the replacement of co-operation by competition within a state that leads to the evisceration of the social energy provided by co-operation. Turchin points to the way in which population growth, particularly amongst social elites, leads to a savage competition for resources and a weakening of both social and state power. Such states become the potential victims of those who have maintained their *asabiya*.

By the 1570s the élan or social energy of the Ottoman empire had begun to dissipate. Over the next 250 years the empire slowly became the "sick man of Europe" as certain regions established their de facto autonomy. According to the sociology of Ibn Khaldun this should have resulted in the next group of socially solid barbarians conquering and replacing them, just as they had previously conquered the Byzantines.

And yet this did not happen. One reason for this was that the Qing Chinese empire in the eighteenth century successfully conquered and subdued the last of the great nomadic empires of Eurasia. For the first time in millennia no barbarian horsemen, no Huns, no Avars, no Mongols, surged across the great plains of Eurasia to sack and pillage Europe, China and the great civilisations of the Islamic world and India.

When a new barbarian empire emerged powerful enough to threaten the Ottomans, and by this I mean the Russian empire, it was successfully checked by the jealousy of the other European powers. It was also into this world of decadence, of empires that were not revitalised by new sets of barbarians, in the Middle East, in India and in China, that the European empires were able to make such inroads from the eighteenth century onwards.

Lepanto was not the victory of Christianity over Islam, nor is its significance to be considered primarily in religious terms or as a clash of civilisations. Of course that does not mean that was not how it was viewed in a celebrating Europe, including Protestant England, and in the many paintings that have come down to us as representing the battle. Yet across the centuries Lepanto also looks like an exercise in futility, a scene of blood, gore and human misery that, at least on the surface, settled so little.

It was the last major naval battle that involved galleys rowed by banks of oarsmen. And it was won, somewhat against expectations, by the side that was willing to experiment with the use of overwhelming firepower in an attempt to blow the enemy ships out of the water rather than use the time-honoured practices of hand-to-hand combat.

In many ways Lepanto can be considered to be a clash of two different types of empire viewed as forms of polity and expressions of political culture and economic practices. On the one hand there was the traditional "plunder empire" as represented by the Ottomans that sought conquest for the sake of plunder in the shape of precious goods and slaves. Selim had

sought to conquer Cyprus, as there was an expectation that a Sultan should keep his janissaries happy at the beginning of a reign by providing them with a prize to conquer. There was little difference between the motives that led the Romans to expand their empire and those of the Ottomans.

The new European empires, as represented by Spain and Venice, were not uninterested in conquest and plunder, especially when one considers the behaviour of Spain in the Americas. But they were also in many ways quite different from the older territorial empires of Eurasia of which the Ottoman was one of the last representatives. And the difference lay in their concern with commerce and trade. Venice did not really want war with the Ottomans because it ruined her trade with that empire, and as soon as possible after Lepanto sought to re-establish that trading relationship.

Lepanto can be seen as symbolic of that transition, described by the nineteenth-century French liberal philosopher Benjamin Constant, from the age of war to the age of commerce. Or as others might say, it can be considered as the birth of modernity. Even the overwhelming use of firepower can be found in the pages of Constant as a feature of the utilitarian approach to warfare favoured by commercial nations. The irony was that the somewhat ramshackle empires of sixteenth-century Europe, with their disorganised finances and administrative apparatuses much inferior to those of the Ottomans, would within 300 years come to dominate the world not because of their superior *asabiya* or virtue but because of their capacity to create modern efficient institutions far superior to the slave bureaucracy of the Ottomans, and because of their ability to deliver superior firepower.

This new European and commercial form of empire supplanted an older, more traditional imperial form. What this meant was that the old rules of empire, of an imperial expansion dictated by the need to conquer to attain booty and slaves and a decline governed by the need to protect its settled possessions from new predators, would give way to a new set of rules. These are the rules of the export and import of capital, as described by Niall Ferguson in his recent studies of the English and American empires.

Nevertheless it is appropriate that scholars such as Turchin direct our attention to the significance of *asabiya* and the importance of the idea of social cooperation as a foundation of a stable and powerful state. It is also important that the story of Lepanto should recover its place in the historical consciousness of the West. Capponi's highly readable and scholarly account does help to achieve that goal. But it should not be read as yet another episode in the seemingly endless war between Christianity and Islam. Rather it should be seen as a battle in which an emerging form of state and empire was able to show its mettle against the last powerful traditionalist empire.

Critical Thinking

1. Why does the Battle of Lepanto have "a major place in the symbolism of the Western-Islamic relationship"?
2. Why was the battle of Lepanto "an enormous psychological boost" for the people of Western Europe?

3. Defend or oppose the claim that Lepanto represented "a 'dynamic, innovative West' pitted against the 'stagnant East'."
4. What is Asabiya and did the Ottomans possess it?
5. Do you agree or disagree that Lepanto is symbolic of the transition "from the Age of War to the Age of Commerce"?

Internet References

Internet Medieval Sourcebook
wwwfordham.edu/halsall/Sbook12.html

Create Central

www.mhhe.com/createcentral

From *Quadrant*, April 2008. Copyright © 2008 by Quadrant Monthly. Reprinted by permission.

Article   Prepared by: Joseph R. Mitchell, *Howard Community College*
and Helen Buss Mitchell, *Howard Community College*

Do Civilizations Really Collapse?

Scholars gather to challenge popular author Jared Diamond's take on societies' "ecocidal" tendencies.

ERIC A. POWELL

Learning Outcomes

After reading this article, you will be able to:

- Understand the features of Jared Diamond's "ecocidal" theory of the collapse of civilizations and discuss the criticisms of this theory.

On a blustery October day atop Tumamoc Hill, a tall butte near the center of Tucson, a dozen social scientists scramble across volcanic rock piles and weave through stands of saguaro cactus to look at traces of human habitation: large rock terraces, or *trincheras,* that cling to the side of the hill, and the faint remains of small pit houses that date from 300 B.C. to A.D. 450. The wind sometimes carries away the voices of their guides, archaeologists Paul and Suzy Fish of the Arizona State Museum. So the cultural anthropologists, historians, and archaeologists strain to hear them describe the desert lifestyle of the people who made their home at this trincheras site, one of the biggest in the Southwest. Paul and Suzy tell a good story, so the scholars don't want to miss it.

This diverse group is visiting Tumamoc Hill while taking a break during a four-day seminar called "Choices and Fates of Human Societies," a gathering where the topic of storytelling is a matter of some urgency. Hosted by the Amerind Foundation, an archaeological research institute in Dragoon, Arizona, the seminar is dedicated to analyzing and countering ideas popularized by Jared Diamond, perhaps America's most well-known storyteller when it comes to the human past. The UCLA geographer and physiologist's two enormously popular books have been credited with turning a new generation on to the science of the past, but at the same time have generated grumbling and even alarm among some specialists, who say Diamond's attempt to reduce the history of societies to one grand narrative obscures the uniqueness of individual cultures.

In the Pulitzer Prize-winning *Guns, Germs & Steel: The Fates of Human Societies* (1997), Diamond offered an ambitious "short history of everybody for the last 13,000 years,"

an account that explained the gulf between the first and third worlds largely as a matter of geographical accident. In his most recent book, *Collapse: How Societies Choose to Succeed or Fail* (1996), Diamond uses "vanished" ancient cultures such as the Classic Maya and Easter Islanders to illustrate how past societies that mismanaged the environment were doomed to catastrophe, committing what he calls "ecocide."

Diamond's vision of history is celebrated in the popular press and even by many academics as a welcome synthesis of a number of different historical disciplines. The fact that his ultimate goals as a writer are to challenge the idea that the West is superior because of racial or genetic differences and to raise awareness of the environmental catastrophe facing contemporary society make his work all the more compelling.

The problem, say many scholars, is that Diamond gets the past wrong. Criticism of his work focuses on a concern that Diamond fails to appreciate the complex role that culture plays in the development of societies. Anthropologists and archaeologists whose lives are devoted to studying the complexity of culture recoil at Diamond's statement that "historical studies of human societies can be pursued as scientifically as the study of dinosaurs."

Some archaeologists are especially concerned with *Collapse,* feeling Diamond cherry-picks data to fit his environmental agenda. They say his concern with using ancient cultures as cautionary tales about environmental mismanagement leads Diamond to reduce the history of people such as the Easter Islanders and the "Anasazi" or Ancestral Puebloans who lived at Chaco Canyon to accounts of the elites whose decisions doomed their societies to failure. Soon after the book was published, concern with its depiction of the Classic Maya and other civilizations as "failed societies" reached such an acute level that at the 2006 American Anthropological Association's (AAA) annual meeting in San Jose, California, a symposium devoted to critiquing Diamond's works drew a standing-room-only crowd. The response was so enthusiastic that two participants, Patricia McAnany of the University of North Carolina Chapel Hill, a Mesoamerican archaeologist, and Near Eastern specialist Norman Yoffee of the University of Michigan, put together the seminar at the Amerind Foundation to explore in greater depth the issues raised at the AAA meeting.

McAnany and Yoffee reached out to specialists in a wide range of fields, from the cultural anthropology of Papua New Guinea to the archaeology of the American Southwest. They invited them to Amerind's Arizona estate to spend four days discussing and refining their critiques of the ideas popularized by Diamond. McAnany and Yoffee also emphasized the need to get their message out to the world beyond specialists, and organized the seminar around the goal of producing a volume of essays written for students and the general public.

It was a tall order. McAnany and Yoffee were asking participants both to dissect hugely complex issues with their peers and to present those issues in papers that could be read by the average high-school senior or interested layperson.

No wonder then, that after three days of intense discussions, the seminar participants seem pleased by the field trip to Tumamoc Hill. The group is content to wander the butte, admiring its views of downtown Tucson and listening to Paul and Suzy Fish tell the story of how the site is far older than they thought it was before excavating here, and how it is still revered by Native Americans such as the Tohono O'odham. For a few hours, *Collapse* and *Guns, Germs & Steel* recede into the background, and the group focuses on the people who lived here 2,000 years ago.

Diamond was not invited to the seminar, but his presence in the Amerind's library, where the scholars meet every day, is palpable. The small two-story room is lined with books on Southwestern anthropology and archaeology. Combined, these books probably have not reached even a fraction of the readership commanded by Diamond's big-picture tomes. (When reached for comment, Diamond declined to answer questions related to the seminar, citing his unfamiliarity with the critiques presented there.)

On the seminar's first day McAnany starts off the proceedings by emphasizing her admiration for Diamonds writing abilities. "The beauty of Diamond is his simplicity," she says. "And the more we can have students read about archaeology and history the better. But how is the story being told? We want to tell a story that's more complex than the one in *Collapse*."

McAnany goes on to outline areas in which the seminar participants are in broad agreement with Diamond. In particular, they concur that the differences between the first-world's "haves" and the third-world's "have nots" are not the results of genetics, a critical theme of *Guns, Germs & Steel*. McAnany also expresses admiration for Diamond's efforts in *Collapse* to raise awareness of environmental problems facing modern society. But that is where their sympathy for his positions seems to end.

The entire premise of *Guns, Germs & Steel*, is flawed, they say, because it seeks to explain the dominance of European civilization as the culmination of a series of historical accidents that started with the first domestication of plant and animal species some 13,000 years ago. Diamond argues that a unique combination of geography and access to domesticated species led inexorably to Europe's domination over the rest of the world. But the

seminar participants maintain that Europe's central place in the world order is a fleeting phenomenon. They argue that it makes no sense to see all of history as a logical progression leading to European ascendancy. To do so, they say, ignores recent political and cultural realities that motivated European conquest and colonization. There was nothing inevitable about the Spanish invasion of the Inca Empire, for instance. Rather, it was the unique cultural values of late-medieval Spain that resulted in Pizzaro leading a coalition of Native American groups against the last Inca emperor, Atahualpa.

The situation is reversed in *Collapse*. Here, Diamond often depicts culture as the villain. He argues that many ancient civilizations foiled largely because leaders obsessed with maintaining power mismanaged the environment. Easter Island is a prime example. In *Collapse,* Diamond revisits evidence that shows the Easter Islanders cut down all their trees in part to build the famous stone heads called Moai, precipitating an environmental catastrophe that had devastating consequences, including a population crash. For Diamond this is a textbook case of "ecocide," an example of a people making poor environmental choices because of their obsession with a cultural phenomenon, in this case the Moai.

If you talk to 20 different historians then you'll get 20 different histories, says Yoffee. We know that. But Diamond is wrong. And he's wrong in ways that matter.

If you talk to 20 different historians then you'll get 20 different histories, says Yoffee. We know that. But Diamond is wrong. And he's wrong in ways that matter.

It's a measure of Diamond's ambition that the papers delivered at the seminar cover such a rich array of topics, and not just the ancient past. Over the course of four days, cultural anthropologists discuss Diamond's analyses of the modern predicaments of New Guinea and Haiti, and the harrowing recent events in Rwanda.

In *Collapse,* Diamond explains the Rwandan genocide largely as a function of overpopulation. In 1994, the country's ethnic Hutus slaughtered nearly 500,000 Tutsis after the plane carrying the president, a Hutu, was shot down. The ensuing bloodshed had an immediate political cause, says Diamond, but ultimately it was the result of stress brought on by too many people occupying ever smaller plots of land, which severely stressed the food supply. Genocide was the society's tragic attempt to regain equilibrium. But Christopher Taylor, a University of Alabama anthropologist who was in Rwanda at the time of the genocide, sees the massacres as the result of a complex combination of political, economic, and cultural factors.

After telling his colleagues how he and his Tutsi fiancée eluded Hutu death squads to escape the country, Taylor explains how he then analyzed political cartoons published in Rwandan newspapers for clues to the horrible events. He says the cartoons showed that modern Rwandans linked the presidency to traditional concepts of sacred kingship and fertility rites. During periods of drought and stress, the king could be sacrificed for the people. At the time of the assassination, Rwanda was going through a drought, and also suffering economically because of a global drop in the price of coffee, the country's main export. The assassination of the president in this context had a symbolic meaning that Taylor argues also played a role in the genocide. Overpopulation by itself doesn't explain the collapse of Rwanda.

When Diamond does consider cultural factors in his accounts, they are almost always the main culprits in a culture's downfall. For instance, Diamond blames the failure of the Norse colony in Greenland in the fifteenth century on the Norse's stubborn refusal to adopt a maritime lifestyle like their Inuit neighbors. By ignoring fish and relying mostly on traditional European livestock, writes Diamond, the Norse were ill-prepared for increasingly cold conditions brought on by the Little Ice Age, a period of global cooling toward the end of the medieval period.

But Joel Berglund, a Danish archaeologist, says that archaeological evidence shows the Norse made extensive use of fish bones as fertilizer for crops. Far from ignoring the sea, they used it extensively for their own purposes. When the Little Ice Age came, the Norse simply left, taking everything they could and moving to other parts of the Norse world. "Why should we see the colony as a failure when it succeeded against all the odds for 400 years?" asks Berglund.

Probably the most anticipated paper at the seminar was given by University of Hawaii archaeologist Terry Hunt, who has a story to tell about the fate of Easter Island that differs drastically from Diamond's. According to Hunt, the evidence for the Easter Islanders deforesting the island is weak. The real culprit, he says, is *Rattus exulans,* the Pacific rat. Brought by the Polynesians, rats multiplied quickly, eventually numbering in the millions. Hunt theorizes that they consumed the island's palm nuts at such a high rate that the trees eventually died out. The Easter Islanders were at fault in that they introduced the rat to the island, but blaming their obsession with Moai for the deforestation and subsequent population crash makes no sense. The Easter Islanders could have been building Moai until the moment they were contacted by Europeans, says Hunt, at which point they became victims of diseases for which they had no immunity. According to this theory, the dramatic population crash was the result not of ecocide, but genocide. The Easter Islanders still alive today are descendants of people who survived the tragedy of European contact, not the failure of their own leaders to manage the environment.

Several participants cite the fact that Diamond seems to ignore the link between "vanished" ancient cultures and their descendants living today. Michael Wilcox, a Stanford archaeologist and Yuma Indian, points out that the people of Chaco Canyon in the American Southwest didn't die out, they became today's Rio Grande Pueblos. "Archaeological sites aren't corpses," says Wilcox. "They're shells."

People living in marginal environments like the American Southwest and Greenland move around, says Wilcox. Abandonment of sites is a strategy, not a result of everybody dying out. In this light, the ruins at Chaco Canyon are not symbolic of that culture's failure, just signs it moved on.

When the collection of essays discussed at the seminar is published, this is the message that might resonate most with readers. While Diamond stresses ecological catastrophe and the failure of societies, the seminar participants emphasize the resiliency of cultures that survive political and environmental change.

On Tumamoc Hill, the wind has died down, and Paul and Suzy Fish are wrapping up their story about the trincheras builders. The climate 2,000 years ago would have been wetter, they say. Perhaps a drought led people to leave the area around A.D. 450. It's possible they eventually became the Hohokam people, who in turn are probably ancestral to the modern Tohono O'odham, for whom the hill is still sacred.

As the sun begins to edge toward the horizon, the seminar participants pile into a van and take the steep road down to Tucson. Tumamoc Hill, its rock terraces visible for miles, is already casting its long shadow across the gleaming, modern city below.

Critical Thinking

1. Explain Jared Diamond's theory of committing "ecocide."
2. What key element do critics think Diamond leaves out of his theory?
3. Why is Diamond's explanation of the Rwandan Genocide controversial?
4. Do you find the challenge to Diamond's claim that Easter Island's deforestation was not the major cause of its population extinction convincing? Why or why not?

Create Central

www.mhhe.com/createcentral

Internet References

Jared Diamond -Collapse 43
   http://homepage.eircom.net/~odyssey/Quotes/Life/Science/Collapse.html

ERIC A. POWELL is a senior editor at ARCHAEOLOGY